POLICE PLANNING

Second Edition, Fourth Printing

POLICE PLANNING

By

O. W. WILSON

Dean, School of Criminology
Professor of Police Administration
University of California
Berkeley, California

CHARLES C THOMAS · PUBLISHER

Springfield · Illinois · U.S.A.

Published and Distributed Throughout the World by
CHARLES C THOMAS • PUBLISHER
BANNERSTONE HOUSE
301-327 East Lawrence Avenue, Springfield, Illinois, U.S.A.
NATCHEZ PLANTATION HOUSE
735 North Atlantic Boulevard, Fort Lauderdale, Florida, U.S.A.

First Edition, 1952
Second Edition, 1958
Second Edition, Second Printing, 1962
Second Edition, Third Printing, 1968
Second Edition, Fourth Printing, 1971

With THOMAS BOOKS *careful attention is given to all details of
manufacturing and design. It is the Publisher's desire to present books
that are satisfactory as to their physical qualities and artistic possibilities
and appropriate for their particular use.* THOMAS BOOKS *will be true
to those laws of quality that assure a good name and good will.*

Printed in the United States of America

D-1

Law Enforcement Code of Ethics

As a Law Enforcement Officer, my fundamental duty is to serve mankind; to safeguard lives and property; to protect the innocent against deception, the weak against oppression or intimidation, and the peaceful against violence or disorder; and to respect the Constitutional rights of all men to liberty, equality and justice.

I will keep my private life unsullied as an example to all; maintain courageous calm in the face of danger, scorn, or ridicule; develop self-restraint; and be constantly mindful of the welfare of others. Honest in thought and deed in both my personal and official life, I will be exemplary in obeying the laws of the land and the regulations of my department. Whatever I see or hear of a confidential nature or that is confided to me in my official capacity will be kept ever secret unless revelation is necessary in the performance of my duty.

I will never act officiously or permit personal feelings, prejudices, animosities, or friendships to influence my decisions. With no compromise for crime and with relentless prosecution of criminals, I will enforce the law courteously and appropriately without fear or favor, malice or ill will, never employing unnecessary force or violence and never accepting gratuities.

I recognize the badge of my office as a symbol of public faith, and I accept it as a public trust to be held so long as I am true to the ethics of police service. I will constantly strive to achieve these objectives and ideals, dedicating myself before God to my chosen profession...law enforcement.

ADOPTED, 1956, THE PEACE OFFICERS' ASSOCIATION OF THE STATE OF CALIFORNIA

To

Ruth
Sally Jo
Patricia Anne

Preface

I T IS the purpose of this book to analyze the planning process in a police department and to discuss the tasks of planning within the police field without regard to their scope. The book is intended to guide the police planner in the accomplishment of his immediate tasks no matter what the level of his planning responsibilities. It is intended to assist the staff of the planning unit in a large department, the part-time plans officer in a smaller department, and the heads of functional units who are responsible for operational planning in their special fields. It is also intended as a guide to a complete police department survey that has as its objective the modernization of the organization structure and all operating procedures.

This broadness of purpose makes it necessary to consider the planning tasks from the point of view of the complete over-all survey. The reader should understand, however, that the component parts are contained within this broad treatment of the total planning task; it encompasses plans and planning problems of lesser magnitude, and the police officer who has a planning responsibility of limited scope will find in the book an analysis and discussion of his special planning problem.

The book also discusses organization for planning and the need for placing responsibility for this process. It analyzes the process of planning so that the planner may proceed, logically and systematically, toward the accomplishment of his purpose. It lists basic data needed in planning. It discusses factors that should be considered in developing the organization structure and in planning operations in each of the special branches of service to deal with both usual and unusual needs. Plans relating to procedures, tactics, personnel, equipment, buildings, budget, and extra-departmental activities are also discussed.

While written principally for the police planner, the book will be found to be helpful to all serious students of police administration.

O. W. W.

Contents

POLICE PLANNING

CHAPTER 1

The Planning Process

THE police chief is responsible for the prevention of criminality and the repression of criminal activity, the protection of life and property, the preservation of peace, and public compliance with countless laws. He is supplied with men and equipment to assist in the attainment of these objectives. These he must organize, direct, coordinate, and control in a manner that will assure the most effective and economical accomplishment of his purpose.

Consideration of the ever-mounting cost of government services and of crime makes apparent the necessity of achieving police objectives in the most effective and economical manner. If police operations are not economical, police service will further increase instead of diminishing the total cost of crime, thus placing an unreasonable additional burden on the taxpayer. If police operations are not effective, their objectives will not be attained. Society may then find itself at the mercy of organized criminals who *today* corrupt public officials so that they may operate with impunity and who *tomorrow*, impressed by the wisdom and economy of direct action, may take over the offices themselves. When public offices are filled by racketeers and other criminals, the democratic way of life will be gone.

Police objectives are achieved most effectively and economically through the efficient operation of three interrelated processes: viz., *planning, doing, and controlling.* Of these, *planning is basic.* Without it, effective direction, coordination, and control are impossible.

Planning Defined

Planning is the process of developing a method or procedure or an arrangement of parts intended to facilitate the achievement of a defined objective.

Plans in life are found in a variety of forms. Architectural and engineering construction plans are on blue prints and in specifications. The budget is a work plan in terms of expenditure requirements. An organization chart represents the arrangement of the component personnel groups of a force. Military plans for field

3

action are recorded in directives, orders, and maps. A directive is a broad outline of action stated in terms of objectives. An order is a more specific plan of action to be taken or procedure to be followed. A procedure is an outline of action to be taken under specified circumstances.

The Value of a Plan

A plan serves a number of purposes:

1. It implements policy and clarifies it by defining more precisely an immediate objective or purpose and outlining what is to be done to achieve it. A failure to plan signifies a lack of policy, or at least a lack of general understanding of policy by the members of the organization.

2. A plan serves as a guide or reference in both training and performance. It simplifies the direction of the members of the group, facilitates the coordination of their efforts, and places responsibility. In terms of tasks to be performed and effort required in their accomplishment, coordination is achieved more readily when the duties of each component member or unit are outlined in the plan and when the relationships are thus officially established. A group operates as a mob in the absence of consistent direction and coordination; through planning, chaos, confusion, and friction are replaced by system, order, and teamwork.

3. The planning process gives continued attention to the improvement of practices and procedures. Consistently uniform and superior methods are thus assured.

4. A plan enables a check on accomplishment. Control is thereby effected.

5. Wise planning assures the most effective and economical use of resources in the accomplishment of the purpose of the organization.

The Nature of Police Planning

Police plans may be classified in a number of ways. To facilitate orderly discussion, they are here arbitrarily divided into *procedural, tactical, operating, extra-departmental, and management plans,* although this classification with its terminology may be controversial. Research is, of course, essential in all planning.

Procedural Plans. Procedural plans include every procedure that has been outlined and officially adopted as the standard method of action to be followed by all members of the department under specified circumstances, regardless of where or when the circumstances arise and regardless of the functional unit to which the member confronted by them may be currently assigned. These plans constitute the standard operating procedures of the department.

Department procedures assure desired action and thus facilitate and expedite suitable operations and lessen the likelihood of errors and confusion. The procedures are applicable unless prescribed otherwise in a special case; thus the flexibility necessary in some situations is retained.

Procedural plans relate to office, headquarters, and field procedures. They include reporting regulations, record-division operations, instructions relating to the operation of any type of equipment, and dispatching procedures.

Other procedures relate to the surrounding of a building in which criminals are believed to be hiding or operating, and the searching of such a building, the immediate surrounding area, and also quadrants radiating from the building. Other examples include procedures to be followed in stopping, questioning, searching, handcuffing, and transporting persons whose actions, in a vehicle or on foot, arouse the suspicions of an officer.

Tactical Plans. Tactical plans also affect all members of the force but they are restricted to methods of action to be taken at a designated location and under specified circumstances. Tactical plans represent the application of procedures to specific situations. An outline or description of action that is to be taken in the event of a jail emergency or when a report is received that a robbery is in progress or has just been committed at a specified location, such as at the First National Bank, are examples of tactical plans. Plans to deal with special community events, such as athletic contests, political rallies, parades, street carnivals, Halloween, or other holiday celebrations that may attract large crowds at designated locations, are other examples. Plans to cope with strikers and pickets at a specific plant also fall within this category.

Operational Plans. Operational plans include the work programs of the line divisions. The work to be done to accomplish the purposes of patrol, crime investigation, traffic, vice, and juvenile-crime control, must be analyzed from the point of view of the nature, time, and place of the component tasks, and measured in terms of man-power and equipment requirements. Men and equipment must be assigned to each branch of service; specific objectives must be defined and methods of action developed for their achievement. Some procedures relating specifically to the accomplishment of these objectives will also be planned.

The work program of the line divisions will be planned on the basis of average requirements over a 12-month period. Fluctuations from the average need occur in all fields and short-range plans must be developed to meet unusual requirements. For example, a sudden surge of robberies may impose an unusual load on one platoon in one or more districts and on the detectives assigned to investigate this class of crime; likewise, an unexpected increase in the accident rate, or in the activity of vice operators or juvenile offenders, may necessitate some variation from the work program designed to meet service requirements based on year-around needs.

Extra-departmental Plans. Extra-departmental plans include those that require action or assistance from persons or agencies outside the police department, or that relate to some form of community organization. An extra-departmental plan may be of particular interest to a special operating division. For example, a local safety council is of special interest to the traffic division; a community council for the control of delinquency is concerned with problems of interest to the juvenile division; and a local crime commission is concerned with organized crime, the special interest of the vice division. These special divisions, therefore, have a greater interest in the development of extra-departmental plans in their spheres of activity than has the department as a whole. The previously mentioned tactical plans to deal with special community events will be extra-departmental to the extent that they involve assistance and action by nonpolice agencies.

Disaster-preparedness plans and civil-defense plans are other examples of extra-departmental plans in the preparation of which the police should assume leadership, or at least participate actively, because they have a large responsibility in these events. These plans, however, are department-wide in scope; no single line division is exclusively responsible for their operation.

Management Plans. Management plans relate to the problems of equipping, staffing, and preparing the department to do the job, rather than to its actual operation as an organized force. They include the organization plan (with definitions of the duties of the component organic units), the budget, and procedures relating to accounting, purchasing, and personnel management (recruitment, training, rating, selection for promotion, discipline, and welfare).

Management must anticipate population growth, changes in the socio-economic characteristics of the population, basic changes in the industrial, commercial, and residential character of the community, future territorial expansion, major alterations in street layouts, and innovations in the laws and customs of the people. Management must plan to provide resources adequate to deal with increased needs for police service resulting from these changes.

Research in Planning. The planning process includes research: facts in a wide variety of forms must be discovered; they must be compiled or otherwise recorded in an orderly, systematic fashion, and they must be critically analyzed to discover the need and to develop the details of the proposal. Research also includes seeking principles that may be applied in the improvement of police service. For example, measuring devices are desired to appraise the requirements for service in every field of police activity; the need may be measured *proportionately*, but an absolute measure of the work load in terms of man-power requirements is also desirable. A measure of the accomplishment of each organic unit and of its individual members is also needed. Research also includes an evaluation of the effectiveness of present procedures. As examples: Are procedures for appointment and promotion invariably selecting the best man for the job? Can present patrol procedures be made more effective?

Much research is needed before the relative merits of many alternative police procedures may be accurately appraised. Controlled experiments will provide basic data from which sound conclusions may be drawn. The relative merits may then be established of one- and two-man patrol car and detective operations, of conspicuous and inconspicuous patrol, of foot and car patrol, of checking the security of business establishments, of the degree of patrol-division responsibility in crime investigations, and of a variety of other controversial procedures.

Scope of Planning

Planning needs are not the same in all departments. The planning effort may be directed at a very small segment of the total organization or operation, or it may involve a complete survey of the whole with a view to developing new plans throughout. Municipalities and other units of government sometimes employ consultants or an outside agency to plan a complete reorganization of the force with a modernization of all departmental procedures. In such an undertaking, research is necessary to provide an inventory of personnel, equipment, and buildings, and to appraise police-service requirements. On the other hand, a department may undertake a similar basic overhauling of its own organizational structure and operating procedures over a somewhat longer period of time. Other departments, on the contrary, have carried on a satisfactory planning program over the years. Their plans are usually stabilized and there may be little to be done except to keep them up-to-date.

Before considering further the specific task of planning, attention must be given to some preliminary preparation that should be made if the planning process is to operate most effectively. The department must be organized to assure that planning will be done both promptly and effectively. This is accomplished by placing responsibility for planning on a designated individual or unit. Each will then know what is expected of him. The steps in planning must be analyzed so that the planner may know how to proceed most effectively toward the development of his plans. Since success in the operation of a plan is frequently dependent on wise timing, consideration must be given to the present feasibility and practicality of the plan. Attention must also be given to the manner in which plans and preliminary studies are drafted and to the recording and publication of related orders, procedures, schedules, and instructions. They must be in easily understood terms and they must be communicated to all involved members by an effective system of dissemination if compliance is to be expected. Finally the plan must be placed in operation and its execution supervised.

Organization for Planning

The chief of police has ultimate responsibility for planning, just as he has final responsibility for all processes operating in the organization. Except in the small force, however, he will not have the time to carry on department-wide planning and to supervise the planning process throughout the department. It is for this reason that provision must be made in the organization structure for a planning unit to be held responsible for plans that are department-wide in scope (organization, procedures, and tactics are examples) and for supervising and assisting the planning process throughout the department. In a small force, planning responsibilities may be placed on a designated officer, such as the personnel officer, for example, in addition to his other duties.

Internal Organization and Functions

The Los Angeles Police Department provides an excellent example of the organization and operation of a planning and research division.[1] It is responsible for the following functions:

1. Development and reporting of potential improvements in police administration, management, and procedures based on studies of current trends and methods.

2. Design and control of paper forms used by the department.

3. Study of current and pending legislation affecting the operations of the department, maintenance of legal-opinion files, and liaison with the city attorney.

4. Compiling, analyzing, interpreting, and disseminating information on crime statistics and the workload of the department.

5. Compilation and maintenance of the department manual.

6. Processing of proposed department orders to insure adherence to policy and accepted format, and to prevent duplication of, or conflict with, existing orders.

7. Assisting in the preparation of the annual report and the department budget, and development of current and long-range budgetary estimates.

8. Preparation of maps, graphs, charts, and other artwork for use throughout the department.

The planning and research division, commanded by a captain, is composed of two sections, one devoted to analysis and the other to systems, and each commanded by a lieutenant. The analysis section is divided into five units (administrative research, budget, cartography, tabulating, and statistics) and the systems section into three units (manuals and orders, legal, and forms). Each unit is headed by a sergeant except two (cartography and tabulating) that are directed by civilian personnel.

Administrative Research Unit is responsible for the following functions:

1. The study of projected trends in socio-economic data which have a functional relationship to the problems of the police as an

---

[1] From the 1956 *Annual Report,* Planning and Research Division, Los Angeles Police Department.

aid in the development of long-range plans and objectives of the department.

2. Basic research in the field of police administration.

3. The creation of administrative research techniques which can be applied by other units of the department in carrying out their activities more effectively.

Budget Unit has the following functions:

1. Assist in the preparation and coordination of the department-proposed budget, including the alteration and improvement program, capital-improvement program, current-level budget, service-betterment budget, and budget organization charts.

2. Preparation of administrative and budgetary reports, surveys, and studies as requested by the chief and departmental staff.

Cartography Unit:

1. Coordinates the printing, mounting, correcting, and coloring of maps ordered by all departmental units and outside agencies through the supply division.

2. Provides technical advice concerning the availability, design, mounting, and surfacing of maps intended for use (a) as an aid in deployment during emergency conditions such as floods, disasters, and stake-outs, (b) in depicting crime trends or occurrences, (c) in locating places of arrest, and (d) for training purposes.

3. Prepares maps for court presentation, emergencies, and special events.

4. Prepares charts, diagrams, floor plans, sketches, and title cards for departmental use.

Statistics Unit:

1. Interprets and disseminates crime statistics and other related material to be used as aids for more effective and efficient operation of the department.

2. Prepares and distributes periodical statistical reports.

3. Prepares special surveys and reports relative to crime trends, *modus operandi,* and special problems.

4. Prepares statistical charts, graphs, and artwork as needed by other department units.

5. Assists other agencies in the analysis of statistical information.

6. Maintains and operates the *modus operandi* files.

7. Processes and prepares crime reports for keypunch and tabulating operations.

Tabulating Unit:

1. Operates electronic and mechanical tabulating equipment.

2. Establishes new and implements existing procedures when electronic or mechanical tabulating equipment is involved.

3. Prepares and compiles machine-processed reports.

4. Maintains and operates all tabulating card files except the *modus operandi* files.

Forms Unit:

1. Examines existing forms and procedures with the objective of eliminating or combining, simplifying, and improving them.

2. Designs new forms and develops procedures to implement their preparation and processing.

3. Conducts field studies to determine the most efficient design and use of forms and methods.

4. Maintains liaison with other government and private agencies in the furtherance of the department's form-control program.

5. Maintains a complete history and alphabetical, numerical, and functional indexes for all forms.

6. Maintains and operates a Vari-typer to serve all departmental units.

Legal Unit:

1. Researches legal questions and problems for the department; surveys departmental orders and practices in the light of actual or proposed changes in state or local law.

2. Furnishes legal advice to staff and field personnel.

Manuals and Orders Unit:

1. Receives, researches, and processes requests for department orders, memoranda, and amendments to the department manual.

2. Furnishes information to members of the department regarding existing procedures, orders, and manuals.

3. Advises and assists members in developing and maintaining bureau and division manuals.

The Duties of a Planning Unit

The duties of the planning unit (or officer) may be best described by saying that it performs planning duties that would be performed by the chief if he had sufficient time. The planning officer is a staff officer who performs designated administrative tasks (planning duties) for the chief; he assists the chief in planning administrative policy.

Likewise, the most precise and effective guide for the planning officer is the rule that he should plan as he would were he the chief of police. Especially in over-all reorganization planning, he should ask himself, "What would I do if I were the chief?"

The duties of the planning officer or unit may be listed as follows:

1. To review and analyze periodically all department plans (including operational plans) in order to assure that they are suitably recorded and up-to-date.

2. To modernize and improve plans that are department-wide in scope.

3. To suggest, either directly to the heads of operating divisions or to the chief, the modernization and improvement of operational plans.

4. To lend such assistance to the operating divisions in the preparation and improvement of their plans as they may desire.

5. To obtain assistance from operating personnel, either directly or through the chief, in the preparation or improvement of plans.

6. To analyze the operation of plans to ascertain their suitability; when a new plan is placed in operation, to discuss its weaknesses with operating personnel and to effect needed improvements in it.

In short, the planning unit will examine the minute detail of every aspect of police organization, operation, and management, and will attempt, by analysis and contemplation, to increase the effectiveness of police efforts and the economy of their operations in every field of operation. The busy workday of line officers with its stress and bustle leaves little or no time for the development of ideas into full-blown plans. This is the task of the planning unit.

The planning unit is primarily responsible for the development of plans that are department-wide in scope. The extent to which it will participate in the development of operational plans will vary greatly among departments and among divisions within the same department; it will be influenced principally by the willingness of the operating divisions to seek assistance in accomplishing its planning duties.[1]

[1] "At the outset the chief can help to establish a favorable reception for a planning unit, although confidence and respect cannot be commanded but must be earned. It should be understood that initially there may be some mistrust and reluctance to present problems to the planning unit for discussion and aid. This attitude can be over-

The Stimulation of the Planning Process. It should be understood at the outset that planning is a process that permeates the entire organization. Planning must be in operation at every level and in every functional unit of the organization. Since this is so, no one person may be given total responsibility for planning.

The purpose of organization for planning is to stimulate the planning process. In so far as the creation of a planning unit accomplishes this purpose, it is achieving its end. The planning unit, however, should not do all department planning. A planning unit or a part-time planning officer is tempted to take over the entire process rather than to stimulate it. There will then be less planning throughout the organization and creation of the unit defeats its purpose. This hazard should be recognized and guarded against.

The planning unit should consider stimulation of the planning process as a first responsibility. It is important to promote the planning process throughout the organization for two reasons. First, the knowledge and experience of the operating personnel, and especially of those who will execute the plan, are essential to effective planning. Without it the plans are likely to be impractical. Second, the success of a plan is dependent on the confidence operating personnel have in it. Such confidence is stimulated when the members who are to operate the plan have a part in its preparation.

The participation of operating personnel in the formulation of plans may be accomplished by the appointment, by the chief, of wisely selected committees to consider special problems and to outline procedures to deal with them. In some instances it may be desirable to assign temporarily to the planning unit one or more members to work on some specific plan. During the process of developing a plan, informal discussions should be held with members of the force whose operations will be affected by it. Modifications based on the experience and opinions of these men will strengthen the plan. The participation of these members will also strengthen their support of the plan.

While all operating personnel may not participate in the prepara-

come rapidly when it is made evident that the unit is not seeking credit at the expense of other divisions of the police department. When it becomes known that the planning unit provides assistance without censure or seeking credit for improvements, it becomes a welcome aid to line commanders. Such a planning unit, integrated as part of the management team, invariably becomes a vital force in the progress of an organization." Richard Simon, Deputy Chief of Police, Los Angeles, in "The Planning and Research Division of the Los Angeles Police Department," *The Journal of Criminal Law, Criminology, and Police Science,* vol. 44, no. 3, Sept.-Oct., 1953, pp. 365-373.

tion of a plan, those who do are influential in convincing the others of its practicality and value.

Steps in Planning

There are five basic steps in planning. (1) The need for the plan must be recognized. (2) A statement of the objective must be formulated. (3) Relevant data must be gathered and analyzed. (4) The details of the plan must be developed. (5) Concurrences must be obtained from organizational units whose operations may be affected by the proposed plan. Provision should be made to assure the accomplishment of each of the steps if the planning process is to operate effectively.

Recognition of the Need for the Plan. If the need for the plan is not recognized, the plan obviously will not be prepared. It is important, therefore, that attention be given to the discovery of the need. Otherwise, essential planning will not be done and the effectiveness of operations will consequently be impaired.

The police must be alert to discover coming events that may impose unusual burdens on them. Seasonal variations in crimes and other incidents requiring attention may justify special operating plans during periods of greatest frequency. Public events that result in the congregation of large numbers of persons in relatively small areas deserve the development of plans that will facilitate the protection and rapid dispersal of the crowds.

Needs are also discovered through breakdowns and failures. When a procedure permits a failure in the accomplishment of a purpose or the occurrence of an unfortunate incident that damages department prestige, there is evidence of need to review and analyze the procedure. Examples of warning signals that indicate the desirability of reviewing and analyzing current plans and operating procedures include: the injury of an officer, an innocent person, or a prisoner while in police custody; the escape of a prisoner; the failure to capture a criminal suspect; the loss of property in police custody; the damage of police property and equipment; a sudden increase in the crime or accident rate or decrease in the percentage of stolen property recovered and of cases cleared by arrest.

It is most desirable, however, to discover weaknesses and deficiencies in a procedure before they cause a breakdown or failure. This may sometimes be accomplished by a critical analysis of the plan. In other instances a need is discovered through analysis of factual data. An apparent need may sometimes be verified by such analysis.

Most needs are discovered through some form of inspection. It is for this reason that the control process (implemented by inspection) is vital to effective operation. Since inspection and planning are thus closely related, and advantage is gained, in departments of suitable size, by combining in one unit the inspection and planning processes.[1]

Line divisions are responsible for the discovery of needs within their fields of special operations. The chief, however, has the ultimate responsibility of seeing that this is done. When he has organized his force in a manner to assure the effective operation of the control process by a system of inspections, he will have greater assurance that such needs are discovered. When this has not been done, the plans officer must accept some inspectional responsibilities in order to assure the discovery of the need. To discover their suitability, he must review and analyze plans and study the use that is made of them.

In practice it is found that most of the original ideas that lead to improvements in organization, operating procedures, and techniques are conceived by the operating units who are aware of problems that adversely affect their operations. It is the responsibility of the planning unit to research the problem, consider the proposal, study its application, and develop suitable procedures to place a workable plan into operation.

Statement of Objective. The second step in planning is the formulation of the mission. It is the answer to the question, What is to be accomplished by the plan? A precise statement of the objective should be prepared as an aid to clarity in thinking; reference to the statement diminishes the hazard of straying from the true purpose. A clear definition assists in gathering and analyzing relevant data, rejecting nonessential facts, and developing the details of a plan designed to achieve the objective.

The importance of a clear and accurate formulation of the objective deserves emphasis. Without this statement to guide him, the planner stands in danger of wasting his time gathering irrelevant facts, exploring sidetracks that do not lead to the achievement of his purpose, and of developing a plan that will not meet the need

---

[1] The advantages of combining the planning and inspectional tasks in one unit are discussed, O. W. Wilson: *Police Administration*, McGraw-Hill Book Company, Inc., New York City, 1950, pp. 78-79.

that has been discovered. The loose thinking that accompanies a failure to prepare an exact statement of the objective frequently results in an impractical plan.

The statement of the purpose should incorporate the answer in general terms to the question, How is the objective to be accomplished? For example, the objective may be to apprehend a criminal. He may be apprehended by placing a watch on pawnshops, by increased patrol coverage, by a cover on places likely to be attacked, and so on. The statement should indicate which procedure it is planned to use. Sometimes, however, the answer to this question cannot be provided until relevant data have been gathered.

Gathering and Analyzing Relevant Data. The analysis of relevant data is intended to provide the planner and the chief with an estimate of the situation on which to base a decision that action is required, to develop the details of the planned action, and to evaluate its soundness.

Some plans, especially operational plans, necessitate the analysis of considerable data. The nature of the data and the manner of its collection, tabulation, and analysis, varies according to the purpose the plan is to serve. As a general rule, data must be obtained that will provide on analysis the answers to the questions: *What? Where? When? Who? How?* and *Why?* so far as these relate (1) to the basic problem and (2) to its solution.

Data that should be available for planning purposes are described in the next chapter. Subsequent chapters discuss the analysis of these data to meet specific planning needs.

Details of the Plan. On the basis of the analysis, the plan is developed. It may be in the form of a simple procedure, or it may be a complex operation involving the organization of personnel and equipment and the drafting of orders outlining procedures and schedules of assignment and relief.

It is in the development of the plan in detail that it becomes helpful to obtain the assistance of operating personnel. The knowledge and experience of those who are currently dealing with the problem in the field are essential to the development of a sound and practical plan.

Obtaining Concurrences. The operations of more than one organizational unit are affected by some plans. For example, procedures that are department-wide in application affect the operations of all members of the force. The personnel of organizational units should always be given an opportunity to review and suggest modifications of any proposed plan that affects their operations. This is best accomplished by informal discussion during the development of the plan. A formal written concurrence should be sought, however, from each affected unit. *Any unit that does not approve the plan or some detail of it should be required to submit a written statement of reasons for non-concurrence.* The planner then has an opportunity to modify the plan to meet the objections. When he is convinced of the wisdom of the plan, however, he should prepare a consideration of the non-concurrence, answering each argument offered by the opposition. The chief should then decide on the action to be taken; that is, he may accept the proposed plan or the point of view expressed in the non-concurrence or some modification of either.

Practicability and Feasibility of the Plan

In the development of the plan, and sometimes as a part of an earlier step, consideration must be given to its practicality and feasibility. A plan may be quite practical under certain conditions and yet be impractical in the present circumstance. *The best plan will fail when the operating personnel are not competent to carry it out or are determined that it shall not succeed.* In considering the practicality of a plan, therefore, consideration must be given to such personnel characteristics as competence, morale, interest, enthusiasm, quality of leadership at lower levels, and so on. The adequacy and availability of both equipment and man power likewise influence the practicality of a plan.

The feasibility of a plan is also influenced by factors outside the department over which the chief has less direct or no control. These factors include community resources as well as the attitude toward the plan and the spirit of cooperation of other community agencies that may be involved to some extent in its operation. Also included are public and official sentiment. The police cannot advance beyond the sympathetic understanding of either the officials who control their destiny or the general public. While practical and perfectly sound from a police viewpoint, a plan may be contrary to the stated or implied policy of the *administration*. A plan may also be contrary to the interest or wishes of *powerful influences* in the community which are in a position to stop its operation or to apply pressures that will result in more damage to the police purpose than if the plan had not been undertaken. *The public*, too, may not be prepared to accept the plan.

While the police chief must not compromise with criminals, he must consider the feasibility of his plans, not with the view of discarding them for all time, but rather to hold their operation in abeyance until conditions are more favorable. While unfavorable factors must be considered in deciding on the advisability and timing of the adoption of a plan, the progressive chief does not permit them to dissuade him from his objective. *He immediately undertakes to eliminate or correct adverse conditions so that these forces will shortly favor the plan.*

Completed Staff Work

Planning officers should be well-grounded in the doctrine of completed staff work. *The staff officer who only points out weaknesses or who merely suggests needed action is not performing his full duty.*

Completed staff work includes the five basic steps in planning mentioned above and, in addition, the preparation of a survey report or study adequately documented with supporting facts and figures and having annexed to it all the implementing documents, such as letters, orders, schedules, maps, and so on, that may be needed to place the plan in operation. The document should have the concurrence of each unit whose operations are affected by the proposal. The chief will then have before him all the facts he will need to reach a decision.

Survey Report. The report of the analytical study should be divided into four principal sections:

1. An introduction or letter of transmittal which should contain a precise and accurate statement of the purpose of the study and a brief summary, without argument or discussion, of the recommendations.

2. An appreciation or estimate of the situation as it relates to the purpose. This section should analyze critically the facts that describe the situation. It should point out weaknesses and factors that deserve special attention in the accomplishment of the purpose.

3. Each element involved in the situation should be discussed and a specific conclusion relating to its correction or improvement should be reached. Argument should be given in support of each proposal. Each conclusion should be followed by a positive, precise, and accurate recommendation. No arguments should be given with

the recommendations.[1] The recommendations should be repeated substantially as they are given in the introduction, except that some or all may be in greater detail. The subject matter should be organized with the factors arranged in a logical and systematic manner.

4. Appendix. Tables, charts, and maps that must be referred to for a clear understanding of the text should be inserted near the point of reference. The appendix may contain raw statistical data and other material, such as floor plans and maps, that do not require examination for an understanding of the text but that should be provided to substantiate the accuracy of refined data and to furnish details that should be available for a close study of the proposals. Such documents as letters, orders, outlines of procedures, and assignment schedules designed to implement recommendations made in the body of the report may also be included in the appendix.

The Plan. The plan is the implementation of the decision to take the recommended action. *Police plans should invariably be recorded.* Their publication in some form establishes the fact of their official adoption and serves as a reference in training and supervision and for guidance in their operation.

Plans will be recorded in a number of ways depending on their nature, how many and which members will be concerned with them, and the use that is to be made of them. Some will be initially in the form of a special or general order that may later become an addition to department rules and regulations or duty manuals. Some may be in the form of assignment schedules, prepared broadcasts, records operations, and so on. Others may relate to special events and will have served their purpose after the event has passed. The recording of department procedures is discussed in some detail in Chapter 14.

Activating the Plan

Since plans do not become effective until they are placed in operation, consideration must be given to the delegation of authority and the placing of responsibility for their activation. A plan is usually placed in operation by general or special order signed by the chief. Operating plans are frequently activated less formally by officers at lower levels of authority.

---

[1] The planning staff should avoid giving alternative, less-desirable recommendations except when alternatives are expressly requested. Alternative suggestions raise doubts as to the merits of the first recommendation and are likely to result in a rejection of the best plan. The motto should be: "Recommend the best—and stick to it."

The planning officer is a staff officer lacking authority to order a plan into operation. Failures to activate plans sometimes occur when a planning unit has been created under pressure of higher authority without the complete sympathy and support of the command group. Planning efforts are then wasted. The command group must favor the principle of specialized planning as well as the product if the planning effort is to be most productive. The support of the command group is often won through discussion incident to obtaining concurrences.

When the plan has been activated, supervision must be provided to assure successful conduct of the operation. The provision of a suitable system of inspection will further enhance the likelihood of success.

Authority of the Chief

The elected representatives of the community establish policy by the enactment of ordinances designed to regulate the general public. The police are charged with the enforcement of these laws. Policy is also established by budgetary appropriations; the budget represents the department work program. If the chief is to be held responsible for the accomplishment of the police purpose within this policy framework, he must have authority to organize and direct his resources to this end.

Many communities unwisely restrict the authority of the chief to manage his force in the manner he considers most effective. Restrictions are frequently imposed on the chief in the management of his personnel and in the organization and direction of his force. The former restrictions are discussed in Chapter 13.

The practice of establishing the organization of the department by charter provision or even by ordinance places the force in a straitjacket. The progressive chief then finds himself powerless to modify the structure of the organization to meet changing conditions. No part of the organization structure should be established by law. The chief should also be permitted to make changes in department rules and regulations, duty manuals, and operating procedures without reference to a legislative body. He should have complete freedom, under the direction of the administrative head of the city, to modify the organization structure and operation of his force in a manner that will enable him to utilize his resources most effectively in the attainment of his objectives.

CHAPTER 2

Gathering Basic Data

A WIDE range of information, available in a variety of forms, is needed in police planning. Much of it will be compiled in statistical tabulations; some, however, will be in the form of inventories, maps, and word descriptions.

Appendix A, page 284, contains a list of basic data required in police planning. Not all of the listed information is needed, however, in all planning operations. The list is designed to meet the requirements of all-inclusive plans necessitating a survey of the entire organization and its operation. Some operational, procedural, and tactical planning may need little or none of this information.

Some of the information has its source outside the department. The municipal charter, civil-service laws and regulations, and ordinances and state laws frequently contain provisions that relate specifically to the police department, its organization, operation, and administration. Data relating to street mileage and the area of the jurisdiction are available in the city engineer's office. Census data reveal useful information relating to the population and its socio-economic-racial characteristics. Other agencies may provide additional information useful to the planner.

The Present Organization Structure

An understanding of the true structure of the organization is dependent on the analysis of the relationships that exist between its principal units. These relationships will be apparent only when the operating and procedural details are thoroughly understood. For this reason it is necessary to analyze procedural and duty manuals in addition to the organization chart itself in order to understand the precise relationships.

It is also desirable to ascertain whether the organization chart and procedural and duty manuals describe the relationships, duties, and procedures exactly as they presently exist. Frequently it is found that the true organization and operating scheme bear little resemblance to the paper plans on which they presumably are based. Deviations in practice from the recorded plan (organization

21

chart and procedural manuals) represent various forms of failures and consequently are significant. They may result from a number of causes. The causes should be considered in planning so as to avoid similar failures in the operation of the new plan. The most common causes of failure to adhere to the adopted plan are a lack of understanding and sympathy with the plan and the actual unsuitability of the plan to its purpose.

Lack of Understanding. The structural and operating plan of the organization may not have been explained in such a way that operating personnel understand it. Without understanding, the plan will not operate successfully.

Lack of Sympathy. Unsympathetic personnel may sabotage the plan because of prejudice against the one who developed it, for "political" reasons, or selfishly in order to further the prestige, influence, or authority of an individual or group within the department.

Unsuitability of the Plan to its Purpose. When the plan is impractical, operating personnel may discover that adherence to it impairs the effectiveness of their efforts. Pressed by necessity, enthusiastic, interested, and understanding officers may cut across lines of authority or otherwise violate the basic principles of the plan so that the organization will more effectively serve its true purpose of channeling the efforts of all members toward the achievement of police objectives.

Ascertaining the Organization Pattern

In some departments there may be neither organization chart nor procedural manuals. The true nature of the organization may be difficult to ascertain under these circumstances. Whether the plans are recorded or not, the planner must obtain by inquiry the procedures followed in actual operations if he is to understand the true structure of the organization in its detail. A variety of opinions are frequently found within the department as to its real organization, and inquiry should not be limited to the opinion of the head of the organization or of key personnel.

Differences of opinion relating to the structure of the organization and its operation must be resolved as far as possible. They cannot invariably be resolved for the reason that variations may actually exist among the several functional, time, and place units.

For example, the district commanders may establish different relationships with special branches of the service at headquarters. One may undertake a greater responsibility in traffic, vice, or juvenile crime control than another. Platoon commanders may do the same. Likewise, one patrol sergeant may require the performance of tasks by his men not required by other sergeants, or he may require their performance in a different manner. Inconsistent variations can be resolved when the deviation is not currently acceptable and is corrected when discovered. When variations are permitted without correctional effort, the procedures must be considered and recorded as alternatives in describing the organization and operation of the force. These inherent differences represent its true character.

Variations in the opinions of officers and doubts as to their relationship to both superiors and subordinates are also sometimes difficult to resolve. Officers in poorly organized departments frequently are not certain to whom they are directly responsible; likewise they sometimes are in doubt as to the scope of their authority over subordinate officers.

Questions as to whom they are responsible and who is responsible to them should be asked of officers in key positions as well as those who have special assignments that differ markedly from the assignments of other officers. Divergent answers and expressions of uncertainty are evidence of faulty dissemination of information, of lack of instruction concerning assignments, and of confusing organization relationships; they are therefore significant. Inconsistencies must be resolved; to these questions there cannot be divergent answers. Someone at a higher level of authority in the department should be asked to reconcile the divergent answers. The reconciled answer should be accepted as describing the organization pattern; the confusion, however, should be noted.

The current operating organization of the force should be drawn in the form of a chart with the duties of the principal units described in broad outline. Later, after the detailed organization of these units is discovered (in the manner described in later chapters), the organization chart should be expanded to show its present form in as complete detail as may be desired.

A chart of the current operating organization is helpful in analyzing its structure and in describing its operation and its weaknesses.

Comparisons between the present and the recommended organization are also more readily made, described, and understood when charts are available for inspection.

Compiling the Data

Most of the statistical information needed in police planning is obtained directly from police records. Its compilation is effected either by mechanical tabulating equipment or by manual sorting and counting.

Manual Accounting. The absence of tabulating equipment need not prevent the police planner from obtaining needed information. Data may be compiled directly from the basic complaint, arrest, and other records. This is accomplished most readily by preparing an index card containing needed information on each incident. Using cards of distinctive colors for the several classes of incidents facilitates the operation.[1] The data are readily compiled by counting the cards that have been manually sorted according to the information desired. Basic records in card form (such as arrest-record cards) may be used for this purpose without the necessity of preparing index cards.[2]

Tabulating Equipment. Mechanical tabulating equipment, *when its use has been wisely planned,* enables the compilation of a wide variety of statistical information with speed, accuracy, and economy. The accuracy of the data thus compiled is limited only by the accuracy with which the basic information was obtained and punched on the cards. The relatively high present-day clerical salaries make tabulating equipment an economic necessity in all but the very small department. Since tabulating equipment is useful to other city departments, small police forces that may not be justified in maintaining such equipment for their exclusive use should utilize the facilities when they are located in some other municipal office. The police, for example, might punch their own cards and run them through the tabulating machines when this equipment is not being used by some other department; or the office having cus-

---

[1] For example, index cards of one color might be used for Part I crimes, and index cards of different colors might be used for Part II offenses, accidents, arrests, and miscellaneous reports.

[2] For a description of a procedure for gathering information by the use of index cards and basic records, see O. W. Wilson: *Police Records,* Public Administration Service, Chicago, 1942, pp. 207-211.

tody of the equipment may run the cards, gathering such statistical information as the police may request.

Tabulating equipment is useful in compiling data for daily and monthly summaries; it is almost essential for making the many special studies that should be made for the police planner. Especially is this true in studies of the territorial and time distribution of incidents that call for police service. The variety of information that can be tabulated is limited only by the nature of the basic information that is punched on the cards.

Data Recorded on Punch Cards. Since the information that may be obtained by the use of tabulating equipment is restricted to that punched on the cards, when planning the installation of such equipment, *scrupulous attention should be given to the nature and form of statistical data that will be desired* and consideration should be given to the design of the cards to provide columns for all information that may be needed. Imagination and foresight will assure that data are recorded to meet future as well as current needs.

Information will be desired for four principal purposes: (1) The preparation, on a daily, weekly, monthly, and annual basis, of comparative statistical summaries of incidents that require police attention. (2) The identification, through *modus operandi,* of a crime as being one of a series committed by the same man, and also the identification of the perpetrator.[1] (3) The analysis of the causes of accidents. (4) The determination of the time and place distribution of incidents that require police action.

Much of the needed basic data relates to Part I crimes, Part II offenses, accidents, miscellaneous reports, and booked arrests. In addition, information is needed on traffic citations and the *modus operandi* of arrested persons; in large departments, information will also be desired relating to personnel and payrolls.

The variety of desired data necessitates the use of more than one form of punch card. The number of distinctive cards that will be needed is influenced by the size of the force and the nature and detail of information to be recorded. As a minimum, different cards should be used in all departments for recording complaints, arrests, accidents, citations, and juvenile case histories. Departments desiring

---

[1] The use of electrical machines in the comparison of the *modus operandi* and physical characteristics of the unknown perpetrator of a current crime with those of known criminals, in order to discover likely suspects, is discussed, p. 172.

more detailed information may add other distinctive cards for crimes against children; vice complaints; lost and found and stolen and recovered vehicles; other lost and found property; the *modus operandi* of arrested persons, and perhaps some others.

Cards used by a police department that prepares suitable statistical summaries may be used as a guide in the design of cards for local use. Likewise, cards used by a department that makes identification through *modus operandi* should be examined in designing cards for this purpose.

Cards recording arrest and citation data should include space for identifying the assignment of the arresting officer. It may be desired to know whether he was a foot or motorized patrolman, a motorcycle officer, a detective, or an officer assigned to the vice or juvenile divisions. It may also be desirable to know whether it was a multiple arrest, whether the arrest was made by more than one officer, and whether it was on-view or the officers were dispatched to the scene.

Recording the Location on the Punch Cards. Information as to the location of incidents that call for police service is essential in periodically checking on the equity of the beat loads and in studying comparisons between police incidents and the socio-economic data tabulated by census tracts. This information is also required in laying out beats and in planning operations against specific types of criminal activity. To meet these needs, the location must be recorded more precisely than by either beat or census tract. It is for this reason that the area of the jurisdiction should be divided into a relatively large number of small districts called reporting areas (150 or more for each 100,000 population) each completely contained in a census tract and a beat. The reporting areas should not be transversed by the boundary of either a census tract or beat, nor by streams, railroad tracks, main highways, or important streets that may form desirable future beat boundaries. The small districts need not be of equal area, but they should contain approximately equal numbers of incidents, although a considerable variation is not especially harmful.

The location of incidents should be recorded on the punch cards in several different ways, *viz.,* by district (when police operations are decentralized among district stations), and by beat and platoon, census tract, and reporting area. The determination of the area (district, beat, census tract, and reporting area) in which the incident occurred should be made by the punch-card operator on the basis of the street address recorded on the complaint sheet, accident report, or arrest card. This operation is simplified, and the opportunity for not-easily-detected errors is lessened by the use of a directory that lists the streets alphabetically (with the numbered streets appearing first in numerical sequence) and under each street name the block numbers that fall within each reporting area. The block numbers are arranged in the directory in three columns. Blocks on street sections that do not form a boundary of a reporting area, beat, census tract, or district should have their numbers in the second column; those that do form a boundary should have their numbers in both the first and third columns but on separate horizontal lines. The first column should be used for the even-numbered street addresses and the third column for the odd-numbered ones. Columns to the right of these three should each contain a number on each horizontal line to designate (1) the district (in departments having district stations), (2) the census tract, and (3) the reporting area in which the block numbers appearing on that line are found. Additional columns, one for each shift or time period of the day during which different beat layouts are provided, are used for recording, in the same manner, the number of the beat in which the block numbers appearing on the line are found for the time of the day during which the incident occurred.

The directory may be in the form of a small booklet, although a Kardex or rotary-type index is used more expeditiously. The punch-card operator looks up the street number appearing on the basic record; when the block number is listed in the second column, the numbers on the same horizontal line in the columns to the right are punched on the card. When the block number does not appear in the second column, the operator ascertains whether the street address is even or odd and then consults either the first column (for even numbers) or the third column (for odd numbers). The numbers on the same line in the columns to the right will represent the numbers for the various areas to be punched on the card.

Recording the Time on the Punch Cards. Time data are needed to discover daily and seasonal variations in the work load which should be considered in planning weekly and annual leaves. These data are also needed to ascertain the most desirable hours for patrol shift changes, to compute the proportional distribution of the force among the several shifts, and to plan special operations to meet specific needs.

Time data should be recorded on all cards in terms of year, month, date, day of week, and hour of day. The hour of occurrence should be recorded on all cards. The time reported, which does not need to include the day of the week, is not needed on arrest and accident cards.

There is justification for using the hour reported instead of the hour of occurrence in Part I crimes in some planning computations. The proportion of cases in which the hour of occurrence is exactly known is sometimes so small as to make the use of the hour reported necessary, especially in the organization of beats, in order to have an adequate sample. This procedure is further justified by the fact that an added burden is placed on the police at the time Part I crimes are reported.

For the purposes of tabulation, any given hour-number, such as 2, will represent the 60-minute period immediately following it, i.e., the period from 2:00 to 3:00. When the exact hour of occurrence is not known, but is given as during a two-hour period, the first hour should be taken as the time. If the time is given as during a longer period, when the period covers an odd number of hours, the middle hour is selected as the hour of occurrence, and when it covers an even number of hours, the first of the middle pair of hours is selected as the hour. When the period covers 24 or more hours, no hour is recorded.

Recording the Data

A card should be made on each incident even though the information may not be complete. For example, the hour of occurrence is of value in determining the most suitable shift hours and in making the chronological distribution even though the location is not known, provided the incident occurred within the jurisdiction. Incidents that are reported as having occurred at headquarters (as has been found to be the practice in some departments in recording the locations of arrests and some other incidents where the location was not readily ascertained) should have the location recorded as unknown. Otherwise the small district containing police headquarters would have a disproportionate share of incidents.

Patrol service is needed at the locations and during the hours of occurrence of incidents that call for police service. Experience has shown that the time and place distribution of these incidents does not vary greatly from one year to the next. When the incidents that occurred on one shift during a year are spotted on a map, the distribution pattern shows remarkable similarity to the pattern for the succeeding year. Their not-too-distant past distribution, therefore, serves as a guide in planning the chronological and territorial distribution of the patrol force.

Patrol service is needed to deal with the incidents at the times of their occurrence and also at other times to prevent them by diminishing the effectiveness of the hazards that induce them. Since the determination of the shift hours and the distribution of the patrol force should be based on the *proportional* time and place distribution of the incidents, it is unnecessary that the number be precisely correct, provided variations from the total are believed to be distributed with reasonable uniformity in time and place. Because of possible seasonal variations, the data should cover a 12-month period if it is to reflect an average need for the year.

The data desired may not invariably be available in the form desired, in which case ingenuity must be used in obtaining data having equal significance. The numbered case reports (complaint or offense and accident records) are the source for basic information on Part I and II crimes, accidents, and miscellaneous reports, and the arrest ledger (blotter) or arrest cards provide the information on booked arrests. These basic records are nearly always available although the information is sometimes incomplete in some respects. Least difficulty is experienced, as a general rule, in obtaining data on Part I crimes, arrests, and accidents. Sometimes numbered cases are not made on all Part II crimes and miscellaneous reports. Search must then be made for records of equal significance. The radio log sometimes serves as a suitable substitute. Frequently there are also found other records that may constitute a portion of Part II and miscellaneous reports; these may be in the form of a daily bulletin or "running sheet" on which are recorded pertinent information relating to unnumbered reports.

When the numbered reports are found to be restricted to Part I crimes and major Part II crimes, there may be justification for accepting the entire category of major crimes as a type of incident instead of attempting to segregate the reports that are not Part I; otherwise the relatively small group of major Part II crimes must be lumped with radio calls or with the incidents recorded on a "running sheet."

Tabulating cards (or index cards) should be prepared on all incidents for a 12-month period. Limitations in clerical staff, however, may make desirable the use of a representative sample instead. For example, cards may be prepared on every other incident or on the incidents that occur on every other day. When a sample is used, care must be exercised to avoid inaccuracies resulting from an inadequate or untrue sample. Special attention should be given to the possibility of hourly, daily, and seasonal variations unduly influencing the sample.

The cards on each type of incident should be segregated according to the hour of occurrence. The number in each of the 24 hours should be expressed in terms of per cent of the total for the 24 hours. These hourly percentage figures for each type of incident will give the proportional time distribution of the incidents. Cards on Part I crimes should be segregated according to the time reported as well.

Some additional information is needed relating to the small districts. The area of each should be computed, preferably by the city engineer's office, and the area should be expressed in terms of per cent of the total area. The total number of store doors to be checked for security should be counted in each district, and this number should also be expressed in per cent of the total number of doors. The total number of establishments in each district subject to patrol inspection, such as dance halls, taverns, bars, bowling alleys, pool halls, and similar places of amusement, should also be counted, and this number should be expressed in per cent of the total.

The number of incidents of each type occurring in each of the small districts on each shift should also be expressed in per cent of the total for that platoon. This computation must be made after the determination of the desired shift hours, and consequently further complications of data must be delayed until this decision is reached. The use of these data for this purpose and for the distribution of the patrol force is discussed further in the chapter on patrol.

CHAPTER 3

Decisions That Influence the Functional Organization

THE functional organization of the force is strongly influenced by the relationship between the patrol division and the special divisions of the department. Before considering the detail of the police organization structure, therefore, it is desirable to reach some basic decisions as to the responsibility that should be placed on the patrolman for conditions on his beat and for action that he should take in the investigation of crimes and accidents, the suppression of vice, the control of traffic, and the supervision of juvenile offenders. A decision must also be made as to the assignment of responsibility for the search of crime and accident scenes for physical evidence. These decisions as well as others relating to the functional organization of the force are influenced by the desirability of specialization.

The Extent of Specialization

Duty manuals and other sources must be examined to ascertain the duties of the beat patrolman in each field of activity and the task of specialized personnel at the level of execution. The duties should be recorded to facilitate analysis and decisions as to needed changes. Analysis will reveal the extent of specialization.

Specialization has some noteworthy advantages. It facilitates the placing of responsibility, the training of the members, the development of experts, and the promotion of *esprit de corps*. It also stimulates special police interest and usually arouses an increased public interest.

Specialization, however, also has some disadvantages. It tends to limit the usefulness of the members and to restrict general police interest; tasks of command are made more difficult and other administrative problems are created. Specialization also tends to hamper the development of a well-rounded police program and to diminish territorial coverage.

The following factors should be considered in reaching decisions as to the desirability of specialization:[1]

1. The quality of personnel.
2. The need for special skill and ability.
3. The importance of the job.
4. The amount of work to be done.
5. The need for readily available services.
6. The existence of intermittent emergency needs.
7. The need for maintaining skill through performance.
8. The need for planning and control.
9. The dissimilarity of the task to other duties.
10. The attitude of the members of the force toward the task.
11. The interference of the task with the performance of regular duties.
12. The size of the force and the area of its jurisdiction.

An examination of these specialization-determining factors reveals that the degree of specialization should not be the same in all branches of police service nor in the performance of all tasks within the particular field of activity. The extent of desirable specialization can be wisely established only after analysis of each operation to ascertain its characteristics in terms of the factors listed above. Specialization may be clearly indicated in the performance of one task in a special field, such as traffic, but not in the performance of another task in the same field.

Patrol Division Responsibility

A superior quality of service is usually provided when all members of the department have some responsibility for the accomplishment of the primary police purposes, which may be considered to be the prevention of crimes and accidents, dealing with them when they occur, and providing a variety of services to the public. When a crime or accident becomes known to the police, they care for the injured, apprehend the perpetrator or suspects, seek witnesses and obtain facts from them and the victims, search for and preserve physical evidence for laboratory examination, establish the identity of the perpetrator, and prepare the case for presentation in court. Crimes against persons and property are usually reported promptly to the police by the victim. Violations of so-called morals laws,

---

[1] Each of these factors and the advantages and disadvantages of specialization are discussed, and arguments favoring the enlargement of the beat officer's responsibilities in the special fields are given in *Police Administration*, pp. 30-35 and 82-89.

however, usually do not involve an aggrieved victim but, instead, all parties are willing participants. The police, therefore, must ferret out these violations as well as violations of regulations that ordinarily do no harm to an individual victim. Ultimate responsibility for the discovery of the nonvictim-type crime and for the arrest of the perpetrators of all crimes is usually imposed on special organic units of the department.

The performance of tasks within each field of special activity should not be the exclusive responsibility of the members of a special division nor should they be relieved of all responsibility for the performance of duties outside the field of their interest. Decisions must be made as to the need for special divisions and as to the assignment of tasks to the specialists, to patrolmen, and to other members of the force. The relationship of the special division to the patrol division is especially important. The specialists should be made exclusively responsible for the performance of some duties, the patrolmen of others, while both should have a joint responsibility for the accomplishment of some tasks.

Decision 1. What should be the basic responsibility of the beat patrolman?

The beat officer should invariably be held responsible for the elimination or reporting of conditions that may induce incidents that call for police service; he should be held to account for crimes committed on his beat. He should be required to prevent crimes and accidents, suppress vice, and protect and control the juvenile as well as the adult population.

The policy of holding the beat officer responsible for conditions on his beat has important advantages. Responsibility is unmistakably placed. It falls on the one member of the force whose duties most readily enable him to discover undesirable conditions and to take immediate corrective action. The continuous personal attention of the beat officer to a designated area affords him an apportunity to acquire firsthand, by observation and inquiry, information regarding conditions on his beat. His continuous presence and his knowledge of police hazards afford maximum opportunity for the prevention of crimes and accidents and the suppression of vice. The need for specialized patrols and for the performance of some inspectional tasks by specialists is diminished when the patrolman is responsible for all conditions on his beat. The number of specialists required is thereby lessened and the patrol division is strengthened proportionately.

Decision 2. When a special division is created, what should be the policy in reference to the assignment of tasks within the special field to motorized beat patrolmen?

Tasks that do not interfere with regular patrol duties and that can be performed substantially as well by the beat patrolman as by the specialist should be assigned to the motorized beat officer.

Several advantages result from the performance by the beat officer of tasks in crime investigation, in vice, traffic, and juvenile-crime control, that do not interfere with his regular patrol duties and that he can perform substantially as well as the specialist.

1. A better quality of service is usually provided by competently supervised beat patrolmen than by specialists. This is true for two reasons: (a) Speed is usually an important factor in the successful disposition of police calls, and the continuous presence and immediate availability of the beat officer in a radio car assures rapid response to calls for service. (b) When investigations and other action are performed by beat officers under the direction of able patrol sergeants and platoon lieutenants, the entire patrol division resources may be brought into operation; the undertakings are then quickly consummated. Information thus obtained frequently leads to the immediate clearance of the crime by the arrest of the perpetrator and the recovery of stolen property. When the undertaking is not disposed of by the platoon on duty, the efforts of the other platoons may be readily coordinated within the patrol division; the plan of action is thus completed without interruption, delay, or change.

2. When the patrol division performs routine tasks for them, the time and energy of the specialists are conserved for investigations that require their special skills. When tasks that may be performed by the beat officer are assigned to specialists, during the night hours either specialists must be kept on duty to answer infrequent calls or investigations and other action are delayed, frequently until the following day. Delay jeopardizes the success of the undertaking. Investigations by specialists assigned to night duty are usually nothing more than preliminary investigations that could be performed equally well or better by the patrol division.

3. The patrolman's sense of responsibility is heightened when he

investigates a crime or other incident that he was charged with preventing.

4. The assignment of tasks in the special field to the beat officer provides an opportunity for patrolmen to acquire investigative techniques and interrogative skills through experience and enables police executives to discover talent in patrolmen that may justify their assignment to special divisions.

5. The value of the beat patrolman to the service increases as he becomes better acquainted with persons and conditions on his beat. The broader his responsibility, the greater the opportunity for him to become well acquainted. The assignment of tasks to specialists that deprives the beat officer of the opportunity to become acquainted with criminals, problem children, and vice conditions on his beat results in a less competent policeman.

6. The assignment of inspectional tasks in a special field to the beat patrolman assures a 24-hour continuous attention that is lacking when he is not given this responsibility.

7. Enforcement in special fields (e.g., traffic and vice control) by an adequately motorized patrol division, because of its complete coverage, is more consistently uniform in both time and place than when it is left to specialists. For example, when every patrolman is a traffic officer, the deterrent effect on motorists and pedestrians is increased and more widely spread. The relatively large number of officers engaged in enforcement reduces the load on each to relatively small proportions; a higher level of enforcement is usually possible, therefore, with less administrative pressure.

8. The supervision of specialists, on duty at hours or locations in such small number as not to justify a supervisory officer from their branch of the service, is not a problem when the patrol division undertakes the performance of their tasks.

9. The assignment to specialists of tasks that can be satisfactorily performed by beat patrolmen further depletes the patrol strength and lessens the effectiveness of patrol service proportionately. When men are not withdrawn from the patrol division for assignment to special divisions, the patrol force is substantially larger than it would otherwise be; the larger size permits smaller beats and more intensive patrol. More intensive patrol is advantageous from the viewpoint of crime, vice, and accident prevention.

10. A superior quality of service is provided by a well-integrated department in which the efforts of all the organic units and their

members are directed toward the accomplishment of the total police purpose.

Decision 3. What responsibility should be placed on the patrolman for vice conditions on his beat?

The beat patrolman should invariably be held responsible for vice conditions on his beat. He should be required to ascertain vice conditions by observation and investigation and to take suitable corrective action under the direction of his immediate patrol supervisor. He should make an arrest for a vice offense committed in his presence. Other vice offenses coming to his notice or discovered by him should be reported to his supervisor who should direct immediate action by the officer, organize an immediate raid using the patrol force for this purpose, or, if he feels that the vice division may be interested in the case or that it has ramifications that justify such attention, he should withhold direct action and report the matter to the specialists, by telephone or in person if it seems urgent. The vice division, in turn, may advise him to proceed, or it may undertake the investigation itself. Violations on which the patrol division is unable to obtain evidence should be reported to the vice division for action. Assistance and advice from the specialists should be freely sought. Reports to the vice division should be in writing although the written report may be preceded by conversation.

Patrolmen should be required to make periodic reports of vice conditions on their beats, stating categorically that there are no known vice activities except those reported. Patrolmen should be held to account for their failure to discover vice operations on their beats.

Decision 4. Should the patrol division or the traffic division be principally responsible for the enforcement of moving-traffic regulations?

To discharge this principal responsibility, the division selected for the task has an obligation to make substantially more than half the stops (*i.e.,* warnings, citations, and arrests) that are made by the department for moving violations. The principal enforcement of moving-traffic regulations by an adequately motorized patrol division has many of the previously mentioned advantages.

There does not seem to be justification for the creation of a traffic-division patrol unit large enough to undertake the principal enforcement of moving-traffic regulations. The tasks of enforcing moving-traffic regulations is not dissimilar to other motor-patrol duties. Special skill and ability beyond the capacity of the beat officer are not required; the amount of work, when the task is divided among all patrolmen, is not so great as to occupy full time; the task does not ordinarily interfere with other patrol duties when the patrol force has been distributed in proportion to the need for patrol service. Traffic violations are the most frequent form of public misconduct, and general patrol should be used in its prevention.

Decision 5. Should the patrolman and his supervisors be responsible for the preliminary investigation of crimes on his beat?[1] *If not, what limitations are to be imposed on his investigation of crimes the final clearance of which is the ultimate responsibility of a special division?*

In considering these questions, distinction must be made between the preliminary investigation of the crime and its continued investigation with ultimate responsibility for the accomplishment of the police purpose. The ultimate police purpose in crime investigation is usually the conviction of the perpetrator, although in the case of the juvenile offender it may mean his readjustment by treatment without court action. The ultimate purpose includes the clearance of the case by the arrest of the perpetrator and the recovery of any stolen property.

There seems justification for making an exception of the distinction between the preliminary and the continued investigation in crimes, such as frauds and worthless checks, which are committed without protest from the victim and which usually are not reported to the police until some time has elapsed. These usually do not re-

---

[1] "Patrol-division duties relating to a reported crime may be classified as noninvestigative (direct action) and investigative (the preliminary investigation). Direct action consists of care for injured persons, apprehension of the criminal at the scene or in flight, protection of the crime scene pending the search for physical evidence, and finally, the recovery of stolen property. The preliminary investigation is the immediate investigation up to the point that postponement of further investigation would not jeopardize its successful completion. The preliminary investigation consists of interviewing the victim, searching for and interviewing witnesses and suspects, and taking suspects into custody if there is sufficient evidence of guilt or when postponement of arrest might permit the suspect to flee." By permission, from *Police Administration,* by O. W. Wilson, p. 116, Copyright, 1950. McGraw-Hill Book Company, Inc.

quire immediate preliminary investigation; their entire investigation, therefore, may be left to the special division.

The principal purpose of accident investigation is to discover violations and to obtain evidence useful in the identification, apprehension, and prosecution of the violator. Accident investigations are therefore included in the term "crime investigation." The question of the assignment of traffic-accident investigations is discussed more fully in Chapter 10.

Choice may be made among four broad patterns of assignment to beat officers and specialists of responsibility for the preliminary investigation and the continued investigation. Members of the detective, vice, traffic, and juvenile divisions are referred to here as specialists.

1. Ultimate responsibility for the complete investigation may be placed on the beat patrolman. In this pattern, the patrolman is held responsible for the final clearance of all crimes committed on his beat by the arrest of the perpetrator and the recovery of stolen property. The specialist has none of these responsibilities except in the types of crime mentioned above that were committed without protest from the victim; he is merely available to the patrolman for consultation and advice.

2. In the second pattern the patrolman has responsibility for the preliminary investigation of all crimes committed on his beat, but the ultimate responsibility for clearance by arrest of the perpetrator and the recovery of stolen property in only designated classes, such as petty theft. In this pattern, the special division has ultimate responsibility for clearances and recoveries in all classes of crimes except those in which this responsibility is placed on the beat patrolman.

3. In the third pattern, the beat patrolman makes a preliminary investigation of all crimes and the special division has ultimate responsibility for their clearance and the recovery of all stolen property.

4. In the fourth pattern, the special division has ultimate responsibility for the clearance of all crimes and the responsibility of the beat patrolman is limited to the preliminary investigation of designated classes of crimes. The special division undertakes the immediate and complete investigation of other classes of crimes. For example, homicides and rapes might be investigated at once by

the detective division, while the beat patrolman might undertake the preliminary investigation of less serious crimes.

No matter which of these four patterns is selected as the most desirable relationship between the patrol and the special divisions, further refinement is necessary in the form of a more exact definition of probable exceptions. For example, if the first pattern is selected, regulations should be drafted relating to the circumstances under which the patrolman would be required to seek assistance from specialists in his investigation. In the second pattern, decision must likewise be made as to which classes of crimes patrolmen should have ultimate and complete responsibility to investigate and clear. While the second and third patterns make no provision for calling on specialists in the preliminary investigation of any designated classes of crimes, it may be desirable to establish regulations that would require their notification and perhaps a request for their assistance in certain crimes, not primarily on the basis of their classification but rather on their seriousness. For example, some but not all homicides, rapes, and aggravated assaults may deserve immediate detective attention. The decision may well be left to the patrol division command within the framework of a general policy statement, rather than arbitrarily to require detectives to be called out in all crimes in that class. In the fourth pattern, regulations must be drafted designating those classes of crimes that are to be investigated immediately by the special division.

While a fifth pattern, in which specialists have exclusive and complete responsibility for the preliminary investigation of all crimes, is found in a few poorly organized departments where the services of patrolmen are greatly restricted, the infrequency with which this procedure is found and its general undesirability render it unworthy of further consideration. The practice of requiring immediate preliminary investigation by the special division of designated classes of crimes without regard to their individual severity (pattern 4) likewise seems ill advised. These procedures make imperative the 24-hour service of some specialists. Since the investigation made at night by a specialist is merely a preliminary investigation, the advantages of specialization in investigation are not gained and the investigation may be performed better by the beat patrolman under the direction of the patrol command.

Placing complete responsibility for the clearance of all crimes and the recovery of all stolen property exclusively on the beat patrolman (pattern one) is also considered undesirable. It makes overtime work mandatory or results in a cessation of the investigation until the patrolman returns for duty; it may also interfere with his regular patrol duties.

The second and third patterns, as described above, seem most suitable. Choice between them must be made on the basis of the relative investigative load and responsibility that it is desired to place on the patrol and special divisions, especially in reference to less important crimes. There seem to be important advantages in giving ultimate responsibility for clearances and recoveries to the specialists in all crimes, as is provided in the third pattern. The previously mentioned disadvantages of giving exclusive responsibility to the beat officer are then avoided.

Specialization in the Search for Physical Evidence

Search must be made for physical evidence at the scenes of crimes and accidents. The evidence must be discovered, identified, recorded, preserved, marked and labeled, and transported to headquarters. This must be done without loss, mutilation, or contamination. Special skill and equipment are needed to perform these tasks satisfactorily. The search should be undertaken immediately in order to lessen the possibility of accidental or deliberate destruction, alteration, or concealment of evidence.

Decision 6. Who should be assigned the task of searching crime scenes for physical evidence?

An examination of current practice among police departments indicates that there are five groups of persons to whom the search of crime scenes for physical evidence may be assigned. They are: the beat officer who makes the preliminary investigation; the detective who has ultimate (and, in some departments, complete) responsibility for the final clearance of the case; the identification officer who may be sent to the scene to search for latent prints and who may expand his activities to include a search for all physical evidence; a member of the crime-laboratory staff; and a specially trained evidence technician supplied with an automobile containing equipment essential for a thorough search and the preservation and transportation of physical evidence.

The assignment of the search for physical evidence to the patrolman or detective charged with the preliminary investigation has serious disadvantages. Each man cannot be supplied with all essential equipment; the cost would be prohibitive and its transportation and care would interfere with the performance of routine duties. Bringing equipment from headquarters involves needless delay. Equipment used by all members of a large group is subject to abuse and neglect; defective equipment and exhausted supplies interfere with effective operation. Each man in so large a group cannot be effectively trained. Skills that must be maintained by frequent performance would be lost owing to the relatively infrequent performance when the tasks are distributed among all patrolmen or detectives. Either the preliminary investigation or the search for physical evidence suffers when both are performed by the same man. The two tasks are dissimilar, they require quite different skills, and they deserve the attention of different officers in order to assure prompt action.

The assignment of the search for physical evidence to either the identification officer or the laboratory criminalist also has serious disadvantages. Delay experienced in getting the specialist to the scene, especially during his off-duty hours when a 24-hour service is not provided at headquarters, retards the search. Imposition on the off-duty time of the identification officer or laboratory man and the inconvenience of locating him and bringing him to the scene sometimes result in these specialists not being called or the search being postponed until the following day. Under either circumstance evidence is lost that might otherwise prove helpful in the identification and conviction of the criminal. The search for physical evidence does not normally merit the services of a highly trained criminalist. To use the services of a highly trained man on a task that does not ordinarily require such costly skills is fundamentally unsound.

Evidence technicians assigned to each platoon, and supplied with automobiles carrying all equipment needed in the search, recording, preservation, and transportation of physical evidence assure prompt and thorough search of all crime and accident scenes. This arrangement has the following advantages:

1. Greater skill may be developed by the evidence technician. He may be selected on the basis of his special interest and ability; he may be given more intensive training than it would be possible to

provide for a larger number, and he improves his skill through frequent performance.

2. More complete equipment may be provided the relatively small number of evidence technicions. Since they are skilled, they may be supplied with more delicate equipment, and it is less likely to be damaged or its care neglected than if it were used by a larger number of less well-trained officers.

3. More thorough searches are possible by suitably trained and equipped evidence technicians; more physical evidence is therefore discovered and preserved for laboratory examination.

4. Twenty-four-hour service in radio-equipped automobiles assures prompt and speedy attention to the search for physical evidence.

Decision 7. Should the same evidence technician search both crime and accident scenes for physical evidence?

The search for physical evidence at crime and accident scenes requires identical equipment and skills. There seems, therefore, no justification for dividing the searching task on this basis. Instead, each evidence technician should search all crime and accident scenes that occur in his jurisdiction.

Decision 8. Should the evidence technician be limited to the search for and handling of physical evidence, or should he, in addition, also make the preliminary investigation of crimes and accidents?

The evidence technician should be restricted to dealing with physical evidence. The combined tasks of preliminary investigation and search for physical evidence are beyond the capacity of one man; one or the other or both tasks suffer when this combination is attempted. The beat officer should concern himself with the investigation of persons while the evidence technician concerns himself with the investigation of physical things.

When these two tasks are combined, two men are needed for their performance. A two-man crew of investigators is then usually created. All of the previously mentioned advantages of the preliminary investigation by the beat officer are then lost. Two-man crews of investigators result in a demand that a crew be assigned to the detective division for crime investigations and another crew to the traffic division for accident investigations. This degree of specialization is undesirable.

Decision 9. To which division should the evidence technicians be assigned?

The assignment of the evidence technicians to the patrol division has the following advantages:

1. The patrol division should be responsible for the preliminary investigation, and the search for physical evidence is an essential part of it. The coordination of the efforts of the officers making the preliminary investigation and searching for physical evidence is simplified when both are members of the patrol division.

2. Since the patrol division is the only division that invariably maintains supervisory officers on all shifts, supervision of the evidence technicians is simplified and made more effective when they are members of the patrol division. In consequence they are more likely to be available for immediate response to calls for service when they are members of that division.

3. When evidence technicians are assigned to the patrol division, they may be effectively employed, in the intervals between calls for their service, in the performance of patrol tasks, designated by the patrol sergeant or platoon lieutenant, that intensify patrol in areas of special current need.

4. The assignment of the evidence technicians to any other division results in their participation to a greater degree in preliminary investigations. This tempts the special division to assume complete responsibility for the preliminary investigation and to provide a two-man crew for its accomplishment. When this is done, the beat officer and the patrol division have no responsibility in the preliminary investigation. Under these conditions the department does not operate as a well integrated unit, but each special branch closes itself off from the remainder of the force and restricts itself to the exclusive and complete performance of all tasks in its special field.

Decision 10. Since many departments today employ accident-investigation cars manned by crews trained to make a complete investigation of traffic accidents, how may these crews be most readily converted into the type of evidence technicians described above?

In reaching a decision in reference to this question, consideration must be given to current practice in the department, the progressiveness of its members (and especially its leaders), and the inertia that must be overcome in effecting any change. Under some conditions it may be wise to undertake the change in two steps. For example, the search for physical evidence at crime scenes might logically be added to the duties of the accident-investigation officers as a first step. Few additions to their equipment and training are needed to prepare them for this added assignment. Their operation at crime scenes, however, should be restricted to the search for physical evidence. They should not make the preliminary investigation of crimes. This task should be left to the patrolman on the beat.

A second step in the development of the desired procedure for preliminary investigation of crime and accident scenes would be to place on the beat patrolman responsibility for the investigation of accidents; the evidence technician, who would then operate the former accident investigation car by himself, would work with the beat officer in both types of investigation. The two would operate as a team, the beat officer concerned with the investigation of persons, the evidence technician with the investigation of physical things.

CHAPTER 4

Organization According to Functions

THE discussion of the decisions that must be made in planning the organization structure of the police force is divided into two chapters. The organization of the level of authority above the heads of the several functional units and the territorial decentralization of the force among district stations will be discussed in the next chapter. The present chapter is restricted to a discussion of the functional organization of the force.

Analysis of Present Organization

Before considering the detail of its reorganization, analysis should be made of the present police organization. Procedures for ascertaining its true character were discussed in Chapter 2. When the complete organization structure with all its relationships is thoroughly understood, an examination should be made of it to ascertain whether it conforms to acceptable principles of organization, and if not, in what respects it violates these principles. As far as the principles are adhered to, the organization may be considered sound; as far as they are violated, it may be considered in need of improvement. The principles to be considered include the following:[1]

1. Tasks similar or related in purpose, process or method, or clientele are grouped together in one or more units under the control of one person. In order to facilitate their assignment, these tasks are divided according to (a) the time and (b) place of their performance and (c) the level of authority needed in their accomplishment.

2. Lines of demarcation between the units are clearly drawn by a precise definition of duties which are made known to all members. Thus responsibility may be placed exactly and duplication in execution and neglect resulting from an unassigned duty may be avoided.

---

[1] This statement of principles is taken from p. 17 and their application is described in Chapters 2 to 4 inclusive, O. W. Wilson, *Police Administration*, 1950. They are reproduced by permission of McGraw-Hill Book Company, Inc., New York City.

3. Channels are established through which information flows up and down, thus permitting the delegation of authority, the placing of responsibility, the supervision of operations, and the coordination of efforts. The individuals and groups are thus tied together into a unified force capable of direction and control. The lines of control must be clearly defined and well understood by all members so that each may know to whom he is responsible and who, in turn, is responsible to him.

4. Each individual, unit, and situation must be under the immediate control of one and only one person, thus achieving the principle of unity of command and avoiding the friction and confusion that result from duplication of direction and supervision.

5. No more units or persons are placed under the direct control of one man than he is able to manage.

6. Each task is made the unmistakable duty of some one; responsibility for planning, execution, and control (implemented by inspection) is definitely placed on designated persons.

7. Supervision is provided of each person at the level of execution regardless of the hour or place.

8. Each assignment of responsibility carries with it commensurate authority to fulfill the responsibility.

9. Persons to whom authority is delegated are invariably held accountable for its use.

The organization structure, relationships, and procedures must be analyzed in terms of compliance with these principles. Special study should be made of conformance with the principles of unity of command and span of control (4 and 5 above); violations are frequent and usually have serious consequences. When the span of control is reduced, the first principle is frequently violated by combining tasks that are dissimilar and unrelated.

Notation should be made of weaknesses discovered in the organization structure and of principles that are violated. These notations will form the basis of the recommended changes in the organization structure.

Factors That Influence Organization Structure

Organization may take a variety of structural forms and still conform to the principles listed above. This is true because there are several factors, both external and internal that influence its construction. These are discussed in the following paragraphs.

Physical and Social Characteristics of Community. The area and population density of the community influence the need for a geographical decentralization of one or more police functions and the extent of desirable specialization. In addition, any physical, social, or economic characteristic that tends to set apart a section of the community, and to give to it some measure of separate community consciousness and identity, emphasizes the need for territorial decentralization. Topographical characteristics that impede easy and direct travel have the effect of separating a section from the whole and of extending distances and thus may make necessary an earlier decentralization than would otherwise be necessary. Lakes, streams, ravines, unimproved sections, and lack of roadways that give easy and direct access, are examples. Homogeneity in race, occupation, and economic status are factors that set apart one section of a community; strong leadership may develop a separate community identity, consciousness, and pride. Demands for a district police station are then sometimes made. The community consciousness of a recently annexed section that was previously an independent community, as well as the distance that may be involved, also sometimes results in a demand for a district station even though the need is not otherwise apparent.

Certain characteristics of the community also influence the nature and extent of the need for police service; they therefore influence police procedures and, consequently, organization. For example, some communities have a greater proportion of retail stores, or of industries, than others; the need for a foot patrol to devote its entire attention to the security of such establishments will therefore vary. The presence of docks with their shipping traffic, of railroad and bus lines with their depots, of important state and federal highways, of a municipal airport and parks that must be policed, create special problems for the police and a demand for appropriate procedures for dealing with them. Transient laborers attracted by seasonal work opportunities, and temporary idlers attracted by recreational facilities during certain months, cause seasonal variation in the need for police service and influence the nature of police procedures that must be followed in coping with the varying needs. The number and nature of recreational establishments, such as bars, taverns, dance halls, bowling alleys, pool halls, skating rinks, and carnival-like activities, and the extent to which they are concentrated in a section of the community, also affect the nature of police problems and the procedures that must be used in dealing with them. All of these, therefore, are factors that must be considered in analyzing police requirements; their presence or absence will influence somewhat the organization structure.

Community Sentiment. Since police service is a service to the people, the sentiment of the people influences its nature. For example, a community that is traffic-safety conscious, and perhaps organized to promote public safety, demands and obtains a greater proportion of police effort devoted to this field. The same applies to juvenile delinquency and to the control of commercialized vice. Strong community consciousness in any of these fields of activity also influence the acceptance by the people of controls that must be applied by the police in the accomplishment of their purpose. Procedures used in any special branch of police service are consequently influenced by the sentiment of the people.

The sentiment of the community is not invariably favorable to procedures designed to accomplish the police purpose. Unfavorable public attitudes may make the immediate adoption of a superior procedure impractical. For example, the people may not favor the level of enforcement needed to assure acceptable traffic safety. Even more frequently they do not favor the degree of repression in commercialized vice necessary to prevent the organization of these unlawful activities with attendant political corruption and terrorism.

A necessary part of the task of achieving police objectives is the development of public attitudes favorable to their attainment. The police, therefore, must be organized to inform the public regarding the significance and consequences of failures in law enforcement and compliance and regarding police requirements and the results of failure to meet them. The police cannot progress ahead of public sentiment.

The development of favorable public sentiment is a relatively long-range project, whereas organization requirements are immediate. The organizational structure, therefore, must be designed to conform somewhat to public attitudes. As public sentiment changes, modification of the structure may be desirable.

Community attitudes are expressed in various ways. Lack of compliance with laws, lack of public resentment against non-compliance, and frequent failures of juries to convict are reflections of unwholesome public sentiment. The policies of elected representatives of the people as expressed in legislation, budget appropriations, and administrative orders are other expressions of community feeling. Opinion stated in the press and by radio also reflect the community will because citizen opinions are influenced by them and also because the press and radio frequently reflect public opinion.

Police Factors. The competence of the members of the force (established by recruitment standards and procedures and by training) and their interest, enthusiasm, and sympathy with policies and procedures, also influence the construction of the organization pattern. As these characteristics become more favorable, the need for specialization diminishes and the acceptance of superior procedures is enhanced. Lack of suitable leadership may prevent the operation of an otherwise sound plan. Limitations in headquarters space and in the opportunity for its expansion and rearrangement may also prevent the creation of the most desirable organization structure.

Functional Organization

Functional organization is the division of the members of the force into groups for the performance of tasks that are similar or related in process, purpose, or clientele. It will be considered here from the point of view of the number of functional units that are needed and of broad definitions of the duties of each.

The police organization includes the detailed arrangement of the principal organic units, and its true structure is known only when the relationships between the several component units have been precisely and completely described by exact definition of duties. Some parts of the design of the police organization, therefore, may not be disposed of completely at this point. These will be dealt with in later chapters in connection with planning within each of the units. It must be understood, therefore, that decisions relating to the organization and duties of the several units will influence the construction of the police organization into its principal units and must be borne in mind in planning the rough skeleton of the organization.

Justification for the creation of a special division is not based exclusively on the need for the performance of tasks by specialists at the level of execution. Justification may be found in the need for specialization in planning and controlling police activities in the special field even though the execution of the plans may be the exclusive responsibility of the patrol division. In only the very small department will there be no need for specialization in planning and control in each field of special activity. When there is justification for the creation of a division for planning and controlling police activities in a special field, however, there are nearly always some members of the force devoting full time to the performance of tasks in that field. These logically will become members of the newly created special division except when the need for their supervision justifies their assignment to the patrol division.

Important decisions must be made as to the extent of specialization at the performance level of line, auxiliary, and administrative duties. Related thereto are decisions as to the need for separate organizational units for the performance of these tasks, and in the event separate units are not needed, the manner in which these duties will be combined with the responsibilities of a presently existing one.

Line Divisions

The performance of the primary police tasks is customarily divided among the patrol, traffic, detective, vice, and juvenile divisions.[1] Even the smallest departments provide a patrol service. In the absence of specialized divisions, the patrol force in the small department performs all primary police tasks. In large departments there is a need for the performance of some tasks by specialists and special divisions may then be created.

Decision 1. Is there justification for the creation of a detective division? a vice division? a traffic division? and a juvenile division?

Sufficient work to occupy the full time of one man in planning and supervising department operations in a special field justifies the creation of a special division even though the patrol division retains substantial responsibilities for performance. When planning and supervision do not occupy the full time of one man, the creation of a special division may be justified if the spare time can be logically devoted to other duties in the special field (and in some

---

[1] Line divisions perform services to the public. The only reason for having a police department is to obtain these services. In contrast, the auxiliary services are services to the line officers; the auxiliary services are intended to facilitate the performance of line operations.

instances to unrelated tasks); the decision must be influenced by the desirability of specialization in the local situation. Detective and traffic divisions are needed in fairly small forces, but vice and juvenile divisions of more than one man are usually not created in departments of fewer than 50 men. Departments of more than 100 men should have a separate division for the performance of each of the primary police tasks.

The assignment of vice and juvenile-delinquency prevention and control tasks to the detective division is ill-advised. When detectives are charged with the investigation of vice offenses, they either win the enmity of the vice operators and lose them as sources of information relating to crimes against persons and property or they effect undesirable compromises. The divergence of objectives of the juvenile and detective divisions clearly justifies their separation. Failure in the prevention of juvenile delinquency is marked by the necessity of locking someone in jail, whereas the locking of someone in jail is usually a mark of detective division success. This difference of objectives sometimes results in clashes between the two divisions.

Vice and juvenile-crime control tasks should be assigned to separate divisions having independence and staff-conference rights equal to the patrol, detective, and traffic divisions. To do otherwise will jeopardize the accomplishment of their purposes.

Delegation of Responsibilities Among the Special Divisions

Whether independent divisions are created or not, it is necessary to divide the crimes to be investigated and related tasks among officers concerned with vice operators, juvenile offenders, traffic violators, or other criminals. This assignment should be considered from the viewpoint of ultimate responsibility.

Distinction should also be made between responsibility for the prevention of crimes and for their clearance by arrest of the perpetrators. Frequently a series of crimes in an area of the city and during a particular time of the day boosts the crime rate to unusual proportions. Under these circumstances the press frequently over-emphasizes the seriousness of the situation and unusual pressures are sometimes brought to bear on the police. Such situations raise a question as to where responsibility should rest within the police force for action against the perpetrators.

Decision 2. Should the patrol or the detective division be respon-sible for action intended to prevent the continuance of a series of crimes?

The detective division is responsible for the apprehension of the criminal who has committed a crime. This responsibility should be discharged by investigation; the criminal must be identified and apprehended. The detective division should utilize patrolmen and all the other resources of the department to this end.

The patrol division, on the other hand, should invariably be responsible for the prevention of crime, or the apprehension of the criminal in the act of its commission, whether it appears in isolated cases or in series by individuals or gangs whose identity may or may not be known. The patrol division should be responsible for initiating the planning and execution of stake-outs, plants, sur-veillance, and intensive patrol intended to capture the criminal while engaged in his criminal act.

This delegation of responsibility between the patrol division and the detective division should be clearly established in the minds of the members of the department, the press, and the general public.

Decision 3. In which classes of crimes should ultimate responsi-bility for the investigation be assigned to each special division?

In considering this question, it is important to bear in mind that the patrol division should be responsible for the prevention of the incident and for its preliminary investigation.

The decision in the case of vice is relatively simple. All cases in-volving violations of laws relating to prostitution, gambling, nar-cotics, and the sale of intoxicating liquor should be the ultimate responsibility of vice officers. An exception should be made of gambling by juveniles which should be assigned to the juvenile officers because this offense is usually not related to adult gambling in place, time, or proprietorship, and gambling by juveniles is usually reported to the police by parents and school authorities and is infrequently discovered by vice-division officers in their sup-pression of commercialized gambling.

The traffic division should be assigned ultimate responsibility for the investigation of traffic offenses including hit-and-run and fatal accidents. Crimes involving injury, death, or malicious damage to property in which a vehicle is deliberately used as the implement, however, should be assigned to the detective division. The preliminary investigations, of course, should all be made by the patrol division.[1]

Juvenile officers should be assigned ultimate responsibility for the investigation of the following cases, the preliminary investigation of which should ordinarily be made by the patrol division.[2]

1. Offenses against the family: domestic relations cases, desertion, abandonment, nonsupport of wife or child, neglect or abuse of child, encouraging or contributing to the delinquency of minors, employment of children in injurious, immoral, or improper vocations or practices, and admitting minors to improper places.

2. Sex offenses, except forcible rape, prostitution, and abortion. Included are sex perversions, licentious advances, incest, statutory rape, bigamy and polygamy, and other offenses against chastity, common decency, morals, and the like.

3. Possession or sale of obscene literature, pictures, exhibitions, and so on.

4. Kidnapping of juveniles by relatives, not for extortion.

5. The theft of bicycles.

6. Gambling by juveniles.

7. All other crimes involving juveniles as victims or offenders, except those regularly assigned to the vice and detective divisions.

8. Missing persons.

9. Mental cases.

10. Other cases in which persons need social welfare service and cases in which designated juveniles are suspected of any offense.[3]

Except for cases assigned to some other special division, the detective division should be charged with continuing and ultimate responsibility for the investigation of all felonies, all offenses that may be felonies, and all thefts.

Decision 4. Should the above listed cases be assigned to the detective division without regard to the probable age of the offender?

The exact age of the offender cannot ordinarily be ascertained

---

[1] Department regulations should also forbid action against traffic violators by officers in plain clothes except in such flagrant violations as driving while obviously intoxicated, hit-and-run, and serious accidents. See Appendix G, p. 328, item 33.

[2] Justification for these assignments to the juvenile division is found in O. W. Wilson; *Police Administration*, 1950, pp. 213-215, from which this classification was taken by permission of McGraw-Hill Book Company, Inc., New York City.

[3] The division that has ultimate responsibility for the clearance by arrest of the class of offnse the juvenile is suspected of having committed should not be relieved of its responsibility by reason of the juvenile suspect. See Decision 4.

before his apprehension—or at least until his identity has been established. The assignment to the juvenile division of offenses that have the appearance of having been committed by juveniles is undesirable. When assignments are made on this basis, the clear-cut line of demarcation between the investigative obligations of detectives and juvenile officers is lost and detectives are given an opportunity to avoid their responsibility by requesting the re-assignment of unsolved crimes to the juvenile division on the ground that they have the appearance of having been committed by juveniles.

It is desirable, therefore, to leave the ultimate investigative responsibility with the detective division without regard to probable age, except in cases where the identity and age of the offender is known. This procedure also enhances the accuracy of measurements of detective accomplishment in terms of percentages of crimes cleared by arrest and of property recovered.[1]

Decision 5. Should the final disposition of the juvenile offender be the responsibility of the arresting division, the division having ultimate investigational responsibility, or the juvenile division?

The purpose of the juvenile division is to save youthful offenders from lives of crime, and since the purpose of the other special divisions is to obtain convictions in court, there seems to be strong justification for placing responsibility for final action against the juvenile offender with the division most concerned, which is the juvenile division.[2]

Decision 6. What relationship should exist between divisions that have a mutual and overlapping interest in juvenile offenders in traffic, vice, and crime?

Other divisions should notify the juvenile division of crimes they are investigating that involve juveniles as offenders or victims. The juvenile division should cooperate in the completion of the investigations. It is desirable that juveniles be questioned in the juvenile-division quarters or at least that a juvenile officer be present during the interrogation. It is especially important that policewomen be

---

[1] Other justifications for detectives to investigate to their conclusion all crimes in the classes of offenses assigned to them, even when juveniles are involved, are found in *Police Administration*, p. 130.

[2] A discussion of the desirability of placing responsibility for the final disposition of the juvenile offender on the juvenile division is found in *Police Administration*, p. 221.

present when juvenile or inexperienced but older females are interviewed as victims, suspects, or witnesses.

Decision 7. When two or more special divisions have a mutual and overlapping interest in possible violations by an enterprise, which should be given primary responsibility in the investigation of applications for license and in the inspection of the premises to assure compliance with regulations?

Such overlapping interest is found most frequently between the vice and juvenile divisions in amusement establishments, such as dance halls and taverns. The division with the major interest is the one that is charged with ultimate responsibility for the investigation of most of the violations. This is the division that usually should be given primary responsibility in regard to licensing and inspections.

Command During Emergencies. Emergencies sometimes arise in police service during the absence of the chief and other high-ranking officers. Provision must be made to assure the presence of someone to take command of emergency situations that require the services of members from all divisions.

Decision 8. In the absence of the chief of police, who should be given his power of command to coordinate the efforts of all members of the force in dealing with emergency situations such as explosions, fires, serious crimes, and other catastrophes?

The alternatives are to have on duty at all hours some high-ranking officer to take personal command of such situations or to vest this coordinating power in operating personnel who are always on duty. The latter procedure is preferred. The relative infrequency of emergencies that require top-level coordination of police efforts does not justify continuous attention. Relatively little of the time of an officer assigned to meet this need will be devoted to coordination; his free time and high rank, and the absence of key personnel in the several operating units, will result in interference with normal routine operations by cutting lines of authority and thereby creating confusion and dissension. Suitably trained operating personnel are able to deal with emergency situations as they arise, especially when plans have been made for them. Officers of higher rank should be notified and may take command of the situation when its seriousness justifies this action.

The patrol division is the logical operating division to command emergency operations involving performance by members of all divisions. The patrol division (1) has the largest force and, consequently, integration of members of other divisions with it is more simple because there is need to impose out-of-the-ordinary control over a smaller number; (2) it is the only operating division that invariably provides 24-hour command service; (3) it is usually the first to learn of emergency calls and to reach the scene of action; and (4) since its duties encompass the entire police field, it has broader powers and greater responsibility than any other division.[1] Department regulations should define accurately the responsibilities of the patrol-division command and the relationships that exist under emergency situations.

Auxiliary Services

A number of services must be made available to the operating divisions: records and communications tasks must be performed; department-owned and other property must be controlled and cared for; provision should be made for criminalistic services; prisoners must be held in custody both safely and securely; and maintenance and other service tasks must be performed. Decisions must be reached as to the need for separate units for the performance of each of these services.

Records and Communications. Police records activities vary principally in the extent of their centralization, the nature of administrative and operating records that are maintained independently in each line division, and the extent of central records-division supervision of their use. Discussion of records that should be maintained by the line divisions is reserved for later chapters.

Decision 9. Should police records activities be consolidated into one centralized system under the control of a records division?

The integration of police records into a single centralized system provides many advantages that enhance their effectiveness and the facility of their use. When records activities are thus concentrated, the smaller number of persons engaged in records activities develops greater skill, and their training, supervision, and control are simplified. A specialized record staff views recordkeeping more

[1] By permission, from *Police Administration*, by O. W. Wilson, p. 55. Copyright, 1950. McGraw-Hill Book Company, Inc.

objectively than operating personnel whose effectiveness is reflected in the records themselves. A greater fidelity and a more consistently uniform classification of offenses are therefore obtained. Information is available to all members and search for records is simplified and speeded up when the various records that relate to a specific incident, person, location, or problem are coordinated, and concentrated in one place. A centralized records system also assists in placing responsibility for the performance of each police task; a system of follow-up (review) insures proper action by individual officers.

The records activities of each operating division should be scrutinized with a view to ascertaining the propriety of their continuance.[1] Decisions in reference to them will be discussed in later chapters.

Decision 10. To which division should communications tasks be assigned?

The communications duties under discussion here do not, of course, include maintenance and service of equipment.

The most common practice is to place communications either in the records division or the patrol division. The assignment of communications tasks to the records division assures greater fidelity in recording incidents that call for police service, because the records staff is less likely to fail to record an incident than a line division whose effectiveness is measured in terms of the number of incidents that are recorded and whose burden of report writing is thereby increased. Also, supervision of the communications officer by the records staff is more essential than his supervision by a line division because the recording of messages occupies most of his time.

Only in the small department, where a communications officer (the dispatcher or desk officer) must actually command the field force during certain hours, does there seem justification for the assignment of communications to the patrol division. Neither does there seem justification for the creation of a communications division independent of the records division in even the largest department.

Property Control. Property control duties relate to two principal types of property, viz., department-owned property (supplies, equip-

---

[1] Operating and administrative records that should be maintained by each line division are listed in *Police Records,* Chapter 6.

ment, and so on) and property temporarily in police possession (prisoners' property, found property, property temporarily stored with the police for safe-keeping, and evidence including recovered property and contraband).

Decision 11. Is there need for a property division? If not, to which division should property control be assigned?

Only in very large departments will there be justification for an independent property division. When the property is in the custody of an independent division, however, property control records in the records division provide some added security.[1] In smaller departments, nevertheless, the records division should be given responsibility for the custody and control of property temporarily in police possession in addition to department-owned property.

The receipt and disbursement of property is expedited by the 24-hour service provided by the records division. This unit also usually has space available for property storage, and restrictions on access to the records area increase the security and facilitate the control of the property. The records division is the logical unit to has custody of clerical supplies as well as of flashlights, batteries, ammunition, and other supplies for which a demand may arise at any hour.

Decision 12. Should the control of all department-owned property (of every kind) be under one person or unit or is there justification for a division of the responsibility, as for example, placing the control of some property in a unit charged with maintenance tasks that require convenient access to the stores?

The decisions will be influenced by the extent of police maintenance and department ownership of property. When the extent of police maintenance and department provision of supplies and equipment is limited, the tasks of property control are simplified.

Supplies and spare parts needed in maintenance and service are more logically stored in the custody of the persons who will use them than in the records division. Time is thus not wasted in obtaining needed material; the using unit is also better able to maintain a check of supplies on hand to avoid unexpectedly running short.

---

[1] Property control records are discussed in *Police Records*, pp. 68-75 and 163-170.

The Crime Laboratory. Two decisions need to be made in reference to the police laboratory.

Decision 13. What are the police department crime-laboratory needs in staff, equipment, and space?

An appraisal of crime-laboratory needs should consider the physical evidence that is likely to be discovered at crime and accident scenes and brought to headquarters for examination, and the availability of facilities for its analysis outside the department. A department that has nearby and readily obtainable laboratory services does not require such complete facilities as a department not so fortunately situated.

The purchase of expensive equipment that may not be needed more than once a year is not justified when examinations that require its use may be made by other laboratories. The purchase of equipment whose operation requires skills beyond the capacity of the laboratory staff is also ill-advised.

Each police department, however, should have some sort of crime laboratory even though its tasks are restricted to the gross examination of physical evidence, the screening of evidence for reference to other laboratories, the coordination of department activities that relate to physical evidence, and the operation of the police dark room.

Decision 14. Where should the crime laboratory be located in the organization structure of the department?

There are advantages in giving the laboratory independent status, reporting directly to the chief or an assistant, and not assigning it to any of the line divisions it is charged with serving. Its findings are more likely to be objective when it is free from their influence. Since the crime laboratory performs a service to line officers, if it must be placed within a presently existing division, it should be placed in the records division since it also performs a service to all operating units.

Jail Duties. In considering jail duties, distinction must be made between the operation of the jail at police headquarters and the operation of a separate prison or workfarm for convicted prisoners. The existence of a city prison of any kind removed from headquarters does not complicate the organization structure. It should be considered a separate organizational unit. Its relationships with the department are not unlike those of the county jail except that it may perform catering, laundry, and other services for the department. Regulations should outline services to be performed by the prison for the department and the manner of their performance. Procedures also need to be formulated relating to the transfer of prisoners, their secure custody and welfare, their work program, clothing, food, and medical care. Attention should be given to commitment and release records in order to assure suitable control, and to other records that will reflect the physical condition and welfare of the inmates.[1]

The jail duties of immediate concern are those that relate to the custody of prisoners in the jail at headquarters. Distinction must be made, however, between custodial responsibilities and the responsibility for decisions in reference to incarceration, release, and restrictions on the privileges of prisoners. The latter responsibility is not considered a jail duty.

Decision 15. Who should be given responsibility for decisions relating to incarceration, release, and restrictions on the privileges of prisoners?

The importance of these decisions to the individual prisoner and the serious consequences of unjustified and illegal restrictions on human liberties by the police make desirable the placing of responsibility for such decisions on experienced line officers of sound judgment.[2] The patrol command seems best suited to this assignment. Commanding officers in the patrol division usually have a valuable background of training and experience that qualifies them to make wise decisions, and the patrol command provides 24-hour service. Department regulations should define this responsibility and the relationship with arresting officers from other divisions in order to avoid conflict and misunderstanding.[3]

Decision 16. Is there justification for the creation of a separate jail division?

In only the large department are jail duties of such volume as to

---

[1] The use of records in the control of prisoners is discussed in *Police Records*, pp. 104-111.

[2] The legality of restrictions on prisoners is discussed on p. 181.

[3] The manner in which the patrol command may discharge this responsibility without undue interference with their other responsibilities is described in *Police Administration*, pp. 266-269.

justify the creation of a separate division. An independent division is not justified unless these duties reach such magnitude as to require the full-time services of one or more officers at all hours of the day and night, and then only when their total number reaches such proportion as to indicate the need for a separate unit.

Decision 17. In the absence of a separate jail division, to which division should custodial duties, or the staff engaged in their performance, be assigned?

Custodial duties should be assigned to either the patrol division or the records division. The choice between these two divisions will be influenced most strongly by the volume of jail duties, because consideration must be given to the manner in which the spare time of the staff may be most productively employed. Since the jail staff frequently drives the patrol wagon, and the ambulance also in communities where ambulance service is provided by the police, consideration must be given to the frequency of these runs in addition to the volume of custodial duties.

There are two principal advantages to the assignment of jail duties (and personnel) to the patrol division. (1) Custodial duties are more closely related and similar to patrol duties than to records tasks. This is true from the point of view of clientele and method or process as well as purpose. (2) Since the patrol division should have primary or overall responsibility for decisions relating to incarceration, release, and restrictions on jail privileges, giving this same division direct control over personnel charged with their implementation is justified.

In departments having a smaller volume of jail duties, a greater proportion of the time of officers assigned to their performance is available for other headquarters duty. Records tasks are well suited to this purpose. Many records tasks are not urgent; they may be performed during periods of slack activity and at any hour of the day or night. Some may also be performed outside the records division by carrying records to be worked on into some other office. In small departments, therefore, jail duties may be assigned to the records division.

In larger departments the advantages of the assignment of jail duties to the patrol division become apparent. When custodial tasks are assigned to the patrol division, some records duties may continue to be performed by jail staff as fill-in tasks during slack periods.

Maintenance. Maintenance duties relate principally to police buildings, vehicles, communications equipment, and traffic-control devices. In considering the maintenance of each class of property and equipment, distinction should be made between servicing, on the one hand, and, on the other, actual construction, installation, or repair. The distinction, in part, is based on the skill and special equipment required in performance. For example, janitorial service must be provided for police buildings; these services require little skill and equipment. In addition the buildings must be repaired and renovated; these operations require greater skill and more equipment. Likewise, police vehicles must be washed and greased and have the oil changed; windows must be cleaned and the interiors swept out; water, gasoline, and air must be replenished; and tires and batteries must be changed and repaired. But in addition, the vehicles must be repaired. Some repairs, such as motor tune-ups, may be in the nature of service; others involve major motor, transmission, and differential overhauls and body and chassis repairs. The latter require considerable skill and equipment. Radio equipment and traffic control devices also require maintenance and repair services that vary widely in the skill and mechanical devices needed in their performance.

Decision 18. What maintenance and repair services should the police undertake to provide, and for which should they rely on central municipal shops or private agencies?

Decisions relating to police performance of maintenance and repair duties should be based on the relative advantage of having them performed by central agencies created to provide these services for all operating departments. Since police departments are created to perform tasks that are quite dissimilar to maintenance and repair duties, the police should be relieved of maintenance responsibilities when these duties may be performed satisfactorily by a central agency that has these tasks as its primary responsibility. Exceptions to this general policy should be made when there is no central agency to provide the service, when the quality of the service is poorer than could be provided by the police themselves, when delays or lost time result from distances to be traveled or lack of adequate or suitably organized servicing staff, and when equipment is kept out of operation for protracted periods as the result of the slowness of the service. Space and equipment for maintenance and repairs, and the feasibility of using trusty labor are also factors to consider.

Some maintenance and repairs may be performed by the police more satisfactorily than by a central agency. The justification for police performance will vary from one city to another. For example, the police in one may provide their own janitor service but not undertake building renovation and repair. In another they may do interior painting and some minor repairs. In one city they may not repair vehicles but may service them; the service may be limited to replenishing gasoline, water, and air, sweeping out the interiors, and cleaning the windows. In another community the service may include lubrication and tire and battery changes and repairs; it may even be expanded to include motor tune-ups, brake adjustments, and front-wheel alignment. Likewise, police participation in servicing and maintaining traffic-control devices may vary from none to the performance of all tasks.

From the above it may be seen that decisions in reference to maintenance duties to be performed by the police are dependent on a number of factors, the principal one being the quality and promptness of the services performed by the central agency. The police must recognize their major responsibility; they must not permit an arrangement that will interfere with the performance of their primary duties or that will impair the quality of their service.

Decisions as to the extent of police maintenance duties should be recorded in precise definition of the tasks that are to be performed by the police and tasks that are the responsibility of some other agency. They should be classified under the headings: buildings; vehicles; communications; traffic; armaments; and others.

Decision 19. Should the police establish one or more separate maintenance or repair units?

Decisions as to the manner in which maintenance tasks will be combined, whether they will be made the responsibility of one or more presently existing line or service units, or whether, instead, a maintenance unit will be created for the performance of all related tasks, are dependent on a number of factors. Availability of space and the similarity of the maintenance duties are factors that influence the desirability of their consolidation. The advantages of consolidation are greater flexibility in the use of staff and equipment and the opportunity that is provided for performing more than one task on a piece of equipment at one time. As a general rule such consolidation is desirable; there may be little justification, however, for combining janitor, tailoring, and armament maintenance with the maintenance of mechanical equipment.

Since the maintenance duties are so markedly dissimilar to other police duties there is little justification for assigning these tasks to other police units except for general supervision. Then there may be justification for assigning them either to the patrol division which usually has a greater interest in the servicing of vehicle and communications equipment and in janitor service than any other division, or to the records-division staff which is always on duty at headquarters to supervise the operations.

Administrative Tasks

Certain administrative tasks must also be performed if the line and service divisions are to operate most effectively. Provision must be made for budgeting, accounting, and purchasing; personnel management involves the performance of a variety of duties; thought must be given to public relations; provision must be made to assure effective planning, as well as control through inspections; and intelligence relating to undesirable conditions in the community and within the department must be assured.

In considering the organization of the department for the effective accomplishment of these tasks, decisions must be made as to which duties will be consolidated and made the responsibility of some presently existing unit and which deserve the creation of an independent unit. Factors to be considered in reaching these decisions are discussed in the following paragraphs.

Budgeting, Accounting, and Purchasing. Some budgeting, accounting, and purchasing tasks must be performed by all departments regardless of their size. As the size increases, the volume and complexity of these duties also increase. Their volume, however, is also influenced by the suitability of services provided by the central accounting and the central purchasing agencies within the governmental structure. When the finance department maintains accounts in a form that supplies all needed information to the police promptly and whenever needed, the accounting tasks of the department are considerably simplified. There are some accounting duties, however, that the police cannot readily avoid; timekeeping and payrolls are nearly always police responsibilities. Budget estimates must also be provided.

A central purchasing agent offers important advantages to the police and his services should be utilized whenever they are available. Even though there is a central purchasing agent, however, the police will have some responsibilities connected with purchases, and as a general rule it is desirable to designate one officer as the department purchasing agent to assist the central purchasing agent in drawing up specifications and in expediting department purchases. The need for such an officer naturally increases with the size of the department. Except in a very large department it will not be a full-time task.

Decision 20. Is there justification for the creation of a separate unit to perform budgeting, accounting, and purchasing tasks? If not, to which division should these tasks, or the personnel who perform them, be assigned?

Even though budgeting, accounting, and purchasing are administrative tasks, there is logical justification for the assignment of these duties to the records division in the small department. No other division has duties that are so closely related; the processes involved are similar to those of records, and in addition, when the records division is responsible for the control of department-owned property, these tasks seem closely related to purchasing. Administrative records maintained by the records division, such as those relating to attendance, are also closely related to the preparation of payrolls.

As a general rule, therefore, these administrative tasks should be assigned to the records division until their volume, or the need for a closer control by the chief's office, make desirable the creation of an independent accounting office. This situation is not likely to prevail except in the large department.

Personnel and Public Relations. Success in police administration is frequently dependent on the efficient performance of personnel-management and public-relations tasks. Decisions relating to these duties, therefore, are important.

Decision 21. Does the volume of work related to personnel management occupy the full time of one man? If not, to which officer should these tasks be assigned in addition to his other duties?

Except in the very small department, one officer should be appointed to perform police personnel tasks in addition to his other duties. He should be selected on the basis of his special interest and ability; consideration must also be given to non-interference with his regular duties.

At some point in the increasing size of a department, there is justification for a full-time personnel officer. He should be a staff officer and report directly to the chief or to an assistant.

The extent and nature of personnel duties will be influenced by the existence and competence of a central personnel agency. The existence of such an agency, however, does not eliminate tasks relating to the management of personnel that must be performed by the police themselves.[1]

Decision 22. Should the police personnel officer supervise police training and the department disciplinary machinery?

It is not intended to describe here the nature of police personnel duties beyond observing that some departments do not assign police training and the department disciplinary machinery to the police personnel officer for general supervision. There does not seem to be a logical reason for removing the supervision of these tasks from the personnel officer. Even though the training officer relieves the personnel officer of the training task, supervision of the training should be under the direction of the personnel officer. Likewise, the department disciplinary machinery should operate under his general supervision.

Decision 23. Should public-relations activities be the responsibility of the personnel officer or should some other officer operating independently of him be assigned these duties?

Relationships between the police and the public are established very largely by contacts between individual policemen and citizens and the favorableness of these contacts is so strongly influenced by training and discipline that there seems justification for combining public relations tasks with personnel duties except in the large department or where some factor peculiar to the local situation makes such consolidation unwise.

Planning and Inspection. Provision must also be made for the

---

[1] For a description of the duties of the police personnel officer and a discussion of his relationship to the central personnel agency, see *Police Administration*, Chapter 19. For an excellent discussion of the duties of the police personnel officer, see Chapter 4, "Personnel Management" by Harry Rosenberg, *Municipal Police Administration*, International City Managers' Association, Chicago, 1954, 4th ed.

performance of over-all planning and the general supervision of the planning process throughout the department.

Decision 24. Is there need for a planning unit with a staff? If not, is there need for a full-time planning officer? If not, to whom should over-all planning tasks be assigned in addition to his other duties?

Separate planning units are needed in large departments and in those in which much planning must be done because of the indifferent attention that has been given to these tasks in the past. Planning duties in other departments usually may be assigned to some officer in addition to his other duties. In departments of suitable size, this may be the personnel officer. In others it may be the responsibility of a staff officer who serves purely as an administrative assistant or as an executive officer. In still larger departments there will be justification for the appointment of a separate plans officer, and in very large ones he should be provided with a staff.

Decision 25. Should planning and inspectional duties be combined, and if not, who should be given inspectional duties?

Staff inspections must be made if suitable controls are to be effected. The inspectional process throughout the organization also needs supervision. The volume of the work and the interest and ability of possible assignees will influence the decision to combine these tasks with planning duties. In a large organization, the inspectional duties will occupy the full time of one or more staff officers. In smaller ones the inspectional and planning duties may be combined under one staff officer. There are some advantages in combining planning and inspectional duties even when they reach such proportions as to require a sizable staff.[1]

Intelligence. In large departments provision should be made for a unit to provide an intelligence service for the chief regarding the integrity of his force, organized crime, subversive activities, and persons and conditions that promote civil disturbances in the community.[2] This information must be obtained in smaller depart-

---

[1] The nature of planning and inspectional duties, the advantages of their consolidation, and the character of the organization to assure their performance, are discussed in *Police Administration*, pp. 78-79.

[2] The duties of an intelligence unit are described in *Police Administration*, pp. 67-68.

ments also, but in them the chief himself, with the help of his vice and detective divisions, will obtain the necessary facts.

Decision 26. Is there need for an intelligence unit?

Factors that will influence the need for an intelligence unit are the size of the community, the extent to which crime has been organized in it, and the probable frequency and seriousness of civil disturbances and of breaches of integrity on the part of the members of the force. Departments that have been poorly administered in the past, that have suffered from inadequate leadership and supervision, that lack prestige and have a damaged morale, and those in which personnel tasks have been indifferently performed with inattention to discipline, stand most in need of such a unit. Likewise, the community that has favored leniency in vice control, and in which there are evidences of organized crime and instances of terroristic efforts to drive competitors from the field, and of the corruption of public officials, has greater need for the services of such a unit than one that has been relatively free of commercialized vice.

Non-police and Quasi-police Tasks

The police in some communities are given tasks that are not directly related to police service but are considered unsuitable for assignment to any other department. The operation of the animal pound, duties related to licensing, and the supervision of weights and measures are examples of such tasks. The imposition of these duties on the police will sometimes affect the organization structure.

Decision 27. Should tasks that are not directly related to police service be assigned to the police, and when they are, how should the force be organized to perform them?

Police performance of some tasks that are not directly related to police service assists the police in the attainment of their principal objectives. As far as they are able, however, the police should avoid duties that are not directly related to police service when their performance does not facilitate the accomplishment of the police purpose. When such a task is imposed on them (usually for the reason that no other city department is so well prepared for its performance as the police), the supervision of its performance should be made the responsibility of the head of a presently existing division in order to avoid widening inordinately the span of control of the chief.[1] The selection of a division for this assignment should be based on the relationship of the task to the other activities of the division as well as on the interest, ability, and available time of its head, and the ease with which the work may be performed under his direction. Examples of logical division selection, when the indicated tasks are made a police responsibility, include: the patrol division for the supervision of the animal pound; the traffic division for the supervision of the licensing and inspection of taxicabs and drivers;[2] the juvenile or vice division for the supervision and licensing of amusement places; the detective division for the supervision of weights and measures.

Disaster Preparedness and Civil Disturbances

The structure of the police organization is also affected by plans for disasters and civil disturbances.

Decision 28. How should the police department prepare itself for disasters and civil disturbances?

Disaster preparedness plans should be developed in cooperation with the local chapter of the American Red Cross.[3] The adoption of the plan will not usually affect the structure of the police organization until it is placed in operation at the time of emergency. All members of the force should be informed on the details of the plan and copies of it should be available for study and for reference at the time of an emergency.

Some departments organize a tactical unit to deal with civil disturbances. The members are specially selected, trained, and equipped for this difficult task. Since the members of the unit are drawn from department operating units, its mobilization will affect the operations of the units from which members are drawn and plans must be made to operate with the diminished force.

---

[1] In some cities the large staff assigned to the control of animals may justify the creation of a separate division for this purpose, with the head reporting directly to an assistant chief in charge of operations. A superior method of dealing with the animal-control problem, however, is to contract for this service with the Society for the Prevention of Cruelty to Animals or some other private humane society.

[2] In some cities taxicab drivers participate so extensively in vice operations that their supervision by the vice division is justified.

[3] See Appendix N, p. 528.

CHAPTER 5

Top-level and Territorial Organization

T HE organization of the level of authority above the heads of the several functional units and the territorial decentralization of the force among district stations must be considered in larger departments. Decisions on these matters will influence the organization structure and operation of the force.

Top-level Organization

In organizing the top level of authority, the usual objective is to establish a workable span of control, and at the same time, to group similar or related activities. The heads of the line, service, and administrative units normally report directly to the chief of police. This arrangement is satisfactory so long as the number does not exceed his span of control. The number is influenced by the size of the organization and the manner in which service and administrative duties have been consolidated so as to avoid the creation of additional independent units. Factors that influence the desirability and manner of their consolidation have been discussed.

Human limitations of the chief make advisable a critical study of the number of his immediate subordinates. A needed reduction may be accomplished by imposing an added level of control between the chief and some or all of the heads of the several organizational units. The added level of control may be avoided by extending the chief's effective span of control; this is done by appointing a staff officer as an administrative aide, in some instances as an executive officer or chief of staff.

Decision 1. Does the top level of command in the department need reorganization, and what patterns of organization should be considered?

A survey of the chief's workday may reveal evidence of a need for top-level reorganization. The desirability of such reorganization becomes apparent when the chief is engrossed in detail; when operations are held in abeyance for protracted periods pending decisions by a chief too busy to give the matter his attention; when immediate

70

subordinates experience difficulty in obtaining an interview with him because of his over-crowded calendar; when citizens occupy a large part of his time discussing matters that could be dealt with by someone else; when heavy demands on his time for ceremonial duties, public meetings, addresses, and official conferences leave too little for the administration of his force; and when he lacks time to study the larger problems of the department, to plan broad and long-range programs, to spot-audit department operations, activities, and conditions, and to make frequent personal contact with his subordinates at every level of authority and in every field of police service.

There are many possible patterns of top-level organization beyond the simple and normal one in which all unit heads report directly to the chief. Only four will be considered here. These seem basic; they are susceptible to variations and combinations too numerous to attempt to describe.[1]

1. Three or More Assistant Chiefs.[2] In very large departments there may be justification for the creation of three assistant chiefs, one in charge of line operations, another in charge of auxiliary services, and a third in charge of administrative functions. This form would normally place all department activities, without exception, under the control of one of the three assistants. A variation of this organization would provide a fourth assistant chief with all line operations divided between two assistant chiefs. One might have charge of all patrol operations including the district stations, the remaining line operations being left to the other. Or one might have charge of the uniformed forces (patrol and traffic) and the other of plainclothes operations (detective, vice, and juvenile).[3]

2. Two Assistant Chiefs. In somewhat smaller departments, only two assistant chiefs may be appointed. One would be in command

---

[1] These organization patterns are described in greater detail and illustrated by charts, and their relative advantages are discussed in *Police Administration*, Chapter 3.

[2] No distinction is made in this discussion between assistant and deputy chiefs. The latter title may be used when preferred.

[3] The Los Angeles Police Department has seven bureaus each headed by a deputy chief. They are: Personnel and Training; Technical Services; Administration; Traffic; Patrol; Detective; Corrections (jails and rehabilitation center). The Technical Services Bureau has the following divisions: Supply and Transportation; Records and Identification; Radio Technical; Communications. The Bureau of Administration has the following divisions: Business Office; Public Information; Planning and Research; Intelligence; Internal Affairs; Administrative Vice. The Juvenile Division is in the Patrol Bureau.

of all line operations, the other of auxiliary services and such selected administrative duties as the chief might consider suitable for assignment. In this form of organization, the chief might properly retain the planning and inspection functions and the intelligence unit under his direct control, assigning personnel, public relations, budget, accounting, and purchasing to the assistant in charge of the auxiliary services.

3. One Assistant Chief. In a still smaller department the chief may create only one assistant chief. Under these circumstances, the assistant should normally be assigned either to operations, or to the auxiliary services and administrative tasks. The decision should be influenced by the relative interests, abilities, and experiences of the chief and his assistant.

4. An Executive Officer. In still other departments it may not be desirable to appoint an assistant chief, or the chief may prefer to postpone the day when he must remove himself by one level of authority from the operating activities of his department. He may lengthen his span of control somewhat by the creation of an administrative assistant who would not have direct authority over any of the units of the department but would operate purely in a staff capacity. This officer might be restricted by assignment to specified administrative duties, or he might serve in a capacity comparable to an executive officer or chief of staff, giving orders to all organic units but only in the name of the chief.

Decision 2. What pattern should be adopted in the reorganization of the top level of command?

When a decision has been made that the top-level pattern of the organization must be changed, a choice must be made from one of these basic patterns, or some modification of one of them. Factors that will influence the choice include: the size of the force; the outside demands on the time and energy of the chief; the chief's ability and interests; the total number of independent units whose heads report directly to him after desirable consolidations have been effected; the competence, energy, intelligence, loyalty, and interests of officers who would probably be appointed to the top posts.

Territorial Decentralization With District Stations

The following are the principal disadvantages of district stations: (1) Planning, directing, coordinating, and controlling police operations are made more complicated. (2) The control of special divisions over members assigned to district stations is weakened. (3) Efforts to tighten this weakened control jeopardize the authority the district commander must have if he is to be held responsible for conditions and police operations in his district. (4) The transmission of information, instructions, and records, and the custody and transfer of prisoners, property, and evidence is made more complicated. (5) District stations are costly; the site and building with its communications, office, jail, and motor equipment require a large capital investment; the operation of the station necessitates additional personnel, utility, and other operating expenditures. (6) District stations, by their easy availability and convenience of location, tend to increase the total amount of wasted time that seems to be inevitable in any police office. They provide opportunities for both official and unofficial persons to pass the time of day, thus wasting expensive police time and in many instances exerting even more unwholesome influences on the police.

The disadvantages of district stations are so great as to prohibit their creation and to justify their discontinuance or consolidation unless the need is clearly established in terms of services provided and of increased effectiveness of police operations.

Decision 3. In a department that does not have district stations, is it desirable to create one or more districts with separate stations, and on the other hand, in a department that now has district stations, is it desirable to discontinue the use of all of them, or to reduce their number by consolidation?

District stations may be needed (1) to provide a greater public convenience, (2) to improve the quality of police service, and (3) to restrict the size of the jurisdiction to match the powers of comprehension of the commander. The patrol division commander should have first hand knowledge of what is going on in his jurisdiction that is of concern to the police. He should be aware of police problems and hazards and of personalities that create them. He should be personally acquainted with community leaders; he should know the identity of trouble makers, vice operators, and other criminals in his city. Also, a smaller number of men within the pyramid of authority of the district command permits a more complete understanding of the strengths and weaknesses of subordinates and increases the effectiveness of their direction, supervision, and control. When the magnitude of the task of "being knowledgeable" is beyond the capacity of one man, there is likely to be justification for a division of the jurisdiction into two or more districts.

In departments having district stations, analysis of the data listed under item 22 in Appendix A will assist in determining the need. Public convenience provided by each district station may be measured in terms of the number of complaints and accident reports filed in person by citizens, the number of citizens who received the return of lost or stolen property at the station, the number of times property has been temporarily stored for citizens, and the number of fines paid and bonds posted by citizens themselves. Police convenience may be measured in terms of the number of prisoners booked, the number of foot patrolmen who work out of the station, and the saving in travel effected by the district station operation. An estimate of the saving in travel may be based on the sum of the differences between the distances from the center of each motorized beat to headquarters and to their district station multiplied by twice the number of times motorized officers have legitimate reasons for coming to headquarters. The capital investment represented by the district station should also be appraised in terms of the value of site, building, and otherwise unneeded equipment. The operating cost should also be ascertained. The following items should be included: salaries for the station-house complement with provision for weekly, annual, and sick relief; annual utilities cost; and annual repair and janitor service.

In departments that do not have district stations, the need for one may be apparent from public demands for its creation. The need may be verified by estimating the probable number of services that will be provided and the saving in police time and equipment use; their value should be compared with the estimated cost of capital outlay and operation of the proposed district station.

Decision 4. What should be the basic responsibility of the district command?

The basic responsibility of the district command may be compared to the basic responsibility of the beat patrolman as described in Chapter 3. *When a district station is established, all tasks that can be performed by the district force substantially as well as by headquarters should be assigned to the district.* Much crime and vice is peculiar to the district and may be dealt with most effectively by district officers who are likely to be well acquainted with persons and conditions in the district. Criminal activities and other operations that are city-wide in scope should, of course, have the attention of headquarters.

When the district force is limited to patrol, the relationship between the district command and the special divisions will be somewhat like the relations between the patrol division and the special divisions in a department having no district stations. The district command, therefore, will be responsible for the preliminary investigation of all crimes and accidents and should have evidence technicians assigned to them to assist in the performance of these tasks. Since the investigation of nearly all accidents may be satisfactorily completed by the beat officer and the evidence technician the review tasks of a chief accident investigator should be performed by district personnel. Accident investigation, therefore, should be made an exclusive district operation. The extent to which the district will continue the investigation of crimes, the ultimate clearance of which is a detective division responsibility, will depend on the extent of responsibility it is desired to give to the district command. There may be justification, however, to extend rather than restrict the responsibilities of the district command in the special fields. The extension of responsibility may justify some specialization within the district force. Decisions must then be made as to the relationship between these specialists and the special divisions in whose field of activity they are working.

Decision 5. In a department that has or contemplates the creation of district stations, what functions in addition to patrol should be decentralized?

This decision is really a series of decisions; a separate and sometimes different decision will be made in reference to each primary, secondary, and administrative police duty. Ordinarily none of the administrative duties is decentralized, except that some accounting tasks (in reference to timekeeping and payroll data) should be performed at district stations. These duties, however, are ordinarily performed by regular officers, not by specialists. Some auxiliary services need to be decentralized. For example, some property control duties (in reference to all types of property) and some maintenance tasks (especially janitorial service) must be performed at district stations. The most important decisions in reference to the auxiliary services relate to communications and records.

The importance of fidelity in reporting and the value of administrative control through records make desirable a central control over the records function. For these reasons a central complaint bureau should be maintained to receive, record, register, and assign all complaints (reports of offenses, accidents, and other incidents the police are called upon to handle). Communication systems over which complaints are received should be centralized in the complaint bureau. The only complaints that would ordinarily be received at district stations are those made in person by the complainant, and these should be immediately reported by tlephone or teletype to the central complaint bureau for recording and registration.

It is equally important that dispatching be centrally controlled. Only in this way may there be assurance that man power will be deployed to deal most effectively with police incidents that require interdistrict action. Lack of central control over dispatching results in delay that may make the difference between success and failure. An independent transmitter for each district station is not ordinarily feasible; the number of channels is restricted, and decentralized control of radio communications makes coordination more difficult. In a very large city, however, district stations that are removed by great distances should be provided with independent transmitters. When this is done, the district stations should have their own independent complaint bureaus. Daily, weekly, and monthly summaries and arrest and identification records should then be forwarded to headquarters.

Since supervision and reporting are the principal purposes of call boxes, control over district call boxes should not be centralized at headquarters but should rest with the district command.

In considering the desirability of the decentralization of line operations (duties related to crime investigation, and the control of traffic, vice, and juvenile crime), it is assumed that the relations between the special divisions and the patrol division (in terms of the duties of beat patrolmen *versus* those of the specialists, as discussed in Chapter 3) have been established and remain unchanged.

Decentralization of line operations takes the form of the assignment of specialized personnel to districts. The need for such territorial assignment is based on the same factors as for patrol, i.e., the volume of services to the public and their improvement in quality and convenience, and the increased effectiveness of police operations resulting from saving in police time and equipment use. It should be noted, however, that when patrol requirements justify district stations, requirements in the special fields of police operation may justify an earlier-than-otherwise decentralization because the facilities already in operation make unnecessary such large capital expenditures and overhead operating costs.

Except in cities where the distances are great or the problems acute, the decentralization of members engaged in vice control is not justified. The district command should be responsible for the suppression of vice activities through his patrol force; as in departments without district stations, when the patrol force is unable to cope with the situation, the district command should report the matter to the vice division for further action.

Decision 6. What authority should district commanders be given over members who are assigned to district stations to perform special police tasks in crime investigation, traffic control, and juvenile work?

There are two recommended arrangements. One is to detach the officers assigned to the district from their special unit and give the district commander complete authority over them; the other is to give him no authority, but to provide the specialists with their own supervisors and have them operate as a unit entirely independent of the district command.[1]

The choice between these two extremes is dependent on the extent to which it is desired to hold the district commander responsible for the specialized operation in his district. If he is to be held completely responsible for the satisfactory performance of specialized tasks, then the members engaged in their performance should be assigned to him outright. One arrangement may be used in reference to the performance of some tasks and the other arrangement in reference to others in the same special field.

When specialized personnel are assigned outright to the district commanders, the operational functions of the headquarters division should be established by department regulations and may exclude the continued investigation of certain types of cases by district personnel. Except for such operations as may be thus established, the central division is a staff agency charged with planning procedures, over-all operations, and district relationships. They should also have inspectional responsibilities in the field of their specialty.

---

[1] These two possible relationships, and arguments against the compromises between the two that are found in some departments, are discussed in *Police Administration*, pp. 317-321.

*Decision 7. When the investigation of crimes and ultimate re-
sponsibility for their clearance by arrest and recovery of stolen
property are made the responsibility of district commanders, and
detectives are assigned for this purpose, which categories of crimes
and what other responsibilities should be assigned to the central
detective division?*

When district-station commanders have complete responsibility
for the investigation of crimes committed in their districts, and
detectives are assigned to them for that purpose, the central detective division should be responsible for the continuing investigation
of designated categories of serious crimes and of crimes that are likely
to have community-wide ramifications. Homicide, arson, bunco, and
some categories of robberies are examples. It should be responsible
for the staff supervision of all crime investigations; it should coordinate crime investigations by district detectives. To these ends it
should have units concerned with auto recoveries, the arrest of fugi-
tives, burglaries, and perhaps some others.

CHAPTER 6

Patrol

Police objectives are promoted through the effective accomplishment of a well-rounded program of activity. Superiority of both program and performance is assured when the patrol division is recognized as the nucleus about which the other line units are grouped and policing is considered a patrol service with the specialists serving as aides to the patrolmen. The principle that should guide the planner in establishing patrol division responsibilities is the rule that *all duties away from headquarters should be assigned to the beat patrolman except those that interfere with the performance of his regular patrol duties and those that are performed substantially better by specialists.*

Patrol-division responsibilities in the investigation of crimes and accidents, the search for physical evidence, the control of traffic, the suppression of vice, and the prevention of delinquency establish the scope of patrol field duties. Basic patrol responsibilities in each of these fields were discussed in previous chapters. More precise decisions must be made, however, regarding the responsibility of the beat patrolman in the field of activity of each of the special divisions. These decisions will establish the character of patrol service and will give some indication of the proportional man-power requirements between patrol and the special divisions. Within this pattern, and with the man power that is available for service, the operations of the patrol division must be planned.

Depletion of Effective Patrol Strength

While the decisions mentioned above will influence the proportion of total police man power that is to be assigned to the patrol division, other decisions must be made that will also affect the patrol strength and the manner in which patrol man power is to be used. As the responsibilities of the patrol division are increased in scope, a greater proportion of its energy will be spent in the performance of duties that are less completely general in character. For example, beat officers may be assigned to locations for irregular or periodic, but less-than-full-time, point traffic duty, or

79

to the enforcement of parking regulations in an area that requires less than the full time of a traffic officer. As far as possible, the routine enforcement of time-limit parking regulations and the performance of crosswalk and intersection duty should be assigned to members of the traffic division. Decisions that must be made in reference to these assignments are discussed in Chapter 10. The police strength and consequently the patrol force is also sometimes depleted by the assignment of policemen to quasi- or non-police duties.

Decision 1. Are policemen assigned to quasi-police or non-police duties who should be returned to active police service?

The duties of policemen who are assigned to other city departments or offices, to other government agencies, and to tasks in the police department that are not of a police character, should be analyzed to discover whether some or all such assignments might be discontinued or filled by less expensive labor. The assignment of a policeman to full-time service in some other department, office, or agency, should be questioned. When the tasks are of a police character, the function should be assumed by the police department and the duties performed under its direction and control by officers who remain attached to the police department. Should the prosecutor's office need investigators, they should be appointed by the prosecutor and carried on his payroll. When the tasks are not strictly police in character, as for example when the officer serves as a chauffeur, information clerk, or receptionist, the assignment should be discontinued.

The Nature of Patrol Service

The nature of patrol and the manner of its performance influence its effectiveness. Since increased effectiveness is tantamount to an increase in man power, a type of patrol should be adopted and it should be conducted in a manner that will provide the most effective, efficient, and economical service.

Decision 2. Which is the most effective, efficient, and economical form of patrol?

Except in sections of the community where conditions justify the use of foot patrol or patrol by more than one man, the most effective, efficient, and economical patrol is provided by one man in a radio-equipped, conspicuously marked automobile who conforms to suitable patrol procedures.[1]

The automobile patrolman has the following advantages over the foot patrolman:

1. He can overtake a fleeing motorist.

2. The surprise factor in his patrol is enhanced because the mobility of the car permits an irregular and not easily predicted patrol.

3. He is able to cover a larger area with less fatigue and to reach the scene of action more quickly and in better physical, mental, and emotional condition.

4. The automobile can be operated under all weather and road conditions and it provides protection against inclement weather.

5. He can carry other officers, prisoners, extra clothing, a riot gun, fire extinguisher, first-aid kit, and other equipment.

6. The automobile radio enables the officer to maintain continuous contact with headquarters, an important safety feature and one that makes the officer immediately available for dispatch.

Automobile patrol is the least expensive form of patrol for the reason that increased efficiency, coverage, and effectiveness permit a saving in man power that compensates for the cost of operating the vehicle. Foot patrol, because of its limitations, is the most expensive.[2] The motorization of a foot patrolman increases the

---

[1] The advantages of a conspicuous one-man automobile patrol are discussed in greater detail in O. W. Wilson, *Police Administration, pp.* 94-107, from which much of this material was drawn by permission. Copyright, 1950. McGraw-Hill Book Company, Inc.

[2] "In 1949 there appeared in a popular magazine the first of a series of melodramatic articles describing serious crime conditions in several large American cities. These were followed by a series of telecasts that argued, as did the articles, that the solution to the problems exposed in each community was to take the policeman from his radio-equipped patrol car and restore him to the old-time job of walking a beat. The author's characters laugh at patrolmen 'buzzing around in automobiles' and maintain that the police 'are forgetting their infantry.' 'The cop has been taken out of the neighborhood and put on wheels. He used to be a watchdog. He knew a neighborhood like the palm of his hand. He knew what was going on. He could spot a stranger.'

"Progressive police executives accomplish this purpose, however, without depriving the patrolman of the many advantages of the automobile. . . .

"It is interesting to explore the adequacy of the patrol that would be provided if all patrolmen were on foot. Take, for example, the incident that was reported as follows: 'Why, we had a woman dragged into a car—right off the sidewalk, over on Pemberton, just a couple of weeks ago. There wasn't any policeman around.'

"Obviously hoodlums don't drag women into their cars from the sidewalk in the

cost of his operation between 12 and 20 per cent; the effectiveness of his patrol, however, is increased several hundred per cent. The economy of this procedure is obvious.

Conspicuously marked patrol cars have the following advantages:

1. Patrol is thereby apparently intensified, an important consideration since the basic purpose of patrol is the elimination of the

---

presence of a policeman. To prevent it in this manner, however, would require a foot patrolman in nearly every block; such coverage would require a police force of staggering proportions. No one can seriously make such a proposal.

"Actually the foot patrolman is not likely to be at the right location at the crucial moment to prevent a crime or to deal with it should it occur. This is so for the reason that foot patrol is so readily predicted that the hoodlums are not likely to attempt a criminal act until they have located the policeman. They can then strike with impunity in a section of the beat some blocks away. Obviously the foot patrolman out of sight of the crime scene cannot prevent the attack.

"And should the hoodlums be so inept as to fail to spot the foot patrolman before they strike, and in consequence drag a woman into their car at night a block away from a foot patrolman who hears her scream, what is the officer to do? There seem to be four choices open to him. (1) He could run to the scene and arrive, exhausted, after the car has driven away. This would accomplish nothing. (2) He could commandeer a private car and pursue the hoodlums. He is not likely to succeed in getting a private car in time to undertake hot pursuit. Further, a one-man chase is not likely to be as effective as a department-wide search—but he lacks communication with headquarters. (3) He could assume that the woman is actually being abducted, and not engaged in a family quarrel, and shoot in the direction of the scream in the hope that he would strike the abductors and not the victim or an innocent bystander. Such action would, of course, be inexcusable. (4) He could call headquarters for help by running to the nearest call-box or, more likely, to a telephone in a nearby store or home. This is the most sensible action, but a neighbor who heard the screams would probably have already made the call. So the foot patrolman would accomplish virtually nothing.

"In contrast to the foot patrolman, an officer in a car is in constant communication with headquarters; he is always available for dispatch. He can be sent a great distance and will arrive quickly and without fatigue. On observing hoodlums in a car (or on foot) he is able to call headquarters for assistance, pursue them, and keep the dispatcher informed on the direction of travel so that other policemen may be sent from many directions to intercept the fleeing car—or to surround a building, a block, or a larger area in the event they are on foot. The motorized force can be rapidly mobilized in any troubled area; it can be deployed in a manner to minimize the hazard to the men and to assure the greatest likelihood of successful accomplishment of its mission.

"As previously observed, hoodlums do not strike unless they have an opportunity to carry out their depredations successfully, which is in the absence of a policeman. But this fact must also be borne in mind: While hoodlums will not strike when opportunity for successful attack is lacking, they also will not strike when they *think* there is no opportunity. The basic purpose of patrol is to create a public impression of police omnipresence so that potential offenders will *think* there is no opportunity for successful misconduct. This can be accomplished by conspicuous, unpredictable patrol—as provided by automobile." Excerpts from O. W. Wilson, "Put the Cop Back on the Beat," *Public Management*, vol. 335, no. 6, June, 1953. pp. 122-125.

belief in the opportunity as well as the elimination of the actual opportunity for successful misconduct. The apparent intensification of patrol has a deterrent effect on criminals seeking opportunities to attack and on opportunists who violate regulations when they think the police are not around; it also creates a favorable impression on the public.

2. Conspicuously marked cars are readily identified as police vehicles. Citizens are thus less likely to flee when the police undertake to stop them; arguments used by some traffic violators' that they were entrapped by being followed in an inconspicuous manner are avoided; the emergency character of the vehicle is easily recognized, thus lessening the accident hazard on emergency runs.

3. The official authority represented by the conspicuous patrol car, like the police uniform, impresses the criminal and the minor offender and places them at a psychological disadvantage which makes them less likely to resist.

4. Patrolmen are less likely to neglect their duty or to drive improperly and their supervision by the sergeant is simplified when they are in conspicuous patrol cars.

One-man patrol-car operation has the following advantages over two-man operation:

1. One-man patrol is more efficient and economical than two because the number of patrol units is thus doubled and the beats are only half as large. Smaller beats enable a more intensive patrol; patrol frequency and the inspection of hazards are thus substantially increased. The cost of the greatly increased effectiveness is only the cost of operating the additional vehicles. Converting two-man patrols into one-man patrols and decreasing the man power sufficiently to compensate for the added cost of vehicle operation will nearly double the frequency of patrol operations at no added cost. This is sound economy!

2. The officer patrolling alone is more effective also because he is more likely to give his undivided attention to police duties. The presence of a second officer results in time spent in non-police activities; two officers are more likely than one officer to be involved in small delinquencies and infractions of the rules. For this reason the effectiveness is more than doubled when two-man patrol is converted to one-man operation.

3. A lone officer is safer than when accompanied by a second officer. Each gives the other a sense of safety out of proportion

to the added protection provided by the second man. When by himself an officer is more likely to take suitable precautions in dealing with a hazardous situation.

Automobile Patrol Procedure

The efficiency and effectiveness of automobile patrol, and consequently its economy, are strongly influenced by the manner in which it is performed. *Unsuitable procedures may cause motor patrol to be more expensive and less effective than foot patrol.* For this reason a suitable automobile patrol procedure should be adopted, the force trained in its use, and supervision provided that will assure compliance with its essentials.[1]

Decision 3. What procedure should be adopted for motorized patrol officers?

In some respects the distinction between foot and motorized patrol is unfortunate. All patrolmen should be thought of as being foot patrolmen and should be required to perform the usual routine patrol duties including inspectional tasks. Owing to the size and other characteristics of some beats, patrolmen assigned to them should have automobiles to expedite their patrol. The vehicle transports the patrolman from one task to another, brings him to the scene with greater speed and less fatigue, and enables him to capture a fleeing criminal.

When the patrolman with an automobile performs all the duties of a foot patrolman, *he must spend a large part of his time on foot.* This provides opportunity for observation and for contact with citizens and thus enables the patrolman to serve as the eyes and ears of the department. Provision must be made for the patrolman to report off the air, when absence from his vehicle makes him unavailable for radio dispatch, with suitable control to prevent too large a proportion of the officers in adjacent areas to be off the air at the same time.

An over-emphasis of the emergency character of automobile patrol, restricting its use to answering calls, indicates a fallacious interpretation of its true purpose. The patrolman who remains in his vehicle hidden in a secluded spot when he is not driving is not providing patrol service. The officer who spends all his time driving

---

[1] Motor patrol procedures are discussed in greater detail in O. W. Wilson, *Police Administration*, pp. 98-107, from which some of this material was taken by permission. Copyright, 1950. McGraw-Hill Book Company, Inc.

neglects his duty to make inspections, to observe, to make himself available for public service, and to make contacts with citizens. Protection against weather and relief from fatigue by occasional periods spent in driving from one location to another are to be used with discretion.

Motorized Patrol Techniques

In order to enjoy the companionship of a brother officer during routine patrol and the comfort of his presence in hazardous situations, some patrolmen are eager to prove that one-man patrol-car operation is unduly hazardous. The death of an officer by bandit gunfire should not be taken as immediate and conclusive proof that one-man patrol-car operation should be discontinued. Since the beginning of police service, officers have occasionally been killed by outlaws, and death by gunfire must still be recognized as an occupational hazard.

Every effort should be made, however, to lessen the hazard by the selection of able men and by their training in suitable techniques to enable them to deal effectively with hazardous situations with minimum risk to their own safety. Procedures should be developed, therefore, that will lessen the hazard to an officer who is sent on a call or who undertakes to stop a car whose occupants have aroused his suspicions.

Decision 4. What procedures should be used to assure that officers are dispatched on calls in a manner and in sufficient number to assure the accomplishment of the mission with minimum risk to the officers?

The nature of the call will determine the number of officers and the manner in which they should be deployed to accomplish their mission most effectively. Only the beat officer need be sent on calls in which immediate capture or pursuit of a criminal is not required, except (1) when a crime or accident scene should be searched for physical evidence, in which case an evidence technician should be dispatched for this purpose; (2) when there may be an attendant need for guarding the premises, or controlling a crowd or diverting traffic as at the scene of an accident or other incident that may cause traffic to be blocked, in which event additional officers should be dispatched for these specific purposes; (3) in cases involving drunk or deranged persons and family quarrels, when at least two officers should be sent, and more when the reported conditions indicate the need; and (4) in cases where the principal objective is to save a life endangered by accident or some non-criminal act, when the force sent should be sufficient to accomplish its purpose.

Cases in which criminals are in the act of committing a crime should be divided into two categories: (1) crimes anticipated by the preparation of a broadcast kept on file at the dispatcher's desk for immediate use in the event of attack[1] and (2) crimes in which broadcasts have not been prepared. As a minimum, radio broadcasts should be prepared for all establishments that have robbery alarms terminating at police headquaters. In cases where criminals are reported to be operating but broadcasts have not been prepared in advance, the area surrounding the point of attack should be divided by the nearest intersecting streets into quadrants designated as NW, NE, SE, and SW. The dispatcher should send, as a minimum, the beat officer, the evidence technician, and four officers, each assigned to the quadrant that lies closest to his beat. Additional officers should be dispatched if the size of the premises or other conditions indicate a greater need. All officers should be informed of the nature of the call and dispatched directly to the scene to surround the premises, four or more of them having their quadrants designated at that time so they may know that they are to make a search of the designated areas in the event the criminals escape.

Since the capture of the criminals is the principal objective, the officers should approach the scene and surround the premises as quietly as possible. The first man at the scene should immediately cover the rear of the premises; on the arrival of the second officer, the first should take a position at one rear corner and the second should take a position at the diagonally opposite corner so that each may cover two different sides of the building. The beat officer is in charge of the operation unless the patrol sergeant or an officer of higher rank is at the scene. When the building has been suitably surrounded, the one in charge should ring the door bell or hammer on the front door in an effort to frighten the criminals into the arms of the officers waiting in the rear. If the results are negative, entry should be effected and search made of the premises.

As soon as the escape of the criminals has been established, the

---

[1] Prepared broadcasts are described in *Police Administration,* pp. 104-105, and in *Police Records,* pp. 246-251, where a sample of a prepared broadcast is reproduced.

officers assigned to quadrants should undertake a search of their respective areas, working out from the point of attack, while the beat officer, in the course of his preliminary investigation, should telephone to headquarters all information helpful in effecting an arrest. At the same time the evidence technician should proceed with a search for physical evidence.[1]

Decision 5. What should be done to lessen the hazard to officers when stopping automobiles whose occupants have aroused their suspicions?

When officers are placed alone in automobiles, the number of patrol cars should be increased in proportion; they should be equipped with special "police stop" lights, and the officers should be trained in the techniques of stopping suspicious cars so as to minimize personal danger.[2]

Inspectional Services

Inspectional services provided by the police vary widely among the many forces with respect to the types of premises that are inspected and the nature, frequency, and time of the inspection. In some communities the police inspect the security of establishments when they are closed to business and check on compliance with laws and regulations of such licensed enterprises as taverns, bars, dance halls, bowling alleys, skating rinks, pool halls, and other amusement establishments. Some also check the security of homes temporarily vacant when the owner is out of town. Other departments, on the other hand, do not provide any of these services.

The thoroughness of the security check extends from a careful "shaking" of the door and a visual inspection of windows and other apertures accessible from the ground, on the one hand, to a cursory visual examination from a moving patrol car with the aid of a spotlight, on the other. The frequency of security checks varies from once each night to two times on each of the night shifts with a third inspection of the more hazardous locations on the after-midnight watch.

Policy decisions must be made as to whether inspectional services

---

[1] The deployment of officers on calls is described in greater detail in O. W. Wilson, *Police Administration*, pp. 103-107, from which much of this material was drawn by permission. Copyright, 1950. McGraw-Hill Book Company, Inc.

[2] The police light is described on p. 297 and a suggested technique is given on p. 102 of *Police Administration*.

will be provided by the police, the establishments that will be inspected, and the nature, frequency, and time of the inspection. The time required for any type of inspection may be measured and, since the number of establishments to be inspected and the frequency of the inspections are known, it is possible to compute the number of man hours and the cost of the inspectional services to the community.

Decision 6. Should the police provide inspectional services?

The primary objective of security checks is to apprehend criminals while they are attacking the premises. The purpose of inspecting the licensed places mentioned above is to increase compliance with laws governing their operation and to maintain some degree of surveillance over patrons, some of whom are likely to be of questionable character.

The number of criminals apprehended during inspections is so small that this accomplishment alone would scarcely justify the cost of the service. Inspections, however, play such an important role in preventing crime, which is the basic patrol purpose, that the cost of the service seems to be justified. This is so because the premises subject to inspection are hazards which attract the criminal and, by requiring the beat patrolman to make inspections, the chief is applying the rule "put the policeman where the criminal is—or is most likely to be." Sound inspection policies force the patrolman to give attention to hazards; without this requirement the patrolman would be likely to neglect these locations.

The performance of inspectional tasks also promotes a desirable routine patrol by forcing the patrolman to move from the location of one task to that of another. These tasks also force the motorized officer to patrol on foot where he is more accessible to persons seeking assistance and giving information.

The inspection of vacant homes, of selected licensed premises, and of commercial establishments closed to business and those open for business that constitute a robbery hazard, are all justified on the basis of the crime-prevention and public-relations value of this service. The public-relations value of security checks of homes left temporarily vacant is especially important. The owner is pleased with the service he receives and his neighbors are impressed with the sight of an officer engaged in this task.

Decision 7. How thorough should inspections be?

For example, during what hours and how frequently should

inspections be made (1) of recreational establishments (taverns, bars, pool halls, bowling alleys, skating rinks, dance halls, and so on); (2) of other business enterprises while they are open for business (to reduce the robbery hazard of some and to check on compliance with regulations and to discover stolen property or persons-wanted in such places as hotels, rooming houses, garages, second hand stores, pawnshops, parking lots, and so on); (3) of business establishments that represent a burglary hazard when they are closed to business; and (4) of homes whose occupants are temporarily out of town? Also, what should be the nature and thoroughness of the inspection of each type of establishment? Decisions must also be made as to the relative importance of the inspection of the various types of places in the light of the time required, so that the man power devoted to inspections may be used to best advantage. The policy should be to provide as extensive, frequent, and thorough inspection as the man power will permit.

The security of the doors should be established by actually "trying" the knob; apertures accessible from the ground should be visually examined. Only in this way may the security of the premises be ascertained. This procedure also increases the likelihood of capturing a criminal who may have gained entrance, and it forces the officer into closer contact with people who may be around at the time.

The security of commercial establishments should be checked twice before and twice after midnight with a third check after midnight of the most hazardous locations. An exception may be made of types of establishments that are infrequently attacked, but even these should be checked at least once after midnight.

The security of vacant homes should be checked daily, preferably during the daylight hours so the officer will be more likely to be seen by the neighbors. Inspections of vacant homes at night are likely to create apprehension when observed by neighbors.

The inspection of business houses while they are open for business should be during the most hazardous hours. The nature and thoroughness of the inspection will be influenced by the character of the enterprise and the likelihood of attack or violation.

Foot Patrol and Two-man Automobile Patrol

Conditions in certain sections of some communities may necessitate deviation from one-man automobile patrol. To the extent that deviations are necessary, effective patrol coverage is diminished;

deviations, therefore, have the effect of decreasing the patrol strength. For this reason, decisions to vary from one-man patrol-car operation should be made with reluctance and only when the conditions indicate clearly the necessity of this action.

Decision 8. How many men are needed for foot patrol and during which hours should they work?

Foot patrol may be justified by the concentration, in a relatively small area, of such a volume of inspectional tasks and of duties that arise from incidents that call for police service as to occupy the full time and continuous attention of one or more men on one or more shifts. Inspections of business establishments are intended to assure (1) security against burglary or robbery and (2) compliance with regulations. Incidents of sufficient frequency to justify the full-time continuous attention of an officer usually occur only in areas containing large numbers of cheap amusement resorts, and then but rarely. The assignment of an officer to foot patrol may also be conceivably necessary owing to his inability to operate an automobile. This situation is seldom met today.

A first step is reaching a decision regarding the justification for foot patrol is to discover whether there are some patrolmen who are unable to drive an automobile with reasonable safety and efficiency. This infrequently found inability may arise from lack of driving experience or physical inability resulting from infirmity, defective vision, or injury.

The second step is to analyze the need for the two types of inspectional service mentioned above in order to compute the man-hours required in their performance and to determine their concentration in time and place. In order to avoid the unnecessary use of costly foot patrol, effort should be made to limit the number of shifts and the size of the area in which it will be used.

Although the establishments requiring attention may be concentrated in such a manner as to permit the creation of one or more foot beats for the assignment of patrolmen to perform inspectional duties exclusively, the advantages of motorized patrol are so great as to justify an attempt to divide the area and the inspectional tasks among a number of motorized beats, thus avoiding the necessity of providing the more costly and less efficient foot patrol.

The third step is to discover whether there is an area of such character that incidents requiring police attention arise so frequently as to require the full-time continuous service of a foot patrolman. Such areas are also rarely found. When there is doubt as to whether an area qualifies for a foot patrol on this basis, the question can usually be resolved by analysis of the manner of initiation of police action to deal with the incidents. When in an area that has a foot patrol, analysis reveals that the majority of the incidents was called to police attention by citizen telephone calls to headquarters and not initially discovered by the officer on the beat, justification for the continuance of the foot patrol is doubtful.

The hourly need for foot patrol will be found to vary greatly. The greatest need for inspectional services is usually found during the evening and night hours. In most communities where a foot patrol is needed to perform these services, it can be limited to one shift, the hours being selected to encompass those of greatest need.

The nature, location, time, and extent of irregular or periodic but less-than-full-time point traffic duty may also be a determining factor in the establishment of a foot-patrol beat.

Decision 9. Which areas have characteristics that make desirable a two-man automobile patrol, and during what hours must it be provided?

The most important factor influencing this decision is the frequency of discovery by patrolmen of incidents that require more than one man to deal with them safely and effectively and that are so urgent that it would be impractical to radio for assistance, in contrast to the frequency of incidents that are reported to headquarters so that a suitable force may be deployed by radio in a manner to assure the safe and effective achievement of the police objective. Arrests that require more than one officer and that cannot be delayed pending the arrival of assistance are an example. A comparative analysis of the arrests initiated by two men in patrol cars, in contrast to those by lone patrolmen, may reveal important information. In the study, consideration should be given to the hour of arrest, the location, whether the criminal was in a car, the offense, whether formally charged, difficulty experienced in effecting the arrest, whether the criminal was armed and whether he attempted to use the weapon; the number arrested in a group, and whether assistance was summoned.

In determining the need for two-man automobile patrol, consideration should be given to the following facts: (1) One-man patrol-car operation is safer and more than twice as effective as two-man operation. (2) Some persons contend that one-man patrol-car operation results in the lone officer avoiding dangerous situations and consequently not taking desirable police action. This point is not conceded, but assuming it were partially true, the increased effectiveness of one-man operation would more than compensate for such infrequent lapses. There is no question as to the desirability and necessity of arresting criminals when they are discovered in their criminal acts, but the necessity for an immediate arrest may sometimes be over-emphasized. (3) Policemen have a normal human desire for companionship, and it is only natural that this desire should cause them to avoid, as far as they are able, assignment without a brother officer to entertain them, and to lend them comfort in hazardous situations. Patrolmen, therefore, may be expected to present strong arguments against one-man patrol-car operation. Since the desire for companionship does not seem to be a valid argument, they usually contend that one-man operation is unduly hazardous and less efficient. (4) Owing to the greater efficiency and economy of one-man operation, areas should be selected for two-man patrol (on foot or in an automobile) with reluctance, and the hours during which two-man operation is provided should be held to the bare minimum. (5) Areas in which foot patrol is carried on by one man should be suitable for one-man patrol-car operation.

Distribution of the Patrol Force

Patrol tasks may be divided into three categories: (1) called-for services to deal with incidents that are induced by hazards; (2) inspectional services designed to lessen identified hazards; and (3) routine preventive patrol intended to lessen the intangible hazards whose presence is made apparent principally by incidents induced by them. Since the patrol force should be distributed in proportion to the need for patrol service, a measure of the need should be developed. This may be done most readily in terms of the above-defined categories of police tasks.

The volume of inspectional duties is determined by policy decisions relating to the establishments to be inspected and the frequency and nature of the inspections.

Decision 10. How may the man-hour requirements for inspectional services be measured?

The man-hour requirements for inspections during any time period of the day may be computed when a policy determination has been made as to which establishments should be subject to a regular inspection by the beat officer, how frequently they should be inspected, and the nature of the inspection.

Study should be made of the average time required for the inspection of the various types of establishments in the manner planned. The number of establishments of each type must be counted. Determination may then be made of inspectional needs during each shift expressed in terms of man-hours required to provide the desired quality of service.[1]

Decision 11. How may the man-power requirements for called-for services and routine preventive patrol be estimated?

The number of man-hours needed for called-for services may be computed by multiplying the number of incidents of each type by the average number of minutes required by a patrolman to dispose of the various types of incidents that require police service. The average number of minutes required may be ascertained by time studies.

The number of man-hours needed for inspectional and called-for services added to the man-hours needed for preventive patrol would then give the total man power needed for patrol. With this figure the police could demonstrate to budget makers their exact patrol man-power needs.

Unfortunately, the exact man-hours needed for preventive patrol cannot be so accurately determined. The fact that a substantial part of a patrolman's time is devoted to preventive patrol further emphasizes the inaccuracy of estimates of man-power requirements based on an estimate of the time required for a satisfactorily effective routine patrol. A study in Wichita, Kansas, indicated that the average patrolman spent less than 10 per cent of his time in called-for services, and less than one third in inspectional services,

[1] For a discussion of the manner in which inspectional needs may be computed in man-hours of time, and for a chart that shows the hourly variation in one city, see *Police Administration,* pp. 495, 496, and 498. An average of 30 seconds was devoted to each "door try."

although during the period from 9:00 P.M. to 7:00 A.M. he spent slightly more than half of his time at inspectional tasks.[1] From this it is apparent that the average officer devoted substantially more than half of his time to preventive patrol while officers on duty between 9:00 P.M. and 7:00 A.M. spent more than one third of their time in routine patrol.

A study, made in 1952, of the man-hours devoted by the London Metropolitan Police constable to the various tasks he performs on patrol, shows that, on the average for all shifts, he spends 54.2 per cent of his time in preventive patrol, 15.6 per cent at "door tries," and 13.5 per cent at called-for services. On night duty, the average constable devoted 28.8 per cent of his time to "door tries." An average of 37.3 seconds were devoted to each "door try."[2]

Man-hour requirements for inspectional tasks can and invariably should be computed. Man-hour requirements for called-for services may also be measured, although the incompleteness of the data is likely to make the measurement inaccurate.[3] Such exact man-hour requirements for preventive patrol are not so readily ascertained.

Since preventive patrol is intended to lessen the intangible hazards, the man-hour requirements seem to be a function of the frequency of incidents that results from these hazards, rather than a function of beat mileage. It would be possible, but probably not desirable, to provide a stipulated amount of time for routine patrol for each incident the patrol is intended to prevent. The amount of time provided for each incident would depend on its nature, since it is more important to prevent serious incidents than it is to prevent the less serious ones. The time thus provided for the various types of incidents would be a policy determination not unlike the determination of the types of establishments to be inspected and the

---

[1] See *Police Administration*, pp. 474 and 496. Time spent going from one inspectional task to another was considered routine patrol in this study. The time spent at inspectional tasks was based on a requirement that the doors of stores that close before 9:00 P.M. should be tried once before that hour; all doors should be tried twice between 9:00 P.M. and 1:00 A.M.; and that the doors of stores that present a great hazard, estimated at 60 per cent of the total, should be checked twice between 1:00 A.M. and 5:00 A.M. and once between 5:00 A.M. and 7:00 A.M.

[2] *Report on the Employment and Distribution of Strength in the Metropolitan Police,* Part II, London, 1953.

[3] In most departments time and location data are incomplete on a portion of the incidents and the time tally must, in consequence, be incomplete. For example, in the Wichita study cited above, the time of occurrence or location was not recorded in 65 per cent of Part II offenses, 19 per cent of miscellaneous reports and accidents, and 10 per cent of the arrests.

nature, time, and frequency of the inspections that are to be made of them.

Man-hour requirements for routine patrol seem to be more accurately measured in this manner than by the time required to cover the beat a stipulated number of times for the reason that the need for the patrol is evidenced by the occurrence of incidents rather than by street mileage or area. The incidents are not evenly distributed over an entire beat; sections having a concentration of incidents deserve greater attention than other areas because the concentration of incidents indicates a concentration of hazards, and the purpose of preventive patrol is to lessen the effectiveness of hazards.

The patrolman spends such a large portion of his time in routine preventive patrol that, since there has not yet been developed an acceptable measure of the need for it in terms of minutes, the distribution of the patrol force exclusively on the basis of time spent in the performance of all patrol tasks seems unsound. To compute the load on each shift or on each beat in this manner seems to be striving for a degree of preciseness beyond that of the basic data, except on foot beats in which nearly all the time is devoted to inspectional tasks. The computation also becomes quite involved when an effort is made to record each task undertaken and measure the time required in its accomplishment. It seems desirable to consider some method of distributing the patrol force that is more direct and less complicated.

For purposes of patrol distribution, it is not necessary to express the need in terms of the exact number of man-hours. The number of men available for patrol is known, and since the man-hours needed for inspectional services may be computed, it is only necessary to distribute the remaining man-hours in proportion to the distribution of the need for called-for services and routine patrol. Proportional distribution may be made with reasonable accuracy even though the basic data are not complete when there is reasonable assurance that the deficiencies in data are evenly distributed in time and location.

The distribution of the need for called-for services must obviously be in proportion to the distribution of the incidents that call for the service. Since the purpose of preventive patrol is to prevent incidents that call for service, the distribution of the need for routine patrol must likewise be in proportion to the distribution of the incidents. Man-hours not spent at inspectional tasks, therefore, should be distributed in proportion to the distribution of the incidents that call for service.

Decision 12. What types of incidents should be used to measure the proportional need for called-for services and preventive patrol?

The following categories of incidents are considered suitable for ascertaining the proportional need for called-for services and preventive patrol: Part I crimes, Part II offenses, miscellaneous reports, accidents, and arrests.

The exclusion of traffic tickets served for moving violations from the above list seems justified. The accidents they are intended to prevent seem a more accurate measure of the need for time for the service of traffic tickets than the actual tickets served, since the latter frequently are not in proportion to accidents either in time or place.

The inclusion of booked arrests in the list of incidents, however, seems justified. They are frequently not related in time and place to the offense for which they are made. Also, a greater amount of time is involved in each arrest than in the service of each traffic ticket.

The incidents under consideration, however, are not of equal importance. The prevention of some (the purpose of routine patrol), therefore, deserves more time than others. Also, some require more time in handling (called-for services) than others. Weights must be assigned to compensate for these inequalities. Weighting a factor consists of multiplying it by a number (the weight) to increase its value.

Decision 13. What weights should be applied to the incidents so that routine preventive patrol will be provided in proportion to the seriousness as well as the frequency of the incidents and so that time for called-for services will be provided in proportion to the time required to deal with the incidents as well as in proportion to their frequency?

Consideration will first be given to the distribution of the need for patrol service among the shifts. The principles developed may then be applied with some modification in the measurement of the need for patrol service during one shift in a small district or beat.

In the Wichita distribution mentioned above, the total daily man-hours available for called-for services and routine patrol was ascertained by subtracting, from the total patrol man power, the man-hours devoted to (1) weekly, annual, and sick relief; (2) inspectional duties; and (3) refreshment, on-duty court attendance, fixed traffic posts, and so on. The remaining man-hours were available for called-for services and preventive patrol. These man-hours were distributed among the shifts in proportion to the frequency of incidents that needed to be handled (called-for services) and whose occurrence should be prevented by routine patrol.

In computing the proportional distribution of the incidents among the shifts, if the incidents are all added together each is given the same weight even though some types may require more called-for-service time and some types may deserve more routine-patrol time intended to prevent their occurrence. For example, if dealing with one type of incident requires three times as much time as another, it should have a weight of three. If one type of incident is four times as serious as another, it presumably deserves four times as much routine-duty time directed toward its prevention, and it should, therefore, be given a weight of four. Another consideration in weighting is the fact that time and location data on some incidents are less consistently available than on others.

The Wichita distribution of the man-hours devoted to called-for services and preventive patrol was based on the proportion of all incidents in each of the five types that occurred during each hour of the day. The five percentage figures were averaged to arrive at the hourly proportion of the total need for called-for service and preventive-patrol time. The proportional need on each shift was then computed by adding the hourly proportions for each. For example, of all incidents whose hour of occurrence was known, the percentage that occurred on the day shift was as follows: Part I crimes, 27.2; Part II offenses, 19.1; miscellaneous reports, 26.3; accidents, 38.7; booked arrests, 18.1. The sum of these percentages (129.4) divided by the number of types of incidents (5) gave the proportional need for called-for services and preventive patrol on that shift, i.e., 25.9 per cent. Therefore, 25.9 per cent of the man-hours available for called-for services and routine patrol were assigned to the day shift.

This procedure seemed to offer two advantages. (1) It partially corrected the deficiencies of the time-of-occurrence data, which varied from 69 per cent in Part I crimes to 10 per cent in arrests. Because of the incompleteness of the time data, to have added the incidents whose hour of occurrence was known would have reduced the value of each incident in proportion to the per cent of incidents of that type in which the time of occurrence was un-known.[1] (2) The number of incidents in the five types varied so that this procedure had the effect of giving each incident in a type a weight in inverse proportion to the number of incidents of that type compared to the number of incidents of other types. This was desirable because the frequenncy of the incidents in each type de-creased with their seriousness and with the length of time required to deal with them.

As previously stated, the assignment of weights to the types of incidents is a matter of administrative judgment. In assigning the weights, it must be recognized that the need for patrol service can-not be measured precisely. The measure is sufficiently precise when the distribution of the patrol force by means of it can be defended by logical reasoning and when patrolmen and their supervisors are not conscious of inequalities in the loads of the shifts and the beats.

In the light of experience, it is recommended that the Wichita procedure for distributing the man-hours for called-for service and preventive patrol among the shifts be modified in the following re-spects: (1) Deficiencies in time-of-occurrence data should be cor-rected by dividing the number of incidents in each type in which the hour of occurrence is known by the percentage of incidents in that type in which the hour of occurrence is known. (2) Arbitrary weights should be assigned to each incident in each type, as fol-lows: One should be assigned to arrests, accidents, and miscellaneous reports. It is assumed that all incidents in these types are of approxi-mately equal importance and require approximately equal time to deal with them. Two should be assigned to Part II offenses and four should be assigned to Part I crimes. It is assumed that Part II crimes are two times and Part I crimes are four times as serious and require approximately two and four times as much time to deal with them, respectively, as the other three types of incidents. In applying the weights, Part I crimes should be multiplied by four and Part II incidents by two. (3) The corrected and weighted number of inci-dents in each type may then be added and the proportion of the total on each shift to the total for the 24 hours of the day may then

---

[1] The data could have been corrected for this deficiency in another manner, i.e., by dividing the number of incidents in each type whose hour of occurrence was known on each shift by the per cent of incidents of that type whose hour of occurrence was known. The corrected number of incidents in each type could then be added and its proportion to the total for the 24 hours of the day computed. Either procedure is considered sound.

be computed. This per cent should then be used to apportion the man-hours to be devoted to called-for services and preventive patrol among the shifts. If the administrator or the planner is not convinced of the validity of the above assumptions, he may make his own and assign weights accordingly.

Decision 14. Which hours should be selected for shift changes, and should one or more overlapping shifts be provided?

The proportional hourly distribution of incidents that call for police service varies considerably among the 24 hours of the day. Since man power is distributed in proportion to an average need for service on each shift in inadequate man power will be available during hours of greater-than-average need, and during hours of less-than-average need the man power will not be used to its full capacity. Shift hours should be selected, therefore, that will result in the smallest total hourly variation from the average need for each shift.[1]

The need for an overlapping shift may become apparent when wide variations in hourly needs for patrol service result in a substantial deviation from the average need. An overlapping shift divides the day into smaller time periods, and man power may be assigned to the short periods in proportion to the average need with less total deviation than would otherwise be experienced. Also, when inspectional services are met by a foot patrol on one shift, it is usually advisable to select the hours for this shift on the basis of the hours of greatest need without regard to the hours of the motorized shifts.

Decision 15. How should the beats be organized?[2]

The number of patrolmen assigned to each shift minus the number of patrolmen earmarked for relief and for foot patrol and the number of beats that will require two-man patrol will determine the number of motorized beats on each shift. Motorized beats should overlap the foot beats, and calls for service should be assigned to the motorized officer. The foot patrolman thus devotes his time exclusively to his inspectional duties.

Beats should be organized on each shift so that all will contain approximately equal needs for patrol service; each should have, as

---

[1] The computation of the proportional hourly distribution of incidents that call for police service and the method used in the selection of the most suitable shift hours are described in *Police Administration*, pp. 490-491, and *Police Records*, pp. 237-239.

[2] A method for laying out the beats is described in *Police Administration*, pp. 499-511.

far as possible, uniform social, racial, and business characteristics. A rectangular shape, approximating a square rather than an elongated area, provides a shorter average distance between points in the beat;[1] this shape has the further advantage of permitting greater variation in routes and better opportunity to back-track, thus increasing the element of surprise. Beat boundaries should follow census tract boundaries as far as possible. Beats should not be transversed by an obstacle to easy travel that has the effect of dividing it into separate parts. Examples include streams, lakes, ravines, undeveloped sections, and railroad tracks with few or no grade crossings. The use of important streets and highways as beat boundaries assures these thoroughfares some added attention. Likewise, locations that deserve special attention receive an increased police service when at an intersection that forms the corners of three or four beats.

The layout of foot beats created for the purpose of providing intensive inspectional service is not difficult. Consideration should be given to the inclusion in each beat of such a number of places that require inspection as to occupy the full time of the patrolman in performing the inspections with the frequency and in the manner established by policy. Since communication with the foot patrolman will be principally by call boxes, consideration should be given to their location in laying out foot beats.

The layout of motorized beats so as to provide approximately equal work loads is more difficult. Each should contain its proportional share of the area of the community, of doors to be tried and establishments to be inspected,[2] and of incidents that represent the services called for and the need for preventive patrol. Thus there is assured a suitable proportion of time for inspections, called-for services, and preventive patrol. For example, when there are to be 10 mortorized beats, each should contain approximately 10 per cent of the load.

----

[1] A business section that otherwise would require some foot-patrol beats may sometimes be divided among several motorized beats that contain noncommercial areas, thus giving each motorized officer a portion of the inspectional tasks that justify foot patrol. This arrangement enables a more complete motorization of the patrol force and avoids subjecting a patrolman to the hardships of continuous foot patrol. It also provides some variety to the tasks of patrol and relieves fatigue, since the officer may alternate his time between foot patrol and automobile patrol of sections that do not require intensive inspectional services. This arrangement sometimes results in greatly elongated motorized beats.

[2] Inspectional services performed by foot patrolmen, whose beats are overlapped by motorized patrol, should not be included.

REPORTING AREA CARD

6″×4″

Factors and Elements	Number	Corrected Element Weight	Weighted Number	Percentage of Total for City, this Shift	Factor Weight	Weighted Percentage of Total
				Reporting Area No. ____		
Part I Crimes						
Part II Crimes						
Miscell. Reports						
Accidents						
Arrests						
Total Incidents	xxxx	xxxx			x 5 =	
Store Doors						
Miscell. Establish.						
Total Inspections	xxxx	xxxx			x =	
Area or Mileage					x =	

Grand Total (Percentage of total city load on this shift found in this reporting area, multiplied by sum of factor weights)   =

Motorized beats may be organized by ascertaining, for the shift under consideration, the proportional distribution of pertinent factors among the small districts or reporting areas into which the community should be divided as described on page 26. Reporting-area cards, 6″ × 4″ in size and of three or more different colors (cards of one different color should be used for each shift), are useful for recording the data relating to each reporting area on each shift. The data on each card are to be corrected for incidents on which the time of occurrence is unknown; each factor is to be reduced to the percentage of the total of that factor for the shift under consideration, and a single consolidated percentage figure is to be computed for each reporting area that will represent the proportional work load of the reporting area for that shift.

The area may be expressed in any desired units provided the measurement is reasonably accurate. Instead of area, street mileage may be used. Street mileage is the sum of street lengths contained entirely within the area plus half the length of streets that form the boundary of the area.[1] The choice between area and street mileage

[1] A "beat mile" on a walking beat is the length of the street on which the officer has responsibility on only one side and twice the length of the street on which he has responsibility on both sides.

should be based on the relative ease and accuracy of the computation of the two measures.

The incident factor should include Part I and Part II crimes, miscellaneous reports, accidents, and booked arrests. The number of incidents in each category that occurred in the reporting area during the shift hours under consideration should be recorded on each reporting-area card. The time of occurrence of each incident will not invariably be known; this deficiency is always most pronounced in Part I crimes. For Part I crimes a choice may be made, influenced in part by the extent of the deficiency in known times of occurrence, between the time reported and time of occurrence. The selection of the time reported is further justified by the substantial amount of tim spent by the patrolman in the investigation of these crimes at the time they are reported. As a general rule, the time reported does not differ greatly from the time of occurrence in the other categories of incidents; in contrast, Part I crimes are often not reported for several hours after their occurrence.

The deficiency in known times of occurrence (and times of reporting when this is the factor selected for Part I crimes) is corrected by dividing the number of incidents in each reporting area on the shift under consideration by the percentage of incidents in that category the time of occurrence of which is known. For example, when the time of occurrence is known in only 40 per cent of Part I crimes and the number of Part I crimes recorded in a reporting area is 8, the corrected number of Part I crimes is 20. In order to reduce the number of computations, this correction may be applied to weights that should be assigned to each factor in a manner to be described later. When incidents with unknown times are less than 10 per cent of the total, there does not seem to be justification for this correction.

Inspectional tasks are divided into two categories, each being distinguished from the other by objective or purpose, by the nature of the object of the inspection, and by the time required. Tasks in one category involve store doors the security of which it to be checked when the establishment is closed to business. Tasks in the other category, to be referred to as miscellaneous inspections, involve establishments open for business the inspection of which is required by department policy. Frequently included in this category are taverns, bars, pool halls, bowling alleys, dance halls, public garages, parking lots, drive-in restaurants, and other places deserving police attention.

While store doors are not tried on the day shift (except on Sunday and other days when they are closed to business), the hazard created by business establishments open for business seems justification for including store doors in the inspection factor on the day watch. Likewise, the number of establishments that should be inspected when they are open for business that might not be open during all the hours of a shift should not be subtracted. The closing hour of many of these establishments is a critical time that adds to the police load even though they are closed the remainder of the shift.

Before the proportion of the total load on each shift that is located in each reporting area may be computed, consideration must be given to weights that should be assigned to each of the categories of incidents so that a single consolidated percentage figure may be computed to represent the proportion of called-for services and routine preventive patrol that are needed in each reporting area. Weights should also be assigned to store doors and miscellaneous inspections for the preparation of a consolidated inspection percentage.

Attention must then be given to the assignment of weights to each of the primary factors (area, incidents, and inspections) so that a consolidated percentage figure may be computed for each reporting area which will represent the proportional work load during that shift that is found in each reporting area. These small districts may then be combined in a manner that will provide the required number of beats containing approximately equal work loads.

Decision 16. What weights should be applied to the several factors so that motorized beats may be constructed that will contain approximately equal needs for patrol service?

In weighing the factors, consideration should be given to the problem of combining the reporting areas into beats. If the five-incident factor and the factors of area and inspections can be combined into a single consolidated factor for each reporting area to represent the proportion of the shift load found on it, the task of ascertaining the proportional loads on beats that may be tentatively constructed is greatly simplified. It consists of totalling the consolidated factors for all reporting areas contained within each beat. The tediousness of the task of laying out the beats is lessened when a single factor is devised to represent the proportional load in each small district for each shift.

The consolidation of the five incidents into one factor also greatly reduces the number of computations to be made in ascertaining the proportion of the total for the shift that is found in each reporting area. The consolidation may be effected in the same manner as in computing the hourly distribution of incidents, i.e., by correcting the number of incidents of each type occurring in an area on each shift, by dividing by the per cent of all incidents of that type in which the time of occurrence and the location are known, and by weighting the incidents by multiplying the corrected number of Part I crimes by four, of Part II offenses by two, and of miscellaneous reports, accidents,[1] and arrests by one.

This computation may be simplified by applying the correction to the weight (i.e., dividing the weight assigned to each category by the percentage of incidents in that category on which the time and location are known) and multiplying the number of incidents in each area by the corrected weight. In order to keep the computations simple, the correction should be approximate rather than exact; that is the corrected weight should be rounded at one decimal point.

The total of the numbers of corrected and weighted incidents may then be taken as a consolidated incident factor. Its proportion to the total for the shift, expressed in percentage, represents the proportion of the need for called-for services and preventive patrol that is found in each reporting area for that shift.

Computations may likewise be simplified by combining store doors and miscellaneous inspections into a single factor. This may be done by multiplying by a suitable weight the number of establishments in the miscellaneous inspections category that are subject to patrol inspection and adding this number to the number of store doors. For example, it may be assumed that on the average ten times as much time on each shift is devoted to the inspection of each of these establishments as is spent in trying each store door. Each such establishment, therefore, should be given a weight of ten.

The weights assigned to each of the five categories of incidents and to miscellaneous inspections should, of course, be adjusted to correspond with the relative time devoted to each under local policies and operating procedures, and with local opinion as to the relative importance and seriousness of each.

Since the percentage-of-incidents factor is composed of 5 elements, it may be multiplied by 5. On the day watch the area factor and the inspection factor may be given a weight of one each. On the other

---

[1] There may be justification for assigning a weight of two to accidents when the number is restricted to those involving personal injuries.

two watches the weight assigned to inspections should have the same ratio to the weight of the incident factor (5) as the ratio of time devoted to inspections has to the time spent in called-for services and routine preventive patrol.

For example, on a shift on which 120 man-hours are spent at inspectional tasks and 150 man-hours are devoted to called-for services and preventive patrol, the inspection factor should be given a weight of 4 ($120/150 \times 5 = 4$). Since the computation will not usually produce a whole number, the number should be rounded at one decimal point.

On the day watch with the area and inspection factors unweighted and the incident factor with a weight of 5, the 7 elements (5 incident elements plus area and inspections) each have a value of $1/7$. Weighting the inspection factor by 4 (as in the above example) would result in giving each of the other elements a value of $1/10$. The area factor should be adjusted or weighted so that it will have a constant value of about $1/7$. This may be done by multiplying the area percentage for each reporting area by a weight derived by dividing the sum of the weights of all factors (with area given a weight of one) by 7 and rounding the result at the first decimal point. The area weight in this example would be 1.4 ($10/7 = 1.4$). While this adjustment does not produce a value for area that is precisely $1/7$, it is exact enough for this purpose.

In each reporting area, the sum of the three weighted factors (incidents, inspections, and area or street mileage) each expressed as a percentage of the total for all reporting areas during the shift under consideration, gives a percentage figure which represents the proportion of the total load that is located in that reporting area on that shift. The total of these consolidated percentage figures for all reporting areas will be 100 multiplied by the sum of the weights applied to these three primary factors. To divide the consolidated percentage figure of each reporting area by the sum of the weights seems unnecessary.

In deriving weights, it is considered wise to sacrifice some exactness to gain simplification of computation. For example, when the weights are whole numbers, the computations may be made mentally and recorded on the area cards without the use of a computing machine or of pencil-and-paper multiplication. Under some circumstances, therefore, when the weight is nearly equal to a whole number, there may be justification for using the whole number in order to avoid a two-digit multiplication.

Decision 17. Does the number of patrolmen require the assignment of more than one patrol sergeant? If so, how will the area of the community be divided into sectors, each the responsibility of one patrol sergeant?

When there are between 12 and 17 motorized beats there is likely to be justification for the assignment of two patrol sergeants. A greater number of patrolmen usually requires a further increase in the number of patrol sergeants. While foot patrolmen are less difficult to supervise than men in automobiles, the presence of foot patrolmen to be supervised by the same patrol sergeant must also be considered in reaching a decision as to the need for more than one sergeant. When the number of foot patrolmen on one shift equals eight or more on adjoining beats (beats not separated by distance) there may be justification for the assignment of a patrol sergeant for their exclusive supervision. When this is done the patrol sergeant should be supplied with an automobile.

The beats supervised by one sergeant constitute a sector. The sectors should contain approximately equal work loads and consequently should have approximately equal numbers of beats. Sectors should be divided by important thoroughfares. This is especially desirable when an evidence technician is assigned to each sector since it simplifies his assignment by the dispatcher.

Other Administrative Problems

Decisions must also be made on other administrative problems. Provision must be made for relief, questions relating to the periodic rotation of shifts and frequent beat changes must be answered, and determination must be made as to the responsibility of the patrol division for the staff supervision of members of other divisions on duty during the absence of their own supervising officers.

Decision 18. How will relief be provided for weekly, annual, and sick leave, for leaves of absence for training and other reasons, and to meet man-power shortages growing out of separations from service? Relief must also be provided for superior officers and the evidence technicians.

When one day of rest is provided each week, a relief officer is needed for each six men to be relieved. When two days of rest are provided each week, two relief officers are needed for each five men to be relieved. The provision of relief on each shift is simplified, therefore, when the officers to be relieved are in multiples of six for one relief day a week and of five for two relief days.

As far as possible relief should be provided within each unit or group of men. For example, it is best that a suitable number of men be earmarked on each shift to provide weekly relief, with some serving as relief for foot patrolmen and others for the motorized officers. On a shift having six foot beats and 18 motorized beats, one officer may be assigned to relieve the foot patrolmen and three to relieve the motorized patrolmen if they each have one day off in seven. The number of beats on a shift are usually such, however, that the provision of relief is not so simply arranged.

When the combined number of foot and motorized beats is not a multiple of six (or five), one relief man will have one or more days when his services are not required. A decision must then be made as to whether he will be used to meet a deficiency on another shift on his free days. The alternatives are to use him for relief for a superior officer or a specialist on his regular shift, or to assign him to some task that deserves occasional attention but does not justify full-time assignment, such as the inspection of certain recreation establishments.

While the periodic progressive movement of a relief officer from shift to shift to meet relief requirements is undesirable in some respects (the irregularity of his work-hours makes difficult an orderly schedule of living), it may be justified in the provision of relief for the evidence technicians because of the importance of the work done by these officers and the greater-than-ordinary skill required. A similar provision for sergeants to relieve other sergeants during their weekly and annual leaves and when they are acting as lieutenants during the absence of these officers is not recommended, however, although it does assure more effective supervision than is provided by patrolmen who act as sergeants. The advantages gained by having patrolmen act as sergeants outweigh the advantage of more effective supervision. This procedure provides training for patrolmen who aspire to be sergeants; they learn the importance of working more closely and harmoniously with their sergeants; they discover the nature of supervisory problems and the need for experience and training in preparation for such positions. This practice also gives police executives an opportunity to discover potential sergeant material and thus reduces the likelihood of unwise selections for promotion.

Study should be made of monthly variations in the work load in terms of incidents that call for patrol service in order to discover whether there are seasonal variations that will enable annual leaves to be taken during periods of slack activity. Man-power shortages resulting from annual, sick, and other leaves of absence, as well as separations from the service, are most satisfactorily met by drawing on the special squad that will be mentioned later. When such a squad has not been created, the needs must be met by the regular patrol force which will cause a diminution of service during the absence of an officer on leave.

Man-power shortages may be met by permitting officers to work shifts on their off-duty time, preferably on their weekly days of rest, and to be paid for this service at the regular daily pay rate. Nearly always there are policemen who are glad to supplement their income in this way. Restrictions should be placed on the total number of shifts they may work each week so that fatigue will not interfere with the effectiveness of their work.

There are two less desirable methods of thus meeting the need. Since foot patrol is the least effective, patrolmen may be withdrawn from foot beats to fill the need. The inspectional duties on the vacant foot beat would then either be performed by the motorized officer (or officers) on whose beat they were located or these duties would be divided between two or more foot patrolmen on adjacent beats. Alternatively, the motorized beat may be divided between two or more officers on adjacent motorized beats. Every ingenuity should be used, however, to keep the beats completely covered at all times; only as a last resort should the beats be divided in the manner described.

Decision 19. Should platoon assignments rotate periodically or should recruits start on the night watch, progress to the evening watch, and finally after considerable service, to the day watch?

This is a policy decision that should be made with a view to the selection of the procedure that will provide the best quality of service. The practice of permanent assignments to platoons with provision for advancement to other platoons as vacancies occur has the following advantages:[1]

1. Some of the advantages of specialization are gained; police

---

[1] By permission from *Police Administration,* by O. W. Wilson, pp. 111-112. Copyright, 1950. McGraw-Hill Book Company, Inc.

hazards, persons abroad, physical conditions, and consequently police duties, vary considerably on the three shifts.

2. Continuity of service and attention to current problems is enhanced by permanent platoon assignments.

3. The physical and domestic welfare of the officer requires that he work regular hours. Regularity of hours contributes to good family relationships and to superior physical and mental efficiency.

4. The rookie policeman assigned to the graveyard shift is concealed from the more critical citizen until he has had sufficient experience to be qualified for service during hours when he will be more prominently in the public eye. Reserving the day watch for older patrolmen is a desirable reward for their years of service, and duty on this shift does not usually require the prime physical condition that is needed on the other two.

5. Assignment to less desirable platoons may be used as a disciplinary measure and to employ patrolmen who have not measured up to desired standards and yet who do not deserve separation from the service.

6. It enables some policemen to work shifts that are considered less desirable by others. Whenever possible, officers should be permitted to work the hours they prefer. They should, therefore, be given a seniority choice in the selection of a permanent shift.

Decision 20. Should there be stability in beat assignments or should they be changed frequently?

The highest quality of patrol service is obtained when officers are permanently assigned to their beats. The ability of the officer to serve is in direct proportion to his knowledge of the hazards and people on his beat and of its geography. Permanent beat assignments enable advantage to be taken of differences in ability and the preferences of patrolmen by assigning them to beats having duties for which they are best suited.

Decision 21. What staff supervisory responsibilities should the superior officers of the patrol division have over the members of the other divisions who are on duty in the absence of their own supervising officers?

Department policy should require every officer at the level of performance to be under the continuous supervision of some superior officer. The patrol supervisors should be given responsibility for the staff supervision of on-duty members of the special divisions in the absence of their own supervising officers. The patrol division is the logical division to be given this responsibility because it is the only division that invariably has supervisory officers on duty at all hours. The responsibility must be exactly defined by department regulations in order that all may know the precise nature of the relationships.

Decision 22. What procedures may be followed in large cities to avoid having all patrolmen off their beats at the change of shifts?

The distances that patrolmen must travel in going to and from their beats in a large city, especially one that does not have district stations, result in all of the beats being uncovered for a substantial period during the change of shifts. The period is lengthened when the vehicles are serviced at the change of shift.

When a city is large enough to be confronted by this problem, each platoon is likely to have two or more patrol sergeants, each heading a squad of patrolmen assigned to beats located within a sector, and at least two lieutenants. The problem can be solved by staggering the reporting time of the force on each platoon so that shift changes will be made at 15 minute intervals over a period of time. Each squad would leave their beats eight hours after going on. One lieutenant would report for duty with the first squad; the other lieutenant would report for duty with the last squad of the platoon.

When servicing the vehicles at the time of shift changes creates a bottle neck in patrol service, provision may be made for their service on a contract basis by the regular commercial service stations on the beats.

CHAPTER 7

Detective Operations

T HE previously discussed decisions relating to the preliminary investigation of crimes, the search for physical evidence, and the classes of crimes to be assigned to each of the divisions for continued investigation will establish the nature of the relationship of the detective division to the other line divisions. In planning the operation of the detective division, decisions must be made in reference to the selection of detectives, the manner in which they will work, the hours best suited for detective operations, the assignment of cases among the members, and the internal organization of the division into bureaus. Provision must be made for weekly relief. Relative responsibilities must be allocated between the detective and records divisions for the preparation, use, and maintenance of operating and administrative records. Related to this question is the need for a detective-division secretary and other clerical assistance.

Decision 1. What factors should be considered in the selection and retention of policemen for detective service?

The word "detective" should be a title of assignment and not of rank. The chief of police should be privileged to select men for this assignment on the basis of their competence and to remove them if they fail to maintain a satisfactory level of performance.

The good investigator usually has initiative, perseverance, and a tremendous physical and nervous vitality; he is alert, observant, and inquisitive. He has an unusually retentive memory and the ability to detect fallacious reasoning. He has a practical knowledge of human beings that enables him to get along well with people. He is persuasive and convincing and is able to win the confidence and friendship of those with whom he deals. He has a wide range of acquaintances and sources of information.

Tests may be devised in the future to measure these qualities. Written examinations used today that are primarily information tests are not especially useful in the selection of the best qualified investigators. A wiser procedure is to select a patrolman tentatively

111

on the basis of his demonstrated performance in the preliminary investigation of crimes on his beat. Trial on the job in the detective division will quickly confirm or deny the wisdom of the initial choice.

In no branch of police service may the accomplishment of the unit and of its individual members be so accurately evaluated as in the detective division. Rates of clearances by arrest, of property recovered, and of convictions, serve as measures of the level of performance. Current accomplishments thus measured, when compared to previous accomplishments in the same class of crime, may reveal significant variations between the accomplishment of the incumbent and his predecessor, or between the present and past performance of the same detective. Similar comparisons may be made between local accomplishments and the accomplishments in comparable communities. Chance may cause an unfavorable comparison during a short period, but when the failure in performance extends over six months or a year, a conclusion of diminished effectiveness seems justified.

A detective division built of members retained on this selective basis is most likely to contain the best investigators on the force.

Decision 2. What plans should be developed by the detective division?

Detective responsibility in crime investigation gives them a right to propose procedural changes in the preliminary investigation of crimes and the search for physical evidence as well as the content and routing of investigation reports. They should also plan the organization of their division, schedules of assignment and relief, and operating procedures for their own members.

Detectives also have a responsibility to plan operations intended to discover evidence, witnesses, and suspects by canvass of neighborhoods, or establishments of one kind, such as all drug stores, although the extensiveness of such operations frequently justifies the use of beat patrolmen for their accomplishment. Plans to effect an arrest and prosecution should be the responsibility of the detective division even though the operation is carried out partly or entirely by the patrol division. In contrast to this, plans intended primarily to prevent criminal acts and to apprehend criminals in operation should be prepared by the patrol division. Operations in both categories should be coordinated between the two divisions;

each division should ordinarily seek the assistance and advice of other divisions that may have an interest in its plans.

Decision 3. Should detectives work singly or in pairs?

All of the reasons that justify one-man patrol-car operation in preference to the use of two men apply with equal force to the detective service. Most investigations may be made more effectively by one man, and the economy of one-man assignment is apparent.[1]

Decision 4. Should each detective be given as a regular assignment the investigation of all crimes in one or more designated classes?

Specialization in detective assignment should be the invariable rule. This procedure assures the assignment of officers in accordance with their special interests and abilities; it enables the investigator to become expert in the investigation of certain classes of crimes and informed regarding the individual criminals and criminal types who specialize in these crimes, their methods of operation, associates, hangouts, and methods for disposing of their loot. Specialization also fixes responsibility and enables a more accurate measure of accomplishment.

Decision 5. How should classes of crimes be grouped for assignment among the members when the number in some classes does not constitute a full work load?

Classes of crimes grouped for assignment to one man or to one unit within the detective division should be similar or related in some manner. For example, crimes such as bad checks, counterfeiting, frauds, shoplifting, and short changing are related because they are frequently committed against retail merchants. A detective assigned to these crimes enjoys some of the advantages of specialization because his field of attention in terms of area and prospective victims and offenders is narrowed. Some classes of crimes may be grouped for assignment purposes because they are related in the sense that one may grow out of another. For example, robberies, aggravated assaults, rapes, and abortions sometimes result in homicide.

---

[1] Arguments favoring one-man patrols are found in *Police Administration,* pp. 101-102 and supra p. 84. Department regulations should require a detective engaged in a dangerous investigation or arrest to obtain needed assistance from other detectives when available and otherwise from the patrol division. See Appendix G, p. 327, item 28.

The final grouping of classes of crimes for assignment purposes must also consider their relative frequency, seriousness, and required investigative time. The most desirable grouping will result from trial and error adjustments.

Decision 6. When the number of crimes in a class is so great that more than one detective must be assigned to their investigation, what should be the basis of assignment to two or more detectives?

Crimes in the same class may be assigned to two or more detectives on the basis of (1) a logical further subdivision of the crimes, as for example, distinguishing between residence and non-residence burglaries; (2) the geographical location of the incidents; and (3) the order of receipt of the reports, each detective receiving an assignment in turn.

The assignment should be based on a further subdivision of the class of crimes, as long as the subdivisions may be made logically and in a manner that promotes the advantages of specialization. The advantages of specialization are promoted when crimes within the subdivision are restricted in area, character or occupation of victims, and to criminal specialists. The last factor may be appraised by ascertaining the degree of persistency of criminals in restricting their operation to crimes within each of the subdivisions.

When logical subdivisions have been made and the number of crimes in them remain more than can be investigated satisfactorily by one detective, the assignment within the subdivision (and within classes that are not susceptible to logical subdivision, such as car theft) must be made on the basis of geographical location. This procedure provides economy in time and transportation. Also, criminals frequently restrict their current operations to a section of the community.

There seems to be no logical justification for assignments based only on the order of receipt of reports of crimes.

Decision 7. What factors should be considered in the selection of assignments for the individual detectives?

The personal characteristics of one criminal are likely to differ, sometimes in important respects, from those of other criminals. The innate characteristics of the criminal influence him in the selection of his specialty. For example, the confidence man has personal characteristics that differ in many respects from those of a bandit or burglar. Also, the characteristics of one confidence man resemble those of another confidence man more precisely than they do those of a criminal in an unrelated field.

The personal characteristics of one detective are likely to differ from those of other detectives in the same manner. Just as the characteristics of one criminal attract him to his criminal specialty and qualify him for the operations of his choice, so do the characteristics of some detectives better qualify them for specific assignments than other detectives. This being true, the selection of assignments for detectives should be based on the characteristics of the man. One will be found better suited for the investigation of frauds, bad checks, confidence games, and so on, than for the investigation of robberies.

Some detectives prefer the investigation of one type of crime to all others. As far as possible, detectives should be given their choice of assignment; they are then most likely to work effectively at it. The seriousness of some crimes and the extent to which they arouse public interest and inflame the emotions, however, justify their assignment to men of experience. Some assignments involve greater personal hazard and require greater physical activity than others. These factors prove attractive to some detectives. On the other hand, after a man has worked in such assignments a number of years, his diminished alertness and vigor may justify his transfer to an easier and less-hazardous task. In some assignments the detective will associate with prominent persons in the business and social life of the community; other assignments will bring him in contact with a rougher element. He should be given the assignment into which he will fit most naturally, where he will be most at ease, and where he will be most acceptable to the persons with whom he is dealing.

Decision 8. What constitutes a fair work load for each detective?

Research is needed to ascertain the optimum work load for detectives more accurately than is possible today. The total work load is influenced in part by the extent to which the patrol division participates in the preliminary and continuing investigations. The case loads of individual detectives must vary according to the seriousness of the crime, homicides obviously deserving and receiving greater attention from the police than the average petty theft. The work load is also influenced by variations in the energy and ability of individual detectives.

Since it is most desirable not to deplete the patrol force by the unnecessary withdrawal of man power for assignment to any of the special branches of service, effort should be made to hold the number of detectives to a minimum. This means giving them heavier rather than lighter work loads. The number of detectives is limited, in the same manner as the total force, by budget appropriations. The number should be restricted to from 8 to 11 per cent of the total force. When it exceeds 11 per cent, there is reason to suspect that the division is overmanned.

When the number of detectives is known, the head of the division should undertake the assignment of cases among them in a manner to provide approximately equal work loads. This may require some adjustment by trial and error. Adjustments must also be made to meet seasonal and other intermittent variations in frequency of certain classes of crimes.

Decision 9. Should the detective division be organized into a number of bureaus or squads?

Just as advantages are derived in small departments when similar or related classes of crimes are grouped for assignment to individual detectives, so advantages result in large departments when detectives assigned to similar or related classes of crimes are grouped in bureaus. The assignment of cases in thus facilitated, and the investigative efforts in related cases are more closely and readily coordinated. Close coordination is desirable because criminals sometimes commit related crimes outside the field of their specialty.

Reassignment of cases to meet frequency variations within the classes and their subdivisions is also simplified when they are made within a bureau. As subdivisions of classes are increased in number, the likelihood of variations necessitating reassignment of cases is increased somewhat.

The creation of bureaus within the detective division also promotes the effectiveness of supervision. Increased effectiveness of supervision alone will justify the creation of bureaus in a large detective force.

When two or more men are assigned to the same class or subdivision of a class of crimes, there are advantages in having them members of a section, with one designated to direct the work. The creation of a bureau or section does not necessarily require the appointment of a detective of superior rank as its head. Such action is desirable when the number within the unit, which is one measure of the responsibilities imposed on its head, jutifies a higher rank.

Decision 10. How may detectives be supervised most effectively?

The nature of detective work necessitates considerable freedom of movement. This fact makes the effective supervision of detectives both difficult and important. Procedures should be developed, therefore, that will assist in detective supervision and in the appraisal of their work.

Attempts to control the activities of detectives by requiring them to maintain diaries or to submit daily activity reports have usually not proved satisfactory. The results do not ordinarily justify the time spent in preparing the account, and frequently the reports do not record true facts, especially when these reflect to the discredit of the detective.

The most effective supervision is provided by an adequate number of supervising officers to check on the hour-by-hour activity of their subordinates. Supervisors who know from one hour to the next the location and activity of their subordinates are in a position to guide them in their work and also to assure strict attention to business.

Decision 11. Should detectives ordinarily be assigned to the evening and night shifts?

The need for detectives on the evening and night shifts is strongly influenced by the extent and quality of preliminary investigations by the patrol division. When the patrol division provides an ordinarily satisfactory preliminary investigation of all crimes assigned to the detective division for ultimate clearance, there will be no need for detectives to be assigned to either night shift except when the frequency of crimes requiring their immediate attention seems to justify it. Analysis of the frequency and justification for calling detectives back to service will reveal the desirability of keeping one or more on duty during some night hours to provide immediate service of a quality or type beyond the capacity of the patrol division. However, even in a large department, such assignments should not be made until the need is clearly established. The man power for such assignments must eventually come from the patrol division, thus further depleting its strength.

In reaching decisions on the desirability and need for nighttime detective service, it is well to bear in mind that an investigation made by a nighttime detective is usually a preliminary investigation to be concluded by a daytime detective assigned to that criminal specialty. Preliminary investigations by a qualified patrol force will ordinarily be not only just as good as a preliminary investigation by detectives, but it will actually be superior in quality because of the large investigative resources that are available in the patrol division in terms of mobile, widespread man power. These resources, directed by a competent patrol sergeant or platoon lieutenant, permit a more rapid, complete, and thorough investigation than would be possible by one or two detectives.

The problem of supervising night detectives is a further argument against their use. Detectives on night duty in the absence of supervisory officers from their own division will come under the supervision of the patrol-division command as previously explained. When the number of detectives exceeds four there is justification for the assignment of a superior officer from the detective division to supervise their work.

Most detective investigations can be conducted to the best advantage during the daytime. The limitation of detectives to daytime duy does not mean, however, that they will not have occasion to make some investigations during the night hours. Their hours of work should be flexible so that they will be able to work at night when their investigations must be made during these hours, which will not be often.

Decision 12. When detectives are assigned to night shifts so as to be readily available for immediate crime investigations, how should they be kept occupied during the hours when they are not investigating crimes?

In reaching a decision on this matter, it must be remembered that the principal purpose of the night assignment is to provide immediate detective service in the investigation of reported crimes. Fill-in assignments, therefore, should not interfere unduly with the primary purpose.

The advisability of using detectives during their spare time to perform clerical duties is ordinarily ruled out because of lack of skill. Street duty of a suitable character for this purpose must be either inspectional or routine patrol. Night detectives can be used for inspectional duties to advantage if they maintain frequent contact with the dispatcher. Calling the dispatcher at 30-minute intervals while out of range of the police radio should be adequate, especially if the patrol division has substantial responsibilities in the preliminary investigation of crimes. Inspectional duties may be interspersed with patrol, which has the advantage of maintaining constant radio communication with headquarters.

Decision 13. How should weekly detective relief be distributed among the days of the week, and how should it be provided?

The most suitable relief day for detectives is Sunday because this day is least suited to investigations. On Sunday people are away from their occupations and often absent from home, and other public agencies related to the administration of law enforcement, or having information helpful in investigations, are closed. In many jurisdictions, this is also true of Saturday. The need for detective service is ordinarily greatest on Monday because it is the first day following a week-end of increased criminal activity and also because of the work load that has accumulated over Sunday.

When detectives have one day off in seven, a skeleton staff should be on duty on Sunday and all who can be spared should be off duty on that day. When detectives have two days of relief in seven, Saturday and Sunday are best suited for relief. In a department that does not utilize its patrol force to its full potential in crime investigation, Saturday will have a somewhat greater need for detective service than Sunday, and it may be desirable to have the Saturday skeleton force reinforced to handle the greater load.

Detectives who are off duty on Sunday or on Saturday and Sunday ordinarily will not need to be relieved by someone to devote full time to the performance of their tasks. Their investigations may be postponed until the following Monday, except for urgent cases that require immediate attention. These may be investigated by the skeleton crew, the case assignments being without regard to their class.

During the week days there is greater need for the immediate investigation of crimes that have been investigated preliminarily by the patrol division. When the number of detectives off duty during the week days is not great, two detectives assigned to similar or related classes of crimes may interchangeably act as each other's relief, each conducting necessary investigations for the one who is off duty.

When detectives are off duty on two consecutive week-days, the need for relief detectives to substitute for those off duty becomes apparent.

Decision 14. What operating and administrative records should be maintained by the detective division?

It is assumed that records and their control are centralized in the records division. Under these circumstances, copies of all complaint sheets and investigation reports should be sent to the detective division for the use of the assigned detective.

Some records relating to prosecutions are also desirable. A summary of each state and federal case on which prosecution is imminent serves to review the police investigation and thus reveal any weak points that deserve additional attention. It also makes available to the prosecutor in a concise form the salient facts relating to the crime, the defendant, the witnesses and their testimony, and physical evidence. A prosecution ledger for state and federal cases assures follow-up on court dispositions and records the success of individual detectives in obtaining convictions when a separate account is kept of each major class of crime.[1]

A monthly summary of the cases worked on by the individual detective is another useful device for appraising his accomplishments and for making comparisons of case loads. The assignment summary for each detective should have recorded on it from day to day each case worked on during the current month including cases from previous months on which clearance by arrest or the recovery of stolen property occurs. Columns permit an indication of the nature of the clearance and of the disposition of the offender.[2]

An attendance record must also be maintained. This is usually in the form of a call-in sheet. Provision should also be made for recording the schedule of individual detectives so that their whereabouts may be readily ascertained at any time.

Some detectives also need certain pawnshop records. Routine processing and permanent filing properly belong to the records division, although the detective secretary may assist in the operation in a not-too-large department.

---

[1] Prosecution reports and the prosecution ledger are described in *Police Records,* pp. 98 and 101.

[2] A monthly detective-division summary is illustrated and its use described in *Police Records,* pp. 143-144.

Decision 15. What are the detective-division requirements for clerical, stenographic, and reception assistance, and how should it be provided?

The need in the detective division for clerical, stenographic, and receptionist assistance is dependent on the size of the force and the office arrangement. In departments of suitable size, the office arrangement may permit one secretary to serve as receptionist and sometimes to perform other tasks for more than one division or office. The need is also influenced by the extent to which dictating and sound-recording equipment is used, and the extent to which the detectives typewrite their own reports.

The desirability of having a stenographer immediately available for recording interrogations, serving as a receptionist, routing complaint sheets and investigation reports, taking telephone calls, making appointments for the detectives and receiving messages in their absence, letter writing, and maintaining detective assignment summaries, prosecution ledgers, and an attendance record with a schedule to facilitate ready contact with detectives who are on duty away from headquarters, justifies the appointment of a division secretary before the volume of these duties occupies her full time. Fill-in clerical tasks, such as indexing pawnshop tickets and wanted notices, may then be assigned to use her spare time to advantage.

CHAPTER 8

Vice Control

T HE relationship of the vice division to the patrol and other divisions and the scope of vice-division investigations and licensing and inspectional responsibilities are established on the basis of previously discussed decisions. Decisions that remain to be made include those relating to the strength of the division, the hours of work, the need for specialization within the division, essential administrative and operating records, the need for secretarial services, and the control of evidence and contraband. Consideration must also be given to the advisability of providing, as a part of the vice division or independent of it, a specialized patrol designed primarily to prevent vice operations in a designated area.

Decision 1. Should a special patrol, justified in a section of the community to 'prevent vice activities, be a part of the vice division or independent of it?

Such a specialized patrol is rarely justified. The creation of a special patrol for this purpose should be avoided until the need for it has been clearly demonstrated. Under ordinary circumstances the most effective results are obtained by holding individual patrolmen responsible for vice conditions on their beats with a vice division to conduct investigations that require skills and facilities not possessed by the patrol division. Under all circumstances the vice division should have ultimate responsibility for ferreting out and eliminating vice.

When there is justification for a special patrol having as its principal purpose and primary duty the suppression of vice activities in a section of the community, it should be a part of the vice division and under the direct control of the head of that unit, except when the small number makes ill-advised the assignment of a supervisory officer; in this case the patrol should be under the direct control of patrol-division supervisors even though their entire time is devoted to the suppression of vice. The desirability of ordinarily placing a special patrol charged with the suppression of vice under the direct control of the vice division arises from the advisability of not dividing this responsibility. Since the vice division is held responsible for the elimination of vice operations, they should be given direct control of officers engaged exclusively at this task, whether they are in uniform or plain clothes.

Decision 2. How many men should be assigned to the vice division, and is there need for women police?

The desirable strength of the vice division is influenced by public and official sentiment and by the extent of patrol-division participation in the suppression of vice activities, the extent to which vice operations have been ignored in the past by the police, and the extent to which vice operations are entrenched in the community. Conditions vary so greatly among communities as to make impractical any attempt to establish, as the most desirable level of enforcement, either a proportion of the force or police man power on a per capita basis. Determination of the man power to be assigned to vice control requires a high quality of administrative judgment. A sound policy is to provide the maximum level of enforcement that the sentiment of the community and the resources of the department will allow. This is so because of the close relationship between commercialized vice and organized crime. Freedom from terrorism and political corruption is assured every community when vice is rigidly repressed. The suppression of vice also reduces the amount of unorganized crime.

There does not seem to be justification for the regular assignment of policewomen to the vice division. Their services should be available, however, so that they may be called on in cases involving young girls and inexperienced women.

Decision 3. Should members of the vice division be given specialized assignments, and should they be assigned to regular shifts?

Except in large cities having more than half a dozen officers assigned to the vice division, the members will work best as a team on the same shift under the direct leadership of the head, without specialization. In larger cities, specialization may be advantageous. Even then the members work most effectively under the direction of the head, on a flexible schedule suited to the current need. Avoiding regular hours serves also to confuse vice operators.

Decision 4. Does the vice division need secretarial assistance?

In terms of number of members, the vice division has greater need for clerical assistance than the detective division because of the necessity of maintaining records independent of the central records system. The need for clerical assistance is further justified by the desirability of having someone to answer the telephone and take messages. Full-time clerical assistance is not ordinarily justified in vice divisions of fewer than a half dozen members, however, nor in larger ones except when the clerical tasks occupy nearly the full time of one person.

Decision 5. What operating and administrative records should be maintained by the vice division?

The vice division should temporarily maintain, independently of the central records system, a file of open cases on which they are working. As these cases are closed by arrest or otherwise, they should be sent to the records office for consolidation into the central records system. At this time care must be taken to avoid including information that may serve to identify undercover operators.

The vice division should also maintain suitable indexes: a name index of all suspects, persons arrested, complainants, informants, undercover operators, and so on; an index of automobile license numbers obtained from cars observed under questionable circumstances; and a location index. They should also maintain a file of reports from undercover operators that do not relate to specific numbered complaints or reports.

The vice divisions in some cities are responsible for the inspection of licensed establishments in which vice operations are sometimes found. The inspections are made to discover violations that may justify action toward the revocation of the license. Some vice divisions maintain a folder or envelope on each licensed establishment, on which are recorded in suitable columns the dates of inspections and by whom made, with spaces in which to indicate by check mark that conditions were found to be satisfactory or unsatisfactory. The folders are filed according to the street and street number of the enterprise.

Inspectional reports are submitted by vice-division members as well as by patrolmen when these officers are given such tasks. Adverse reports, which are prepared separately, are filed in the folder. This procedure provides evidence of inspections when charges are made that the police have ignored unsatisfactory conditions at a designated place. It also lessens the likelihood of inadvertent neglect of duty. A record of warnings for previous violations also strengthens the case for a license revocation.

The disbursement of undercover funds must be made and recorded in such a manner as to lessen the likelihood of charges of misappropriation of funds and at the same time safeguard the identity of undercover operators except under circumstances of dire necessity. A prosecution ledger should also be maintained, to assure suitable and positive follow-up on court dispositions and an accurate summary of the results. If the vice division is responsible for the custody of evidence and contraband, inventories and records of the disposition of this property must also be kept.

Decision 6. Should the vice division have custody of evidence and contraband?

Placing responsibility for the custody of vice evidence on the property clerk ordinarily relieves the vice division of much detail work and inconvenience. The safe custody of vice evidence, however, is of great importance; lost, stolen, or altered evidence may not only result in a dismissal of an important case or an acquittal, but it may also irretrievably blacken the reputation of the department. Failure of the department property-control facilities and procedures to assure absolute protection of vice evidence justifies the assignment of the custodial task to the vice division. Unreasonable delay or other inconvenience experienced by the vice division in obtaining evidence for presentation in court from the property clerk further justifies this assignment.

Decision 7. How may the vice division discover persons, enterprises, and locations that deserve their special attention?

Sources of information that should be utilized to discover evidence of vice violations include complaint and arrest records, classified newspaper advertisements, beat patrolmen, informants, and undercover operators. Arrests for drunkenness, narcotic addiction, and disorderly conduct, complaints by citizens who have been annoyed by solicitations or disturbances, reports by health officers of cases of venereal infection and by vice patrons who have been swindled or diseased, indicate the likelihood of violations and frequently reveal information as to the identity of offenders and the locality of their operations. Some types of thefts and other crimes sometimes indicate the operation of narcotic addicts. Classified advertisements of massage parlors and other personal services may reveal the operation of prostitutes.

Observations by beat officers that reveal the nature of suspected establishments and the character of their patrons sometimes result in the discovery of illicit operations. Beat patrolmen are frequently able to obtain useful information by skillfully interrogating patrons observed leaving suspected establishments. Patrolmen and vice-division members alike should develop information sources that will keep them informed of vice activities. The occupations of some persons afford them an opportunity to learn of vice operations. For example, door men, cab starters, transportation dispatchers, bell boys and captains, barkeepers, and employees of pool halls and other recreational establishments, are unusually good information sources. Police officers should cultivate their friendship in order to profit from their knowledge. The informants, of course, must be carefully protected. Undercover operators who spend time in recreation establishments and bars are also able to pick up useful information and to develop their own unwitting informants.

The information received from any of these sources may justify an immediate raid. More frequently, however, the information will be used to guide an undercover operator in obtaining additional evidence.

Decision 8. Should the police use Nalline tests to detect the use of opiates?

Under the leadership of Chief Wyman W. Vernon, the Oakland, California, Police Department examines selected persons to establish whether they have recently used morphine derivatives. The program was developed through a conference with judges, the district attorney, and probation and parole authorities. Those subject to the test are probationers and parolees with a history of narcotic addiction and persons arrested on narcotic charges.

The test is administered by a physician who first makes a brief physical examination of the subject to discover any abnormalities and to measure the diameter of the pupil of the eye, using for this purpose a "pupillometer," which is a small card containing along one edge a series of black dots varying in diameter from 1 to 5 mm.

A subcutaneous injection is made of 3 mg. of Nalline (N-Allylnor-morphine), which is an opiate antagonist that induces abstinence symptoms in the person who has recently used such drugs. Larger doses would cause the addicted subject much pain and discomfort, but the small dosage used is adequate to cause a measurable pupillary reaction without acute discomfort.

The Nalline injection causes the pupils of the person who has not been using opiates to contract by from 0.5 mm. to as much as 2 mm. The pupils remain unchanged in size when the subject has been using opiates occasionally but is not addicted. In contrast, the pupils of the addicted subject will increase in diameter from 0.5 mm. to 2 mm., depending on the degree of addiction.

The local judges agreed to sentence all convicted narcotic users to from three to five years on probation conditioned on their submitting to a Nalline test once each month on a one-day notice from the probation officer. A similar program has been developed for periodically testing parolees with a history of narcotic use. There is already considerable evidence that the knowledge that he will be returned to custody if he fails the test has a strong deterrent effect on the former addict.

Each subject is required to sign an authorization-and-waiver form before he is examined. Of 494 persons arrested for violations of narcotic laws, only 31 have refused to submit to the test. Of 207 persons brought to trail, only four not-guilty verdicts have been returned; in these cases there were no needle marks or other corroborating evidence.

The Nalline tests have increased the conviction rates in narcotic-use cases to heights that were formerly considered impossible of attainment. Types of crimes most popular with narcotic users have declined sharply, and the experienced officers in the narcotic detail of the Oakland department are impressed with the absence of narcotic addicts on the streets of their city.[1]

---

[1] The above information was taken from an article by R. E. McDonell, Director of Research and Planning, Oakland Police Department, "The Nalline Test and its Effect on the Oakland Crime Problem," published in *Oakland's Health*, vol. 12, no. 1, January, 1957.

CHAPTER 9

Delinquency Control

THE independence of the juvenile division and its relationship to the detective and vice divisions are determined by previously mentioned decisions. There remain to be established the nature and scope of its function; its relationships to the patrol and traffic divisions; the organization, hours of work, and relief of its members; its administrative and operating records; and its clerical staff. Attention must also be given to the development of operating plans and procedures.

Juvenile-division Function

The nature and scope of tasks to be assigned to the juvenile division will be influenced in part by the prevailing concept of police responsibility. The nature of some tasks clearly indicates the desirability of their assignment to the juvenile division, provided they are to be assumed as police responsibilities. The primary question is whether the police should undertake their performance.

The police should deliberate over the advisability of accepting responsibility for the performance of the following tasks. Each is to some extent related to the prevention of delinquency.

1. The investigation of cases that relate to the delinquency of juveniles or the prevention of criminality, or that have social-welfare significance.

2. The inspection of locations and enterprises that may constitute juvenile-delinquency hazards or afford an opportunity for delinquent acts.

3. Tasks related to the licensing of enterprises whose activities may stimulate delinquency.

4. The elimination of unwholesome influences that may stimulate juvenile delinquency. This is accomplished in part through investigation, inspection, and licensing, but the task, in addition, includes an aggressive search for unwholesome influences and effort toward their elimination that may extend beyond ordinary police procedures. For example, strong community pressure is sometimes

128

needed to obtain legislation to eradicate or correct an unwholesome condition when the proposal is resisted by vested interests.

5. Provision of wholesome influences. As in the elimination of unwholesome influences, the provision of wholesome influences is being considered, not from the point of view of one child, but of many children. It relates to recreation and other character-building activities that may be made available to the entire community or to a section of it, rather than to the needs of the individual child.

6. Coordination of community effort in the sense of directing the attention of agencies and groups toward conditions and individuals in whose correction or adjustment they have some responsibility.

7. Treatment of the maladjusted. The police may participate to some degree in the correctional treatment of the child who has displayed some personality difficulty.

That the police should undertake the first three of the tasks listed above seems beyond argument. Otherwise they will fail to prevent crime and delinquency. The extent to which the juvenile division will participate in the performance of these three tasks is determined by the previously discussed decisions as to the responsibilities in these fields of the patrol division and of the other specialized units. Consideration must now be given to the advisability of the police undertaking the performance of the remaining four tasks. If these tasks are a police responsibility, they should obviously be performed by the juvenile division.

Decision 1. Assuming that unwholesome influences which stimulate juvenile delinquency should be suppressed by license control and orthodox inspections and eliminated in individual cases brought to attention through complaint or investigation, should the police aggressively strive for the discovery and elimination of unwholesome influences wherever they may be found?

Unwholesome influences most frequently result from lack of suitable regulation of enterprises or activities, or from a failure to enforce such regulations. Inadequately regulated places of recreation frequently provide unwholesome influences that represent a hazard to the youth of the community. Dance halls, taverns, bowling alleys, skating rinks, pool halls, and other places where young people may gather, afford an opportunity to the greedy and vicious to prey on youth. Gambling establishments, houses of prostitution, and places that sell alcoholic beverages to the youth are other examples. Employment of young people at places, hours, or occupations that jeopardizes their health or morals also constitutes an unwholesome influence. Young people on their own initiative sometimes engage in unwholesome practices. These may result from a lack of adequate and attractive leisure-time activities in the recreational and character-building fields, or from a failure on the part of the police to regulate the formation and conduct of gangs and other groups waywardly inclined.

The regulation of the conduct of youth and the elimination of unwholesome conditions that arise from the failure to enforce laws are clearly police responsibilities. Obtaining legislation that may be needed to eliminate unwholesome conditions of the kind described above also seems to be a police responsibility, even though public opinion must be aroused to demand its enactment.

There are other unwholesome influences that sometimes have their roots intertwined among the traditions of the people and deeply imbedded in the economic, social, and political life of the community. It seems likely that any condition that promotes depravity, dishonesty, poverty, or ill-health, may also contribute to some extent to criminality. Such conditions, therefore, are unwholesome and should be eliminated. Their roots, however, are frequently so deeply imbedded as to require the organized effort of the community to uproot them.

Decision 2. Should the police initiate action and take the lead in organizing community sentiment to correct deepseated, unwholesome conditions that jeopardize the physical, moral, and emotional well-being of the people?

Police responsibility here also seems apparent. If the police are to accomplish their purpose of preventing delinquency, they must eradicate all conditions that stimulate criminality and that promote crimes by affording opportunity for their commission.

Decision 3. Should the police assume leadership in organizing the community for the prevention of delinquency?

Since the police department is the one agency in the community charged with the prevention of crime, it should initiate, as a part of its program, the organization of the community for the prevention of delinquency. The coordination of agencies that play some part in the prevention of delinquency, the expansion of their facilities, the promotion of needed additional agencies and facilities, and the direction of their efforts to areas of the city and segments of the youth population in greatest need, are all tasks that deserve community effort. The eradication of unwholesome conditions is sometimes impossible without the organized effort of the entire city.

Decision 4. Should the police provide or promote the provision of wholesome influences in the form of recreation and character-building group activities?

In considering this question, the administrator should understand that there may be two advantages to police participation in the provision or promotion of group activities, i.e., improved public relations as well as the prevention of delinquency. While group activities of the kind under discussion undoubtedly make better citizens of normal, well-adjusted participants, the success of these endeavors in appreciably reducing delinquency, preventing the development of criminality, and correcting the maladjusted personality, has not yet been demonstrated with certainty. The public-relations value of police participation in such group activities is more readily apparent. A concomitant delinquency-prevention value is found in any activity that brings the police in close and friendly touch with youth. So, while there may be doubt as to the inherent delinquency-prevention value of group activities, it seems likely that at least its potential value is enhanced by police participation.

In considering police participation in community group activities, distinction must also be made between promoting and providing the activities. The provision of recreational and character-building activities is the responsibilty of other departments of government and groups in the community. For the police to compete with other agencies in a duplication of their work seems ill-advised. The police have an unquestioned responsibility, however, to discover evidences of need for group activities in sections of the community, or for segments of its population that are neglected, and to promote the expansion of the activities to meet these needs.

Participation by the police in the actual provision of group activities is justified only when a need can be met in no other way, and then only temporarily until an agency responsible for such activities is organized or expanded to provide the service.

Recreational and character-building activities are organized, not for the dèlinquents or pre-delinquents, but for the total youth population. The activities tend to concentrate themselves in areas where the demand and support for the services are greatest. These are usually areas of less rather than greater delinquency. Also, some agencies fear the contamination of wholesome youth by the delinquent and pre-delinquent; they not only do not actively seek to serve the delinquent or problem child, but they frequently bar him from the activity.

The police are not primarily responsible for making better citizens of normal youth. The police have some responsibility, however, for the prevention of criminality, and if the facilities of the community fail to meet the needs of the delinquent and pre-delinquent population, they are justified in providing the facilities themselves. Justification for police participation in such group activities is in direct proportion to the delinquency or threatened delinquency of the group.

The police, therefore, should promote the expansion of group activities by other agencies into the areas and for segments of the population in greatest need; they should restrict their participation in group activities to meeting needs that can be met in no other way; they should focus their attention on the delinquent and pre-delinquent rather than on the total population. The police may justify their participation beyond this point, not on the basis of delinquency prevention, but on the basis of public relations.

Decision 5. Should the police participate in the correctional treatment of the child (or adult) who has displayed some personality difficulty?

Correctional treatment may be considered to include a reprimand or caution; a friendly and informal association; a more formal supervision with some restrictions on activities and a periodic inquiry into conduct and progress; a program of adjustment that includes action by one or more other community agencies, such as the school, church, health and psychiatric clinics, and relief, recreation, and character-building agencies. Finally, the treatment may mean action by the juvenile court. A decision as to police participation in correctional treatment will be influenced by the nature of facilities available in the community and the competence of juvenile-court probation-office staff.

Juvenile-court action is a step toward penal treatment and a criminal career. The police delinquency-prevention objective is to forestall a criminal career. It seems likely that each passing year brings added maturity to the individual and with it a diminution of the likelihood of criminal behavior.[1] Each year that the police succeed in preventing behavior whose seriousness may justify court action brings the youth one year closer to a maturity that lessens the likelihood of serious misconduct.

There is no proof today that the experience of a prison sentence makes a better citizen of an adult. On the contrary, there seems some evidence that the experience is an unwholesome one that frequently confirms the criminality of the convict. This does not mean that penal institutions should be abandoned. They serve to protect society from the depredations of criminals who are unreformable or who have not yet matured out of their criminal ways; they may also serve as a deterrent to others who may be tempted to misbehave. It seems likely, however, that many now in penitentiaries would have been better citizens, and they and society would have been better served, had they not been sent to prison.

Likewise, there is no assurance that making a child a ward of the juvenile court enhances the likelihood of his successful maturation. On the contrary, the experience may handicap the youth in his development into a useful citizen. This does not mean that juvenile-court action should never be taken any more than that penal institutions should be abandoned. It does mean, however, that so long as there is reasonable hope for the adjustment of the child without such drastic action, juvenile-court action should not be taken.

Further justification for police participation in correctional treatment is found in the fact that the large number of children who become involved in small delinquencies is beyond the capacity of the juvenile-court probation office to handle. The choice in the case of more than half the children dealt with by the police must be between no treatment at all and some treatment and attention by the police. The desirability of police action to prevent a recurrence of misbehavior by the individual child seems apparent.[2]

There also seems justification for the police to provide or promote the provision of correctional treatment for some adult offend-

---

[1] Statistics in support of this view are found in *Municipal Police Administration*, International City Managers Association, Chicago, 4th ed. 1954, p. 182.

[2] For a detailed discussion of the justification for police participation in the treatment of juvenile offenders, see *Police Administration*, pp. 204-209.

ers. Just as the police may save a child from a life of crime by sympathetic and understanding action short of actual prosecution, so also may the police, by intelligent treatment, save adult offenders from experiences that may confirm them in their criminal misconduct. The case for treatment rather than prosecution and punishment for alcoholics and sex deviates seems apparent; an equally strong argument exists in the case of some other accidental or occasional offenders.

Decision 6. On which juvenile offenders should the police file petitions in the juvenile court?

There is no arbitarary rule for the police to apply in deciding whether a petition should be filed in juvenile court on an individual offender, or whether he should be treated by the police themselves or with the assistance of other community agencies, or referred to one agency alone for some specific treatment. Decisions will be influenced by the conditions that need correction; the attitude of the child; the persistency of his misbehavior; the seriousness of the offense; the facilities of, and relationships between the police, the juvenile court and its probation department, and community agencies interested in some phase of the problem.

A proposal that the line of demarcation between police (or other community) treatment and the filing of a petition in juvenile court should be based on the seriousness of the offense (for example, filing on all felony cases and treating all lesser offenses within the local community) does not seem sound. The interests of the child and of the community are sometimes best served, even in felony cases, by treatment short of court action. On the other hand, some children guilty of minor offenses may be so badly in need of correctional treatment as to justify immediate juvenile-court action.

A sound policy calls for police treatment (directly or through other community agencies) of all juvenile offenders when a preliminary diagnosis of them does not reveal a maladjustment or other problem that seems unlikely of correction by the local community. This policy cannot be implemented by a categorical rule, but conferences between interested agencies will bring about a sound working relationship that will further the welfare of the children and at the same time protect the community from the results of their misconduct.

An exception to the above policy may be indicated when the

seriousness of the offense has aroused public opinion to demand decisive action. Repeated misconduct on the part of the child may also deserve juvenile-court action.

The coordination of the interested agencies is facilitated by the maintenance of a central index of juvenile offenders, preferably operated by the probation department of the juvenile court. Law enforcement agencies within the jurisdiction should forward each day an index card of suitable size and form on each juvenile dealt with, listing the name and case number and other pertinent but not detailed information. These cards, filed in the central index, provide other agencies with information relating to youthful offenders within the area and inform the juvenile-court probation office of offenders currently being dealt with by local police agencies. In populous jurisdictions, 24-hour telephone service should be provided so that any enforcement agency can obtain information at once on a juvenile offender with whom they are currently dealing.

Decision 7. Should some offenders be placed under voluntary police supervision?

Some juvenile offenders, guilty of normal childhood mischief, need only a mild reprimand. The incident should, of course, be reported to the parents. Others, however, deserve more intensive treatment. Those who do not need the attention of other community agencies may be placed under voluntary police supervision.

Voluntary supervision is the practice of having the juvenile offender report his activities in person to the police at periodic intervals, such as once each week, over a relatively short period of time, such as six months or less. During this time he may be subjected to some restrictions on his activities, such as an early curfew or a limited number of shows, and he may be required to perform certain stipulated household tasks and yard duties at his home. The officer to whom he reports should insist on compliance with these conditions, reprimand the child for his failures, and admonish him against misconduct. Voluntary supervision should be agreed upon by the child and the parents.

Voluntary supervision assists the parents in the control of a problem child, restricts his liberties, and brings him into close association with the police. Acquaintanceship with the officer to whom he reports has an opportunity to ripen into a friendship that may be lifelong. This association assists in reorienting the child, gives him a new set of values, helps him to break away from undesirable associates and habits, and frequently is all that is needed to stop his wayward behavior.

Decision 8. Should the police attempt the adjustment of offenders requiring more intensive treatment than voluntary supervision, using all available community resources?

The diagnosis of the offender sometimes reveals conditions whose correction requires the attention of one or more community agencies. The police have a responsibility to direct the attention of other agencies to children needing their services and to follow-up on the results.

In the adjustment of the problem child, the police should leave no stone unturned to accomplish their purpose. The likelihood of adjustment is enhanced when favorable attention is focused and steadily maintained on the child; such attention may provide needed affection and a sense of his own worth. The assistance of the home, the church, and the school should all be solicited. The school counsellor and sometimes the class teacher should be urged to assist in the solution of the problem. Some departments use voluntary workers as big brothers to assist with the individual child. University and college students in criminology, social welfare, and psychology are frequently interested in carrying on such work as a part of their training.

Decision 9. To what extent should the patrolman on his beat participate in the department juvenile crime-control program?

Patrolmen should participate as actively in the prevention of delinquency as they do in traffic and vice control and in the preliminary investigation of crimes. In dealing with incidents assigned to the juvenile division, patrolmen should have the same relationship to the juvenile division as they have to the detective and vice divisions in dealing with incidents in their special fields. Patrolmen should investigate offenses involving juveniles either as offenders or victims, supervise recreational establishments and areas containing delinquency hazards, and assist in the adjustment of the individual delinquent.

The patrolman may render important services in the adjustment of the individual delinquent by supervising and making friends with problem children on his beat. The juvenile division should keep him informed regarding the identity of problem children and the nature of their difficulties; it should give him suggestions as to procedures for dealing with the individual child. In this way each patrolman serves as the big brother of the delinquent boys on his beat and maintains an interest in their welfare and a watch for undesirable influences.

The patrolman should establish friendly relationships with all boys on his beat and promote in them a respect for law and a favorable attitude toward its enforcement. He should be alert for evidence of persons and places undesirably influencing children and youth; he should be persistent in his efforts to eradicate these influences and to direct youthful activities into wholesome channels.

Decision 10. Should the juvenile division or the traffic division be responsible for such juvenile group safety activities as schoolboy patrols, junior safety councils, junior traffic courts, bicycle-rider clubs, and so on? Also, which of these two divisions should be responsible for dealing with the juvenile traffic offender in the event he is dealt with informally by the police?

There are a number of advantages to placing responsibility for youth safety activities on the traffic division rather than the juvenile division. The objectives of the two divisions are quite different. The juvenile division is primarily interested in preventing delinquency; the traffic division is primarily interested in safety. The youth safety activities are designed to promote safety, although as previously stated, police participation in any group activity that results in a friendly relationship between children and the police is likely to have important delinquency-prevention value. Since the primary purpose of the activity falls within the jurisdiction of the traffic division and a failure in its attainment will reflect against the traffic record, it seems logical to place responsibility for youth group safety activities on the traffic division. The members of this division are also more likely to have a greater interest and enthusiasm in the projects than the members of the juvenile division. The juvenile division, however, should cooperate with the traffic division in their projects and assist them in every way possible.

The individual juvenile traffic offender, however, should be referred to the juvenile division for final disposition or treatment. This is so because the traffic offense, especially when repeated, may be symptomatic of deep-seated ills that deserve special attention.

Also, the juvenile division will frequently have a previous record on the offender and will be able to relate the present offense to previous behavior; the treatment should then be related to the action taken by the division in previous incidents. An exception is made in the operation of any form of traffic court conducted by juveniles themselves.[1]

Juvenile-division Organization

The organization of the juvenile division into bureaus or sections and the assignment of duties to each is influenced by the size of the division and the nature and scope of its operations as determined by the previously discussed decisions. Decisions must also be made on the following questions in order to establish the organization of the division.

Decision 11. What bureaus should be established in a juvenile division of a size to justify their creation and which duties should be assigned to each?

The duties of a juvenile division may be divided into three broad categories, i.e., investigation, patrol and inspection, and special. Special duties encompass licensing tasks; adjustment work; coordination of community agencies concerned with the prevention of delinquency or the treatment of the delinquent or pre-delinquent; the provision of wholesome influences; and planning police delinquency-prevention activities. In divisions of suitable size, there may be justification for the creation of three bureaus to perform these three classes of tasks. They will be referred to hereafter as the investigation bureau, the patrol bureau, and the coordinating bureau.

The relationship between the investigation bureau and the other juvenile bureaus should be similar to that between the detective division and the entire department. The relationship between the members of the juvenile division and beat patrolmen should be similar to the relationship between the detectives and the members of the patrol division.

The juvenile-division investigator should have ultimate responsibility for the clearance by arrest of all cases assigned to the juvenile division in the same manner that the detective-division in-

---

[1] See Ralph W. Daniel, "A Juvenile Jury for Young Traffic Offenders," *Focus*, Vol. 29, No. 1 (January, 1950), pp. 23-26.

vestigator has ultimate responsibility for the clearance of cases assigned to that division. Likewise, patrolmen (in the patrol division as well as in the juvenile division) should have responsibility for the preliminary investigation of crimes assigned to the juvenile division.

The need for juvenile-division members to devote their full attention to inspectional duties is usually less than the need for investigational staff. In consequence, the need for a bureau to perform these and related duties will usually arise, in the growth and development of a department, after the need for an investigation bureau has been met.

Inspectional tasks are usually assigned to juvenile-division members engaged in patrol duties. Inspectional duties that occupy the full time of a person off the street (that is, on private property or in an area restricted to amusement resorts) is an exception and may be performed by a specialist not engaged in routine patrol. The dance-hall supervisor, found in some departments, is an example.

Members assigned to the patrol bureau are charged with patrolling areas containing hazards to the youthful population during the hours of greatest need. In addition to inspectional duties and routine patrol, the members should make preliminary investigations of cases initially assigned to the juvenile division and consequently not investigated by the patrol division. They should also assist in the supervision of problem children in the community as a service to the adjustment officers.

The size of the patrol bureau will be influenced principally by the extent of inspectional services that cannot be satisfactorily performed by the beat patrolman and by the size of areas of the community of such great hazard to youth as to justify a special patrol. It will also be influenced, in departments where the juvenile division is closed during the night hours, by the desirability of having a juvenile-division officer immediately available to deal with juvenile offenders that may be picked up by beat patrolmen.

Advantages gained from participation of the beat patrolman in the delinquency-prevention program of the department are so great as to justify placing responsibility for the performance of the above-mentioned patrol duties on the beat officer up to the point that the need for a special juvenile-division patrol becomes clearly apparent.

The need for a coordinating bureau will be influenced by the extent to which the police have assumed responsibility in eradicating unwholesome influences and in promoting or providing wholesome group activities; treating the maladjusted; and coordinating community effort in the prevention of delinquency.

The investigation of license applicants and the issue of licenses may not be the exclusive responsibility of one bureau. For example, the officer charged with the investigation of bicycle thefts may be responsible also for their registration or licensing. Likewise, the dance supervisor may logically undertake the investigation of applicants for dance licenses.

While not all juvenile divisions will be of such size as to justify the creation of three separate bureaus as indicated above, the functions must be performed regardless of the number of members. The internal organization of the division, therefore, may not invariably follow the pattern indicated. In some departments there may be no specialized juvenile patrol even though there may be justification for the appointment of a specialist to make inspections of such places as dance halls. In others, the police may not have assumed their full responsibility for the prevention of delinquency and the tasks that are undertaken in this category may be so minor as not to justify the creation of a special coordinating bureau.

Decision 12. To what extent should juvenile-division personnel be assigned to work during the evening and night hours?

The members of the investigation and coordinating bureaus should normally work during the business hours of the day in the same manner and for the same reasons as the members of the detective division. The need for regular night duty becomes apparent only in the patrol bureau. Leisure time in the evening hours, and the operation of amusement resorts to profit from it, make the evening and early night hours especially hazardous to the youth population. As a general rule, the need for routine patrol and inspection is greatest during the evening hours, and consequently if there is a need for such service by the juvenile division, the patrol should operate in the evening and at night.

Decision 13. Which days of the week are most suitable for weekly relief for members of the juvenile divisions?

With the exception of the patrol bureau, the need for the services of the juvenile division is usually less on Sunday than on any other day of the week. In departments that provide one day of rest in seven, all members of the juvenile division, except a skeleton staff, should be off duty on Sunday. In departments that provide two days of relief each week, the majority should be given Sunday and Monday as relief days, with the remainder scattered through the week. There is a greater need on Sunday for the services of the members of the investigation bureau than for the services of the coordinating bureau staff. Saturday has a greater need for the services of juvenile-division personnel than any other day of the week and consequently this day should not ordinarily be used as a relief day.

The need for patrol services is usually less on school days and weekly relief for the members of the patrol bureau should be provided during this time. An exception is found in some communities where dances are closed on Sundays; Sunday is then a suitable relief day for the dance supervisor.

Administrative and Operating Records

The organization of the police records system, which is discussed in a later chapter, will influence the nature of records that will be maintained by the juvenile division. For the moment it is assumed that a central records system exists that will encompass juvenile case records in the same manner as adult records. In addition to the records of the central system, however, there is need for some administrative and operating records that should be maintained by the juvenile division itself. While the juvenile-division operating records are related to the central system of case records, they may be independent of and physically separated from them.

Decision 14. What administrative and operating records should be maintained by the juvenile division?

The juvenile division has need for attendance records similar to those described for the detective division. For the investigation bureau, a monthly summary, similar to that used by the detective division, provides a control and a continuous check on the load and accomplishments of individual investigators. A large juvenile division (one having a dozen or more members, for example), is also justified in maintaining a prosecution ledger such as the one described for the detective division.

Other records that should be maintained by the juvenile division will be determined by the nature of their work. For example, if adjustment work is carried on there will be need for an intensive juvenile case history on each offender with whom the division is deal-ing.[1] Likewise, licensing or registration of bicycles, dances, and other places will necessitate other operating records and indexes. Plans for the eradication of unwholesome conditions in the com-munity, the promotion or provision of group activities, the coor-dination of agencies in the community, and other special activities of the juvenile division will necessitate other operating records.

A juvenile index should be maintained by the juvenile division to permit ready access to information relating to the history of offenders. A copy of the card to be forwarded to the previously men-tioned central index should be filed in the juvenile division. In addition, of course, the records division will index the names of juvenile offenders for the general name index.

Spot maps should be maintained in the juvenile division showing the location and class of juvenile offenses. Similar maps should show the residence of juvenile offenders and the nature of their offenses. These or other maps showing the location of schools, playgrounds, recreational establishments, scout troops, and other group activities sometimes reveal startling deficiencies in the provision of group activities and recreational facilities in areas of great need.

An inventory should be maintained of community agencies con-cerned in any way in the prevention of delinquency. The facilities and services they provide should be shown for each. Other services and facilities in the community that may be helpful in the treat-ment of the individual offender or in the solution of other juvenile-division problems should also be included.

Secretarial and Clerical Staff

Decision 15. What are the requirements of the juvenile division for secretarial and clerical staff?

Justification for a secretary is usually found in the juvenile divi-sion before the need for one becomes pressing in a detective division with an equal number of members. This is so because the juvenile division will ordinarily maintain more operating records than the detective division. Particular reference in this connection is made to the juvenile case-history file, the juvenile-offender index, spot maps, licensing, registration, and some other special operating records.

---

[1] See *Police Records, op. cit.*, Form 39, p. 145, for an example of a juvenile case his-tory.

The extent to which these records will be maintained by the central records division is influenced in part by the size of the juvenile division. In a small department, a division secretary may not be justified; then the maintenance of the records should be shared between the records division and the members of the juvenile division. Under these conditions, the records division should be relied on for all possible records service; the operating staff of the juvenile division should undertake only those records tasks that they are better able to perform than the records division.

There are advantages in the maintenance of the previously mentioned operating records by a division secretary. These advantages may justify the appointment of a secretary earlier than would otherwise be feasible. On the other hand, when the secretarial load becomes so heavy as to make impossible the maintenance of these operating records, there then may be justification for relying again on the central records division for some records services rather than appointing a clerk who may not be kept fully occupied. As the volume of work increases, however, it will finally reach such proportions as to justify clerical assistance within the division.

In large departments that maintain 16- or 24-hour service in the juvenile division quarters, the free time of the officer assigned makes him available to perform some clerical tasks when he possesses the necessary skill.

CHAPTER 10

Traffic Control

THE organization and operation of the traffic division are influenced by the extent of patrol-division participation in the enforcement of moving-traffic regulations and in the investigation of traffic accidents as well as by the extent of traffic-division participation in records keeping and analysis and in public education in traffic safety. They are also influenced by the location of traffic-engineering facilities in the city government and by the nature of any special activities the traffic division may undertake.

Consideration should be given to the principal functions that are properly the responsibility of the traffic division. The three pillars of engineering, education, and enforcement which support a suitable traffic-control program are customarily considered fundamental. Decisions must be reached as to the extent of police responsibility in the performance of tasks in each of these three fields and where within the police organization the responsibility is most properly placed. Some police traffic operations will also be found to cut across two and sometimes all three of these basic functions, involving as they do problems in enforcement, education, and engineering. The assignment of responsibility for such operations within the organization structure of the police department or of the traffic division then necessitates some deliberation, and sometimes the coordination of the three functions in a single operation creates other problems that must be solved.

Engineering

Decisions must be made to establish police responsibility for certain traffic-engineering tasks and to determine the need for a police traffic engineer and the most suitable location for him in the organization structure of the department.[1]

---

[1] A more detailed discussion of police traffic engineering is found in O. W. Wilson, *Police Administration*, pp. 137-141, from which some of this material was drawn by permission of McGraw-Hill Book Company, Inc. Copyright, 1950.

Decision 1. Are there some traffic-engineering functions that may be properly considered police tasks and, as such, assigned to the police department?

Traffic-engineering tasks may be divided into two broad categories: (1) General traffic-engineering tasks which include large-scale, long-range planning and construction of major improvements in the street and highway system. New streets, freeways, elevated highways, grade separations, and other elements of the road system that require much time, money, and effort in their planning, promotion, and accomplishment are examples. (2) Police traffic-engineering tasks which are primarily concerned with the discovery and remedy of accident and congestion hazards. Surveys, studies, compliance checks, and the tabulation of accident and enforcement facts provide data relating to accidents, traffic flow and volume, and parking and driving practices. Unsatisfactory conditions that cause accidents and congestion may frequently be remedied by the use of signs, signals, markings, islands, median strips, intersection redesign, loading and parking facilities, and improved street illumination.

The police traffic-engineering activities listed above are an integral part of the traffic-control program. Without them the police cannot provide maximum safety in traffic movement with minimum inconvenience and delay.

Traffic control is a primary police task. It is more important than the process of traffic engineering which assists in its accomplishment. Police traffic engineering must be carried on by the police department if it is to provide safe and expeditious traffic flow. The police, therefore, should undertake police traffic-engineering tasks.

Decision 2. Should a qualified traffic engineer be appointed to perform police traffic-engineering tasks?

Decisions relating to any of the traffic facilities listed in item (2) above whose use may remedy conditions that cause accidents and congestion should be based on analysis of need by a traffic analyst who should be a qualified traffic engineer. Without a traffic engineer, unqualified policemen will undertake many police traffic-engineering tasks themselves. Solutions to traffic problems attempted without traffic-engineering skills are little more than guesses and often prove to be expensive experiments. A fully qualified traffic engineer should, therefore, be appointed to the police force.[1]

This decision does not mean that the police traffic engineer should undertake general traffic-engineering tasks. In the absence of a city traffic engineer he might be called on for some general traffic-engineering work. With the appointment of a city traffic engineer, however, the police traffic engineer would not ordinarily concern himself with general traffic-engineering problems beyond giving his suggestions to the city traffic engineer. There must, however, always be close coordination between the two traffic engineers.

Decision 3. Where in the police organization structure should the police traffic engineer be located?

Since traffic engineering is a tool to be used in the police control of traffic to facilitate its safe flow, the police traffic engineer should be attached to the staff of the traffic division under the direct control of the head of that unit.

Education

Somewhat similar decisions must be made in order to establish the extent of responsibility of the traffic division in a community program of public safety education.

Decision 4. To what extent should the police carry on a program of public education in the field of traffic control?

The police usually recognize their responsibility in the promotion of traffic safety through public education. Many community agencies will participate in the educational program when their efforts are directed and coordinated. The schools, press, radio, theaters, advertising firms, civic clubs, and other groups in the community have facilities to promote public education. Someone must arouse their interest and direct their activities. Local safety councils sometimes provide the needed initiative, coordination, and direction. The ultimate responsibility, however, lies with the police. For this reason they should take an active part in organizing community facilities to educate the public in traffic safety. The police should also develop their own program of public education, using their own man power and facilities to this end.

---

[1] Arguments favoring the appointment of a police traffic engineer and a description of his duties and the relationships between a police traffic engineer and a municipal traffic engineer are found in *Police Administration*, pp. 137-141.

Wise expenditures in public safety education will ordinarily provide more immediately greater returns in accident reduction than equal expenditures in either enforcement or engineering. For this reason the police should accept responsibility for providing the most effective program of public safety education that lies within their ability.

Decision 5. Should such community events as parades, public meetings, and drivers' schools be held in the interest of public safety?

Any event or activity that will promote safety consciousness and safety education is considered desirable. While the organization, promotion, and carrying out of the event may be undertaken by a local safety council or safety committee of some civic organization, the police have primary interest in such activities and should initiate them. The extent of police participation will depend upon the nature of community organization for safety; in well-organized communities the police may need only to suggest the project and some community organization will plan it in detail and carry the undertaking to its successful conclusion. In less-well-organized communities, however, the police must carry a heavier burden; in some it may be necessary for them to accept the principal responsibility for the entire project. Even in the well-organized community, the police must participate actively in the planning and accomplishment of the project. They should bear in mind, however, that their objective is to obtain greater public cooperation and assistance from increasing numbers of the civic organizations. The more the community can be brought to participate, the greater the public educational value of the project.

Decision 6. Should such devices as bill boards, thermometers, and dials be used to show the current accident rates, and should marks on the pavement be used to indicate the location of fatal accidents?

Any device or procedure that will call public attention to the hazards of driving and that will make the general public more safety conscious is desirable. The most important safety factor is the attitude of motorists and pedestrians. Any activity that will tend to produce a more desirable attitude is worthwhile. The police, therefore, should initiate and promote activities designed to accomplish this purpose, utilizing the assistance of community organizations as much as possible. The ultimate responsibility for the success of these activities rests with the police.

Decision 7. Should the development and operation of a program of public safety education be the responsibility of the traffic division or of the department public-relations office?

The public-relations officer, in departments that have one, is responsible for the development and maintenance of a satisfactory relationship between the police and the public. Informing and educating the public is a part of this responsibility. The public relations-officer has the responsibility of stimulating operating personnel toward this accomplishment, coordinating the activities of all units of the department, and lending them such assistance as may be desired or required. The existence of a public-relations officer, therefore, does not relieve the traffic division of their responsibility to promote and carry on programs of public safety education, utilizing community resources as well as the resources of the department toward this end. This work should be coordinated with other department public-relations and education activities by the public-relations officer.

Enforcement

Decisions made in reference to the enforcement of traffic regulations will influence the traffic-division man-power requirements for street duty and the nature of their assignments. These decisions will also establish the nature of the relationship between the traffic and patrol divisions and the extent to which the traffic division will rely upon the patrol division for the execution of their traffic-control plans. These in turn will influence the extent to which the traffic division must undertake staff supervision and inspection of traffic tasks performed by the patrol force.

Decision 8. Should the traffic division make strong effort to eliminate the need for congestion assignments (crosswalk or intersection duty and the enforcement of parking regulations), and should it fill such assignments only when the need is clearly apparent?

The cost of police man power is so great that every effort should be made to lessen the need for congestion assignments and to avoid meeting it unless it is clearly justified. This is so even though officers on congestion assignments may have some public-relations and crime-deterrent value. Pressure is frequently applied by influential persons and groups following an isolated accident that may stampede the police into making an assignment that cannot be economically justified. The need for crosswalk and intersection assignments should be carefully studied on the basis of accidents and vehicular and pedestrian volume before such demands are met. If the police do not resist unreasonable demands, their costly man power will be occupied at relatively unimportant tasks, and the primary police purposes will not be served.

Likewise, in assignments for the enforcement of parking regulations, only such force should be used as may be clearly needed to accomplish the purpose of preventing congestion and assuring a reasonable conformance with parking regulations. In such assignments also, the police will frequently meet unreasonable demands by retail merchants on the basis of a single incident that may, if complied with, rob the force of much man power at a cost to the taxpayer beyond the benefits derived.

Many pedestrian and vehicular traffic-control problems can be solved by the use of signal-control devices. Signs, markings, roadway redesign, and regulations may also be helpful. The attention of the traffic engineer should be directed at all points requiring frequent point traffic duty in the hope that signalization may free expensive man power from this routine task that is usually more effectively performed by mechanical means than by a policeman. Officers should not be posted at signalized intersections, or at other intersections and crosswalks, until the need for such assignment to keep traffic moving smoothly and safely becomes clearly apparent.

The use of schoolboy patrols, suitably selected, equipped, trained, and directed, will eliminate the need for policemen at school crossings. Traffic signal lights manually controlled by the schoolboy patrols at locations of fast and heavy traffic flow facilitate the operation of the patrols. The large number of boys who may be engaged at such tasks makes possible more effective control than by one or two policemen. Resistance to this use of school children should be overcome through public education. When the police fail in this endeavor, they have no alternative but to use expensive police man power or to employ women, retired policemen, or other less costly labor for the service. These procedures are expensive, and the practice of using policemen complicates the administrative task of uniformly providing patrol man power in proportion to need.

Decision 9. *Which locations (intersections and crosswalks) need full-time point traffic duty and which need intermittent or regular but less-than-full-time duty, and on what days and for what hours (periods of time) must the service be provided?*

Examples of point traffic duty include downtown intersections and crosswalks where at times the pedestrian traffic may necessitate special attention; school crossings not supervised by junior traffic patrols; industrial plants whose shift changes result in a heavy concentration of pedestrian and vehicular traffic; theater and other public meetings that result in the sudden ejection of large numbers of people; and Saturday morning matinees for school children at neighborhood theaters.

When the locations that seem to require such service have been determined, study should be made to establish the genuineness of the need and to attempt the development of a system of control that will make unnecessary the use of expensive man power at some locations. Steps must then be taken to fill the remaining assignments.

Decision 10. *What areas require regular or intermittent time-limit parking supervision? Which areas may be most economically supervised by full-time traffic officers and how many officers are required? Which areas, removed from the others, have a less-than-full-time need for the supervision of time-limit parking?*

Areas containing time-limit parking restrictions are established by ordinance. All such areas are not invariably given continuous police supervision. The extent and frequency of police checks on compliance with time-limit parking restrictions is influenced by public demand, usually by retail merchants, by the adequacy of police man power, and by the policy of the chief toward enforcement at times and in locations where the demand for parking facilities is not great. Man-power requirements are usually less in metered zones than in other areas. Man-power requirements in metered zones will also be influenced by the policy of marking cars to prevent their remaining in a stall beyond the time limit even though the meter does not show them to be in violation.

Sound policy in the enforcement of time-limit parking regulations is to apply no more man power than is necessary to win a compliance that will be satisfactory to the retail merchants.

On the basis of the above information, routes should be laid out for traffic officers who will devote full time to checking over-time parking. Decisions must also be made as to the assignment of a less-than-full-time task of checking over-time parking in an area removed from the central section.

Decision 11. Should parking regulations be enforced by men on foot or on three-wheel motorcycles?

The three-wheel motorcycle provides many advantages in both metered and unmetered time-limit parking enforcement. When the patrol force is distributed among the shifts in proportion to need, the day watch will have a minimum force on duty. Since bank robberies and other serious crimes are sometimes committed during these hours, officers assigned to parking enforcement on radio-equipped three-wheel motorcycles constitute a reserve force that may be deployed to assist in dealing with these infrequent but grave offenses. They are also available for dispatch to supplement the patrol force in less serious situations when patrol man power may for some reason be depleted.

The greater efficiency of the officer on this vehicle as compared to the officer on foot is evidenced by the greater number of traffic tickets issued and arrests made by the motorized officer. It may also be forcefully demonstrated by having the foot man carry a pedometer so that the miles covered on foot may be compared with the miles on the cycle. The officer on a three-wheel motorcycle can provide an intensity of enforcement equal to that of a man on foot on a route approximately five times longer than can be covered by a foot man. In other words, an officer on a motorcycle can do the work of five foot patrolmen.

The mobility of the cycle justifies the establishment of one or more routes containing outlying zones, thus relieving some beat officers of time-limit parking enforcement in neighborhood shopping centers and some other areas.

Decision 12. Should civilians or women be used for parking enforcement?

The use of a motorized time-limit parking-enforcement unit as a reserve to assist in dealing with bank robberies and other serious daytime crimes as well as to supplement the patrol force in less serious situations requires commissioned officers for this assignment. The use of civilians or women for this purpose is false economy. The deterrent and called-for-service value of this reserve far outweighs the difference in salaries.

Decision 13. How should parking-enforcement assignments be made?

The practice of dividing the parking district into area beats for assignment purposes leaves the manner of coverage to the discretion of each officer. While such discretion is desirable for a general patrol, the complicated problem of parking enforcement presented by one-way streets and metered and unmetered zones of various time limits makes it necessary that the manner of travel over the area be planned in great detail. For this reason assignment should be made to routes containing approximately equal work loads and so designed that the movement of the officer from one block to the next will be designated, to assure the best possible manner of coverage.

A well-designed route will be far from simple. Some blocks of streets will be covered more frequently than others, owing to one-way streets, which must usually be ridden twice to cover both sides, and to extraordinary needs created by short time-limit zones.

A section of a large-scale map with disproportionately wide streets should be used to outline each route. The route should be shown in the form of a continuous line from a starting point and return to the same location, with arrows to indicate direction of travel. The route map should be mounted on the motorcycle to guide the officer on his complicated tour. The officer may, however, start his tour at any point along the route.

While the mileage of each route may be computed from the map, conditions on one route may require more time for coverage than on other routes of equal mileage. Only by having one officer time himself, as he performs the usual police tasks while covering each route, may a fair determination be made of the equality of work loads among several routes.

Decision 14. To what extent should traffic-congestion tasks (crosswalk or intersection duty and the enforcement of parking regulations) be performed by traffic-division members? When should the patrol division be called on for assistance in such assignments?

Traffic officers should be used on all congestion assignments that occupy the full time of a man. When several less-than-full-time tasks can be combined to occupy the full time of one man they should be assigned to a traffic officer. Some less-than-full-time point duty may be assigned to traffic officers in addition to their other duties, as for example, when an officer engaged in the enforcement of parking regulations spends a part of his tour at an intersection or crosswalk.

Likewise, when there is a traffic squad for the enforcement of moving-traffic regulations, its members may be used for short-time assignments at crosswalks and intersections in widely separated sections of the community. It is not usually wise, however, to make such assignments to a traffic squad created primarily to meet unusual needs and secondarily to enforce moving-traffic violations; attention to unusual needs will upset schedules so frequently as to make such assignment ill-advised.[1]

Enforcement of parking regulations should also be placed on members of the traffic force, except in areas where the need for this and other traffic duty does not justify the full-time assignment of an officer. In such areas, a determination must be made as to the relative desirability of assigning the less-than-full-time parking supervision to the beat officer in contrast to a traffic officer who might come into the area periodically from the location of his principal duty. Factors that will influence the decision will include the amount of time involved and the hours when the service must be provided; the importance of the task (how strong are the pressures on the police for its provision and, from a police viewpoint, whether something less than complete enforcement would have serious consequences); the time that would be spent in travel by a traffic officer assigned to some other location who might periodically move to the area in question, and the extent to which such added assignment would interfere with his regular duties; the extent to which the performance of these duties by the beat officer would interfere with his regular patrol duties; the relative efficiency of performance by a traffic officer equipped with a three-wheeled motorcycle as compared to a beat officer on foot or in an automobile.

The traffic division should attempt to fill all congestion assignments with their own officers as far as this may be done without leaving one or more unoccupied or unproductively employed during a part of the tour of duty. Short-time congestion assignments beyond the capacity of the traffic-division members must be handled by the patrol division, using beat officers to fill intermittent and less-than-full-time needs.

The patrol division is nearly always confronted with the necessity of filling some of the need for intermittent or less-than-full-time

[1] Such a squad is described, *infra.*, p. 274.

point traffic duty. Such assignments, however, should be held to the bare minimum.

When responsibility has been placed on the patrol division for point traffic duty at selected locations and for checking on over-time parking in isolated sections, ingenuity and cooperation be-tween the patrol and traffic divisions will be required to fashion a schedule designed to meet the need with least disruption to regular patrol. Once the assignments have been agreed upon and the sched-ules drafted, the traffic division will have a continuing staff-inspec-tional responsibility to assure themselves that the assignments are being filled regularly and promptly and that the tasks are per-formed in an approved manner.

The man-hours devoted by beat patrolmen to congestion assign-ments must be considered in laying out the beats in the manner described in Chapter 6.

An exception to the rule that the traffic division should use its own members is found when these officers, because of their small number, location of duty, or hours of work, do not justify the ap-pointment of a traffic supervisor. Under these conditions there may be justification for the assignment of certain full-time traffic duties to the patrol division in order that the officer engaged in their per-formance may have suitable continuous supervision. For example, in a small department there may be an insufficient number of traf-fic officers on street duty at one time to justify the appointment of a traffic sergeant, or the insufficiency may be found during hours when the main traffic force is off duty. Also, in somewhat larger departments, there may be traffic officers, of insufficient number to justify the appointment of a supervisor, working full time on con-gestion assignments in a section of the community so far removed from the location of a traffic sergeant as to justify their assignment to the patrol division in order to assure supervision.

Decision 15. Is a traffic-division unit or squad for the enforce-ment of moving-traffic regulations ever justified?

Two conditions may justify the creation of a traffic-division squad for the enforcement of moving-traffic regulations: (1) An inade-quately motorized patrol force, or a failure to give principal re-sponsibility for the enforcement of moving-traffic regulations to the motorized patrol force. (2) A need for man power to meet un-usual and irregular needs in traffic control, such as parades, street carnivals, athletic events, political rallies, and other assemblages of people who must be protected and have their dispersal facilitated.

Even when the principal responsibility for the enforcement of moving-traffic regulations is given to an adequately motorized patrol force, there may be justification for a traffic squad to meet the second need listed above. When a traffic squad is provided for the primary purpose of meeting irregular and unusual traffic needs,[1] they should be used, during intervals between events requiring their services, to supplement the enforcement of moving-traffic regulations by the patrol division. They should be assigned to the hours and areas of greatest need. Since such assignments will be intermittent, the members of this squad will not be available for regular short-time congestion assignments nor for the principal enforcement of moving-traffic regulations. This squad may also be directed against criminals whose activity at certain hours and locations has created a greater-than-ordinary need for covers or plants or intensified patrol.

Decision 16. Should a system of notices of violation be instituted that will enable the notice to serve as a warning except when the driving history of the offender justifies other action?

The notice of violation serves as a written warning. The written warning is superior to the verbal warning in the following respects: (1) When filed in a driver index, it provides a complete permanent record of the driving history of the motorist. A complete driving history of the motorist is helpful in deciding on action to be taken by both the police and the court. (2) It establishes proof of the occurrence, since it contains the signature of the motorist. (3) The formality of a written notice has a more salutary effect on the erring motorist than a verbal warning; this is further enhanced by the written copy retained by the motorist. (4) It serves as an accurate measure of performance and consequently stimulates officer activity. Substantially more stops are made by officers who use written warnings than by those who do not.

The notice of violation relieves the officer of the necessity of making a decision as to the action he should take against the offender; he merely reports the facts of the violation and the circumstances surrounding it, instead of deciding whether to cite or merely to warn. Relieving the officer of the responsibility of de-

[1] The organization and operation of such a squad is described, *infra.*, pp. 274-276.

ciding whether to cite or to warn has the following advantages: (1) The decision will be more objective and usually more sound when it is not influenced by emotions which are frequently aroused, sometimes quite unconsciously, by a clash of personalities, the current state of the officer's and motorist's physical and emotional health, the officer's attitude toward traffic violations and department policy, or by extraneous factors, such as incidents that relate to the chase and stopping of the motorist, rather than to the violation itself. (2) The action to be taken should be based on the complete driving history of the offender. This information is not readily available to the officer at the time of the arrest. Analysis of the motorist's record may be made at the time the notice is filed in a drivers' index. A sound decision may then be made as to action to be taken based on a schedule of combinations of the current offense with past offenses and accidents that justify the issuance of a summons. This procedure assures uniformity of treatment and expedites the work of the file clerk. (3) The officer is relieved of some emotional strain because he is merely reporting the incident, not citing the offender. Since the action that will be taken is based on the past record of the motorist, the notice of violation is only a warning in the event the record is favorable. Being relieved of some emotional strain, the officer will perform his duties more effectively and more cheerfully and he will make more stops than he otherwise would.

The notice of violation operates successfully only when the motorist's driving record is on file and readily available for analysis. When a substantial proportion of the motorists are from out of town, other provision must be made to assure the availability of their driving history if the plan is to work satisfactorily. This is accomplished when all cities in a region or a state agree to establish drivers' indexes and to cooperate with the others by furnishing the driving record of their residents who commit traffic offenses in other communities. A copy of each notice of violation served on an out-of-town motorist is then sent to his residence where it is filed in the local drivers' index. At the time of filing, a report of his driving record is forwarded to the city that served the notice; on the basis of this record a decision is made as to the action to be taken.

Accident Investigation

Since one of the principal purposes of police traffic control is to prevent accidents, facts relating to the causes of accidents and where and when they are occurring must be compiled and analyzed to guide in the application of engineering, education, and enforcement activities. Accident investigations enable the police to obtain facts essential (1) to the wise direction of their efforts and (2) to the successful prosecution of drivers who commit serious violations. Decisions must be made as to which accidents deserve investigation, who is to investigate them, and the manner in which the accident reports should be filed.

Decision 17. Which traffic accidents should the police investigate intensively?[1]

In seeking the answer to this question, consideration should be given to the purpose of accident investigations. The wise direction of police effort in engineering, education, and enforcement must be based on information as to the most frequent types of violations that result in accidents and the classes of drivers involved; where and when (by days of the week and hours of the day) they occur most frequently; and physical hazards resulting from the unsuitability or inadequacy of the roadway, adjacent areas, signs, signals, markings, or regulations. Accident facts also serve as evidence of violations and thus assist in convicting violator-drivers.

The conviction of the driver is important in accidents involving the drinking driver and in those resulting in manslaughter, hit-and-run violations and, in some cases, personal injury. In other accidents, however, there seems to be no greater justification for the conviction of the accident driver than for the conviction of a driver guilty of the same violation that did not result in an accident; the first-accident driver is not so likely to have a second accident as is the repeater-violator to have an accident, and the cost of the accident stands as a heavy penalty to the motorist for his carelessness and violation.

A complete investigation of accidents, including measurements and photographs of the roadway and adjacent areas, of skid marks, the exact place of impact, and detailed statements from drivers and all witnesses is a costly undertaking that is justified principally to gain convictions. Information essential to the direction of police effort in engineering, education, and enforcement can be obtained

---

[1] A more detailed discussion of the investigation of automobile accidents is found in O. W. Wilson, *Police Administration*, pp. 145-147, from which much of this material was drawn by permission of McGraw-Hill Book Company, Inc. Copyright, 1950.

in suitable detail and with satisfactory accuracy in less serious accidents by less time-consuming methods.

A sound policy is one that differentiates between (1) accidents involving the drinking driver, the hit-and-run driver, other violations on which prosecutions are likely, personal injuries, damage to public property, and defects in the roadway or other conditions or circumstances that might result in a damage suit against the city, and (2) all other accidents. The former should be recorded and registered as numbered cases and thoroughly investigated in complete detail. Skid marks should be measured and the location of other objects involved in the accident should be established by measurements; photographs should be taken of skid marks, vehicles, and other objects, and sketches should be made.

Such complete and detailed investigation of the non-injury accident that does not fall also in any of the other categories listed above is unnecessary. Its investigation should be restricted to obtaining information necessary to fill in the National Safety Council type of motor-vehicle accident-report form (or a local state-adopted modification of it). The officer at the scene should identify the drivers and automobiles and obtain other essential facts. The drivers, of course, should be required to report to police headquarters. State laws and city ordinances almost invariably require drivers involved in accidents that result in property damage, in excess of a designated amount, to report the facts on an approved form to the police of the city in which the accident occurred.

The reports by the drivers and by the investigation officer (when one was at the scene) are the only reports that are ordinarily required in non-injury accident cases that are not complicated by other factors. These reports contain all the information needed in the preparation of collision diagrams and in summarizing the time and location of accidents, the types of contributory violations, and the classes of acident drivers. Detailed measurements of the roadway and significant parts of the adjacent area are made by the traffic engineer in the preparation of a condition diagram of an accident-frequent location.

Decision 18. Who should investigate traffic accidents?

The investigation of traffic accidents in the above described categories should be made by the beat patrolman assisted by the evidence technician in the same manner as they undertake the preliminary investigation of crimes and the search of crime scenes for physical evidence. The evidence technician is charged with searching the accident scene for physical evidence; identifying, recording, preserving, and transporting it to headquarters for examination; making measurements of skid marks; locating and establishing the place of impact; taking photographs; and otherwise assisting the beat officer in the investigation. The advantages of placing responsibility for the investigation of traffic accidents on the beat officer are the same as in the investigation of crimes.

The ultimate investigative responsibility in traffic accidents rests with the traffic division. A chief accident investigator in the traffic division should continue accident investigations as detectives continue the investigation of crimes whose ultimate clearance is the responsibility of their division. The relationship of the chief accident investigator to the officers who make the preliminary investigation of traffic accidents is the same as that of the detectives to the officers who make the preliminary investigation of their crimes. Most traffic accidents, however, are disposed of during the preliminary investigation; the chief accident investigator is principally concerned with hit-and-run and other important cases on which there will be prosecution.

Special Operations

The performance of a number of special activities designed to promote public safety cannot be left to community organizations so readily as the events mentioned in the section on public education. If these special activities are to be carried on, the police must accept most of the burden. Included in this category are traffic-violator schools, bicycle-rider schools or clubs, schoolboy traffic patrols, and junior safety councils. Decisions must be made, therefore, as to the desirability of the police undertaking such projects. Similar decisions must be made in regard to the inspection of vehicles and certain licensing duties.

Decision 19. Should the police operate a traffic-violator school?

The purpose of police action against violators of moving-traffic regulations, of course, is to reduce the frequency of the violations, because as the violations are reduced in frequency the accident rate is likewise reduced. It has been demonstrated that the traffic-violator school is approximately 25 per cent more effective than a fine in reducing the frequency of moving-traffic violations.[1] This is the equivalent of increasing the number of fines assessed in court by 125 per cent of the number of traffic-violator school graduates; the effectiveness is 25 per cent greater than if they had been fined. The cost to the police, in money and damaged good will, of obtaining this increased effectiveness through the operation of a traffic-violator school is considerably less than obtaining it by increasing the number of traffic officers by the number that would be necessary to obtain the increased number of fines indicated above.

Since the traffic-violator school is both effective and economical, the police seem justified in using this device in their traffic-enforcement program.

Decision 20. Should the police organize and operate a bicycle-rider school or club?

Rewards in the form of increased safety obtained by the operation of bicycle-rider schools or clubs are not so great as in the traffic-violator school, although the public-relations benefits of the former may justify their operation. From a safety viewpoint alone, there does not seem to be justification for their operation, although an exception is found in communities that have an unusually high bicycle accident rate.

Decision 21. Should the police establish a schoolboy traffic patrol?

The effectiveness of a properly selected, trained, equipped, and directed schoolboy patrol alone justifies its operation. In addition to safety advantages, the operation has an economic advantage to the taxpayer; expensive police man power is relieved of school-crossing duty by a force that is able to perform the task more effectively and over a much wider area than is possible by the police themselves. Also, the close relationship of the police to the participants has a clearly discernible public-relations value, and the friendliness of the relationship provides some delinquency-prevention benefits. The experience of all other school children in complying with the directions of their playmate traffic officers constitutes valuable training in the important civic virtues of conforming with regulations and complying with the directions of authority. The experience of children at schools that employ junior traffic patrols

---

[1] The measurement of the effectiveness of the traffic-violator school is discussed in *Police Administration*, p. 163.

trains them in law observance. This feature of schoolboy patrols is important not only to the police but to the parents and the community as well.

In some communities it is difficult to overcome the resistance of parents to the idea of their children serving their playmates as policemen. The police should not rest, however, until their community is convinced of the wisdom of using schoolboy traffic patrols. The practice is justified from the point of view of child safety, economy to the taxpayer, and its value in training children in important civic virtues.

Decision 22. Should the police organize some form of juvenile traffic court to be operated by young people?

The juvenile traffic offender presents some unusual problems. He is not subject to action by adult courts and the procedure necessary to bring him before the juvenile court is so cumbersome and time consuming that the police often take no action against him. Informal treatment, usually on the basis of a voluntary agreement with the offender and his parents, is sometimes provided by the police in order to impose some restriction on the juvenile driver without time-consuming appearances before juvenile court.

Some communities, with varying degrees of success, have experimented with various forms of juvenile traffic courts operated by high school boys. As in the case of junior traffic patrols, the operation of juvenile traffic courts has advantages beyond the field of safety; the experience of the participants as well as of the offenders is useful in the development of a desirable sense of civic responsibility.

While a high priority should not be given to the operation of a juvenile traffic court, the advantages derived from it seem sufficiently great to justify police interest in its development. The promotion and operation of juvenile traffic courts, however, might well be left to some agency in the community other than the police.

Decision 23. Should the police undertake the inspection of vehicles for defects?

The annual compulsory presentation of motor vehicles for inspection is an expensive and time-consuming annoyance from the point of view of the motorist. There is serious question that the economic saving in life, limb, and property effected by such inspections is equal to their money cost, to say nothing of the damage to good will that usually results.

If compulsory vehicle inspection is to be undertaken, it should be restricted to older vehicles, such as those older than some designated age between five and 10 years. More than half of the vehicle defects that are contributory causes of accidents consist of defective brakes, tires, and lights. Although relatively new motor vehicles are subject to these defects, it would be erroneous to conclude that the new vehicle is as likely to be defective in these respects as the older one because the owner of the new vehicle has greater pride of ownership and is more likely to have the means to maintain the car in proper repair. The older vehicle is also more subject to other types of defects that may contribute to accidents than the newer one.

Compulsory annual inspection of the older motor vehicles is a suitable undertaking for a state motor-vehicle administration, rather than a municipality. The inspection may be a prerequisite to the issuance of the annual vehicle license. Only when vehicle defects are an unusually frequent contributing cause of accidents does there seem to be justification for the compulsory inspection of the older vehicles by the municipality.

For the same reasons as those listed above, the operation of a squad to make indiscriminate inspections of all vehicles does not seem justified. A preferred procedure is to require all officers to be alert for vehicles whose condition appears to justify inspection. The inspection of these vehicles, when there is reasonable ground to believe that they are defective, may be accomplished by the issuance of a notice of defect.[1] The operator may then take the vehicle to any garage and have the defect corrected; the repair or correction may be noted on the notice of defect which is then returned to the police department.

Decision 24. Should the police undertake tasks related to the issuance of city licenses for vehicles or drivers?

Some municipalities impose a wheel tax; others license taxicabs and cab drivers. The collection of taxes and license fees is a task the police should avoid; this is a proper duty of the finance department. The inspection of vehicles used as common carriers and the examination of their drivers is more properly a police task. Such inspections and examinations have a safety purpose; unsafe vehicles

---

[1] Notices of defect are discussed in *Police Records,* pp. 121-122.

and incompetent and untrustworthy drivers should be barred from common-carrier operation.

Decision 25. What policy should the police adopt in reference to towing away and impounding improperly parked vehicles?

Public relations are damaged when vehicles that are parked in violation of a traffic ordinance are towed away and impounded, and consequently the police should avoid this practice whenever possible. A vehicle that is parked or left in a manner to jeopardize safety or to impede seriously the regular flow of traffic should be shoved to a suitable location when this can be done; otherwise it must be towed away and impounded.

Hours of Work and Relief

There is considerable hourly, weekly, and sometimes seasonal variation in the need for traffic work. Consideration must be given to these variations in the selection of hours of work and weekly and annual relief.

Decision 26. Which hours of the day are most suitable for members of the traffic division?

The head of the traffic division should invariably work during the day shift. Some special evening events may make work during other hours necessary on rare occasions. The chief accident investigator should also work during the day hours for the same reasons that detectives should. Officers, such as those engaged in educational, engineering, analytical, and clerical tasks, should also usually be assigned to day duty.

Officers assigned to congestion assignments will nearly always work during the day hours; only in large cities will there be sufficient congestion-assignment duty in the evening hours to justify the regular assignment of traffic officers. The selection of hours of daytime work for officers on congestion assignments will be influenced by conditions prevailing in each community. In smaller communities it may be possible to select an eight-hour period which will encompass the total need for congestion assignments. In larger cities, however, the need is often spread over more than eight hours, thus necessitating two overlapping shifts; some of the officers should then report for duty one, two, or three or more hours later than the others.

The decision to use the patrol division for the principal enforcement of moving-traffic regulations will influence the selection of the hours of work of the traffic patrol. When the principal enforcement effort is a traffic-division responsibility, the traffic patrol should be distributed among the shifts in proportion to the distribution of traffic accidents among the shifts. When the principal enforcement of moving-traffic regulations is a patrol-division responsibility, the traffic patrol (usually with the primary responsibility of coping with unusual events) will be used to supplement the traffic-enforcement efforts of the regular patrol. Their assignment, therefore, should not be a regular and continuing one, but should be during the hours and at the locations of greatest accident frequency. As a general rule this will be during the late afternoon and evening hours.

Decision 27. Which days of the week should be selected for weekly relief for traffic officers?

Traffic-congestion duty requirements vary greatly among the days of the week, being somewhat in proportion to business activities. The peak nearly always occurs on Saturday in the retail business section; Sunday nearly always has little or no need for officers on congestion assignments. For this reason, in communities that provide one day of relief in seven, all officers on congestion assignments should, as a rule, work on Saturdays, and all that can be spared from duty should be off on Sundays.

The relief-day problem becomes complicated when the number of weekly relief days is increased to two. In the case of traffic officers who work daylight hours, the problem may be readily solved, however, by accepting, for assignment to these greatly desired shift hours, officers who are willing to take nonconsecutive off-duty days. All of these officers would then have Sunday off duty (except such number as may be needed for traffic duties on that day) and the second off-duty day for these men would be distributed among the remaining days of the week, taking into account variations in work load from day to day.

The headquarters staff should ordinarily be off duty on Sunday when one day of relief is provided each week. When the number of relief days is greater than this, the previously mentioned complication arises. This relief can also be provided, however, in the manner described above. The duties of some may permit their being off duty on Saturday and Sunday without relief. In most instances, relief must be provided the chief accident investigator.

Conditions in the local community will indicate the most desirable days of rest for officers on traffic patrol. Week-end days usually experience the heaviest traffic volume and accident toll. When this is true, rest days for officers in the traffic patrol force should be distributed among the week days.

Some communities experience a seasonal variation in traffic that clearly indicates the periods during which the principal part of the force should take their annual leave. In others the need is nearly constant; annual leaves should then be distributed throughout the year.

Administrative and Operating Records

The traffic division, like all other units in the department, needs some administrative and operating records. The previously discussed advantages of a central records division justify holding the records operations of the headquarters traffic staff to a minimum. Decisions therefore must be made as to the division of records tasks between the traffic and the records division.

Decision 28. Which administrative records should the traffic division maintain with its own staff?

The only administrative record that the traffic division seems justified in maintaining, and then only in the large force, is an attendance record. In smaller forces the attendance record can be more effectively maintained by the dispatcher or desk officer in conjuction with the attendance record of the patrol division.

Decision 29. What operating records should the traffic division maintain?[1]

In view of the advantages gained from the consolidation of records operations in a central records division, a sound policy for the traffic division is to avoid undertaking any records tasks except when overpowering advantages to traffic operations are thus gained. The maintenance by the traffic-division staff of some special operating records, such as those that relate to the operation of the traffic-violator school, the schoolboy traffic patrol, bicycle-rider schools or clubs, juvenile traffic courts, educational activities, and police traffic-engineering tasks, may be justified. Even many of these records, however, may be more satisfactorily filed and summarized by the records di-

[1] See *Police Records,* pp. 139-142.

vision. In police departments that maintain traffic signs, signals, and markings, the maintenance records can usually be most effectively managed by gearing them into the procedures followed in handling other maintenance records, with provision for their follow-up, filing, and summarizing left the responsibility of the central records division.

The advantages derived from the integration of traffic-enforcement and accident records with other police records make desirable the consolidation of these records in the central records division. The traffic division is relieved of a mass of detail when the records staff processes these records; this is a specialized task totally dissimilar to other traffic duties. Since the traffic division has ultimate responsibility for traffic conditions in the community, and since traffic records are essential tools in traffic control, it is important that the traffic staff obtain from the records division all information relating to traffic records that they may require and in a form that is most suitable to their needs. This means, therefore, that the traffic division should have a voice in the manner in which traffic records are processed and filed.

The traffic staff will need certain spot maps in their offices. The traffic division should indicate the information they wish spotted; the spotting task should be a records-division responsibility. Likewise, daily, weekly, and monthly summaries of enforcement and accident facts, and special studies as well, should be provided by the records division in a form agreeable to the traffic division. A performance summary for each traffic officer is an important administrative record that should be provided by the records division at stated intervals and in a form satisfactory to the traffic administrator. When the principal responsibility for the enforcement of moving-traffic regulations rests with the patrol division, similar records of accomplishment in traffic enforcement by each motorized patrol officer may be provided.

The analysis of traffic-records information is the responsibility of the traffic-division staff. This task is not time consuming when the records information is provided in a form that permits ready understanding and comparison.

Secretarial and Clerical Staff

Decision 30. What secretarial and clerical staff should be provided for the traffic division?

In proportion to man power, the traffic division has less need for secretarial and clerical staff than any of the other special divisions. The traffic-control job is found on the street; it is there where the accidents and congestion are found, and it is there where enforcement and directive effort must be applied. The administrative head, and a small staff in large forces, should spend some time at headquarters analyzing the information provided by the records division and in planning traffic operations. The need for clerical assistance, in addition to that which may be supplied by the records division, is dependent largely on the success of the traffic division in having records tasks performed satisfactorily by the records division and on the need to assist motorists who call at headquarters to report traffic accidents. In all but large departments, desk officers or information clerks in conveniently located positions may supervise the preparation of accident-report forms.

CHAPTER 11

The Auxiliary Services

T HE organization of the force to facilitate the provision of auxiliary services was discussed in Chapter 4. Records and communications tasks play important roles in police operations. Efforts directed at improving the effectiveness and efficiency of police operations should include a survey of the manner in which these and other auxiliary services are performed.

The effective accomplishment of records and communications tasks, and the provision of ambulance, patrol-wagon, and tow-car service necessitate the preparation and control of suitable forms and the assignment of many tasks. Decisions relating to the assignment of these duties will further delineate the structure of the organization.

Police Records

Police records serve three principal purposes. (1) They record all discovered facts relating to the incident and the action taken by the police in dealing with it and thus serve as a history of police actions. This account is useful in day-to-day operations: any interested member can learn from it what action has been taken on any specific incident; it enables assigned officers to refresh their memories as to what has been done on each case; identifications can be made from it of persons and property and similar methods of operation. (2) Police records enable supervisors, through a report-review (follow-up) officer, to exercise effective control over police operations. (3) Police records serve as the basis for statistics relating to incidents and police action. Statistics are useful in ascertaining crime and accident rates and the effectiveness of the police in preventing and dealing with these incidents, and in measuring the need for police service in terms of the work load. To fulfill this statistical function, data must be recorded relating to the classification of the incident, the time of occurrence by date, day of week, and hour of the day, and the location by reporting area. Information relating to the difficulties involved in, circumstances of, and clearances by arrests must also be tabulated.

The consolidation of all police records into a single integrated system supervised by a central records division and the desirability of using mechanical tabulating equipment were discussed in earlier chapters. The present discussion is concerned with the operation of a consolidated records system and the forms that should be used. First, however, it is advisable to consider the hours of work for the records staff and measures to safeguard the security and good order of records.

Decision 1. Should the records office and records cabinets be accessible to all members of the department?

Accessibility to records cabinets should be restricted to records-division members. Otherwise some records will disappear and others will be misfiled and thus lost to use. The loss of records relating to a crime may seriously impair its investigation; when the case is important, the consequences may be serious. Also, when the case has political implications and when it relates to vice operations or to incidents that may reflect on police integrity or indicate police brutality or dereliction of duty, its innocent loss may be construed as deliberate by officials, the press, and the public, and the police reputation may thus be blackened.

Each index card belongs between two certain cards; otherwise it is misfiled. Since index cards are filed in reference to cards already in the cabinet, a misfiled card serves as a seed against which other cards will be filed, thus establishing two locations in the index where a card may apparently be correctly filed. An index represents a large investment in the salary of the file clerks who have built it. It is sound economy to protect this investment. As cards are misfiled, the value of the index is diminished; a misfiled card cannot be found except by accident or costly search.

Some departments attempt to lessen the likelihood of the disarrangement of records by a regulation that forbids line officers to remove index cards and forbids those who remove a case file or an identification record to refile it, requiring instead that the records be placed in an out-of-file drawer from which the clerk responsible for maintaining the file may obtain and refile it. The results of this arrangement are not usually satisfactory. The regulations are frequently violated, sometimes inadvertently, and the files become disarranged.

The wisest procedure is to restrict access to the filing cabinets to records clerks, who are skilled in the use of indexes and other files. Compliance with regulations governing records operations may be gained more readily from this small, well-trained group than from other members of the department.

In order to avoid tempting the line officers to make a search of records, the records office door should be kept locked and service provided over a counter. In order to avoid the ill will that may be engendered by refusal to admit line officers to the records room, it is best that the door be located at a point removed from the counter; requests for entry that must be refused are then less likely to be made.

Decision 2. What other precautions should be taken to safeguard the security and arrangement of records?

Responsibility for filing each class of record should be definitely assigned to one or more designated clerks, and other clerks should be required to place records removed from the cabinets in an out-of-file drawer to be refiled by the assigned clerk. In order to place responsibility for misfiled cards when more than one clerk operates an index, or when assignments are changed, each file clerk may be required to mark the side of each stack of index cards about to be filed with a colored pencil, each clerk being assigned a different color. The mark should not be placed on the top edge of the card, however, where it would be worn off by the fingers in the course of searches.

Clerks should be assigned to go through indexes, card by card, in search of misfiled cards. The frequency of such searches will be influenced by the size and condition of the files. Large departments are justified in having a clerk devote full time to this task when the volume requires one or two years to work through all of the cabinets.

Charge-out sheets, to be placed in the file at the locations from which records have been removed, should be used to assure the return of the records removed from the records office and to place responsibility for their safekeeping on the officers who have withdrawn them.

Decision 3. During which hours should the records office be open for business?

When access to records is denied to the line officers, it is essential that records clerks be on duty to provide service to them at all hours of the day and night and on all days of the year.

Complaint Records

Complaint records serve to record incidents that are discovered by or reported to the police for action; to facilitate the assignment of cases and the control of their investigation and disposition; and to permit a tabulation of the incidents and of the police action taken. By complaint records (also variously called incident and case records) is meant those forms on which are recorded incidents that call for police action. In addition to Part I and Part II crimes, there are included, as police incidents, accidents of every description, lost and found persons, animals, and property, and a variety of other occurrences reported to the police that may not fall within any of these groups.

Within the category of complaint (incident) records are included such forms as offense reports (and separate forms are usually used for a number of classes of crimes, such as robbery, burglary, larceny, auto theft, bicycle theft, bad checks, and so on), casualty reports, motor vehicle accident reports, lost and found reports, and miscellaneous reports. These report forms serve as the number one item in the case and are sometimes called the case or face sheet to which are attached in chronological sequence all investigation reports and other forms and documents relating to the case. In cases where a separate offense report is not made, a copy of the arrest report becomes a complaint record.

Although communications records are discussed later (page 197), since complaints (reports of incidents) are usually communicated to police headquarters, a discussion of the manner in which they are recorded, and registered for control purposes by having a serial number stamped on each report, must include the receipt of the information by the dispatcher (in small departments) or by a complaint clerk (in larger departments), the original record that is made of it, the assignment (usually by radio) of officers to deal with it, the report on the assignment by the dispatched officers and, finally, the preparation of the form designed for the type of incident reported.

In some departments, especially the small ones, complaint (incident) reports are typed by headquarters staff on the basis of incomplete information received from the complainant. Since this information must be amplified by facts developed by the investigating officer, the incomplete complaint record must be supplemented by investigation reports and, in crimes involving fraud, theft, and violence, by a preliminary report form[1] to assure the recording of all pertinent facts. This practice results in the so-called complaint report serving as the face sheet to which are attached all subsequently prepared reports. It is not, in a true sense, a complete complaint or offense report. In other departments, the complaint report (then called an offense report) is prepared by the investigating officer, thus serving also as a preliminary and investigation report.

The decision as to whether the complaint report form will be executed by headquarters staff or by line personnel assigned to deal with the incident will determine the basic character of the complaint records. Decisions must also be made as to the types of incidents that are to be recorded, the manner in which they will be recorded and registered, and the nature of record forms needed in the process.

Decision 4. Should complaint reports be prepared by headquarters staff on the basis of information received from the complainant, or should they be prepared by the officers assigned to deal with the incident?

The following facts seem to justify the preparation of complaint reports by the officers assigned to deal with the incident.

Delay in the preparation of complaint reports is necessary when lack of knowledge as to the classification of the incident makes impossible the selection of the complaint form designed for incidents of that class; lack of other pertinent information prompts further delay; postponement in preparation of the complaint form invites permanent avoidance of the task; the incident is then not recorded and the history of police action is incomplete and a true measure of service rendered by the police is consequently impossible.

Complaint reports prepared by headquarters staff cannot ever be as complete as when they are made out by the officers assigned to deal with the incident. This makes the use of a preliminary report form essential; the preliminary report is, in fact, the complaint (offense) report.

The preparation of the complaint report by the officers assigned to deal with the incident relieves the headquarters staff of this burden;

---

[1] Preliminary report forms, described in *Police Records*, pp. 62-64, are actually nothing more than an offense report containing spaces for detailed information relating to the *Modus Operandi* characteristics and other details of the crime. Its use is made necessary when an incomplete complaint report is prepared by headquarters staff. When the offense report is prepared by officers assigned to the incident, the preliminary report becomes in fact the complaint report.

it eliminates the need for a preliminary report in crimes of fraud, theft, and violence, since the complaint report serves its purpose; it eliminates the temptation of headquarters staff not to "make a case"; and it eliminates from the case file reports on incidents that, on investigation, are found not to be qualified for inclusion.

Decision 5. When complaint reports are prepared by officers assigned to deal with the incident, in what way should headquarters staff record the incident so that effective control may be exercised over police treatment of it?

An 8" × 5" assignment record[1] should be used to record, with a ballpoint pen, information relating to the complaint and complainant and officers assigned to deal with the incident. The form should contain spaces for recording the nature and location of the incident, the name, address, and telephone number of the complainant, and a larger space for writing in details relating to the incident. Some departments facilitate recording the nature of the incident by printing on the form a number of the most frequent types of incidents each followed by a check box. Spaces should also be provided for recording, with an automatic time stamp, the date and hour (1) the information was received, (2) and officer was dispatched, and (3) the assigned officer reported back in service.

One corner of the assignment record should contain an assignment block to facilitate recording the radio call numbers of officers assigned to the case. The assignment block consists of three squares of different sizes. The medium-size square has its corners on the midpoints of the sides of the large one; the small square has its corners on the midpoints of the sides of the medium-size one. The call number inserted in the small square is that of the officer on whose beat the incident occurred and who is responsible for preparing the incident report, when one is required. The call numbers of officers assigned to the scene to assist the beat officer are inserted in the corners of the medium-size square; when there are more than four, some are inserted in the small square in parentheses. The call numbers of officers assigned to quadrants are inserted in the corners of the large square.

Assignment records should be serially numbered by the printer to assure suitable follow-up control.

---

[1] Sulphide paper of 16 pound weight is suitable stock for this form. The form will not be subject to much use; it can be stored after one year and destroyed after three.

The assignment record is prepared by whoever receives the complaint or report. It is forwarded to the dispatcher who inserts the call numbers of officers dispatched to deal with the incident. When the assigned officers report back in service, the assignment report is forwarded for processing.

While the assignment record serves a purpose somewhat similar to that of the complaint or case report prepared by the headquarters staff in some departments, the assignment record has some notable advantages: First, only one form is used for the assignment record regardless of the nature of the incident, and second, it is prepared *immediately* on receipt of any information requiring the dispatch of a policeman, whether it be the report of a crime or accident or the request of another policeman or a citizen. No policeman should ever be dispatched except on the basis of an assignment record. In consequence, all police action is more likely to be recorded than when some other procedure is used.

Decision 6. How should the officer assigned primary responsibility for dealing with the incident (usually the beat officer) report on the results of his investigation and on the action taken?

Various forms are used by police departments to report designated classes of incidents. Department regulations indicate the classes of incidents that are to be recorded on each of the forms. The officer assigned primary responsibility for dealing with the incident must report that he has prepared the required form; when a form is not prescribed, he must report the action that he took. A report on assignment, also 8″ × 5″, accomplishes both of these ends.

The report on assignment should contain a printed list of all incident reports used by the department, each followed by a check box. When the matter has been disposed of by the preparation of any one of these forms, this accomplishment is indicated by a check in the appropriate box. When none of the indicated forms was prepared, the officer will give the details of the assignment and action taken in a brief sentence or two.

In departments without district stations, the report on assignment may be printed on the reverse of the assignment record form. The assignment records are then distributed to the assigned officers at the end of their tours of duty so that they may complete their reports on assignments. In departments decentralized among one or more district stations, the report on assignment must obviously be a separate form.

Decision 7. What incidents should be recorded and registered by a numbered report?

If police records are to fulfill their purpose, all occurrences in the following categories must be recorded:[1]

1. Violations of federal and state laws and city ordinances (except isolated traffic violations ordinarily handled by notices of violation) reported by citizens or other agencies or discovered by the police in any other way. Exceptions are also made of city ordinance violations which are observed by the police (not reported to them) in which action consists only of a warning which is accepted without protest.

2. Calls on which officers are dispatched, except those that (a) are merely requests for information, (b) are handled by a special service report,[2] and (c) result from traffic violations not endangering life or property.

3. Warrants and subpoenas, and arrests not disposed of by citation.

4. Lost and found persons, animals, and property.

5. Reportable automobile accidents; reports of personal injuries, bodies found, suicide attempts, damage to public property, sick cared for, and mental cases.

6. Cases in which a police officer is involved in any way in the damage of public or private property or the injury of any person or animal.

7. Miscellaneous cases, general and special orders, violations of rules and regulations, and any other incident that a commanding officer desires to have recorded.

Decision 8. What incident report forms should be used for reporting occurrences the police are called upon to deal with?

The number of separate incident report forms that are used by a department is determined in part by its size. In cities up to 100,000 population, the following are adequate:

Crime Report (for crimes for which other forms are not provided)
Vehicle Report (for lost or stolen, abandoned, or towed-away automobiles, motorcycles, bicycles, and other vehicles)

---

[1] This list is taken from O. W. Wilson, *Police Records*, 1942, pp. 41-42, by courtesy of Public Administration Service, Chicago, Illinois.
[2] *Ibid.*, pp. 80-82.

Lost and Found Report (for lost and found animals and property except vehicles)

Lost and Wanted Persons Report

Casualty Report (for personal injuries, bodies found, suicides and attempts, sick cared for, mental cases, and damage to public property, but not for motor vehicle accidents)

Motor Vehicle Accident Report

Arrest Report

Larger departments find it advantageous to use separate report forms for such crimes as robbery, burglary, larceny, bad checks, frauds, as well as separate forms for motor vehicles and bicycles, and perhaps some others. Forms should not be multiplied unnecessarily; a new form should not be adopted until the need for it has been clearly demonstrated.

Decision 9. Should incident reports be approved by the supervising officer before being forwarded to the records division?

The practice of many departments of requiring a supervisory officer to approve reports submitted by subordinates is undesirable for a number of reasons. The approval is either (1) a "rubber-stamp" approval made without reading the report and consequently a meaningless gesture which gives a false sense of reliability to the report, or (2) the supervisor spends a great deal of time at a clerical task reading stacks of reports to detect minor irregularities when his time should be devoted to actual on-the-job supervision of his subordinates. A report-review (follow-up) officer should be assigned the task of reviewing all police reports and, in a staff capacity, calling the attention of supervising officers to deficiencies in the reports, of their subordinates.[1] The report-review officer serves, in a sense, as the secretary of all supervising officers, relieving them of a tedious but important task that is all-too-frequently performed by a perfunctory "rubber-stamp" approval and that can be better performed for them by someone who devotes full time to this task. Supervising officers, in this way, have more time to supervise their subordinates on the job, a task that is ineffectively performed in most police departments.

---

[1] The report-review process is described in *Police Records,* pp. 194-201, and in *Police Administration,* pp. 243-245.

Decision 10. How should incident reports be registered?

Incident reports (not including arrest reports) should be delivered or sent to the records office by the officer charged with their preparation. Immediately on receipt, the records staff should register each incident report by stamping on it a serial number, the same serial being used for all categories of incidents. An automatic number-stamping machine should be used for this purpose. The copies of the incident report should then be distributed according to department regulations. The originals, which should remain permanently in the records division, are logged in, in consecutive order, on a daily bulletin.

A clerk should each day check reports on assignment, on which the preparation of an incident report is indicated, against the daily bulletin to assure the receipt of the report. This clerk should also check the assignment report file to discover, by the absence of consecutive numbers in the series, whether any reports are missing.

Decision 11. What should be the size of complaint records?

Complaint sheets and investigation reports are either of letter-size or 8″ × 5″. The advantages of the letter-size are: cases on which there is considerable investigation are less bulky; the sheets can be bound more readily; uniformity in the size of the sheets is less essential; and correspondence does not need to be trimmed to 8″ × 10″ size for folding to fit the 8″ × 5″ form. A greater number of carbon copies can usually be typed because the letter-size sheets are frequently of thinner stock.

The smaller size has some economic advantages; most reports do not require more space and there is therefore a saving in filing space and paper. Since the 8″ × 5″ complaint sheet is usually made of sextant bristol board, the individual case can be filed more readily by itself.[1] In contrast, the letter-size sheet usually requires the use of

---

[1] The Wichita, Kansas, department uses an end-opening envelope 8″ × 5½″ with the complaint form printed on its face. The envelope is stuffed by the printer with a thin carbon and an 8″ × 5″ sheet of blank white paper which serves, when the envelope is typed and number-stamped, as the duplicate complaint sheet (case card) for the assigned special division. The original copy of all investigation reports and other documents related to the case are filed by placing them in the case envelope. The nuisance of paper clips and staples are thus avoided and the likelihood of items becoming detached from the case and lost by slipping under other cases in the file is diminished.

a manila folder in which are inserted a number of cases. The number that can be filed in each folder is not uniform because the individual cases vary in bulkiness and search is therefore made more difficult.

Either size may be used satisfactorily. Frequently the size of available filing cabinets will influence the choice.

Decision 12. How many copies should be made of the complaint sheets?

In departments that do not have district stations, it is usually wise to provide a carbon copy of the complaint sheet for any specialized division that is assigned responsibility for the continued investigation. Otherwise a carbon copy is not needed. As a general rule a copy is not needed in casualty cases because their investigation is ordinarily disposed of by the patrol division. In larger departments additional copies of complaint sheets must be provided.

Decision 13. What should be the form of the department daily bulletin and what information should it contain?

The purpose of the daily police bulletin is to disseminate information among all members of the force. Its form, therefore, will be influenced by the type of information most needed that can be readily contained in it. The members of the force need information regarding cases to which they are assigned, administrative matters (general and special orders and notes on the bulletin), persons wanted and stolen property and their cancellations, and general information regarding criminal activities in the community.

In all but the large departments, this information can be contained in bulletin sheets continuously typed by the complaint clerk or an assistant. In larger departments this procedure unfortunately becomes impossible, owing to the need of district stations or patrolmen who do not report to headquarters before taking their posts, or to the fact that the material requires screening before being disseminated merely because of its volume. When any of these conditions prevail, a decision must be made as to the material that should be contained in the daily bulletin. Under all circumstances it is desirable that the bulletin contain all administrative matters and all possible information regarding persons wanted and stolen property (and cancellations) as well as a general picture of criminal activities in the community. This information in a large department may be contained in a printed daily bulletin; slightly smaller departments will reproduce it by mimeograph. Deviation from the continuous daily bulletin that provides complete information regarding department activities to all members should be made only when conditions clearly require it.

When an abbreviated form of the continuous daily bulletin is used, other means must be adopted for informing patrolmen of cases to which they are assigned. District stations should then provide for their own members a continuous daily bulletin of district incidents as a supplement to the printed bulletin issued from headquarters. Special divisions, particularly the detective and juvenile divisions, will also find helpful a continuous bulletin containing brief resumes of cases assigned to their members.

Arrest Records

Arrest records include all records relating to persons arrested except complaint and identification records. Decisions must be made as to who is to prepare arrest records, the nature of the information they should contain, and the type of records that may be helpful in the control of the prisoner and his property.

Decision 14. When and where should the prisoner be booked and his personal property taken from him, and who should do it?

The prisoner should be booked as soon as a decision is reached at the police station that he is to be charged or held in jail. A booking room should be provided for this purpose. When correctly designed and located, a booking room enables the police to hold prisoners securely and safely, with little supervision required, pending decisions relating to their disposition, booking, or transfer. The arrest data should be recorded by a booking officer in an adjoining room. A grilled wicket in the partition will enable the booking officer to obtain needed information and also to observe prisoners in the booking room.

A jailer should have custody of the prisoners and should search them and remove their personal property within view of the booking officer. Property should not be removed from a prisoner at the station except in the sight of a second officer. The property should be delivered to the booking officer, at the time it is taken from the prisoner, for the preparation of the prisoner's property receipt. The property should be stored by the booking officer in a prisoners' property cabinet for return to the prisoner on his release. In smaller departments the arresting officer may perform the jailer's duties of assisting the booking officer and searching the prisoner.

Decision 15. Should an arrest card be used or, instead, should a ledger (blotter) be used for recording pertinent information relating to the prisoner and the circumstances of the arrest?

An individual record-of-arrest card for each person arrested has the following advantages: (1) It may be typed and thus is more legible. (2) A carbon copy of the upper half of the arrest card may be made to provide information for the court clerk for the preparation of a court docket; after recording the court disposition in spaces provided in the lower half, the court clerk may send this copy to the records division where it may be placed in the case file. (3) The original may be sent to the records office for a search of records to ascertain whether the prisoner is wanted; it may also be placed in an alphabetical index located at the booking counter or in the jail until the prisoner is released, the index thus serving as a jail register. (4) In the absence of mechanical tabulating equipment, arrest cards may be readily hand-sorted at the end of the month for the purpose of compiling data for the monthly report.

The advantages of the individual arrest cards justify their supplemental use in jurisdictions where the law requires the recording of information on arrested persons in a bound book.

Decision 16. What information should be recorded at the time the prisoner is booked?

In addition to any information that may be required by statute, the following are essential data to be entered on a record-of-arrest form: (1) the full name and address of the arrestee; (2) the day, date, and hour of arrest; (3) the place of arrest; (4) the charge with space for additions or modification of the original charge at the conclusion of the investigation; (5) the name of the arresting officer or officers; (6) the manner in which the arrest was made—on sight, by warrant, or on other authority; (7) whether the arrest was made as the result of the officer being sent by headquarters; (8) whether a multiple arrest, and if so, how many; (9) whether the arrestee had a dangerous weapon; (10) whether the arresting officer summoned assistance; (11) the circumstances of release or delivery and who authorized it; the date and hour; to whom delivered if to another authority; (12) the arrest number; and (13) the case number.

In addition to these essential facts, the arrest record should contain space for a number of additional items of information: (1) sociological and identifying information: nativity, race, sex, age, length of time in the county, state, and the United States, marital status, and occupation; (2) information regarding the condition of the prisoner, especially as to whether he had been drinking; (3) the name of the officer who booked the prisoner and the name of the officer who entered information regarding the arrest on the daily bulletin; (4) information regarding any previous record, indicating (a) that a search has been made of the general name index, the nature of the previous record discovered, and to whom reported and (b) who fingerprinted the subject, who searched the fingerprint file, the nature of the previous record found there, and to whom reported; and (5) the fact that the court clerk has been notified of any change of charge and of the trial date, whether he was notified by telephone or by written report, who notified him, and the date and hour of these notifications.[1]

Decision 17. What records are needed to assure suitable control over restrictions on the privileges of prisoners?

The police have a reasonable time in which to take a person they have arrested before a proper judicial officer.[2] During this period the prisoner does not have the rights of a free man. The police,

---

[1] Taken, with slight modification, from *Police Records*, pp. 91-92.

[2] "It is ordinarily the duty of an officer after making an arrest, either with or without a warrant, to take the prisoner, within a reasonable time, before a justice of the peace, magistrate, or other proper judicial officer having jurisdiction, in order that he may be examined and held, or dealt with as the case requires. It is sometimes said that this must be done immediately, or forthwith, or without delay. These requirements are construed to mean no more than that this duty must be performed with all the dispatch and promptness possible under the circumstances. Accordingly, an officer may detain a person arrested in custody for a reasonable time until he can conveniently and safely take him before a magistrate, if the circumstances are such as to preclude an immediate examination, hearing, or trial, as when the arrest was made at night or on Sunday; when the court was not in session; where the prisoner himself occasions the delay, as where he is drunk; or where the arresting officer is unable to find a judicial officer. Similarly, a person arrested may waive his right to be taken before a magistrate, or consent to accompanying an officer without being taken before a magistrate. An officer may not detain a person arrested in custody longer than is reasonably necessary under the circumstances, or arbitrarily refuse to place a formal charge against a prisoner, thus preventing him from obtaining bail; nor may an officer detain the person arrested for any purpose other than to take him before a magistrate, and accordingly, it has been held that a peace officer may not keep a person arrested in his custody for an unreasonable length of time in order to procure evidence from him, or to obtain his confession." 6 *Corpus Juris Secundum* 618.

however, should grant reasonable privileges to prisoners in their custody when doing so does not jeopardize the success of their investigation.

Some arrested persons, however, should be investigated by the detective or some other special division. When members of the special division are not on duty, this action means holding the prisoner for them within the limits of the period considered to be reasonable. The police objective is sometimes but not invariably jeopardized when such prisoners are permitted to communicate with accomplices, relatives, or friends, by telephone or by other prisoners acting as intermediaries. Such privileges should not be denied except when clearly warranted by circumstances, and then only during the period of time indicated above.

The authority to deny such privileges should be restricted to designated commanding officers. The privileges should not be withheld when justification for their denial no longer exists. Procedures should be established to assure prompt investigation by the members of the special division for whom the prisoner is being held. Records should be devised to safeguard the interests of both the police and the prisoner and to place positive responsibility for oversight or poor judgment.

A form prepared by the booking officer on a prisoner to be held for investigation may contain spaces for such pertinent information as that relating to the circumstances which justify holding the prisoner, the date and the hour the authorization was signed by the commanding officer, the circumstances that justify the denial of communications in cases where this action is taken, the date and hour on which the right of communication was restored and by whom. This form, with a duplicate of the investigation report prepared by the arresting officer, when forwarded, serves to notify the special division of the facts and the need for immediate attention. Regulations should require the completion of the investigation and the return of the form, properly filled out and signed, to the booking officer before the end of that business day. A failure to adhere to this time schedule should be referred to the chief or to some commanding officer designated by him for a decision as to holding the prisoner under investigation for a longer period.

A duplicate of the form may be clipped to the arrest card in the jail index; the custodial staff is thus notified of restrictions imposed on designated prisoners and a supervisory officer may detect failures to complete the investigation before the end of the day by an inspection of the index. Small departments may indicate restrictions of privileges on the arrest card and thus make the use of this duplicate unnecessary.

Some departments prepare an extra copy of the arrest card to inform the members of the detective division of persons in jail who require their attention. This procedure is wasteful of paper, since only a small proportion of the prisoners need to be investigated by the special divisions; it wastes the time of the detectives by requiring them to scan all arrest records; responsibility for the investigation is likely to be confused, and detectives may then undertake to investigate prisoners held for other special divisions.

Decision 18. Is there need for a jail sheet or register to show persons in jail each morning?

A jail register containing the names of all persons in jail each morning, prepared with a suitable number of copies, has the following uses: (1) A copy provides information to each division as to persons in jail; similar information is provided to the sheriff's office or other police department that may undertake the daily exchange of jail registers. (2) The register facilitates accounting for prisoners at the end of each shift and their control at all times; restrictions on privileges are noted on it. (3) The register serves to establish the cell location of prisoners; it gives information which is needed in an investigation of a crme alleged to have been committed in jail and reported after the release of many or all prisoners present at the time.

The register of the previous day, checked against the alphabetical jail file for accuracy, serves as a copy from which a new jail sheet is made each morning. The old register is then filed in the records office. The original of the jail register is used by the jailers during that day. As restrictions on privileges are imposed or removed, notations are inserted; as prisoners are placed in jail, their names are added, and as they are released, their names are crossed off; as they are moved from one cell to another, corrections are made.

Identification Records

Identification records include fingerprints, photographs, and records of the physical characteristics of arrested persons. Decisions must be made as to where, when, by whom, and on which prisoners identification records are to be prepared, and the nature of the records that are to be made.

Decision 19. Where should prisoners be fingerprinted and photographed and by whom?

Prisoners should be fingerprinted and photographed in the jail area or in an office immediately adjacent to the jail area and so located as to permit entry of its single door without passing through a public space or an area containing escape routes. These restrictions on the location of the fingerprinting room lessen the escape hazard; when the room is within the jail area, time is not wasted in taking the prisoner from and returning him to jail.

Prisoners should be fingerprinted and photographed by the jail staff rather than by identification officers. Time spent in going to the jail from the identification quarters is thus saved. This procedure also makes 24-hour service by identification officers unnecessary since it assures that prisoners will be fingerprinted regardless of the hour of their release. The necessary skills may be easily acquired by any patrolman.

Decision 20. Should a chronological record be kept of prisoners who are fingerprinted and photographed?

A chronological record of all persons fingerprinted and photographed should be kept in a bound book, showing the identification number, the name, date, and fingerprint classification. This record permits determination of the identification of any person by his identification number; when not all who are fingerprinted are photographed, this record is essential to ascertain the number that has been photographed or fingerprinted during the current month.

Decision 21. Which prisoners should be fingerprinted?

The advantages of identification by finderprints are so great and the cost is so small as to justify a policy of fingerprinting all prisoners permitted by law. Many departments follow the practice of fingerprinting every person who is placed in jail as well as those immediately released on bail whose offense permits such action. The police should attempt to increase rather than to reduce the number fingerprinted. Local persistent offenders who may be jailed at frequent intervals and whose identity has only recently been established by fingerprints should, nevertheless, be fingerprinted each time they are placed in jail on a new offense.

One exception should be made to the policy of fingerprinting as many prisoners as possible. The psychic harm that may be done to most juvenile offenders and the relatively small identification value of the fingerprint in the case of most juveniles raises serious question as to the advisability of fingerprinting them as a general rule. An exception should be made of the persistent offender, especially one who specializes in crimes where latent prints may be left at the scene. The exception, however, should be authorized by the head of the juvenile division or by the chief of police.

Decision 22. Should a copy of all fingerprints be forwarded to the F.B.I. and to the state bureau of identification?

In order for fingerprints to serve their maximum usefulness to the local department and to all other law enforcement agencies it is imperative that copies be sent to both the F.B.I. and the state bureau. Other police agencies who may have arrested the subject in the past are thus informed of his present whereabouts; the identification sheet sent by the federal or state bureau will give the local department the past criminal record of the subject and also inform them of future arrests reported to these bureaus by fingerprints.

Decision 23. Should a separate folder or envelope be placed in a cabinet for each fingerprint card in the file?

Many departments maintain cabinet drawers filled with manila envelopes or folders, one for each fingerprint card. These envelopes or folders are usually filed according to the identification number but some departments file them alphabetically. In the envelopes or folders are usually placed identification sheets received from the F.B.I. and the state bureau, extra fingerprint cards, extra photographs, the photograph negative, investigation reports, correspondence, statements or confessions, and other documents relating to criminal trials in which the subject has been the defendant.

This procedure is ill-advised. A substantial portion of the space is taken by the folders themselves. The cost of cabinets, floor space, and folders or envelopes, makes this procedure expensive. The procedure also causes some confusion in filing and searching for documents relating to a criminal case. Documents relating to a criminal case should be filed in the case file. Extra copies of photographs must be stored in a readily accessible location so that copies may be delivered to authorized enforcement officers. The most desirable procedure is to file all extra copies according to identification number in cabinet drawers of a size to accommodate the photographs. The negatives should be filed in drawers of suitable size in a fireproof cabinet located in or near the dark room. It is considered illadvised from a point of view of fire hazard, time lost in transfer, and added danger of loss, to store the negatives in the records office. When these procedures are followed, there remain in the folder only the identification sheets.

A criminal history file should be created to store identification sheets received from the F.B.I. and the state bureau. Only the latest sheet from each bureau should be retained. The criminal history file will thus consist of nothing more than identification sheets filed according to identification number. These will occupy relatively little space.

Decision 24. Should all prisoners who are fingerprinted be photographed?

The fingerprint, which is the basic identification record, is supplemented by the photograph. The photograph does not provide such positive and irrefutable identification, although it has a value in visual identification lacking in the fingerprint. The photograph is several times more expensive than the fingerprint. The decision to photograph prisoners must be based on the advantages of identification by inspection of a photograph weighed against the added cost.

Criminals seen by their victims or by witnesses may be identified by means of their photographs. A relatively small proportion of all persons placed in jail will be guilty of crimes that will enable their identification by this means. While it is manifestly impossible to foretell with certainty which prisoners are likely to be observed in future crimes and thus be susceptible to identification from their photographs, those who have been guilty of such crimes in the past are more likely to offend similarly than those who have not. In view of the expense of photographing all prisoners, therefore, it seems wise to adopt a policy of photographing only selected categories of prisoners. For example, photographs may be taken of those charged with felonies, larcenies, frauds, and certain sex offenses, as well as exceptional prisoners ordered photographed by a commanding officer. Color photography is used advantageously by some departments.

Decision 25. Should full-length photographs and group photographs be taken of some prisoners?

The identification value of a photograph is increased as it includes a greater portion of the body. For this reason full-length photographs of very serious offenders are desirable. There are also advantages in taking group photographs of criminals who operate together. Identification by the victim or a witness who has seen the criminals operating together is more likely from a full-length photograph of a group of two or more criminals than from individual photographs of their heads and shoulders.

Decision 26. How should photographs of criminals be filed?

Photographs of some criminals should be filed according to their criminal specialty in a Kardex type file. The criminal specialties used in classifying the photographs will be influenced by the relative frequency of the several types and would ordinarily be restriced to major offenses. For example, sections of the file may be established for sex crimes, burglaries, robberies, frauds, checks, auto theft, and grand larceny. When the number of Negroes justifies, a separate subdivision may be established for them. The photographs within each group should be arranged according to height. The photograph of a criminal may appear in more than one place in the file in the event he has demonstrated a varied criminal specialization.

Decision 27. Should a single-fingerprint file and a physical-defects file be established?

Two factors must be considered in determining the justification for the creation of either a single-fingerprint file or of a physical-defects file: (1) the size of the community; and (2) the extent to which crimes are committed by transient or out-of-town criminals. The creation of either of these files is not justified in the department in a small community, or in a larger suburban community in which much of the crime is committed by out-of-town criminals. The police in large communities, especially those in which much of the crime is committed by local criminals, should maintain both files. The large department should provide identification service based on the use of there files to suburban communities; this service further justifies their maintenance.

Decision 28. Should a questionable-character file be established?

The desirability of maintaining a questionable-character file is also influenced by the two factors that influence the advisability of installing a single-fingerprint file or a physical-defects file. A police department is justified in establishing a questionable-character file, however, before there is justification for the installation of the other two. The file should include all known sex offenders.

A questionable-character file, used in conjunction with a map on which the residence and location of employment of the subjects are spotted in a manner to indicate their criminal specialty provides officers with information regarding potential offenders in areas where criminal attacks have occurred. They also inform officers of potential offenders who may reside or work on their beats, and thus assist patrolmen to give these persons suitable attention. A locator file, with dividers to correspond to the map grid coordinates or street names and block numbers, facilitates the identification of each person spotted on the map.

Decision 29. How may the modus operandi and physical characteristics of the unknown perpetrator of a current crime be compared with those of known criminals in order to expedite the discovery of likely suspects? Also, how is it possible to ascertain whether a recent crime was probably committed by the same unknown person who has committed other crimes of the same class?

M.O. *(modus operandi)* searching may be said to fall into three general categories: (1) when an offender is in custody and some pattern can be identified in his criminal behavior, files may be searched for all recorded offenses which he may have committed, (2) files of uncleared offenses may be searched to discover those with M.O. patterns similar to a current unsolved crime, and (3) when a method of operation is observed in a series of uncleared crimes, search may be made against the M.O. patterns of known offenders in order to pick out likely suspects. The objective is the same in all three categories, *i.e.*, to discover cases that match in a given number of M.O. characteristics. When any volume of reports is involved in M.O. searching, consideration should be given to mechanical equipment available for this purpose.

Identification through M.O. characteristics can be effectively accomplished by the use of an electrical test-scoring device, although the use of this apparatus requires an operator to note the dial reading on each sheet, which is a slow process as compared to the punch-card collator which automatically selects cards that are alike in certain specific characteristics. The following procedure makes it possible to ascertain, by a test-scoring machine, whether a recent crime was probably committed by the same unknown person who has committed other crimes of the same class:

The M.O. characteristics of all crimes are coded on suitably designed sheets, similar to test-scoring sheets, using a special soft lead pencil for this purpose. The current crime has its M.O. characteristics similarly recorded. The sheet of the current crime is placed in the scoring machine, thus serving as the key to "right answers." The M.O. sheets of previous crimes of the same class are then placed in the machine, one at a time; the number of M.O. characteristics of each that are similar to the characteristics of the current crime is then indicated by a needle on a dial which shows the number of "right answers." Crimes that resemble the current one in any desired number of M.O. characteristics may thus be discovered; the corresponding cases may be drawn from the files for more careful scrutiny to discover the likelihood that they were committed by the same perpetrator. Likewise, when the M.O. characteristics of known criminals are thus recorded according to their criminal specialty, the sheets may be put through the scoring device in the same manner in order to discover known criminals who have committed crimes with M.O. characteristics similar to the current crime in any desired number.

The advantage of the electrical test-scoring device lies in the fact that all sheets that are alike in any desired number of M.O. characteristics may be discovered in a single run. With a punch-card collator many runs must be made to accomplish the same purpose. For example, if in a given class of crime 25 M.O. characteristics are recorded on test-scoring sheets, the operator may select all sheets that have 5, 10, 15, or any other desired number of characteristics similar to the current one without regard to which of the 25 characteristics they are. The number of similar characteristics that should be taken as the cut-off point (those having this number or more similar characteristics then deserve more careful scrutiny) will obviously vary with the class of crime.

The electrical test-scoring apparatus may also be used to advantage in the identification of probable suspects by means of the verbal description of the criminal furnished by the victim and witnesses. The description should be as detailed as possible; it should include the height, weight, age, hair and eye color, build, complexion, marks, scars, and deformities and peculiarities; it should also include a detailed description of the features as well as the idiosyncracies of movement and mannerism of the criminal. When the scoring device is arranged to compare the described characteristics of the criminal with those of all known persons engaged in this criminal specialty, sheets containing the descriptions of persons in this group may be run through the machine. The operator should select those having any specified number of characteristics identical to those of the wanted man. The photographs and descriptions of the selected suspects may then be scrutinized by the victim and witnesses in the hope of identifying the wanted criminal.

The IBM 101 statistical machine, although more expensive than either the test scoring device or the collator, accomplishes the purpose more rapidly and effectively than either of the others. This machine is designed for the purpose of high speed classifying and counting and for the preparation of printed statistical reports. There is combined in one unit the functions of selecting, editing, counting, accumulating, printing, and balancing. The machine automatically distributes cards into 13 pockets according to the type of data being selected. Through the wiring of a flexible control panel, the selection in any one pocket may be the result of the card meeting several conditions or any desired combination of conditions. For example, in a series of burglaries in which 15 distinctive characteristics are noted, the M.O. file on known burglars will reveal in a matter of minutes all known offenders whose patterns of operation correspond with these characteristics in any designated number whatever without regard to which of the 15 characteristics they are. This equipment can also be used to identify suspects from a physical description given by the victim or witnesses.

Indexes

Maximum usefulness of records is assured through indexes that enable the speedy and certain identification of records, persons, and property. Decisions must be made as to the kind of indexes that should be installed.

Decision 30. Should separate name indexes be maintained or are advantages gained by the consolidation of some or all into one?

Name indexes maintained by some departments are legion; complaint, arrest, identification, accident drivers, nicknames, and correspondence indexes are sometimes further multiplied by having separate ones for each calendar year. Sometimes valuable information concealed in a separate index is overlooked, whereas one general index enables a determination in one search of all contacts the police have had with the subject. The identification of badly wanted persons is sometimes made through such simple and relatively innocent incidents as accidents, complaints, correspondence, and arrests for drunkenness and other minor offenses. Such identifications are not likely to be made unless the two index cards bearing the pertinent information are brought together in the same index. No matter whether the subject is currently a complainant, a suspect, a person under arrest, an accident driver, or a correspondent, the history of his relationships with the department is helpful to the police. One name index also lessens the possibility of an index card being inadvertently filed in the wrong index. One general name index is, therefore, considered essential for speedy and effective operation.

In spite of the maintenance of one general name index, there may be justification for maintaining carbon copies of certain index cards in a cabinet at a location removed from the central records office. For example, correspondence files may be maintained by the chief and division heads for letters that do not relate directly to police incidents. This correspondence should be indexed in duplicate; the original index card should be filed in the general name index; the copy may be placed in an index near the correspondence filing cabinet to facilitate its search.

In departments that issue a large number of citations, and especially in those that use notices of violation with action based on the driving record of the motorist, the volume of tickets may make it impractical to file them in the general name index. In these departments a driver index should be established for this exclusive purpose. This arrangement also permits the index to be placed at a location where an officer, held at a post for important but infrequent tasks, may occupy his spare time operating the index. Carbon copies of index cards for accident drivers and for traffic offenders who are booked should also be filed in the driver index;

the original copy of these index cards should be placed in the general name index.

Decision 31. Which names appearing in an incident report (offense, miscellaneous report, lost and found, or accident) should be indexed?

Index cards should be prepared for every name appearing in the reports, including aliases and nicknames but excluding the names of witnesses, possible witnesses, and police officers. The names of officers should be included, however, when they are involved in the incident as a victim, complainant, or offender.

Decision 32. Should index cards be removed from the file for the purpose of inserting additional information?

The addition of new information on an index card already in file necessitates a search before the indexing operation can be undertaken. This is a costly operation not justified by the saving of a few index cards. Index cards should be prepared from the basic reports; when correctly filed they will be placed beside other cards on the same person already on file.

Decision 33. Should name indexes be arranged purely alphabetically or should a phonetic system be used?

The principal advantage claimed for the phonetic system is that names not accurately spelled are found more speedily and certainly than by the alphabetical system. Experience with the phonetic system in police service has not been sufficiently extensive to permit a sound conclusion as to the relative merits of it and the alphabetical system. The phonetic system is by code. The use of a code may introduce elements of error and delay; inexperienced clerks would seem to be unable to search the phonetic index as rapidly and accurately as the alphabetical index. The cost of converting to a phonetic system is also a serious disadvantage to its use. Future experience must reveal which of the systems is superior.

Decision 34. How should a stolen- and lost-property index be organized?

Departments file index cards bearing descriptions of stolen and lost property either (1) alphabetically by the name of the article described; or (2) in main sections such as athletic goods, books and stationery, building material, cameras, clothing, and so on. Alphabetical filing by the name of the article requires less skill in searching the index and there is less possibility of misfiling. The advantage claimed for classifying the property under general heads is that persons who steal one type of property may also be guilty of the theft of other property of the same type; the stolen-property index thus brings together cards having this common *modus operandi* characteristic. The greater simplicity, accuracy, and speed of operation of the alphabetical arrangement, however, seem to make this system superior to the other.

Decision 35. What number, inscription, and nickname indexes are needed and how should they be organized?

Nicknames and aliases should be filed in the general name index; a separate nickname index is not required. Initials and monograms on stolen and lost property should be filed in an inscription index according to the last letter and subdivided according to the other initials in the same manner as in an alphabetical name index. Full names should be filed in the inscription index in the same manner as in an alphabetical index.

Number indexes should be organized to arrange the numbers as though the digits appeared in reverse order. For example, the number 3456789 should be filed as though it were 9876543; it would be filed under the primary divider 9, the secondary divider 8, the tertiary divider 7, and so on. This is done to assure a more even distribution of the cards throughout the index.

Several number indexes are justified, the number dependent on the volume of cards to be filed. Separate number indexes should be maintained for autos, watches, guns, bicycles, and in larger departments for other selected classes of property bearing serial or motor numbers.

Decision 36. Should printed forms of index cards, and index cards of different colors be used?

The use of printed forms for index cards does not seem justified. Typing time is not saved for the reason that clerks may insert the information on a blank card in a designated order so that the location of the data on the card indicates its nature; superfluous words do not need to be added. A blank card permits greater flexibility in recording needed information than a printed form. Also, printing the form adds to the cost.

Using index cards of different colors for designated purposes facilitates filing and searching and lessens the likelihood of misfiling a card in the wrong index. It enables the file clerk to distinguish readily, in stolen-property, number, and inscription indexes, between property reported lost or stolen, and property pawned or found. Index cards of distinctive colors also call the attention of the file clerk to persons who are wanted, who are on probation or parole, who have licenses subject to revocation, or who have registered personal property.[1]

Decision 37. How should pawn tickets be indexed and filed and by whom?

Immediately on their receipt, pawn tickets bearing numbers and inscriptions should have this information indexed on cards of a color different from those recording stolen property. Clerks who file these cards should report in writing to the detective division any apparent identification with cards already on file. A search of the stolen-property index may be made at this time, but the chance of identification does not justify making a card for this index. Some departments rely on the pawnshop detail to make identifications through the stolen-property index but not through the number and inscription indexes. The advantage of filing an index card on pawn tickets lies in the fact that the article may be reported stolen after it has been pawned; with a card on file, it may be identified when its loss is reported.

The detective secretary, in not-too-large departments, may index the pawn tickets in addition to her other duties.

Decision 38. When mechanical tabulating cards are used, is there need for complaint classification cards?

A duplicate of the "victim" name index card, called a complaint classification index card, is ordinarily made on each offense report or complaint, regardless of its classification (Part I or II, lost and found, casualty, or miscellaneous). The complaint classification index cards are filed according to their principal classification (Parts I to V inclusive), subdivided according to class. Even though tabulating equipment is used, these index cards are needed to identify cases when the name of the victim is not known. They are also useful

---

[1] Red cards are hard on the eyes and for this reason should not be used.

in obtaining other information without the necessity of running large numbers of cards through the mechanical sorting equipment.

Miscellaneous Records

In addition to complaint, arrest, and identification records and their indexes, a number of miscellaneous records are needed. Some incidents that do not justify the preparation of a numbered report should be recorded to assure follow-up, to enable a summary of police activity, to simplify recording the accomplishments of individual officers, and to provide a record for future reference. Summaries must be provided, and provision must also be made for recording and filing general and special orders and other administrative matters, personnel data, inventories, and correspondence that does not relate to numbered cases.

Decision 39. How should officers' reports on unnumbered cases be filed?

A department-memo form is useful for reporting activities and other incidents for which special forms are not used, to enable follow-up, ready reference, and monthly tabulations of police accomplishments. Illness and injury of officers, notes for the daily bulletin, lanterns placed on street obstructions, reports of speeches and of visitors who are taken on tours of inspection of police headquarters, are examples of incidents that may be recorded. Files may be established for each classification. Others that are not so readily classifiable may be filed alphabetically in an officer's report file.

Decision 40. What files should be established for unnumbered cases (cases that do not fall within the categories listed under Decision 7)?

Some incidents, such as store inspections, citations, vacation homes, and so on, are handled by special forms. Those that do not justify a separate form may be recorded as an item on an 8″ × 5″ card by the desk officer or dispatcher when they are reported by patrolmen. The date, hour, location, and officer should be recorded for each incident. Included in this category are doors and windows found unlocked and safe lights not burning, unfounded bank and other alarms, and ambulance calls when the police rely on ambulance service from some other agency. When the police provide ambulance service, a log of ambulance runs should be kept by the drivers.

Some incidents are a special service to other city departments or to public utilities. Included in this group are street-light outages, broken watermains, fire and health hazards, and so on. A special-service report[1] serves to record these items, assures reference to the agency concerned the following business day, and permits a monthly tabulation of the services rendered. In departments that do not use a special-service report, these incidents may be recorded by the desk officer on cards kept for this purpose as described above.

Decision 41. Should a store-report file be maintained and if so, where?

Store reports are a useful device to assure that patrolmen make periodic contacts with the business men on their beats; the reports assure discovery and correction of physical and procedural security weaknesses; they provide the residence addresses and telephone numbers of the managers and their assistants. These advantages justify the use of store reports.[2] They should be placed on file in the communications room where they may be consulted by the dispatcher. They should be filed according to street number under the names of the streets arranged alphabetically.

Decision 42. What form of daily and monthly summaries should be prepared?

The International Association of Chiefs of Police designed Consolidated Daily and Monthly Report forms. The information called for in these two reports should be considered a bare minimum. Key personnel in the smaller departments should be given a daily summary containing more detail than is provided in the Consolidated Daily Report; all departments should have more detailed information on a monthly basis than is contained in the Consolidated Monthly Report. Deviations from the Consolidated Report forms, however, should scrupulously avoid omitting any information contained in them.[3]

---

[1] See *Police Records*, pp. 80-82.
[2] See *Police Records*, pp. 82-84.
[3] Daily summaries and monthly report tables containing greater detail than the Consolidated Reports are shown in *Police Records*, Chapter 9.

Record-forms Control

Attention must be given to the design and routing of record forms in order to increase their utility and the efficiency of office operations. Design effort should be directed at the simplification and standardization of forms and the reduction of their number by consolidation. Control of the ordering of forms is needed to prevent accumulating unnecessary quantities and to prevent their requisition on the eve of a change in design. Study must also be made of the suitability to use of current forms with a view to improvement in design, and search should also be made for forms whose use is no longer needed.

Decision 43. What provision should be made for record-forms control?

Control of the design and ordering of record forms should be made the responsibility of one person who may be identified as the record analyst. His mission is to reduce paper work involved in preparing, reading, processing, analyzing, distributing, and filing forms, and to effect economies in paper and printing costs. In the design of a new form or the modification of an old one, the analyst should give attention to the purpose of the form (the source, value, and use that is to be made of the information that is to be provided by it); to possible consolidation of report forms or the revision of a present form to fill the need for the proposed new form; to the sequence of entries on the form; to the standardization of the size and format so that typewriter tabs set for one form will serve for other similar forms; to the exclusion of space for unessential information; and to the routing of the form.

Communications

Police communications are carried on through telephone, teletype, radio, telegraph, and mail. Since the receipt of complaints and the deployment of the force are both dependent on some form of communication, consideration must be given to the assignment of communications tasks. The location of the communications unit in the organization structure was discussed in Chapter 4.

Decision 44. What duties should be assigned to the communications unit?

The recording of communications is an integral part of the

communications task. In many departments the communications room is called the complaint room; complaints are received by some form of communication, they are recorded, and officers are dispatched by radio, call box, or telephone. The tasks to be performed in the communications or complaint room, therefore, consist of the operation of communications devices and the recording of messages received and sent.

The central complaint or communications officers should operate the telephone PBX board, the radio, teletype, and call boxes, except that, in departments that have district stations, call-box operation should be decentralized with each district station in control of the boxes within its jurisdiction. Records tasks that must be performed consist of the preparation of the radio log,[1] radio assignment records, and the call sheet for recording routine box calls by patrolmen in departments that do not have district stations.

Decision 45. Which of the communication and records tasks listed above should be assigned to the radio dispatcher?

A categorical answer cannot be given to this question. The answer will be influenced by the volume of work, the physical location of communications devices, and the ready availability of records clerks to assist during unexpected peak periods. The volume of work will fluctuate widely but regularly during the hours of the day and night. During some hours the dispatcher may be assigned more tasks than on others. In the interest of economy, the dispatcher should be assigned as many of the tasks as he can manage; this may be done without jeopardizing effective operations when the communications room is located contiguously to the records office so that a clerk may assist when the dispatcher's work is too heavy.

As the volume of work increases, the dispatcher should be relieved first of the operation of the PBX board, the teletype, and call boxes. Dual broadcasting equipment enables the assignment of two dispatchers during peak hours, one to dispatch officers on a previously received complaint while the other is receiving another complaint by telephone. Dual dispatching loses most of its advantages when the load during the hours of least need is so great as to justify two dispatchers.

---

[1] The superior practice of sound-recording all radio transmissions makes unnecessary the burden of maintaining a radio log.

Decision 46. What prepared broadcasts should be filed at the dispatcher's desk?

A broadcast, which the dispatcher may read when an alarm is sounded, should be prepared in advance for each robbery alarm that terminates at police headquarters. This preparation assures that the force will be effectively deployed in a manner planned by the command group and approved by the chief.[1]

Miscellaneous Services

Provision must be made for ambulance, patrol-wagon, and tow-car service and for the storage of abandoned and recovered automobiles. Some policy decisions must be made relating to these facilities.

Decision 47. Should the police department provide ambulance service?

The municipality has a responsibility to provide ambulance service. The police should avoid this task when other arrangements can be made, although some public good will may result when generous police-ambulance service is provided. The alternatives include the provision of this service by the health department or municipal hospital or by contract with private agencies or hospitals. In some communities the morticians eagerly seek the privilege of rendering free ambulance service; the competition between them for the privilege and the necessity of strict impartiality frequently creates a serious problem that is solved by alternating calls or by using the service that is nearest to the scene of the emergency. These procedures, however, are never completely satisfactory; a contract with one reliable firm is the best procedure.

Decision 48. Which officers should be assigned to operate the patrol wagon and the ambulance, and what duties may they perform between runs?

The jail staff is usually best qualified to drive the patrol wagon and ambulance. While they are on such runs, the records staff may perform any needed jail duties. In smaller departments the records staff may manage the jail and also operate the patrol wagon and ambulance. Records duties are suitable fill-in tasks for the ambu-

---

[1] See *Police Records*, pp. 246-252.

lance and patrol-wagon crews, and the jail staff also, when they
are not members of the records division.

Decision 49. ~~What should be the policy of the department in
reference to the transportation of prisoners to headquarters by the
arresting officer in his patrol car?~~

~~The transportation of prisoners to headquarters by the arresting
officer in his patrol car is economically sound; it saves the time of
the patrol-wagon crew and also the time of the arresting officer while
waiting for the wagon. Hazard to the arresting officer should be
guarded against by department regulations that forbit carrying
fighting drunks, or prisoners in the back seat of a patrol car by one
officer, and by training officers in approved procedures in searching
and handcuffing prisoners. Time can sometimes be saved by dispatching an officer from an adjoining beat to assist in the transportation of more than one prisoner instead of dispatching the patrol
wagon. The second patrol car can be left at the scene; after the
delivery of the prisoners, the officers return for the car. To facilitate
the transportation of prisoners, some departments use sedans
equipped with a plexiglass partition to separate the driver's seat from
the rear compartment. Removal of rear interior door latches lessens
the likelihood of escape by the prisoner. After transporting a prisoner, the officer should inspect his automobile for weapons or evidence that may have been concealed in it.~~

*Decision 50. Should the police maintain a tow-service and stor-
age garage for abandoned and recovered vehicles?*

When the police operate their own automotive maintenance
shop, provision must be made for towing disabled police vehicles.
When repairs are made by a central municipal shop, tow-service
should be provided by it. The police should not undertake to provide a tow-service or storage for abandoned and recovered automobiles. These facilities should be obtained by contract with private
garages, the fee being collected from the owner of the vehicle concerned and not from the police department.

CHAPTER 12

The Police Building and Equipment

IN SURVEYING the needs of a police department with a view to increasing its effectiveness, analysis should be made of the headquarters office layout and of police equipment. The suitability of police buildings and equipment to their use strengthens the effectiveness of police operations. Decisions relating to the construction or remodeling of a police building and the selection of equipment, therefore, deserve careful consideration.

The Police Building

If the police building is to serve its purpose most effectively, attention should be given to its location, to the offices to be housed in it, and to its design to assure maximum effectiveness in use.

Decision 1. Where should the police headquarters building be located?

The police receive services from some city departments and render services to others, and conferences between the chief of police and the chief administrative officer of the city are both necessary and desirable. The location of police headquarters near the city hall strengthens interdepartmental relationships. There are advantages, therefore, in locating the police building at a suitably situated civic center.

When lack of space near the city hall, or the unsuitability of its location, necessitates the construction of the police building elsewhere, a site should be selected with the following specifications: (1) The ground area should be adequate to permit off-street parking for all vehicles owned by the department and its members and the public on police business, the addition of wings to meet expanding needs, and the construction of a building of not more than two floors above the ground level in order to lessen stair-climbing by the police and the public and to avoid the need for elevator service except for prisoners. (2) The location should not be far removed from the centers of the area and population served. (3) It should be served by mass-transportation facilities that provide convenience to the maximum number of citizens. (4) It should be so located in reference to the street layout as to permit ready access by automobile to all sections of the community.

Decision 2. What offices besides those of the police should be in the headquarters building?

Space should be provided for the court, judge, clerk, and a traffic-violations bureau as well as for the prosecuting attorney. There are also some advantages to housing the city attorney and his staff in the police building. The economic and service advantages gained by a closer integration of the police and fire forces justify space in the police building for the fire department headquarters staff and its central communications.[1]

Decision 3. What space provisions should be made in the headquarters building for parking, servicing, and repairing police vehicles, and for maintaining traffic devices?

Some garage space should be provided in the police building, especially in sections of the country subject to severe winters. While it may be impractical to provide space for all police vehicles, as a minimum there should be facilities for the storage of all police vehicles that are not in 24-hour service. It is impractical to store abandoned and recovered automobiles at police headquarters.

In order to facilitate supervision and to utilize trusty labor to best advantage, space should be available to house such maintenance and repair services as the police may provide. Facilities at headquarters for trusties to replenish gasoline, oil, and water, clean the windows, and sweep out the interior of vehicles at shift changes, provide more complete supervision of the operation and thus assure more prompt posting of the patrolmen.

Decision 4. What should be done to facilitate the identification of the building and offices within it?

The building should be identified by a suitable sign, preferably of green neon, readily visible from the street. An easily understood building directory should be placed immediately inside the entrance. The information counter should be identified by an attention-demanding neon sign. The room number and a sign showing

---

[1] The integration of police and fire services is discussed in *Police Administration*, pp. 113-114. See also, Charles S. James, *A Frontier of Municipal Safety*, Public Administration Service, Chicago, 1955. 169 pp.

the identity of the unit housed in each office should be placed on the wall at eye-height near the casing that accommodates the door latch. Arrows in corridors should indicate the direction of the location of offices. The name of the officer on duty should be shown on desks and counters.

Decision 5. What general principles should guide the design and construction of the police building?

The police building should be earthquake-, fire-, and flood-proof. It should be designed to resist, with a minimum force, an attack by a mob, and to lessen the danger of sabotage, especially to communications. Its design should enable operations with a greatly reduced force when maximum man power may be required on the street, and with a greatly enlarged force when emergency demands impose a heavy burden on communications and other services.

The building should be designed with first thought to utility and second to servicability and maintenance. The construction material should require as little repair, painting, and maintenance as possible. The floors should be of a material without crevices that permits easy cleaning. The interior should be of a light color. The walls should be of an easily cleaned material, or a six foot wainscoting of such material should be provided.

Attention should be given to acoustics, ventilation, and illumination. The large rooms and corridors will require acoustical treatment. Soundproofing may be needed in the target range area. Ventilation should be assured, especially in areas that are not supplied with windows, such as small questioning rooms, holdover rooms, and prisoners' corridors connecting the booking room, courtroom holdover, and show-up room with the jail. Illumination deserves special attention in offices where clerks are on duty throughout the 24 hours.

The design of the building should also provide for future expansion. In this connection, special attention should be given to partitions that may be readily moved to change the office arrangement, and to ample conduit space for future power, telephone, and communications-cable requirements.

The number of private offices and small rooms should be kept to the minimum required for effective operation. They should be constructed of clear-glass partitions except those that actually require privacy. Unnecessary partitions should be avoided; space separation may be effected by counters.

The police building should also be designed to protect the public from offensive sights and sounds and to lessen the hazard of escape through windows or doors *en route,* in the transportation of prisoners from the street into the booking room.

Windows outside the jail area should be made escape-proof by the use of ornamental grilles. Window and grille construction should permit cleaning the windows readily from the inside.

Doors to rooms from which the general public should be excluded but to which all officers should have access may be equipped with locks operated by the same key. All members of the force may then be supplied with one all-purpose key. Maximum convenience is provided when these doors are equipped with locks that are operated by the key that opens the call boxes.

Decision 6. What principles should guide in the location of the offices in the police building?

First consideration should be given to the location of the records and communications offices and the booking room. When they are located together, maximum service can be provided with minimum man power. Records duties can be used to occupy the spare time of communications officers and the booking clerk; the records staff is available to assist during periods of peak load. This arrangement also simplifies searching records for reports on prisoners and for information that may be needed by the dispatcher.

The detective division has most frequent need for police records information and for taking prisoners from jail for interrogation. Consideration, therefore, should next be given to the location of detective quarters near the records office and booking room.

The office of the patrol-division captain, usually used by his lieutenants on the night shifts, should be located contiguous to the communications room when this can be done. This arrangement simplifies reference by the dispatcher to the patrol commander of important or difficult problems, and it enables the patrol commander to exercise close supervision of important operations. This location also usually places the patrol commander's office nearer the booking room, thus facilitating his supervision of this operation and review of the circumstances that justify the arrest and sometimes restrictions on the privileges of prisoners.

Offices most frequently used by the public should be placed nearest the entrance. Rooms that serve large numbers of citizens, however, should be located so as to avoid crowds in corridors at points that will interfere with routine operations. This applies especially to the location of the courtroom and the traffic-violations bureau. Ample reception space should be provided in some quarters to avoid the use of a corridor as a waiting room.

The vice-division quarters should be located with a view to providing unobtrusive access. A location that will permit informers and undercover operators to call without being observed by other members of the department is most desirable. The juvenile-division quarters likewise should be in a location removed from the principal police activity where juveniles will not come in contact with or see adult prisoners.

The location of the traffic division will be influenced most strongly by the need of this division for considerable floor space. Its relationship to other offices is relatively unimportant; ready access to records is desirable.

The desirable location of the chief's office is also more strongly influenced by the need for space than for relationship with other offices. Provision should be made for a reception room and a conference room. The location of the chief's office near the center of operations is desirable but not as essential as for the detectives and the patrol commander.

Decision 7. What principles should guide in the location and construction of the jail?

The top-floor location of the jail provides maximum security. It is most desirable to connect the jail with the booking room by a jail elevator. When the building design makes impractical the location of the booking room contiguous to the records office, and no other lower floor location has tasks that would occupy the spare time of a booking officer to advantage, the booking room may be placed within the jail area at the exit from the elevator, which may then be of the self-service type.

The jail areas for both male and female prisoners should be designed to prevent the escape of prisoners except through the booking room even though the jailer should be overpowered and his keys taken from him. Passageway doors leading to the court holdover and the show-up room, and the emergency jail door, should be operated by keys not carried by the jailer except when accompanied by a sufficient force to make a jail break unlikely. To avoid placing prisoners in a passageway when the door at the far end is unlocked, a signal light over the door at the jail end should burn except when the door at the far end is unlocked.

The jail area should contain a room for fingerprinting and photographing prisoners, a storeroom for blankets, a pantry or kitchen, a room equipped for medical examination, the jail side of visiting rooms, a padded cell, one or more cells for drunks, one or more cells where the prisoners will lack opportunity to communicate with others, trusties' quarters, and a suitable number of other cells. A room for testing the extent of intoxication of some prisoners, with facilities for making motion pictures of some of the tests, is also desirable. It may adjoin the booking room. Breakproof rooms with reinforced concrete walls and jail windows but not having the characteristics of cells should be provided for some of the female prisoners and for some juveniles.

In the design of the jail, it may be desirable to have some rooms serve both the male and female jail areas. Examples include the room for fingerprinting and photographing prisoners, the show-up room, a room for medical examinations, and the kitchen. When this is done, the women's jail, under the control of a matron, should be recognized as a weak point; steps should be taken to prevent the hazard of having the doors into the rooms from both jail areas unlocked simultaneously. Regulations prohibiting this practice may be enforced by an arrangement that sounds a loud gong when both doors are unlocked at the same time.

A street call box, operating as a station off the PBX board, should be bolted to the wall in each jail area for the convenience of prisoners and the jail staff. This type of installation will withstand considerable abuse, and calls can be controlled by locking the door and also by the PBX operator.

When the continuous presence of the jailer is not required in jail and he is assigned fill-in tasks at some other location, a warning bell should be installed in the booking room, to be operated by a trusty in the cell block, to summon assistance in the event of an emergency such as the attempted suicide of a prisoner.

A solid steel emergency door should be provided to facilitate the evacuation of the jail in the event of a catastrophe. This door also permits the entry by some means other than by the regular route in the event of a jail emergency such as an uprising of the prisoners.

Decision 8. What principles should guide in the location and characteristics of property storage?

The police building should be designed to facilitate the receipt and disbursement of property and to safeguard its storage. A table, supplied with wrapping paper, twine, and labels, should be located near the vehicle entrance to the building for the convenience of officers who bring recovered and found property to headquarters. A nearby storeroom, preferably unlocked by a call-box or other key in the possession of all officers, permits the temporary storage of bulky articles of no great value until the following day when the property clerk may move them to a permanent storeroom. Articles of greater value and small bulk should be delivered to the booking officer, an information or records clerk, or other clerk at a conveniently located post that provides 24-hour service. Storage space should be provided for safeguarding this property until it is removed to a permanent storeroom.

Maximum convenience is provided by a storeroom located within the records-office layout. The records office should also have a storage room for office supplies; this room may also be utilized for other department supplies. An archive for old records should also be provided.

A locker for storing physical evidence should be supplied for each evidence technician with keys restricted to one for the investigator and one for the laboratory staff.

The security of vice evidence is usually increased by providing a vault for its safekeeping within the vice-division quarters. The bulk of such articles as furniture and some gambling equipment, however, justifies their storage in the custody of the property clerk in a storeroom designed for this purpose.

Parts and supplies needed in any repair or maintenance tasks performed by the police should be stored in the area in which the service is rendered. Storage space should be provided for them.

Decision 9. What provision should be made for the transfer of records?

The physical transfer of records from one office to another becomes more difficult as the size of the building makes necessary a greater separation of offices that perform tasks involving the use of the same records. Especially is this true when the booking officer or the complaint clerk are removed from the records office. These records may be quickly transferred from one point to another in the police building by pneumatic tube. In a large headquarters building, pneumatic tubes may also be used to transport records to the chief's office, the detective quarters, and other locations a considerable distance from the records office. When one location is immediately above another, some form of dumb-waiter may be installed to expedite the transfer.

The distribution of records among operating units is facilitated by the use of a form of mailbox in a counter at a central point through which the records normally flow. Slots in the counter permit the attendant to drop records into the appropriate boxes; the contents may be periodically removed by members of the unit for which they are intended by a door on the corridor side. Similar boxes for traffic tickets and reports are a convenience for the officers.

Decision 10. What provision should be made for locker space and lavatory facilities?

Within its own area, each division should have a lavatory and a locker room with space for a locker for each member and a full length mirror. Lockers in a room designed for another purpose are undesirable.

Decision 11. What provision should be made for showing prisoners?

A show-up room has greatest facility when installed in the squad room used by the patrol division. Show-ups may then be held at each shift change, and members of other divisions may attend. The show-up room should be connected with the jail areas by separate passageways; when the squad room is not on the jail floor, spiral stairs may be a part of the passageways. A locked door at the show-up end of each passageway should exclude prisoners from the show-up stage until admitted by the officer in charge.

A screen of black net in front of a suitably illuminated show-up stage will permit officers to view the prisoners but at the same time prevent the prisoners from seeing the spectators when the squad-room lights are off.

Decision 12. What provision should be made for storing department-owned firearms and gas equipment?

The police arsenal should be under the control of the property clerk. Some weapons, however, should be stored in a cabinet located at a point where it will be under the surveillance of a clerk at a post requiring 24-hour duty, and by which headquarters officers will pass when leaving the building on an emergency call requiring such weapons. The cabinet should contain a suitable number of rifles, machine guns, gas guns and grenades, and bullet-resisting shields. It should be equipped with an electrically operated door.

Equipment

Consideration must also be given to the adequacy and suitability to its use of communications equipment, vehicles, armaments, and other equipment. Decisions must be reached in reference to the ownership of some equipment. Should it be purchased by the department, rented from a private firm, or furnished by the officer either with or without remuneration?

Communications Equipment

The communications equipment that deserves attention in surveying the needs of the department include the telephone switchboard and its stations; the radio, teletype, call-box, and re-call signal systems; and the intercommunicating devices.

Decision 13. How many telephone trunk lines are needed to meet the demands for service?

Trunk lines should be provided in sufficient number to make it unlikely that a person would receive a busy signal when telephoning police headquarters during the hour of most frequent telephone calls. As a service to its users, the telephone company checks the frequency of busy signals on request. Peak hours on the days of heaviest volume of telephone calls should be selected for the checks, and they should be made at least annually to avoid the possibility of seriously overloading the trunk capacity.

Decision 14. How many positions should be provided on the private branch exchange (PBX) switchboard?

The volume of telephone calls will influence the need for more than one position. When the ordinary peak load may be handled by a one-position board, the availability of the equipment to meet unusual needs (such as on Halloween) that may occur once or twice a year may justify the installation of a two-position board. The equipment is then available to handle the added load that results from any catastrophe. When the cost of maintaining a two-position board for meeting infrequent needs is considered ill-advised, the unusual load may be handled by having temporarily installed in the records office or other suitable room a telephone instrument for each trunk, plugged in so that calls may be taken by operators stationed at each instrument. Provision must then be made for the transmission of the calls (recorded on memos or radio assignment sheets) to the dispatcher by runner or other means.

Decision 15. Where should telephone instruments be placed as stations off the PBX board?

Each office and desk having an officer assigned during a tour of duty should have a telephone instrument. Provision should likewise be made for telephones in the jail, garage, service quarters where personnel may be employed, and squad room. In areas where the use of the telephone may be abused, the instrument may be housed in a call box with a locked door to be opened by the key carried by all officers.

Decision 16. Should two- or three-way radio be installed?

All police vehicles including motorcycles should be equipped with two-way radio. Transmitters in police vehicles that permit a communication between cars provide some advantages, but confusion as to who is in command and abuse in use for non-police purposes argue against its installation. When three-way equipment is installed, the temptation to use this equipment for non-police purposes must be curbed by strictly enforced department regulations.

Decision 17. Should a call-selector be installed?

When motorized patrolmen follow the previously described patrol procedure they will spend a substantial part of their time on foot; the inspection of store doors may take them some distance from their vehicles. When officers are to be out of ear-shot of their radio for some time, they should report off the air. There is an advantage, however, in having equipment which will enable the dispatcher to summon an officer who may be out of ear-shot of his radio.

A call-selector, by a dial control, enables the dispatcher to actuate a relay on any selected police vehicle that will sound the horn or turn on a signal light mounted on the top of or inside the car. This arrangement converts each police vehicle into a mobile visual or auditory re-call signal. The advantages are obvious.

Decision 18. How may the dispatcher be kept informed regarding the availability of officers for radio dispatch?

The effective deployment of officers on calls requires that the dispatcher be continuously informed regarding their availability for service. A beat map should be provided for each shift on which the availability of the beat officers is indicated by some device that will show that the officer has been sent on a call or has reported off the air.

The simplest and least expensive indicator of the avaibility of a motorized beat officer is a small bar magnet. When the maps are mounted on sheet metal, a magnet on each beat may be placed on its base, side, or end, to signify that the officer is available for dispatch, has been sent on a call, or is off the air.

A more satisfactory but expensive device for this purpose is a system of lights, one for each beat, arranged with three-position switches that enable the lights to be turned on bright (to indicate the availability of the beat officer), to burn dimly (to indicate that the officer has been dispatched on a call), or to be turned off (to indicate that the officer is off the air). While the officer who has been sent on a call should not ordinarily be dispatched on another call, in the event of a serious incident it is sometimes possible to reach him before he reports back.

The dispatcher should also have information regarding the availability by radio of officers who are not assigned to beats. Included in this category are patrol sergeants, evidence technicians, motorized traffic officers, and specialists from other divisions (detectives and juvenile-division officers are the principal ones) and officers of higher rank in the patrol division who may spend part of their time driving radio-equipped vehicles. Information as to the availability of officers for radio dispatch who are not assigned to beats may be provided by a panel of lights (readily placed on the side of the beat map) to burn in the above described manner.

In some departments switches operated in the offices of division subordinates actuate a similar panel of lights on the desks of division captains and secretaries so that the presence of an officer at headquarters is readily ascertained. His availability by radio is made known to the division secretary by a second row of lights on the panel tied into the circuit operated by and serving the dispatcher. When the latter lights are arranged to be turned on or off by switches at the desk of both the dispatcher and the division secretary, the specialist may report off and on the air to either point. When this is done, two-position, three-way switches must be substituted for the previously described three-position switches to activate the lights.

Decision 19. What files should be readily available to the dispatcher?

The dispatcher should have, at his desk, files that contain information that may be requested by patrolmen or that may assist in their deployment. Included are store reports, frequently used telephone numbers, prepared broadcasts on each establishment equipped with direct-line robbery alarms, and sketches of the floor plan including streets and alleys of all establishments equipped with ADT or other burglar alarms. Provision should be made for ready communication with records clerks so that information from the records office may be quickly obtained.

Decision 20. Should a reserve transmitter be provided?

A reserve transmitter on the headquarters-station wavelength should be available for use in the event of sabotage or a catastrophe that disables the headquarters instrument. When the reserve transmitter is mounted on a truck or trailer it may be stored some distance from headquarters to lessen the chance of damage by the circumstance that disables the headquarters set. This arrangement also provides a flexibility that proves useful when a transmitter is needed in the direction of police operations some distance from headquarters.

Decision 21. Should an emergency electric-power supply be provided at headquarters?

The vulnerability of the commercial electric-power supply to sabotage, strike, flood, storm, and other incidents that may cause a power failure makes it imperative that the police install at headquarters a generator powered by a gasoline engine. The generator should provide sufficient power to operate the radio transmitter and lights at important points in the headquarters building. The equipment should be arranged to go into operation automatically on a power failure.

Decision 22. Should call boxes be installed, and if so, what type should be used and what factors should be considered in determining the number and their locations?

Police radio does not eliminate the need for call boxes. They are essential for communicating with foot patrolmen, for detailed and lengthy conversations with motorized patrolmen, for communications deserving greater secrecy than is provided by the radio, and for the convenience of officers telephoning their reports for sound recording. The call box establishes the location of the officer making a routine time call, a feature still lacking in radio communication. The call box enables telephone conversation with headquarters without the necessity of using a business or private telephone or a pay station. Business and private telephones lack secrecy and their use may be an imposition on a citizen. Pay stations are sometimes not available, especially late at night. Regulations should forbid an officer to accept a key that provides access to a private telephone at night.

Call boxes installed by the local telephone company as stations off the PBX board are preferred to private installations. The police are thus freed of maintenance tasks and are provided a superior service. This arrangement also provides greater flexibility in communications. The call from an officer at a call box may be transferred to any office at headquarters and the officer may be given an outside line to make a needed telephone call.

The number of essential call boxes is influenced by the area of the community and the number of foot beats. The boxes should be concentrated in areas patrolled by men on foot who have no other official means of communication with headquarters. As a minimum, foot patrolmen should have call boxes within three blocks and motorized officers within a half mile of any part of their beats. On sparsely settled motorized beats, the call boxes may be spaced a greater distance. They should be at strategic locations where they will serve the largest number of patrolmen and where their presence may cause a desired concentration of man power.

Decision 23. Should a system of re-call lights be installed?

While re-call lights are not as essential as call boxes, their value in communicating with foot patrolmen justifies their installation when the cost is not great. The installation cost must be weighed against the cost of other needed equipment in reaching a decision.

Decision 24. Should teletype be installed?

Departments within a state-operated teletype network should make themselves members of it. District stations should invariably be tied to the central communications room by teletype. Teletype may also be used to advantage in large headquarters buildings in the immediate transmission of a copy of a typed daily bulletin to division offices.

Decision 25. What type of interoffice communication should be provided?

The desks of commanding officers and some subordinates at key positions should be tied together with a system of interoffice communication that will permit any one to speak by means of a transmitter on his desk to any selected station in the system. Loud speakers at strategic locations in the headquarters building enable the transmission of messages, including selected radio broadcasts, to selected locations or throughout the system. This arrangement facilitates locating an officer who may be temporarily away from his desk.

Motor-vehicle Equipment

Consideration must be given to the condition, ownership, adequacy of number, and suitability to their use of motor vehicles, and to their assignment in a manner to assure maximum use.

Decision 26. What principles should guide in the selection of motor vehicles for patrol and general police service?

Operating cost should be the primary consideration in the selection of motor vehicles for general police service. The operating cost is determined by the initial cost and probable trade-in value, gasoline and oil consumption, and the cost of repairs necessitated by breakdown and collision or upset. Body, fender, and chassis repairs are more expensive on some cars than on others. As a general rule small, light cars are more economical and maneuverable than heavier ones. The small size of the vehicle, however, should not hamper the movements of the occupants nor prevent them from quickly alighting from it.

High performance in speed and acceleration should be considered in the selection of a police vehicle, but its importance should not be overemphasized. These performance qualities invariably increase the operating cost. While it is desirable for the police to overtake speeding motorists, it is not essential that they be supplied with vehicles that are faster than any other on the road. It is better for the police to have an adequate number of less-powerful cars than a deficient number of very powerful ones. The specialists do not need powerful, expensive vehicles, although traffic officers need fast ones.

The closed car is best suited for police service. It affords protection from inclement weather, can be readily heated, and protects the occupants when upset in an accident. The two-door coach body is usually less expensive than the sedan, their wider windows usually afford a less obstructed view, and prisoners may be transported in the rear seat by two officers with less opportunity to escape. Some departments use, for patrol, sedans with plexiglass partitions separating the front and rear compartments, as described on page 200.

Decision 27. What type of vehicle should be provided for traffic service?

The solo motorcycle should not be used in police work because its operation is excessively expensive. The high cost of operation results from the usual practice of assigning a machine to the exclusive use of one rider, the need for replacement at a lower mileage than an automobile, the relatively heavier accident-repair costs, the salary increment usually paid to riders, the loss of time resulting from injuries, the cost of pensions paid to disabled riders and to the dependents of those who are killed, the cost of maintaining crippled riders on the payroll to perform tasks for which they are unsuited, and the salary loss represented by ineffectively used riders during inclement weather when motorcycles are not permitted to operate. To the prohibitive financial cost of solo motorcycles must be added the lives of officers killed each year in their operation.

The automobile should be used for the enforcement of moving-traffic regulations. It is safer and less expensive to operate than a motorcycle,[1] it has greater maneuverability at high speeds, it is an

---

[1] The City of Louisville Department of Finance, in 1950, reported a per-mile cost of $.0710 for operating police patrol cars as compared to $.0625 for solo motorcycles. The figures were restricted to actual operating costs.

all-weather and all-road vehicle, and it provides protection from inclement weather. The solo motorcyle has only two advantages over the automobile. It can be turned around to proceed in the opposite direction more readily and it can be ridden through narrow spaces between lines of traffic where a car could not pass. The necessity for turning around to pursue vehicles traveling in the opposite direction seems unimportant since there are usually a sufficient number of violators traveling in the same direction as the officer to keep him occupied. Since he cannot hope to arrest all violators, the escape of the one going in the opposite direction should not ordinarily be considered especially serious. The need for getting through narrow lanes also does not arise with sufficient frequency to justify the use of the solo motorcyle for this reason alone. The three-wheeled motorcyle may be used in congested areas; it may be driven through most spaces that will permit the passage of a solo machine.

The three-wheeler is especially well suited to the enforcement of time-limit and other parking regulations. It may be operated with little hazard, it does not require the operation of a stand when the rider dismounts, and it permits travel with less attention to its operation than the two-wheeled machine. An officer on a three-wheeler is able to check from five to ten times as many blocks of time-limit parking as an officer on foot.

Decision 28. What are the patrol-wagon, ambulance, and emergency-vehicle requirements in police service?

Patrol-wagon requirements will be influenced by the size and character of the population, the extent of drunkenness, and the policy in regard to the transportation of prisoners in patrol cars. Patrol wagons should be constructed so that the rear door may be fastened from the outside so that an officer will not need to ride with the prisoners or on the rear step. The interior should be illuminated by a protected light controlled by a switch in the driver's compartment. The driver's compartment should be separated from the prisoners' section by a substantial partition with an aperture to permit an officer in the front to observe the prisoners but so constructed that a prisoner can not injure him through it with any weapon except a gun. The interior should be free of articles that may be used as weapons, including bars and supports that may be wrenched from their moorings for this purpose. Patrol wagons should be equipped with stretchers so that they may be pressed into ambulance service in the event of an unusual emergency and also to enable them to handle stretcher cases when the need arises in routine operations.

When the police are required to furnish ambulance service, a suitable vehicle should be used for this purpose. Care should be observed not to send the ambulance on drunk calls and other cases in which the patrol wagon is a more suitable conveyance.

Some municipalities maintain elaborate equipment on heavy-duty vehicles designed to assist in accidents where heavy objects must be moved, steel plates cut through, and other tasks performed that require construction skills and equipment. Some also maintain boats, diving equipment, and grappling hooks for use in water accidents. The nature of the equipment and the work to be done with it seem more closely related to fire-department operations than to police activities. Fire departments are more likely to have space for the storage of such equipment and men skilled in its use than the police. For these reasons it is recommended that the fire department be charged with the maintenance and operation of such equipment instead of the police.

Decision 29. How should police vehicles be identified for control purposes and what equipment should they carry?

Each police vehicle should be allotted a department number to facilitate assignments and the preparation of service and maintenance records. The number should be stenciled near the gasoline-tank cap and also under the hood to facilitate the recording of the number when the vehicle is serviced.

Police vehicles should be equipped with small portable fire extinguishers; small first-aid kits; a dome light so located as to provide suitable illumination for an officer making notes at night; a socket on the dash for inserting a spot light on a flexible cord to enable the officer to shine a beam into dark areas; and a clip board bolted to the cowl, with the outer edge at an angle slightly below horizontal, to hold a note pad and a list of wanted cars. All police vehicles should carry a supply of flares. Patrol cars should be furnished with seat straps to prevent the officer from being thrown from the vehicle during an accident.

The laws of most states require that police vehicles be equipped with sirens and red lights in order to qualify for the right-of-way as emergency vehicles. Patrol cars should also be equipped with an oval shaped light, with a frosted lens bearing the words "Police—Stop" in red letters, mounted ahead of the right front door with the lens parallel to the side of the car and at such a height that the top of the light is no higher than the bottom of the windshield. The light should be controlled by a switch mounted on the dash where it may be readily reached by the driver.[1]

Some patrol cars and some three-wheelers should be equipped with public-address equipment.

Decision 30. Should vehicles be purchased beyond the number required for current operations in order that some may be available for use when other vehicles are out of order, and if so, how many reserve vehicles should be provided?

Reserve vehicles should be provided to enable the force to operate in the manner planned even though some vehicles are currently out of .order. The cost of man power, and the fact that it is used ineffectively if not actually wasted during periods when vehicles are not available, make it economically important that spare vehicles be provided for this purpose. The number needed for spares is dependent on their condition (older vehicles are more frequently subject to breakdown), the promptness of repair service, the accident frequency of the force, and the period of the day and its duration when the department meets its peak demand for vehicle use. It is most important that vehicles be provided to meet the requirements of the patrol division. As a general rule, a minimum of one spare should be provided for each ten in operation; the factors listed above may justify some deviation from this number.

Decision 31. How may vehicles be assigned so as to assure maximum use of them and thus reduce the number that must be operated?

Flexibility in the assignment of police vehicles assures their maximum use. It is most important that the patrol division be kept supplied with vehicles. Patrol requirements are heaviest in the evening and lightest during the day shift when specialists work. When the specialists are not provided cars for their exclusive 24-

---

[1] The use of this light is described in *Police Administration*, p. 297.

hour use and when an adequate number of cars is provided for the hours of heaviest patrol, it is possible to meet most of the needs of the specialists by the assignment, to the special divisions, of patrol-division cars that are not in use during the day shift.

Specialists, except vice-division officers, should not have cars assigned to them on a 24-hour basis. Vice-division work does not readily fit into a regular schedule, and these officers may be called into service at unusual hours. The fact that a car is not needed for each member of the vice division further justifies providing a small vice division with vehicles for their continuous and exclusive use.

Patrol cars should be conspicuously marked and specialists sometimes demand that they be provided with inconspicuous automobiles. The specialists (except the vice-division officers) should be persuaded that conspicuously marked police cars do not ordinarily hamper their operations. This fact is especially true when all police cars reveal their identity by red lights, radio antennae, and sometimes distinctive license plates. A limited number of vehicles may be inconspicuously marked and used by specialists who have the greatest need for plain automobiles during the day and held as spares during the hours of peak need. The need for police cars can be substantially reduced by requiring superior officers and specialists who have infrequent need for transportation to use a spare car, held in reserve for replacement during the repair of a regular vehicle, and when it is not available, to use the motorized patrol to meet spot transportation needs. The use should be restricted to delivering or picking up the officer at a designated location; it should not include waiting for him. With prompt radio service, waiting should not be necessary.

Instead of the assignment of vehicles on an individual basis, large departments may provide car pools for the use of specialists and of superior officers who make infrequent use of automobiles. The provision of vehicles in the pool, however, should be adequate to meet the need during peak hours. Sound economy demands that qualified officers on substantial salaries should not have their operations impeded by the lack of relatively inexpensive transportation. On the other hand, regulations may be needed to prevent the depletion of the pool during the noon hour by specialists driving vehicles to lunch.

The specialists usually work until 5:00 P.M. and patrol requirements usually increase before this hour to the point that additional vehicles are needed to meet the need, sometimes as early as 3:00 P.M. Sometimes this short-time need can be met by arranging repair services so that vehicles under service or repair will be available for use at this hour. Sometimes it may be necessary, at 3:00 P.M. or 4:00 P.M., to reassign to the patrol division a car that has been used by a specialist during the day. When this is necessary, the specialist who loses his car at an earlier-than-usual hour should be selected so that work will not suffer in consequence. Some specialists have a lighter load during these hours and may arrange their work so that these hours may be productively spent at headquarters.

With the exception of the vice division, police cars not in the service of on-duty officers should be housed in the police garage at night. To do otherwise subjects the police to justifiable criticism for using police vehicles for private purposes.

Decision 32. Who should own the police vehicles?

Police cars rented from the officers who drive them assure motorized patrol or transportation for each officer during emergencies, relieve the department of repair problems, do not subject the officers to the unsatisfactory condition in which the cars may be left by former users, and enable the officers to own their own cars more readily. The disadvantages, however, outweigh the advantages. Cars cannot be conspicuously marked and used privately; the cost of purchasing and installing such accessory equipment as radio, sirens, and police lights, becomes a heavy expense to the department when the number of pieces is more than doubled; the transfer from one private vehicle to another of department-owned armaments becomes a problem; the patrol may not be as intensive, and essential driving risks may be avoided; and the department can usually own and operate their own cars at a lower cost than must be paid to officers as rental.

Police cars may be rented from a dealer, in which case the department has exclusive use and all of the advantages of department ownership. The factors to be considered in such an arrangement are the rental costs as compared to depreciation and department operating cost. When the dealer is able to provide more satisfactory and prompt service than the police or municipal garage, this plan may have merit. In large cities, however, department ownership is usually more economical.

Other Police Equipment

In surveying department needs, attention should be given to police armaments and office furnishings and equipment. The ownership of weapons and uniforms and some supplies must also be decided.

Decision 33. What type, caliber, and size of sidearm should be used by the police?

The rigid-frame revolver is the regulation firearm of most American police departments. It has been preferred to the automatic because it does not jam, and a misfired cartridge does not need to be ejected before the weapon may be fired. These favorable characteristics have been considered especially important in police service because most officers do not keep their weapons well cleaned and some departments do not require that old ammunition be replaced at regular intervals.

The automatic pistol, however, has some advantages over the revolver. The cartridge clip holds more rounds than the revolver and a fresh clip may be inserted in an automatic more quickly than six cartridges can be placed individually in the revolver cylinder.

The relative desirability of shocking power and penetrating power should be considered in deciding on the caliber of the weapon. The .38 special is generally considered a caliber that suitably combines the two and is used by most American police forces. The .45 caliber provides greater shocking power but is less effective than the .38 in penetrating automobile bodies and seats.

The great penetrating power and range of the .38 magnum makes the use of this weapon undesirable for general municipal police service.

A short barrel on the sidearm has the advantages of an easier draw from its holster and a lessened likelihood of its being wrested from the officer in hand-to-hand conflict. The added accuracy of a slightly longer barrel is not a matter of serious consequence in ordinary police service. A barrel length of four inches is recommended.

Decision 34. Should riot guns be carried in patrol cars?

Patrol cars in cities should be equipped with racks for carrying riot guns (12-gauge pump guns with 18- to 20-inch barrels). The rack should be equipped with a lock with the key carried on the vehicle ignition-key ring, or the lock should be electrically controlled by the ignition circuit so that it is unlocked when the ignition switch is on. The cartridge cases, loaded with "O" buckshot, should be specially treated and fitted with a fiber plug to protect the crimp. They should be frequently inspected to detect any damage that might jam the gun.

Decision 35. What use should be made of bullet-resisting shields?

Bullet-resisting shields are better suited to police service than bullet-resisting vests. The shield covers a greater part of the body; it is more conveniently used because it unfolds into its shield form when it is picked up and may be discarded instantly when it is no longer needed; its solid steel surface stimulates the confidence of the officer who carries it and destroys the confidence of the criminal who is faced with it. Regulations should require the shield to be used on hazardous missions.

Decision 36. What special armaments should be carried in the cars assigned to the evidence technicians and patrol sergeants?

Arrangements should be made to assure the presence of bullet-resisting shields, and gas guns, grenades, and masks, at the scene of action where they may be needed. It is not feasible to supply each patrol car with this equipment. Automobiles assigned to patrol sergeants and the evidence technicians are invariably at the scene of action. The above-mentioned armaments, therefore, should be standard equipment for these cars.

Decision 37. What factors should be considered in the purchase of office furniture, lockers, and filing cabinets?

Furniture at police headquarters is subjected to hard service and some abuse. Only the most substantial furniture should be considered. Aluminum chairs and metal furniture and filing cabinets usually have longer life than those made of wood. Lockers and filing cabinets should all be of the same make so that any that are added or shifted from one office to another will match those already in place. Filing cabinets of the same make also permit moving the contents of the drawers by transferring the entire drawer to the new location in another cabinet.

Decision 38. What supplies and equipment should the department provide, and which should officers be required to purchase?

The question of department *versus* officer ownership arises most frequently in reference to uniforms, sidearms, flashlights and their batteries, Yawara sticks or batons, and holsters and Sam Browne belts. Department ownership assures greater uniformity. Private ownership assures better care of the articles. Uniformity in private ownership may be assured by rigid adherence to department specifications. It is believed that equipment of this kind should be provided by the individual officer. Provision may be made for the purchase of equipment for the recruit by city funds with provision for deductions from pay checks in small amounts until the account is settled.

CHAPTER 13

Personnel and Public Relations

THE QUALITY of police service is more strongly influenced by the competence of the individual members of the force than by any other single factor. The competence of policemen is established by the method of their selection, the adequacy and suitability of their training, the fairness, promptness, and strictness of their discipline, the absence of morale-destroying influences, and the manner in which they are selected for promotion to assure competent supervision and wise, courageous, and inspiring leadership.

The fact that the quality of personnel determines the quality of police service makes personnel management the most important administrative task of the police chief. This fact also makes important a survey of personnel-management procedures and an appraisal of personnel at every level of authority within the department. Deficiencies thus discovered and corrected will have more lasting effect on the quality of police service than any changes in organization structure or operating procedure.

Police service must not only be of high quality; it must also be acceptable to the general public. The police cannot hope to progress beyond the sympathetic understanding of the administrative head of the city, the governing board, and the public. Competent personnel providing a superior quality of service usually wins support for its program. The support may be hastened and strengthened, however, by special attention to the relations between the police and the public and to the organization of the community toward this end.

It is the purpose of this chapter to inquire into the management of police personnel, to appraise its end result, and to review the relations of the police with the public. Items 6, 7, 8, and 20 in Appendix A (pages 289 and 294) will provide needed information. Study of charter provisions, state laws, and local ordinances must also be made to ascertain restrictions imposed on the chief of police in the management of his personnel.

A clear understanding of the local situation will make apparent weaknesses that deserve correction. Decisions must then be made as to the manner in which they should be corrected.

The Authority of the Police Chief in Personnel Matters

The most common weakness found in police service stems from a failure on the part of the chief of police to exercise suitable authority in the management of his personnel. The failure sometimes results from lack of courage or lack of appreciation of the need for action, and sometimes from ignorance as to methods to use in the administration of personnel. More often, however, and with increasing frequency, the failure results from restrictions that have been unwisely imposed on the chief in the management of his personnel. Some civil-service charter provisions defeat their alleged purpose by making difficult if not impossible the application of sound principles of personnel administration. They take from the chief important authority over the control of the members of his department. A police chief cannot be held responsible for the qual-ity of service rendered by his force under these circumstances.

That civil service has improved the quality and security of policemen is evident. These worthy accomplishments, however, do not excuse continued bad practices by individual civil-service agencies. To say that the universal demand for personnel administration on a merit basis and for job security for honest and competent policemen can be attained only through civil service is to ignore the fact that some of the best police agencies at local, state, and federal levels are not under civil service and actively resist all efforts to take from them the management of their personnel. The Detroit Police Department, the New York State Police, and the F.B.I. are examples. On the other hand, to say that the release of all police forces from civil service would not result in some unfortunate consequences is also unrealistic. No one wants a return to the spoils system, but this danger recedes as police administrators become more professional.

Personnel administration is a function of management. To deny to management essential control of personnel is to take from the executive head of the operating agency his one most important function. In theory, civil-service agencies are to provide the police chief with a high quality of technical assistance in the management of his personnel. If this, and only this, were done, there could be no quarrel with civil service. In practice, however, civil-service agencies go far beyond providing technical assistance in personnel management; they are prone to take from the chief much of his personnel-control authority.

A number of facts explain the present unsatisfactory relationship, found in many jurisdictions, between the police and civil-service agencies that serve them. Perhaps most important is the failure of civil-service agencies to recognize that police service has some unique personnel requirements that differentiate it markedly from other branches of public service. Civil-service board members attempt to apply to the police the philosophies of service and deportment that have served them so well in important business and industrial positions. Levels of morality and standards of conduct that would not interfere with industrial and business employment may be quite unsuited for police service. Personnel technicians also fail to recognize the unsuitability to the police of standards that are satisfactory in other branches of public service.

The police chiefs themselves must accept some of the blame for present unsatisfactory relations. Lack of foresight, a feeling of incompetence in personnel matters, and a desire to be rid of unpleasant tasks have caused many police chiefs to adopt a *laissez faire* attitude toward civil service, just as some now do toward the unionization of their forces. Such indifference on the part of police leaders is evidence of a need for civil service. As police chiefs become more professional, they recognize the importance of their control of personnel; they then insist on their right to establish personnel specifications and standards of service and conduct and on the obligation of civil service to meet the specifications and to deal forthrightly with deviations from established standards. Public opinion will, in the long run, force civil-service agencies to meet justifiable police demands for personnel administration designed to meet the unique requirements of police service.

The police chief has the inescapable responsibility of seeing that persons appointed to the force are qualified for police service. To this end he must evaluate procedures used in the selection of men for appointment; he must assure himself that only intellectually, emotionally, physically, and morally qualified men are appointed; he must see that those who fail to measure up to prescribed standards of performance in the training school and on the job are dismissed during their probationary period; he must remove from the force those who demonstrate their indifference, incompetence, or dishonesty at any future date in their service.

The competent police chief knows that money spent wisely in recruitment is money that will be saved tenfold in the future. One misfit may do irreparable damage to the reputation of the department. Indifferent, incompetent, and stupid policemen cannot provide a suitable quality of police service. It is the responsibility of the police chief to see that they are not appointed to his force and that they are removed when they are already on. This responsibility cannot be discharged without authority. The police chief must be given the necessary authority.

Decision 1. Has the force been suitably disciplined, and if not, what has prevented it?

Items 6 and 7 in Appendix A (page 289) will provide information as to the nature of disciplinary procedures and the disciplinary action that has been taken in recent years. Analysis of the frequency and severity of disciplinary action for various offenses will indicate its suitability. Special attention should be given to the frequency of dismissal of probationers.

When evidence is discovered of lax discipline, a review of the disciplinary machinery and the procedures used in dealing with disciplinary cases may reveal the cause. When lax discipline is found in spite of the fact that the police chief has requisite disciplinary authority, the blame is his. Recommendations should then be made to strengthen discipline. When the police chief lacks essential authority, the blame rests with the device that has deprived him of his natural and necessary power. This device is found outside the police department, usually in the form of a civil-service charter provision or law. Recommendation should then be made that disciplinary authority be restored to the administrative head of the city and his chief of police.

Decision 2. What authority should the police chief have to manage his personnel?

The police chief should have authority to select for appointment and promotion and to assign and remove policemen from service, subject to the direction of the administrative head of the city. The police chief should reach a clear understanding with his superior as to: (1) matters that require pre-action consultation and approval; (2) action that the chief may take without prior clearance but on which a report is desired; and (3) other matters on which no report is desired.

Decision 3. What action should be taken to prevent restrictions being imposed on the chief's authority over police personnel?

The most certain safeguard against encroachment on the authority of the police chief in the management of his personnel is the wise application of sound principles of personnel administration. When the best procedures are used in the selection of persons for appointment and promotion, when the members of the force participate in the administration of a discipline that is just, prompt, and certain, when consideration is given to the welfare of the members, when morale is high and public relations good, there is little likelihood of a successful demand to restrict the powers of the police chief. The police chief who has the requisite authority should guard it jealously and should avoid jeopardizing it by capricious abuse. It is more difficult to regain the lost power than it is to retain it in the first instance.

Decision 4. What action should be planned when the chief's authority over police personnel has been restricted?

Once civil service has engulfed a department, the chief is not likely to succeed in winning back all the authority he previously held. Instead, he must direct his efforts toward making the machinery work to the best interests of the police and the public. He can do this by submitting sound personnel specifications to the personnel agency and urging that they be met. Failure of the personnel agency to meet the specifications can be dealt with by testing the appointees during their probationary period and eliminating the unfit. For example, when the chief specifies a minimum intelligence quotient of 112 and the personnel agency certifies candidates who do not meet this specification, those deficient can be eliminated by examining all appointees during their training period, using a validated group general-intelligence test. Failure of the personnel agency to support the chief in disciplinary cases means that more careful investigation and preparation of cases must be made in the future. This is good practice in any event and argues for the development of department machinery and procedures that will assure the recording and registering of all complaints against members so that their investigation and disposition can be controlled. The chief is not likely to be reversed in suitably documented disciplinary cases.

At the same time, effort should be made to relax the controls of the central personnel agency and to restore authority to the chief. In order to forestall abuse by an incompetent chief, civil service should serve as an auditing agency to assure that superior policies and procedures are adopted and that disciplinary power is not used capriciously. Its authority, however, should be restricted to informing the public and the chief's superior of any failure to apply sound and progressive personnel policies and procedures, and of any unwise disciplinary acts. Civil service should also be given the responsibility to demand that the appointing authority remove a chief who clearly thus demonstrates his incompetence.[1]

Decision 5. What action should be taken to persuade the members of the force of the wisdom of not restricting the authority over personnel to the administrative head of the city and his police chief?

Policemen, sometimes combining their forces with firemen, are frequently active in the initiation of proposed restrictive civil-service laws and charter amendments. This action on the part of policemen is based on the mistaken notion that civil-service restrictions on the authority of the head of the city and his police chief will protect the force from political influences and assure security to its members. It is therefore argued that the restrictive civil-service provisions are good for the department and will enable it to render a higher quality of police service than it otherwise could.

Policemen must be shown the consequences of civil-service provisions that unduly restrict the authority of the chief. The quality of police service is impaired instead of improved by such provisions. Only the well-disciplined force is able to provide a high quality of service; unduly restrictive civil-service provisions produce poorly-disciplined forces that are incapable of a high quality of service. Policemen should realize that whatever impairs the quality of police service is bad for their department and whatever is bad for their department is bad for them as individual members of it. Civil-service restrictions protect principally the incompetent and dishonest. Competent and honest men do not need protection beyond that provided by sound personnel practices. Sound personnel administration protects the interests of the employees because what benefits employees as a group benefits the department and the city. Promo-

---

[1] See O. W. Wilson, "Toward a Better Merit System" in *New Goals in Police Management*, The Annals of the American Academy of Political and Social Science, Philadelphia, January, 1954. pp. 87-96.

tion of the best qualified and removal of the incompetent and dishonest are to the advantage of competent and honest policemen, and a high quality of police service is thus assured.

Conferences should be held by the chief with the members of the force in order to provide a free discussion of the rights of individual policemen and the need of the chief for authority over his personnel. The consequences of depriving the chief of this power should be explained. The desirability of a departmental disciplinary board or board of rights to advise the chief on disciplinary matters should also be discussed.

Decision 6. Is there need for a police personnel officer in a city where there is either a central personnel agency under the direct control of the administrative head of the city or an independent civil-service board?[1]

The existence of a central personnel agency does not diminish the need for a police personnel officer. He should serve as a liaison officer between the police department and the central agency; he must establish suitable working relationships between the two. The conditions of service and the police personnel requirements differ from those found in other departments; a knowledge of the nature of police service is consequently needed to assure a wise application in that department of the principles of personnel administration by someone otherwise technically well qualified. The objective of the police personnel officer is to assist the central agency in the application of the techniques of personnel management to meet the unique needs of police service. The confidence of the central agency in the police personnel officer frequently results in most if not all of the department work being done by the police personnel officer, but under the general direction and with the approval of the central agency.

Decision 7. What duties should be assigned to the police personnel officer?

The police personnel officer should be charged with the development of procedures and their application to facilitate the accomplishment of his objective in five broad fields. (1) Selection of

---

[1] A more detailed discussion may be found in O. W. Wilson, *Police Administration*, pp. 330-335, from which much of this material was drawn, by permission of McGraw-Hill Book Company, Inc. Copyright, 1950.

persons best qualified for appointment, assignment, and promotion. (2) Appraisal of the value to the service of each member. (3) The control of members by supervision and discipline. (4) Promotion of the welfare of the members. (5) Recruit, continuation, and special training. The department personnel officer will actively assist the central personnel agency, when one exists, in the promotion of police recruitment, in the establishment of satisfactory eligibility standards for appointment, in the development and application of reliable testing procedures for selection and promotion, and in the development and use of suitable measures of accomplishment and service ratings. He will train and assist supervising officers in the evaluation of their subordinates. He will assist in the creation and supervise the operation of disciplinary and grievance machinery and procedures. He will promote and direct police training and further the welfare of the members of the force.

Selection for Appointment

The selection of persons for appointment as policemen is the foundation of the personnel program. The capacity of the members for training, their individual competence, and the quality of supervision and leadership that they will provide on promotion are determined by the success of methods used in their initial selection. The quality of police personnel and its leadership and consequently the quality of the service it provides can be no better than the quality of the recruits. Recruitment methods are intended to obtain the highest quality recruit. The methods should be analyzed to ascertain whether they promote or hamper the accomplishment of this purpose. For this reason it is important to appraise their product.

Analysis of the information provided in item 6 of Appendix A (page 289) will reveal strengths and weaknesses. Special attention should be given to the intelligence quotients, formal education, and ages of the members as a whole, by divisions, and by ranks.

Decision 8. What eligibility standards should be established for applicants?

Restrictions on the eligibility of applicants are frequently found in the form of certain minimum standards of citizenship, residence, education, age, height, and weight. Those who do not meet the established standards are thus not eligible to compete as candidates for appointment.

United States citizenship should be required of all candidates. Residence requirements prior to appointment, however, should not be imposed. Backward departments sometimes have residence requirements; progressive departments usually do not. The best men cannot be recruited when some are screened out by an artificial and entirely unjustified preemployment residence requirement.

Persons who will be 21 years of age on or before their appointment date should be admitted to candidacy. To impose a higher minimum age limit is unjustified and works to the disadvantage of the service. The younger man is less likely to have experienced failure in some other field or to have skills that may tempt him to leave the police service; he has more potential years of service and is consequently a lighter burden on the retirement system and operating budget than the older man. The younger man ordinarily has greater physical endurance, he is more easily trained, and he is more adaptable to the conditions of police service than the older man. When the young man who possesses the qualities desired in police service is not appointed at the time he is available, he will

SCORING TABLE FOR AGE, HEIGHT, AND EDUCATION

Percent-age score	Age	Height (less than 6 ft. 4 in. but more than)		Education
100	21	6 ft.	1 in.	Master's degree in criminology
98	22	6	0	
95	23	5	11	Master's degree
90	24	5	10	A.B. or B.S. degree
85	25	5	9½	3 years college
80	26	5	9	2 years college
75	27	5	8¾	1 year college
70	28	5	8½	High school graduate
65		5	8¼	
60	29	5	8	
55		5	7¾	3 years high school
50	30	5	7½	
45		5	7¼	
40	31	5	7	2 years high school

nearly always find his place in some other occupation and his services are then lost to the police forever. Time and experience quickly correct the youthful immaturity of otherwise well-qualified men.

For the above reasons a maximum limit of 29 years of age at the time of appointment should be established.

Height has advantages in police service that justify a minimum standard of 5'9". A maximum height of 6'4" should also be established to eliminate possible glandular disorders. The weight should be in proportion to the height. When the examining physician decides the suitability of weight to height, there is less likelihood of injustice being done to the candidate whose build may warrant a weight out of the usual proportion to height. A minimum educational requirement of high-school graduation should also be imposed.

Decision 9. Should eligibility standards be adhered to strictly or should those who may be slightly deficient in one or more qualifications be admitted to candidacy when they excell in others?

A table that establishes a scale of percentage scores for deviations in age, height, and education permits a desired flexibility that does not eliminate the applicant who excels in some respects because of slight deficiencies in others. The operation of the table, for example, would qualify applicants who have had some college work even though they are slightly deficient in height or slightly more than 29 years of age. Likewise, a young applicant of good height would not be eliminated even though he has not completed high school.[1]

Decision 10. How should qualified candidates be attracted and what procedure should be followed when they make application?

All available media should be used by the police in bringing notice of police examinatiions to the attention of individuals and groups of persons who may be qualified for police service. As a general rule, a large group of candidates contains a greater number with superior qualifications than a small group. For this reason, effort should be made to increase the number of applicants by every

---

[1] The table referred to is taken from O. W. Wilson, *Police Administration*, p. 339, by permission of McGraw-Hill Book Company, Inc. Copyright, 1950. A minimum qualifying score of 240 is recommended.

means, and they should be permitted to file up to the hour of the first examination when to do so is administratively feasible.

Applicants should not be required to submit to a personal interview at the time they file their application. Such a procedure is wasteful of the time of both the applicant and the police. Information regarding the conditions of service and eligibility qualifications, in greater detail than is given in the announcement of the examination, should be contained in a brochure available for general distribution and presented to each applicant. A pamphlet used by one department is reproduced in Appendix B, page 297.

A simple application form on a 8" x 5" card is most suitable. It may be used as a control for recording the results of the tests, notices sent to the candidates, and so on.[1] Detailed information relating to the candidate must be obtained on a personnel questionnaire during his character investigation.[2] Since many applicants will be eliminated before the character investigation stage of the selection process is reached, time and paper are saved and inconvenience avoided by not requiring this information until it is needed.

Examinations should be held frequently, at least once each year and more often when the requirements of the service demand. Appointments from eligible lists more than a year old usually result in less highly qualified recruits. Previous appointments from the eligible list have removed those with the highest qualifications. A new crop of youth has become old enough for police service since the last examination, and its members are likely to contain some with higher qualifications than those who remain on the old list. Those remaining on the old list should be urged to file a new application.

Decision 11. How should candidates be tested and examined, and what standards should be established for appointment?

Tests and examinations should be designed to assist in the appraisal of the intelligence of the candidate; his muscular coordination, strength, and agility; his medical, neurological, and psychiatric condition; and his personality, emotional stability, and character.

Tests of intelligence should invariably be used in the selection of policemen. A minimum intelligence quotient of 112, as measured

---

[1] A sample form is shown in *Police Administration,* p. 341.

[2] Information that should be included in a personnel questionnaire is listed in Appendix C, p. 301.

by a validated group intelligence test such as the Otis or a revision of the Army Alpha should be required. Information tests designed to measure the knowledge of the candidate on police subjects are not considered suitable because relatively few candidates have had preemployment police training. When most candidates in a locality have had preemployment training, tests designed to measure their knowledge in the police field may be used in addition to the general intelligence test. Until this condition prevails, candidates with preemployment training should receive some added weight in the final selection.

Candidates should be tested to eliminate those who lack suitable muscular coordination, strength, and agility.[1] Care should be observed in designing these tests not to subject candidates to physical strains that may permanently injure them. Standards should not be set so high as to eliminate an undue proportion of otherwise qualified men. Great weight should not be given to variations in strength and agility in the final selection from the group who meet the minimum qualifications.

Medical and neurological examinations should be thorough and doubts regarding the physical condition of the candidate should be resolved in favor of the department. Failures in this respect prove costly to both the operating budget and the pension fund.

The character investigation should include fingerprints cleared with the F.B.I., the state bureau, and the police of any city in which the candidate may have resided.[2] Personal interviews should be held with teachers, former employers, associates, relatives, and the immediate family. If the candidate is engaged to be married, his fiancée should also be interviewed and her attitude toward police service ascertained. The investigator should search for evidences of emotional instability on the part of the candidate.

The personality and emotional stability of the candidate is difficult to appraise but effort should be made to do so. An oral board composed of members of the department may be used for this purpose. It seems likely, however, that a more accurate appraisal may be made by selected members of the force holding a private interview with each candidate for this purpose. Each member who inter-

---

[1] The administration and scoring of tests of strength and agility are outlined in Appendix D, p. 305.

[2] Character investigation is described in detail by Richard L. Holcomb, *Selection of Police Officers*, State University of Iowa, 1946.

views candidates, either privately or on a board, should be required
to sign a statement on a personal-qualities rating sheet[1] categorically
recommending either the appointment or rejection of each candidate, and when rejection is recommended, a statement in support of
his view. A qualified psychiatrist on an oral board or by private interview will greatly lessen the likelihood of the appointment of emotionally unstable candidates.

The tests and examinations should be designed to screen out the
least competent and those otherwise disqualified rather than to serve
as the final determination of the most competent. Candidates disqualified by any one test in the series should not be examined
further. When suitably high standards are established, it may be
assumed that all who are not eliminated by the tests and examinations are qualified for service. The remaining problem is to select
from this group those who are most highly qualified.

*Decision 12. How should the most highly qualified be selected for
appointment from all qualified candidates?*

A procedure that seems to be fair to the candidates and at the
same time provides desirable flexibility to adjust for detected
weaknesses is one that ascertains the relative standing of each candidate by arranging all of them in a descending order of their scores
in each of their written examinations, in their total strength and
agility scores, and in their total personal-appraisal scores, and then
ascertains the combined relative standing for each by adding his
positions in each of these lists and dividing by the number of lists.[2]
The personnel officer should then examine all documents relating
to each candidate, especially those reporting on his character and
personality and the results of his physical, neurological, and psychiatric examinations, to discover information that did not warrant rejection but that seems to justify moving the candidate up
or down on the list, thus providing an adjusted combined relative
standing. The previously mentioned application card should contain spaces for recording this information.

Candidates on the adjusted list should not have a right to appointment in the order in which they are listed. Doubts in regard to the
character, personality, emotional stability, or physical qualities of

---

[1] A personal-qualities rating sheet is shown in *Police Administration*, p. 351.
[2] This procedure is described in greater detail in *Police Administration*, pp. 350-
352.

the candidate should be resolved in favor of the department. The chief should be free to make his selection from the adjusted list. In doing so, he should consider all of the scores and other pertinent data relating to each candidate. He may be assisted in his final selection by the personnel officer and other members of the department in whose judgment he has confidence.

Decision 13. Should a probationary period be provided and if so for how long?

A period of probation should be considered a vital step in the selection process. No matter how carefully the candidates are examined and tested, final proof of competence must be sought in trial on the job. During the probationary period, supervising officers should record their appraisal of the accomplishments and abilities of the recruits. Especially in departments where the right of the chief to dismiss incompetent policemen is restricted by civil-service regulations, attention should be given to the discovery and removal of unqualified officers before the end of their probationary period.

The period of probation should be one year. A shorter period may not reveal weaknesses; a longer period may injure morale.

Service Ratings and Selection for Promotion

Accurate evaluation of the competence and productivity of individual policemen is extremely difficult. An appraisal of the service value of policemen must be made, however, in order to make wise assignments and promotions and to evaluate recruitment procedures.[1]

Decision 14. How may the service value of the individual policeman be appraised?

Service ratings should be designed to force the superior to designate 10 per cent of his men as the most competent and another 10 per cent as the least competent. Those who consistently remain in the upper bracket should be considered for promotion and special assignment while those who consistently remain in the lower bracket are those who need special training, reassignment and, when on probation, consideration for separation from service. An accurate appraisal of the service value of the policeman of average ability is not important.

---

[1] The procedures discussed are described in greater detail in *Police Administration*, pp. 354-364.

Supervisors should also be alert to discover and record incidents that indicate the presence or absence of desirable qualities in their subordinates. The service ratings and a summary of the significant incidents enable the personnel officer to identify the most competent and the least competent. Records of accomplishment are also useful in detecting the most productive in a group performing comparable tasks. The relative ability of the most competent may be judged by the significant incidents, service ratings, and records of accomplishment.[1]

Records of the type described above must be simple. When they are complicated, their use is not easily understood and their preparation is burdensome; then they usually fail to accomplish their purpose.

Decision 15. On what basis should officers be selected for promotion?

Promotion in police service brings with it ever-increasing need for the qualities of leadership. For this reason, selection for promotion should be based principally on these qualities.

It is sound policy to discover qualities of leadership and utilize these talents by promotion to ever-higher ranks as quickly as the experience of the talented officer justifies and opportunity presents itself. Qualities of leadership are not necessarily enhanced by length of service nor do acts of heroism invariably reflect these attributes. Length of service and acts of heroism should not, therefore, be considered in selecting officers for promotion except when all other factors are equal.

The practice of basing promotions exclusively or largely on written tests of police knowledge is not considered a wise procedure. Professional knowledge is a necessary attribute of the leader but it is not the most important one. Written tests of police knowledge should be made, but the principal weight should be given to the qualities of leadership reflected in service ratings and summaries of significant incidents. Promotions to positions above the rank of sergeant should also be based on the qualities of leadership demonstrated in the lower supervisory position.

Promotion in a department that has not used general intelligence tests in recruitment should be limited to those who have a mini-

---

[1] A description of these records is found in *Police Administration*, pp. 355-360.

mum intelligence quotient of 112. Intellectually inferior officers do not usually make successful supervisors of their intellectual superiors.

A qualified psychiatrist should interview each candidate for promotion and submit a confidential report of his conclusions to the chief of police.

Decision 16. Should oral-board members from outside the department be used to appraise the personal qualities of candidates for promotion?

A personal-qualities rating sheet should be prepared on each candidate for promotion by officers senior in rank under whom he has served. These officers know most about the candidates and should be best qualified to judge their personal qualifications.

The limited number of officers of senior rank available to appraise the personal qualities of candidates for the higher ranks in the department may make desirable an oral board for this purpose composed of outsiders. Appraisals made by wisely selected outsiders are also more likely to be objective than those made by members of the force who may be unduly influenced by their personal relationships with the candidates.

Decision 17. Should eligibility for promotion to higher rank be restricted to those in the immediately lower rank?

Service in lower ranks is ordinarily a desirable experience in preparation for promotion to higher ranks. An exception to the general rule of promotions exclusively from the immediately lower rank should be made in departments whose unsatisfactory recruitment procedures have provided a force with limited leadership qualities. Violation of the rule in such a department is necessary to avoid promoting obviously inadequate officers.

Decision 18. Should promotional opportunities be restricted to members of the department?

With the exception of those for the position of chief of police, promotional examinations should not be open to officers from other forces except in departments where the lack of the desired qualities makes this action desirable. The importance of the office of chief and the desirability of avoiding the evils of in-breeding make it desirable to hold nationwide examinations for the top position.

Discipline

The fact that discipline strongly influences the quality of police service has been mentioned. The importance of discipline in this respect must not be discounted. Appraisal of department discipline has been discussed. There remain to be made decisions in regard to disciplinary machinery and procedures.

Decision 19. Who should investigate complaints of officer misconduct?

Complaints of police misconduct must be promptly and thoroughly investigated in order to protect the officer when his conduct has been proper and to develop facts to guide disciplinary action when he has acted improperly. The department is thus shielded from unwarranted criticism.

To accomplish this purpose, procedures must be established so that reports of officer misconduct, whether submitted by private persons or members of the force, will be recorded and registered, investigation will be initiated and followed up, and the matter finally will be disposed of by department disciplinary machinery in the event the investigation sustains the complaint.

The seriousness to the officer, the department, and the public of allegations of misconduct justifies placing on one officer or on one unit responsibility for supervising the disciplinary process. Large departments should create a special internal-affairs unit to supervise the investigation of reported breaches of discipline, to assist in or actually conduct the investigation in some cases, to report to the chief the findings and recommendations of commanding officers, to supervise the operation of department disciplinary machinery, such as a disciplinary board, and otherwise to insure the proper functioning of the disciplinary process. In somewhat smaller departments, the investigative functions may be performed by the intelligence unit and in still smaller ones by the personnel officer or someone temporarily assigned by the chief to deal with a specific case.

The immediate supervisor of the officer complained against should ordinarily investigate the complaint and report his findings through channels except when its serious nature or other characteristic, or circumstances related to it, seems, to the commanding officer or the chief, to justify the assistance of, or complete investigation by, the internal-affairs or intelligence unit or by an investigator designated by the chief.

Cases growing out of financial difficulties and others that relate to the social welfare of the officer rather than specifically to the manner of performance of police duties also sometimes deserve exception and should then be assigned to the internal-affairs unit or to the personnel officer. These cases, however, should almost invariably be discussed with the officer's superiors because such matters should rarely be concealed from them and never except with the consent of the chief.

Superior officers charged with the investigation of complaints lodged against their subordinates should be privileged to take non-punitive disciplinary action when in their judgment none other is required. When in doubt, the question should be referred to higher authority for decision. In all cases a complete written report of the complaint, findings, and action should be made.

When the superior officer believes that punitive disciplinary action should be taken, the matter should be referred through channels to the chief for decision. In the absence of a disciplinary board, commanding officers, through whose hands reports of the incident and of its investigation must pass, should make their recommendations as to disciplinary action that should be taken, if any. In departments having a disciplinary board, the commanding officers should recommend whether or not the case should be referred to the board.

Discipline should be recognized as a function of command, and the creation of an internal-affairs unit or the existence of an intelligence unit do not relieve command of its responsibility. These are staff units designed to assist command in the performance of its duties; they are not intended to perform command tasks.

Effort should be made to increase rather than decrease the acceptance of disciplinary responsibility by line officers. The consciousness of disciplinary responsibility should be awakened and nourished at the lowest level, and at all other levels, in the hierarchy of command. In all cases that deserve more than a reprimand, the decision as to the disciplinary action to be taken must be the chief's responsibility. He will be guided by the recommendations of the commanding officers or of the disciplinary board. The punishment should be administered by the highest ranking officer in the line of command above the offender with whom he ordinarily comes in daily contact, since this is the person who represents the authority of the administration to the delinquent officer.

Decision 20. Should a department disciplinary board be created to consider punitive disciplinary matters, and if so, what should be its functions and membership, and how should it be created?

A disciplinary board composed of five members of the force to review the facts in the case and to recommend action helps the chief in his decision, lessens the danger of hasty or capricious action, and thus serves the best interests of the department. The board may be appointed by the chief or be drawn by lot by the accused from officers superior in rank to him but excluding those in his own organic unit. One or more may be drawn in excess of the number needed, with the accused privileged to select the board members from the total number drawn. When drawn by lot, the board should elect one of its members to serve as chairman.

The authority of the board should be restricted to an inquiry designed to establish the true facts and to recommend action to the chief. They should have the power to investigate the case more intensively than was done initially by the officer's superior, although they may base their judgment on his findings. Their investigations, made by themselves or by other members of the department designated by the chief for that purpose, should be in the nature of any police investigation.

The board should be privileged to hold informal private meetings to discuss the investigations made and to arrange for such additional investigation as may be deemed necessary. At the board hearing they should be permitted to request the attendance of the complainant and of such witnesses as they desire. The accused officer should be given an opportunity to appear before the board to make any statement or explanation that he wishes and to answer any questions the board may wish to ask him. He should not be represented by an attorney but he should be permitted to obtain the services of any member of the force to represent him. Legal training should not bar the officer he selects.

Decision 21. Should a report on the action taken be made to a citizen who has complained regarding the conduct of an officer?

The citizen complainant should be informed that suitable action will be taken or that it has been taken. To inform him of the nature of the action sometimes results in further complaint against its inadequacy. Some police chiefs adopt the policy of refusing to provide information regarding the action taken except when ordered to do so by the administrative head of the city.

Decision 22. What should be police policy in reference to concealing facts relating to the misconduct of policemen?

The chief is justifiably concerned with the good repute of his force and in consequence is frequently tempted to conceal facts relating to the misdeeds of members lest the public conclude that such misconduct is common police practice. Experience has clearly shown, however, that its reputation as a well-disciplined department is enhanced by complete frankness in reporting such cases to newspaper representatives and, conversely, that when the police attempt to conceal such facts, the reputation of the department is almost certain to suffer.

These are the salient facts to bear in mind when considering this policy question: The public is not so much concerned with the fact of police misconduct as they are with the fact that action has been taken against the offender by police authority. The public is quick to construe any attempt at concealment as evidence that the misconduct is prevalent and that police authorities take no action against it, but instead condone this behavior, except when they are forced by the press to take a stand against it.

Welfare and Conditions of Service

Consideration must be given to the conditions of service and the welfare of the members of the department. Analysis of the data provided by item 6 of Appendix A (page 289) will indicate whether salaries, hours of the work week, and annual and sick leaves are suitable. When the conditions of service are found to be less desirable than those in comparable cities and in local employment, recommendations should be made for their improvement. The determination of salary scales and conditions of employment is an administrative decision to be recommended to the appropriating body and should not be effected by a vote of the people.

Consideration should also be given to morale-destroying influences in the department and to the need for improved procedures for dealing with grievances held by members of the force. The policy of the department in reference to the right of policemen to organize should also be established.

Decision 23. What restrictions, if any, should be imposed on the payment of overtime and on its accumulation by members of the department?

Overtime should be allowed for time ordinarily off-duty that is spent in court and on special details ordered by the head of the department to meet unusual crime, traffic, and other emergency needs. Compensation should not be made for time spent in completing an investigation or writing a report that originated during the regular tour of duty. To allow overtime for the completion of a task initiated while on duty creates a heavy bookkeeping burden, the practice is subject to abuse, and it reduces the police profession to the level of artisans who punch time clocks. Members of the special divisions such as detectives should be permitted by their superior officers to vary their work hours so as to make any necessary investigations at night when their regular hours of work are during the day, without the need for overtime.

Time spent in organized training during off-duty hours should be compensated at half the regular rate of pay; time spent in training on a full-time basis, however, should be in lieu of regular work and on the regular salary.

Overtime should be compensated by time off, known as recovery time, or by payment at the regular salary rate. Payment for overtime is administratively more desirable than granting time off; work schedules are not interfered with and the force is not depleted by this procedure. As a general rule, policemen also prefer the cash to recovery time.

When overtime is compensated by time off, officers should be prevented from accumulating large amounts that will permit them to be absent for protracted periods. This may be accomplished by a regulation that requires officers to use their recovery time within 12 months of the time it was earned, with provision for an extension through a period of emergency that may require the cancellation of leaves to all officers.

Decision 24. Should a grievance committee be created to consider complaints made by the members of the department, and if so, how should it be formed, what should its functions be, and what authority should be granted to it?

A grievance committee bolsters sagging morale by bringing morale-destroying influences to light where they may be effectively dealt with. It enables the members of the force to initiate action against unsatisfactory conditions. It also affords a wholesome vent to the pent-up feelings of the more timid and a suitable channel for the spleen of the chronic malcontents.

The grievance committee, preferably composed of five members, may have two members designated by the chief and three elected by all members of the force. The committee should elect one of its members as chairman. The committee should serve a year but there should be no restriction on the re-appointment or re-election of its members. It should meet on the call of the chairman to consider matters brought to its attention by any member of the department.

The grievance committee should be privileged to consider any matter it desires and to make recommendations to the chief. Its objective should be to develop satisfactory solutions within the jurisdiction of the department. Action outside the department needed in the solution should be recommended to the chief. The committee should not be privileged to appear before the governing board or the administrative head of the city except with the consent and presence of the chief.

Decision 25. What restrictions, if any, should be imposed on the right of policemen to participate in politics?

Policemen should not belong to any political club or organization, take an active part in behalf of any candidate for political office, or actively participate in politics. Every officer should be urged to vote at each election, but his participation should end there. He should not solicit or contribute money or other things for political purposes. He should be required to resign from the department before filing as a candidate for any elective office.

With the approval of the administrative head of the city, however, all members should be permitted to campaign actively to improve their security and the conditions of police service, and to obtain bond issues for police buildings. Under the same condition, they should also be permitted to campaign for or against local, state, or federal legislation the enactment of which would materially assist or hinder their operations.

Decision 26. What restrictions, if any, should be imposed on the right of policemen to organize?

Policemen should be forbidden to join a labor union, any organization that maintains the right of its members to strike, any organization opposed to minority groups, any organization that attempts to interfere with the administration of the police force, that might in any way exact prior consideration and thus interfere with efficient and effective police operations, or any organization that is affiliated with any of the above.[1]

---

[1] See Appendix G, p. 377.

Policemen should be urged to join professional associations of recognized standing whose purpose is to promote the professionalization of police service and to improve its quality generally or in some special branch. Worthy associations are found at national, state, and sometimes regional levels.

Associations of the members of the local force (sometimes for all members and sometimes with separate organizations for different ranks) designed for social purposes or to provide sick and death benefits (sometimes through group insurance) and to promote the welfare of the members are desirable when they do not violate the restrictions on participation in politics. Local associations are sometimes helpful in promoting the provision of recreational facilities, in facilitating the operation of a grievance committee, in the management of a police loan cooperative, and otherwise in furthering the welfare of the force.

Decision 27. What should be done to promote the physical wellbeing of the members of the force, and should they be subjected to an annual physical examination?

The physical well-being of policemen is dependent on regular and suitable exercise. Gymnasiums, especially those that contain swimming pools and courts for such games as squash or handball and volley or basketball, stimulate the attention of policemen to their physical condition.

Policemen should be subjected to an annual physical examination to detect incipient diseases and physical weaknesses that may be corrected by early treatment. Special attention should be given to the heart condition and weight. Those who are overweight should be required, under the guidance of a physician, to spend a designated number of hours in the gymnasium each week at a prescribed course of exercise until the weight is reduced to normal.

Police Training

Information supplied in item 8 of Appendix A (page 289) will assist in surveying the department training facilities, evaluating its programs, and ascertaining the extent to which outside training facilities are utilized. Conclusions must be reached as to the adequacy of the training that is provided, and recommendations must be made to meet any deficiencies that are discovered.

Decision 28. What training facilities should be provided by the department?

The extent of training facilities and the number on its staff are influenced by the size of the force, its rate of turnover, and the extent to which outside training facilities are utilized. The importance of training deserves emphasis because its extent and quality strongly influence the value of police service and the relationship that develops between the police and the public. Facilities should be provided, therefore, that will assure adequate training.

Training should be made the responsibility of one officer. In a small department he may supervise the training function in addition to other duties such as those relating to the management of personnel. In a large department, the director of police training must be supplied with one or more assistants.

It should not be the responsibility of these officers to provide all training by themselves. Instead, they should consider themselves administrators of the training process; they should instruct in only those subjects in which they have special competence. It should be their responsibility to promote police training; plan curricula and schedules;[1] arrange for instructors from both within and without the department; supervise the preparation of course outlines and lesson plans;[2] provide classroom space, teaching aids, and other facilities; and supervise generally the operation of the program.

The management and direction of a police school involves detail beyond the scope of this book. Some basic decisions will be considered here but the training officer must plan far beyond their limits.

Decision 29. To what extent should facilities outside the local department be utilized by the chief in training his policemen?

Outside facilities may be considered under three heads: (1) basic or recruit training programs provided by state agencies (state police or state boards for vocational education) and by nearby large police departments;[3] (2) specialized training courses such as those offered by the National Police Academy, the Traffic Institute at

---

[1] Model curricula are contained in *Municipal Police Administration,* International City Managers' Association, Chicago, 1954, 4th ed., pp. 195, 203, 208.

[2] A sample lesson plan is reproduced in Appendix E, p. 311.

[3] Police training by state departments of education is described in *Municipal Police Administration,* pp. 192-193.

Northwestern University, the Delinquency Control Institute at the University of Southern California, and shorter institutes in specialized fields conducted by state boards for vocational education and by state universities and colleges; and (3) regular courses offered at local educational institutions such as criminal law, court procedure, evidence, and courses designed specifically for training the police, as well as courses that are less directly related but nevertheless useful to policemen, such as English composition, public speaking, introductory and advanced courses in psychology, introductory political science and other courses in government and public administration.

When the local police department is of sufficient size to warrant the facilities, it should provide its own basic recruit training. When outside facilities are conveniently available, however, the provision of a complete recruit training program may be longer delayed than when the department must rely exclusively on its own resources. Even though outside facilities are used for basic training, the department must train its recruits in local ordinances and government structure, and in police policies, procedures, and reports.

A wise procedure is to gear the department recruitment program with the schedule of basic courses being offered nearby and to send all members appointed at that time to the school. On their return, the recruit training should be completed to meet local needs. Those appointed at other times should be given recruit training in the local department. When the recruit training is not complete, the recruits should be enrolled in the next basic course.

Utilizing basic training facilities in the manner described has a number of advantages. The instruction is usually superior to that provided locally, from the point of view of course content, length of the course, and the ability of the instructors. The association with members of other departments, in discussions in the classroom and during leisure hours, helps to indoctrinate the recruit with a sound philosophy of police service and to orient him in the police profession. Friendships with members from other departments prove useful to the recruit in his future service and help to maintain friendly relationships between nearby departments.

Every department should utilize the facilities of the specialized training programs mentioned in item (2) above by assigning some members to attend sessions of these schools each year. Larger numbers should be sent to short institutes that may be held in their region.

All departments should utilize their local educational institutions to the utmost in promoting the continued education of their members. The police should urge the creation of special courses to meet their needs; policemen should be urged to complete their university training and to work for advanced degrees when they are offered, especially when courses of study are designed especially for them.

Professionalization of police service must be based, among other things, on a cultural foundation in the liberal arts composed of the requirements for the Associate in Arts degree as a minimum. Additional tool courses in English, speech, psychology, human biology, and statistics are also desirable.

Decision 30. How extensively should recruits be trained before they are assigned to street duty on their own resources?

It is most desirable that recruits should receive three months of intensive training before being placed completely on their own resources, although limited instructional facilities and the urgency of their need in service may necessitate reducing this to six weeks.

During the three months of basic training, the recruit should receive considerable experience on the street under close but gradually relaxing supervision. The supervision of the recruit on street duty during and immediately following the completion of his basic training is extremely important. A serious mistake is made when a recruit is placed under the guidance of an older officer who may be incompetent, ignorant, disloyal, inattentive to his duties, disdainful of regulations, and lacking in an appreciation of his responsibility as a police officer and in a proper philosophy of police service. Officers should be carefully selected as field instructors or supervisors on the basis of their ability, knowledge, philosophy of service, personality, and ability to handle people.

An outline of a sample recruit manual designed to assist the field instructor in supervising and training his charge is shown in Appendix F, page 326.

Decision 31. What provision should be made for the continued training of the members of the force?

Continuation training for all members of the department, in contrast to specialized training, should be conducted continuously at roll call by discussion of daily training bulletins by the commanding officer.[1] Officers should preserve the bulletins in loose-leaf binders. The members of the department should be periodically subjected to short written quizzes based on the subject matter of recent bulletins. Quiz scores should be recorded in the officers' personnel files.

A continuously operating program of in-service training designed to give each patrolman an annual refresher course of a minimum of 40 hours requires an increase in the patrolman complement of about 2 per cent so that all may receive the refresher training in 50 weeks without depleting man power needed for essential assignments. The results gained more than justify the increase in man power needed for this purpose.

Decision 32. Should conferences be held regularly for training and other purposes?

Conferences are an effective means of stimulating active participation by subordinates in the administration of police affairs and thus increasing their interest in their work and in the problems of the department. Conferences afford an opportunity to criticize present and suggest new or modified policies and procedures relating to all aspects of the police organization and its administration and operation; they therefore promote improved practices and general efficiency. They improve morale by affording subordinates an opportunity to air grievances, offer suggestions, and otherwise demonstrate their worth. Conferences also facilitate coordination and instruction and simplify the explanation of plans and procedures.

Conferences should be held periodically, preferably once each week. In small departments, the chief should hold a daily meeting with his division heads and a weekly conference with all members who can be relieved from duty. He should also hold a separate weekly session with the superior officers. In larger departments, division heads should hold meetings with their division members. The burdens imposed on the chief in a large department may restrict

---

[1] Samples of daily training bulletins used by the Los Angeles Police Department are shown in *Police Administration,* pp. 380-381, and in *Municipal Police Administration,* 4th ed., pp. 201. Bulletins 1-173 are contained in *Daily Training Bulletin,* Charles C Thomas, Publisher, Springfield, Illinois, 1954, p. 274.

him to daily conferences with his immediate subordinates and weekly meetings with the next lower rank; provision should also be made for sessions with a part of the force on a district basis each week.

Civilian Police Department Employees

The extent of employment of both men and women civilians at tasks for which they are well qualified varies widely among police departments. Also, some departments appoint policewomen at relatively high salaries and assign them exclusively to clerical tasks similar to those performed in private employment by clerks and stenographers at substantially lower wages. Some departments employ patrolmen for most clerical tasks; some pay them a higher salary than other patrolmen because of their clerical skills. Some departments also assign patrolmen to various property-control and maintenance tasks.

In some departments persons with unusual skills are appointed as policemen, usually with a rank above that of patrolman in order to provide suitable compensation. Criminalists and laboratory technicians, skilled lie-detector operators, traffic engineers, and radio technicians are examples. These specialists are frequently not otherwise well qualified for police service. The tasks performed by them do not ordinarily require a police authority beyond that enjoyed by any private person.

Decision 33. What should be the policy in reference to the employment of civilians for the performance of tasks that are non-police in character?

The argument usually presented against using civilians at records tasks is that the confidential nature of the reports makes it essential that they should be read only by police officers. The armed-forces' practice of using civilians to work with top-secret documents indicates the fallacy of this argument.

Two arguments are usually offered against the use of women at these tasks:

1. Some reports contain lurid accounts of sex crimes and other obscene matter the reading of which might prove harmful to women. This mid-Victorian argument does not seem sound. Modern women past 20 years of age are usually informed on such matters and, while

they may be shocked, they are not likely to be morally damaged by reading the reports.

2. Men officers engaged at such tasks are available for street duty during emergencies. This may be a logical reason for using police officers at clerical tasks in small departments because of their limited man power. The infrequency of the use of such officers on street duty, however, raises serious question as to the validity of the argument in other departments.

Some headquarters duties involve dealing with prisoners. Such tasks, as a general rule, should be performed by policemen when the prisoners are men and by policewomen or matrons when the prisoners are women. An exception may be found in departments where the infrequency of arrests of women may not justify keeping a matron or policewoman on duty on each shift. In their absence a woman civilian member of the force may assist the arresting officer in disposing of the prisoner.

The police planner should analyze all non-police tasks (clerical, property control, technical, and maintenance) to discover those that can be performed satisfactorily by civilians. Since tasks that should be performed by police officers frequently do not occupy full time, reassignment of some duties may lessen the number of positions that cannot be filled by civilians.

Tasks that can be performed by civilians should be further analyzed to ascertain any that require male strength. Property control in a large department is an example. Women clerks and stenographers are usually more efficient at office tasks than men.

The employment of civilians at tasks that do not require police authority provides several advantages:

Economy. Civilians can usually be employed to perform these tasks, except those requiring unusual technical skills, at a lower wage than is paid to the police. This applies in particular to clerical, property control, and maintenance tasks. Women clerks and stenographers are nearly always paid lower salaries than men. The professionalization of police service will inevitably result in higher police salaries. The higher the police salaries, the greater is the justification for restricting the use of police personnel to tasks that require their special qualifications. Police salaries are also more likely to be raised if the process does not include raising the salaries of persons engaged at tasks for which they are paid substantially less in private employment.

Efficiency. Many of the tasks that may be performed by civilians require skills not ordinarily found in policemen. Not many policemen are highly skilled clerks, stenographers, artisans, or technicians. The employment of less well-qualified policemen at tasks requiring special skills is certain to impair the efficiency of police operations. The large reservoir of civilians available for appointment to these positions assures an increased likelihood of the selection of persons with superior qualifications.

Simplification of Personnel Management. Personnel-management problems are simplified when civilians are employed at tasks that do not require police authority. In appointment, assignment, and dismissal, the police chief is usually granted a greater control over civilian employees than over police officers. The employment of policemen at tasks that may be performed by civilians also usually results in more frequent reassignments; the lack of promotional opportunities and the dull monotony of many of the tasks frequently cause the policemen assigned to them to become dissatisfied. Since the officers are often not well qualified to perform regular police duties, their assignment to these tasks is likely to result in diminished effectiveness. Frequent turnover of personnel assigned to such tasks further impairs the effectiveness of operations; the new assignee must be trained for the job and during this period the quality of the work is likely to be substandard. Frequent reassignments, coupled with the need to find and train substitutes, present additional personnel-management problems.

Improved Atmosphere. The presence of women clerks, stenographers, and secretaries improves the atmosphere of the police offices. Where they are employed, officers unconsciously curb conduct and talk that otherwise might prove offensive to persons transacting business with the police. Also, some women will call at police headquarters with less trepidation when they know that women employees are present.

Public Relations

Public relations in police service encompass all of the relationships that exist between the police and the public they serve. Public relations are influenced by the attitude of the public toward the police and by the attitude of the police toward individual citizens. Unfavorable attitudes on the part of either party create unsatisfactory relationships.

Police attitudes toward the public are influenced largely by their training, supervision, and leadership. Incompetent personnel, of course, cannot be suitably trained.

Public attitudes toward the police are influenced by their experiences with individual policemen; when the police attitude is unsatisfactory, the experience is invariably distasteful to the citizen. Public attitudes are also influenced by police methods and procedures; a feeling that a restrictive procedure is purposeless, or that police methods fail in their objectives, damages public regard for the police. Citizen attitude is also influenced by other people, the press, and the radio; in consequence, unfavorable attitudes are amplified like gossip that is exaggerated at each telling. From this it may be seen that the attitude of the public is strongly influenced not only by their personal experiences but also by their understanding of police policies and procedures.

Citizen attitudes are reflected in official attitudes and in consequence the police relationships with the administrative head of the city and the governing board are also impaired when their public relations are unsatisfactory. The police cannot progress, in establishing superior procedures and in obtaining needed facilities, beyond the understanding of the public, the administrative head of the city, and the governing board. Information regarding police operations and their plans and needs, therefore, is vital to the sympathetic understanding that assures a satisfactory public and official relationship.

From what has been said above, it is apparent that the quality of police service is influenced in more than one way by public relations. The development of satisfactory public relations, therefore, deserves careful and continuous attention.

Decision 34. What duties should be assigned to the police public-relations officer.[1]

The duties of the public-relations officer may be considered in terms of four objectives: (1) To evaluate public opinion and attitudes with respect to the policies, methods, and personnel of the department. (2) To advise the chief with regard to the public-relations aspects of new or revised department programs, policies, pro-

---

[1] The duties of the police public-relations officer are described in greater detail in *Police Administration,* pp. 387-419.

cedures, and activities. (3) To plan and carry on informational activities designed to keep the public informed on police activities. (4) To provide a staff supervision of all police activities that may influence public support.

In the accomplishment of his objectives, the public-relations officer should first assure himself that all is in order on the police side of the line; then he should undertake to inform the public regarding it.

The first task involves training personnel in favorable attitudes and techniques, modifying police policies and procedures to assure that they are publicly acceptable, providing special services to the citizens and merchants, and physically and mentally putting the force, its quarters, and equipment on dress parade.

When the police house is in order, the public-relations officer should disseminate information through the press, department publications, and a speaker's bureau, and arrange special department contacts with the public, such as tours of inspection of headquarters and special demonstrations, displays, and exhibits.

Decision 35. What should be the relationship of the public-relations officer to the line divisions?

The public-relations officer is responsible for the relationship between the police department and the public. To discharge this responsibility, he must be kept informed of the public-relations activities of all units and members of the department so that he may coordinate and supervise them in a staff capacity.

The appointment of a public-relations officer should result in more, not less, public-relations work being done by all members of the department. The public-relations officer must rely on the line officers to carry out the public-relations program, and he should eagerly stimulate activities on their part which tend to promote the program.

Police-Press Relationships

The relationships between the police and the press are related to and strongly influence public relations. The publication of news is an important public service in which the police have some responsibility. The public interest is best served when the police and the press work hand in hand in obtaining and disseminating news.

Also, the press serves the police by informing the public regarding police problems in which public support and cooperation are needed.

Decision 36. What should be the policy of the police in reference to withholding information from the press?

The police should adopt an attitude of complete frankness with press representatives and should not withhold information except (1) that relating to subversive activities and current vice investigations; (2) the names of juveniles under any circumstance short of murder, and of female victims in sex crimes when the victim is not killed or of ill-repute or guilty of conduct that provoked the attack; and (3) facts the public knowledge of which would interfere with crime investigations or the apprehension or interrogation of suspects.

Decision 37. What news-release procedures should the police adopt to implement this policy?

Procedures should be developed and instructions given to the members of the force that will enable reporters to gather their news facts rapidly, accurately, completely, and promptly following the receipt of the information by the police. To this end, the daily bulletin and most other police records should be made readily available to the reporters.

Records relating to subversive activities and to current vice investigations should obviously be concealed from reporters as well as from members of the force who are not concerned with the investigations. When agreement is reached that the press will not publish the names of juveniles or of female victims in sex crimes, with the exceptions noted above, these cases do not need to be withheld from the press. Otherwise they should be stamped "No Publicity." Cases containing information which if made public would interfere with the investigation, or the apprehension or interrogation of suspects, should also be stamped "No Publicity."

"No Publicity" cases should be delivered to the chief in small departments and to a designated commanding officer on each shift in larger departments. Officers having information relating to them should be informed of the action taken and should refer press inquiries to the designated officer who should discuss the case with the press representatives in a group, stating the position of the department and seeking agreement from the reporters to withhold publication. When the relationships are suitable, the press representative who is unable or unwilling to refrain from publication will so notify the police who may then discuss the matter with the city editor.

Competitor papers are jealous of their news rights and resent any evidence of news being withheld from release until after their deadline. The chief of police should assure the release of news as cases are reported, and he should watch closely for any evidence of newspaper favoritism on the part of members of the force.

Community Organization

Community organizations are helpful in maintaining suitable public relations and in winning public support for police programs, and they should be utilized by the police in achieving their public-relations objectives. In addition to the usual community groups, however, the police should promote the organization of some designed to assist in the solution of specific police problems. These organizations should be created to accomplish the following purposes:[1]

1. Coordinate participating public and semi-public agencies in programs that necessitate the action of several.

2. Protect the community, legislative bodies, courts, prosecutors, police, and other officials from influences of selfish groups that are contrary to public interest.

3. Influence officials to act in conformity with public welfare by supporting the adoption of desirable programs, regulations, and procedures, and by opposing the adoption of undesirable ones.

4. Obtain public support of programs designed in the public interest in order that facilities essential to their accomplishment, in the form of space, equipment, and personnel, may be made available.

5. Popularize these programs so that the people will favor their accomplishment and the enforcement of incidental regulations; obtain public cooperation in the form of compliance with regulations and an active intolerance of their violation.

Decision 38. In which fields should the police promote community organization?

---

[1] This classification was taken by permission from O. W. Wilson, *Police Administration*, pp. 422-423. Copyright, 1950. McGraw-Hill Book Company, Inc.

In some fields of activity more than others, the achievement of the police purpose is dependent on public and official support and on the effective cooperation of several agencies and public officials, and is more likely to be hampered by selfish interests contrary to public interest. The control of traffic, juvenile delinquency, and organized crime present unusual problems which usually require the efforts of organized groups to win the public and official support essential to their solution.

For these reasons the police should actively promote the organization of local safety councils, community councils for the prevention of delinquency, and crime commissions designed to assist in the fight against organized crime.[1]

---

[1] The organization of the community in these three fields is discussed in *Police Administration*, Chapter 24.

CHAPTER 14

Procedures and Tactics

THE procedures mentioned in the previous chapters relate principally to the organization and administration of the line divisions. The planning officer must appraise the adequacy of the procedures used by them and take steps to have weaknesses corrected. Some other procedures also deserve his attention. They fall into two categories: those that relate to police operations in contrast to those that relate to the management of the department.

Procedures should be designed to guide police operations in the field and at headquarters. Headquarters procedures relate to the assignment and method of performance of records, communications, and other headquarters tasks. Field procedures relate to the assignment and method of performance of police tasks away from headquarters. In addition there are special operating procedures used by the special divisions to guide line officers in the performance of their special tasks. Some of these have been mentioned previously.

Procedures must also be designed to guide staff officers in the performance of certain administrative duties. For example, accounting and purchasing procedures must be established, and other procedures are needed to implement policy in the management of police personnel.

Tactical plans must also be developed or appraised and modified.

Many of the procedures mentioned above will be based on previously discussed decisions. Other decisions must also be taken in planning some of the methods. It is not feasible, however, to analyze all decisions that must be considered in the development of all department procedures. Instead, procedures in use by a number of departments are included in the appendix. These procedures may not be the best available; also, their adoption in their present form is not suggested. They are offered only as examples; they should be tailored to meet local needs before adoption. These examples or similar ones obtained from other departments may be used as a starting point in planning procedures for local application.

259

The Duty Manual

Plans must be recorded or published in a manner to assure ready availability if they are to serve effectively as guides in the performance of police tasks. Before considering procedural and tactical planning, therefore, decisions should be made as to the manner of recording plans that affect all members of the department.

Decision 1. How should procedural, tactical, and other plans that affect all members of the department be published so that each member may have a copy readily available?

The police department should publish a duty manual for distribution to all its members.[1] The manual should contain the department rules and general duties, definitions of terms and order of ranks, and an organization chart with a description of the duties of each organizational unit, rank, and position, as well as outlines of selected procedures and tactical operations. It should also contain law, ordinance, and charter provisions relating to the organization and administration of the department and to the authority of the chief of police.

In a large department, the volume of material for inclusion in a duty manual may necessitate its publication in more than one volume. For example, in addition to a general duty manual for all members, a separate procedural manual may be published to guide the members of each division having special procedures of justifiable volume. Management practices and some headquarters, office, and communications procedures that are not of general interest may also be published separately or otherwise recorded to serve the needs of the members whose tasks are thus outlined. When this is done, however, some procedures, or parts of them, that are of interest to all members, should be reproduced in the general duty manual. Procedures relating to discipline and promotion are in this category.

In some communities the chief of police does not report directly to the chief executive of the municipality; instead, the chief, usually with one or more other department heads, is under the direct control of a director of public safety, commissioner of police and fire, or a manager of safety and excise. There also remain a few cities where the chief is under the direct control of a board of police commissioners or a single lay commissioner.

---

[1] Excerpts from a duty manual are reproduced as examples in Appendix G, p. 339.

The division of decision-making responsibilities between the police chief and his immediate superior, whomever he might be, should be precisely defined. This division of responsibility will make apparent the desirability of the publication, under the authority of the chief's immediate superior, of police regulations delineating the functions, responsibilities, and authority of the police department (in part by quoting charter, statute, and ordinance provisions); all policy matters that are within his province; general rules that apply to all members of the force; and the duties, responsibilities, and authority of the chief of police, including a definition of matters on which the chief should not take action without prior consultation and of those on which he might take action but on which his superior would expect early notification.

Within the framework of the legal provisions and the restrictions imposed by his superior, the chief should publish a duty and procedural manual on his own authority. This manual should establish the organization of the force; the functions of its organic units; the duties of members assigned to specific posts or tasks; and standard operating procedures intended to guide all members engaged on designated projects.

Failure to define the division of decision-making responsibility between the chief and his immediate superior aggravates the weaknesses of this dual control of the police force by tempting the superior not to restrict himself to policy-making and administrative matters and, instead, to engage in department operations. When suitable relationships are established and adhered to, the superior will leave the details of the organization and operation of the force, including the development of the minutiae of operating procedures, to his chief of police. Otherwise the force is likely to be held in a strait jacket of regulations, whereas its organization should be flexible and subject to adjustment to meet changing conditions.

Decision 2. In what form should the duty manual be published?

The duty manual may be either mimeographed or printed. When printed, it should be in loose leaf form to facilitate making additions and amendments. Bolts provide more secure and permanent binding than lacing; ring binders are least satisfactory.

The paragraphs of the duty and procedural manuals should be numbered by a decimal system which will permit almost unlimited expansion without change in the basic organization of the material.

An example of such a numbering system is shown in Appendix G, page 339.

~~The duty manual does not need to be of pocket size.~~ When it contains all essential material, it cannot usually be printed in pocket size except with undesirably small type. Suitably trained officers will not ordinarily need to refer to the manual during their tour of duty. Should occasion demand such reference, the question at issue may be resolved by telephoning to headquarters.

Decision 3. What should be incorporated as department rules in the duty manual?

~~Since compliance with a rule is a duty, there is no sharp line of demarcation between rules and duties.~~ The distinction that rules are prohibitive and relate to personal conduct, whereas duties are affirmative and describe action that must be taken under given circumstances, is not always clear cut. An outline of duties is a set of rules, and rules in turn are requirements related to action. ~~Department rules, therefore, are somewhat the same as general duties imposed on all members and both are wisely combined in one section.[1] They may also be called Regulations.~~

Decision 4. Should general rules and duties be restricted to important points or should they cover all points in some detail?

The question of the brevity of the duty manual arises most frequently in reference to department rules. Some administrators are of the opinion that the rules should be drafted in broad terms to deal with principles rather than to cover nearly all possible situations in detail. The manual should be considered a guide and reference book, however, rather than a set of prohibitory laws. ~~Its training value is increased when it sets forth in considerable detail the provisions of department rules and procedures. The philosophy of service is also more readily inculcated by a detailed account of the regulations.~~

Decsion 5. What terms should be defined in the duty manual?

To avoid ambiguity with attendant misunderstanding and confusion, definitions should be given of commonly used police terms.

---

[1] See Appendix G, p. 346.

The following should be included:[1]

Member; civilian employee; officer.

Superior officer; commanding officer; ranking officer; length of service.

On duty; off duty; special duty; leave of absence; sick leave; death leave; suspension.

Department regulations; duty manual.

Order; general order; special order.

Through official channels; report.

Post; route; beat; sector; district.

Division; bureau; section; platoon.

Decision 6. How should the order of rank be defined?

The order of rank should be defined in such a manner that no question will arise in the mind of any member as to who is in authority regardless of who may be absent in the hierarchy of command.[2] Each member should also know without doubt to whom he is immediately responsible and those who are under his direct control. These relationships should be made clear in the description of the organization of the functional units. In addition, the duty manual should be explicit in regard to changes in the normal lines of control that occur automatically under specified circumstances.

Decision 7. Which ranks and positions should have their duties outlined in the duty manual?

In the preparation of a duty manual, the planner should proceed from the general to the particular. General rules and duties that apply to all members of the force should be given first. General duties should then be listed for the superior and commanding officers, the chief of police and his deputies, and the captains. Since the more specific duties of captains, lieutenants, sergeants, and other members will vary according to the division assignment, the duty manual should contain a list of the duties of each position in each division. If the duty manual is to serve its purpose, it should contain a detailed outline of the general and special duties of each rank and position in the department.[3]

---

[1] Definitions of these terms are found in *Police Administration*, pp. 12-13 and 16-18.

[2] See *Police Administration*, p. 16.

[3] Appendix G contains an example of general rules for superior and commanding officers, pp. 380-388, and of the duties of the chief and his staff, pp. 391-407. Examples are also found of the duties of the dispatcher and turnkey, pp. 409-414.

Decision 8. How should the functions and organization of the divisions and other organic units be described?

~~The functions of the divisions should be described in sufficient detail in the duty manual and with such clarity as to avoid misunderstandings that may result in friction from apparent or real overlapping of responsibilities or in neglect of important police tasks from failure clearly to place responsibility for their performance. The organization structure of each division should be described with equal detail and clarity.~~ The functions and organization of the divisions are further clarified by describing the functions and organization of each of the subordinate organic units found in the divisions, and the duties of the officers assigned to each. Obviously the ~~description of the functions and organization of the divisions cannot be taken from the manual of some other department.~~ They must conform to the local organization pattern.

The duty manual referred to in Appendix G. includes sections on the function and organization of the communications office (page 409) which are not included in the text.

Procedures

The general and special duties of the officers in various positions in the divisions will outline many department procedures. For example, the duties of the dispatcher, listed on pages 409-413, describe all procedures followed by this officer. Likewise, the duties of the turnkey (page 413) describe procedures in reference to the control and custody of prisoners.

~~The procedures mentioned above could be recorded, not as the duties of the specified officers, but as practices to be followed in dealing with prisoners in court and in operating the jail. Either method of recording the procedure is satisfactory. The description of the procedure in terms of the duties of specified officers, however, has the advantage of placing responsibility for the accomplishment of the procedure more precisely.~~

Since either method may be used for recording procedures, decisions must be made as to which regulations should be recorded in terms of the duties of specified officers and which are more suitably recorded as methods to be followed without reference to the specific officers who are to perform them.

Decision 9. What types of regulations are more suitably recorded as procedures without reference to the specific officers charged with their performance?

Procedures designed to guide a limited number of officers in the performance of duties that relate specifically to their assignments seem to be best outlined in terms of the duties of their positions. The previously mentioned duties of the dispatcher and jailers fall in this category.

In contrast, procedures to guide all officers are best presented as an outline of the approved method without reference to the duties of specific officers. To do otherwise would necessitate repeating the procedure in listing the duties of officers in all positions. Officers not assigned to specific posts are usually not required to be well informed on the duties of those so assigned, while all officers are expected to be informed on all procedures that relate to their work. For this reason, procedures with which all members should be familiar are best recorded independently of the duties of the various officers. References to the procedures may be made, however, in listing these duties.

Procedures recorded separately in the manner described above may be included in the duty manual. Some of restricted interest, such as those relating to records-division operations, should be recorded in some other manner.

Decision 10. Which procedures are suitable for recording in a separate section of the duty manual?

The procedures will be considered under two separate headings: i.e., field procedures and headquarters procedures.

Field Procedures. Field procedures that are to be followed by all officers when confronted by a specified circumstance must be made known to all who are likely to find themselves in the designated situation. They should, therefore, be published in a manner to assure their distribution to all members. They then may serve as training aids and as guides to individual officers in performance and supervision.

Listed below are procedures to be followed by officers when confronted by circumstances in which failure to take immediate, decisive action will jeopardize the police purpose. The list is not all-inclusive; it contains only the minimum requirements. The inclusion of other procedures is justified in many departments.

Examples of procedures used by some departments to meet designated situations are listed in Appendix H and I, pages 417 and 423. Again it must be emphasized that the examples given may not be the best; also that they must be modified to meet local needs. Each procedure must be approved by the command group and all members should be convinced of its practicality and value.

1. A procedure that has been carefully planned in advance, to be followed by the police when a criminal is reported to be in operation, assures most effective action.[1] Its use avoids the delay, indecision, and poor judgment that sometimes result when speedy action is needed under conditions that usually create some emotional stress.

The procedure should outline the action to be taken by the dispatcher on receipt of calls of various types. He then only needs to ascertain the nature of the call and follow the planned procedure. The classification of the calls according to their nature, in order to assure the suitable deployment of an adequate force to accomplish the mission with minimum hazard to the officers, was discussed on page 85. The procedure should also outline the action to be taken by the several officers dispatched to the scene.

2. General instructions should also be prepared to guide the dispatcher and officers sent on reports of the robbery of banks and other establishments that constitute special hazards. The general instructions are for all officers; they supplement the specific tactical plans that should be developed in the form of prepared broadcasts for business houses that are connected to police headquarters by robbery alarms.[2]

3. The actions or appearance of persons in automobiles frequently arouse the suspicions of motorized officers and justify a challenge. The stopping of some may be especially hazardous. Procedures should be planned, therefore, to guide officers in making such stops, both in the daytime and at night. Departments that still use some two-man patrol cars should develop procedures to guide both one

---

[1] A procedure developed by one department is found in *Municipal Police Administration*, 4th ed., pp. 278-286.

[2] General instructions prepared by one department are reproduced in Appendix H, p. 417. Prepared broadcasts to be used when banks are robbed are contained in *Police Records*, pp. 246-250.

and two men in making the stops.[1] These procedures are not intended for stopping the ordinary traffic violator.

4. In questioning suspects and in searching, handcuffing, and transporting prisoners, officers should be guided by procedures that assure their safety and the security of the prisoner.[2]

5. Desperate criminals in a building create a serious situation that deserves the advance preparation of procedures that will assure the greatest likelihood of the capture of the outlaws with least risk to the participating officers and citizens.[3]

6. Procedures should also be prepared to deal with well-armed, violently insane or other mentally ill persons as well as desperate criminals who may open fire on the police from behind an effective barricade. Under these circumstances the police are confronted with the necessity of dislodging their opponents with least risk to themselves and the general public. They are also concerned with avoiding injury to the mentally ill and those who are temporarily disturbed emotionally.[4]

7. Grave emergencies sometimes arise that necessitate calling out all available off-duty members of the force. When this is done, more than the usual number of dispatchers, jail staff, lieutenants, and sergeants will be on duty, and the number of patrolmen will usually be in excess of the available number of police vehicles. Procedures should be prepared in advance for obtaining additional vehicles and for utilizing each officer most effectively. Otherwise the men will stand around, waiting vainly for an intelligent order that will enable them to proceed effectively toward the accomplishment of the police purpose. An example of a procedure developed by one department is found in Appendix H, page 419.

8. Since most police contacts with the public are related to driving offenses, procedures should be developed for dealing with traffic violators that will lessen the likelihood of damage to public relations. Special attention should be given to the attitude of the officer, his facial expression, tone of voice, demeanor, and words used.

---

[1] A procedure developed by one department for stopping suspicious cars is described in *Police Administration*, p. 102.

[2] Examples of such procedures are found in *Municipal Police Administration*, 4th ed., pp. 283-284. See also *Methods of Transporting Persons Under Restraint*, California Department of Corrections, Sacramento, 1951.

[3] An example of a procedure for dealing with such situations is found in *Municipal Police Administration*, pp. 284-285.

[4] A suitable procedure is found in *Municipal Police Administration*, pp. 285-286.

The procedure should prohibit the officer from asking unnecessary questions; it should require him to make affirmative statements in dealing with the offender. An example of a procedure used by one department is found in Appendix H, page 420.

9. The difficulty of convicting drivers charged with intoxication has caused many departments to develop specific procedures to be followed by the officer who arrests an intoxicated driver. The procedures are designed to test the extent of intoxication. Some departments restrict their procedure to the observation of the physical manifestations of intoxication while the subject undergoes a prescribed series of tests; others take motion pictures of the subject during the testing procedure; some also use chemical tests of the degree of intoxication. Whatever procedure may be used, it should be outlined for the guidance of the officers and their supervisors.

10. Strikes and industrial unrest invariably place the police in a difficult position where they are subject to criticism regardless of the action they take. The critical nature of situations that develop during a period of industrial unrest makes it desirable that police have procedures prepared in advance for dealing with them without regard to their location or exact nature. These regulations must be supplemented by more precise plans for dealing with specific situations.

11. Disorderly crowds and mobs create situations that require unusual caution by the police. Serious rioting may spread over the entire community or a substantial part of it. Poor judgment displayed by one policeman may have serious repercussions. The danger to life and property and the damage to social relations that result from such disorders justify special attention to tensions in the community that may presage impending trouble. The police should be alert to the activities of partisan groups and to rumors designed to incite disturbances. Procedures should be prepared to guide individual policemen and their supervisory and commanding officers in dealing with disorderly crowds in order to assure the most effective management of them and to lessen the likelihood of ill-advised action by the police. An example of a procedure is contained in Appendix I, page 423.

Tear gas and smoke sometimes prove effective in dispersing rioters and the curious spectators who may join the melée if not driven away. A procedure used by one department for dispensing smoke and gas is shown in Appendix I, page 436.

12. Police duties at the scenes of crimes and accidents also require procedures to guide the officers in the accomplishment of their duties. The procedures should be outlined in a manner that will clearly place responsibility on the individual officers sent to the scene for the performance of specific tasks. Confusion and the neglect of important duties are thus avoided; the police, under the guidance of such procedures, make their investigations and dispose of the matter in a businesslike manner. Special attention should be given to the designation of the officer who is to be in command; to the duties of the officers in the order of their arrival at the scene; and to the search for and preservation of physical evidence. Procedures to be followed at the scenes of crimes and accidents in use in one department are reproduced in Appendix J, page 441.

Headquarters Procedures. In addition to the field procedures listed above, other procedures are needed to guide officers in the performance of tasks at headquarters. Since some procedures involve officers both at headquarters and in the field, the line of demarcation is not always distinct.

1. Regulations assure the proper care and suitable use of department-owned equipment: motor vehicles; radio, telephone, teletype, interoffice communications, dictating, sound-recording, and public-address equipment; and bullet-resisting shields, gas weapons and masks, and all types of firearms deserve regulations designed to assure proper maintenance, service, care, and technical operation, as well as the approved use of the equipment. Appendix H contains procedures relating to the care of department-owned firearms (page 422) and to the use of public-address equipment (page 421).

2. Uniform regulations should establish the specifications of uniforms and the manner in which they are to be worn. The specifications of equipment to be furnished by the officers, such as the sidearm, holster, belt, cuffs and pouch, and ammunition pouch, should also be established by regulation.

3. Procedures should also be outlined to guide officers in the wrapping, labeling, and delivery of all types of property. The procedure may be somewhat different for evidence, especially of certain types, than for found property. The procedures may be sufficiently involved to justify its separate publication in the duty manual; on the other hand, when it is not complicated, it may be recorded as a part of the general duties.

4. In departments that regularly hold show-ups of the prisoners, a

procedure should be designed to assure that the operation will be conducted properly, with security against escape, and without subjecting the prisoners to ridicule.

5. Reporting regulations are published by most departments in some form. They are designed to guide all members in the preparation, routing, and use of all department forms and reports. Forms should invariably contain, in fine type at the bottom, instructions to guide officers in their preparation and routing. There are, however, some additional reporting requirements that should be recorded in a procedural manual on police reports, especially in large departments.

Decision 11. Which procedures or regulations do not deserve dissemination among all members of the department, and hence, although they should be recorded, do not need to be included in the duty manual?

Some department operations are of little or no interest to all members. Regulations governing these operations, therefore, do not need general distribution. Administrative procedures and records-division operations fall in this category.

While these regulations do not deserve general dissemination as a whole, parts of them that have general applicability or interest should be distributed to all members. This may sometimes be done by incorporating them in the duty manual.

Records-division operations should be outlined in great detail to assure the performance of the many varied operations that are interrelated but frequently accomplished by different clerks. When records-division operations are suitably recorded on cards, colored tabs may be used to indicate the assignment of the operations to the individual clerks and to guide them in performance. The cards also assist in the supervision of records tasks that sometimes become quite complicated. They thus assure adherence to the prescribed procedures by lessening the likelihood of a failure to detect inadvertent or willful deviations.[1]

Purchasing, accounting, property control, and personnel management procedures also deserve to be recorded so as to establish their official adoption, to facilitate their critical analysis, and to aid in the supervision of their performance. Personnel procedures that deserve

---

[1] The record-division operations used by one department are recorded in Appendix C, *Police Records*, pp. 272-287.

special attention include those relating to recruitment, selection for appointment and promotion, evaluation of accomplishments and value to service, and to discipline, training, and welfare.

Tactical Plans

Tactical plans are made to guide officers in dealing with situations at designated locations where the terrain and other factors may be appraised in advance and detailed plans made accordingly. Plans to meet unusual needs created by special community events and sudden surges in criminal activity are discussed in the next chapter.

Decision 12. What tactical plans should be developed and how should they be recorded?

Tactical plans on which all officers should be informed should be recorded in the duty manual. Included in this category are plans for dealing with jail emergencies and for resisting an attack against headquarters. An example of a plan of action to be used in a jail emergency is found in Appendix H, page 418.

Other tactical plans, while affecting all officers, are designed primarily to guide the dispatcher in the deployment of the force. While all officers should be familiar with the general plan of operation, it is not esssential that each be supplied with a copy. Instead the plans are in the form of prepared radio broadcasts; they should be filed at the dispatcher's desk, available for instant use.

Broadcasts should be prepared in advance for all establishments that are connected with headquarters by robbery alarm. Blockade plans to be used by the dispatcher under certain circumstances are also prepared by some departments.[1]

Tactical plans must also be made for dealing with industrial disturbances. It is neither feasible nor necessary to prepare such plans in advance for each industrial plant or other establishment that conceivably may be involved in a labor dispute requiring police attention. The advance drafting of plans to deal with such disorders at some of the more critical plants is desirable, however; the preparation of the plan will frequently reveal important decisions that should be taken by the chief of police or the executive head of the

---

[1] *Police Records* contains an example of a broadcast prepared by one department for use in the event of a bank robbery, pp. 246-250, and an example of a blockade plan, pp. 250-253.

city as well as opinions that are needed from the city attorney. A plan devised for one plant may be used for others with some modifications.

Plans for dealing with industrial disorders at designated plants should not be published for all members of the department. They should be approved, explained to the members who may be assigned, and filed for future reference.

Planning of Procedures and Tactics

The planning officer is responsible in a staff capacity to see that the need for procedures and tactics is discovered and to initiate their development. He should invariably study procedures used by other departments as a guide in developing similar ones to meet the needs of his own department.

Decisions involved in the development of procedures and tactics are usually beyond the capacity of the planning officer; he must rely on operating personnel for them. For this reason, the use of committees appointed by the chief to make recommendations relating to procedures and tactics for the consideration of the command group is an effective method to follow. The more active the operating personnel in their development, the more likely are the plans to be practical and acceptable to the officers who must use them.

The ultimate responsibility of the planning officer in reference to the development of procedures and tactics deserves emphasis. When needed plans are not developed and officially adopted, there is undeniable failure on the part of the planning officer to discharge his obligations as a staff officer.

CHAPTER 15

Meeting Unusual Needs

ORDINARY police operations are designed to meet an average need. The appraisal of the average need will take into consideration seasonal, daily, and hourly variations of the work load. On the basis of this appraisal, the force is organized, division and platoon strengths are established, beats are laid out, police operations are planned, and men are given their regular assignments.

This organization and plan of operation should be kept intact as far as possible. The withdrawal of men from their regular assignments, and the failure to fill vacant assignments, disrupt the regular police service. Vacant beats and the failure to maintain other regular assignments indicate that the average need is not being met. This should not be permitted except when there is no alternative.

The police, however, must deal with situations that impose greater-than-average work loads on them. Public events, such as athletic meets, parades, and so on, place unusual burdens on the police. These events are usually predictable; some occur periodically. Other situations that require above-normal police effort, however, are unpredictable in time, place, and character. Sudden surges of criminal activity, labor disturbances, riots, unusual community events, earthquakes, fires, explosions, and war are examples.

When these extraordinary work loads are imposed on a force organized to meet an average need, the regular police service is bound to suffer. Depletions of the regular force by separations from the service, prolonged absences for training or other purposes, and sick and annual leaves, also disrupt the regular service. Man power should be provided so that nearly all unusual needs may be met without interference with the regular police service.

Organizing to Meet Unusual Needs

When the shift assignment and territorial deployment of policemen are based exclusively on the average need, a more-than-ordinary need imposes a heavy burden on the force. In the absence of a reserve force, the extraordinary load must be carried by overtime

work, by utilizing auxiliary police, or by reducing the force designated to meet the normal need by withdrawing them from their
regular assignments. While one or all of these procedures may be
utilized to meet unusually heavy loads, such as those imposed by
catastrophes, their use should be avoided when the need can be
otherwise met. Since the need can be otherwise met only by reserving man power for this purpose, consideration should be given to
the creation of a special unit in the department for this purpose.[1]

*Decision 1. How should the force be organized to provide man
power to meet out-of-the-ordinary needs?*

The frequency of situations that create above-average needs for
police service is somewhat in proportion to the size of the community. In small communities the situations occur infrequently; in large
ones they occur so frequently that the extraordinary need is nearly
continuous. When the need is continuous, there is clear justification
for a unit of the force to meet it. When the need is not continuous,
but is nevertheless frequent, such a unit is justified when it can be
used effectively during intervals between the situations that create
the above-normal need.

With the exception of catastrophes and public disorders, the situations that create extraordinary needs arise either from traffic or
crime. When the frequency of these situations in both fields is nearly
continuous, as is often the case in a large city, a separate unit for
each is desirable. For convenience, one will be called a special traffic
squad and the other a crime-crusher squad. In smaller cities the
frequency of the situations may not justify the creation of separate
units; one unit should then be created to deal with both crime and
traffic situations. Such a unit is not justified in small communities
where the infrequent extraordinary need must be met by the force
assigned to deal with the average need.

Although the above-average need may be nearly continuous, it
will never be regular. Variations in the man power needed to deal
with situations that require more-than-ordinary police effort further
complicate the problem. Special squads created to meet unusual
needs are not likely to be adequate to deal with all situations. One
unit must be used to supplement the other in some situations. Likewise, the force normally used to meet the average need must be used

---

[1] A directive creating a Mobile Reserve in one department is reproduced in Appendix K, p. 175.

in some situations to supplement the efforts of both. For example, the entire force is likely to be pressed into overtime duty when disaster strikes. The existence of the special reserve units, however, diminishes the frequency and extent of such requisitions of man power from their regular assignments.

The special squads may also be used as a man-power reserve to fill vacancies in regular assignments resulting from separations from the service, sick leaves, and prolonged absences for training and other purposes. When annual leaves are taken during favored months, without a corresponding seasonal slump in the demand for police service that justifies a reduction in the number of beats, the standard of regular service may be maintained by drawing on the special units for vacation relief.

Decision 2. How may the need be measured so that the creation of special squads may be justified?

The need for a special traffic squad may be measured rather accurately in terms of man hours of overtime work and of service lost in consequence of officers being withdrawn from their regular assignments in order to meet the unusual need. Man hours of sizable proportions and situations of nearly continuous frequency are proof of the need for a special traffic squad.

The need for a crime-crusher squad is more difficult to establish statistically for the reason that, in the absence of such a squad, the entire burden of extraordinary need is carried by the patrol division, and since the patrol must not fail to meet regularly the average need, effort is usually not made to meet the more-than-normal need except by the individual beat patrolman. Unusal needs become apparent, however, in a high crime rate and low rates of clearances by arrest and of stolen property recovered. They also become apparent when intensified criminal activity is frequently concentrated in time, place, and specialty.

Justification for the creation of either special squad is enhanced when they are used effectively during intervals between the situations that create above-normal needs.

Decision 3. How should the special squads be fitted into the structure of the police organization, and who should direct their efforts?

When two squads are created, the special traffic squad should be assigned to the traffic division, and the crime-crusher squad should be assigned to the patrol division rather than to the detective division. (See Decision 2, page 52 and Decision 2, page 112.) When only one squad is created to meet both needs, it should ordinarily be assigned to the traffic division; unusual needs for extra man power usually arise more frequently in traffic than in crime control.

The head of the traffic division should have freedom to direct the efforts of the special traffic squad to meet current needs in the control of traffic at public events, while the head of the patrol division should have equal freedom to deploy his crime-crusher squad in dealing with crime problems. When members from one squad are needed to supplement the efforts of the other, they should be assigned by the chief or an assistant chief. The division head in whose field the need occurs should then direct the efforts of the combined force.

In the absence of a crime-crusher squad, the assignment of the special traffic squad to deal with crime problems should be at the direction of the chief or an assistant. Members temporarily assigned to crime control should be under the direction of the patrol division.

An officer should be appointed as the head of each unit. The members of each squad should ordinarily work as a unit, all on the same shift. The squads should have flexible schedules, the hours of work should be planned by the head of the division to which they are assigned, by the squad leader, or by a planning unit. (See page 477.)

Decision 4. How may these special squads be used most effectively during the intervals between situations requiring more-than-average police effort?

The special traffic squad should be used during normal times to strengthen the enforcement of moving-traffic regulations. It should operate under the direct supervision of the traffic division which should select the hours, locations, and nature of its enforcement effort. When selectively directed, this effort will sufficiently supplement enforcement by the motorized patrol to overcome objections to the assignment of primary responsibility for the enforcement of moving-traffic regulations to the patrol instead of the traffic division.

The crime-crusher squad should be used during normal times to intensify patrol in areas of greatest need. Care should be observed, however, to avoid a general patrol; the crime-crusher squad should be restricted to areas and times of greatest need and should, in each instance, be given a specific mission to perform. Failure in this respect results in a waste of man power.

Plans for Unusual Needs

In planning for unusual needs, the five steps listed in Chapter 1 must be taken: (1) The need for the plan must be recognized. (2) A statement of the objective must be formulated. (3) Relevant data must be gathered and analyzed. (4) The details of the plan must be developed. (5) Concurrences must be obtained from police units and outside agencies whose operations may be affected by the proposed plan. Just as the success of the planning effort is dependent on a precise formulation of the objective, so is the success of the plan dependent on a precise statement of the mission. The squad leader must understand his mission exactly; subordinates must likewise understand their objectives and instructions. Confusion or doubt as to their objectives invariably leads to failure and a waste of man power. This point deserves emphasis.

As in procedural and tactical planning, varied factors must be considered in the development of plans to meet unusual needs. In consequence, many decisions must be reached. Instead of discussing each possible decision, examples of plans developed in some departments are contained in the appendix. The plans are offered only as examples; they must be modified to meet the needs of specific situations.

Plans for Unusual Criminal Activities. The need for more than ordinary patrol-division attention to criminal activity usually becomes apparent in the form of a series of criminal acts, often in the same section of the community, during the same hours of the day, sometimes during the same days of the week, against the same type of persons or property, and frequently in a manner to indicate that they are committed by the same criminal or criminals. The need is sometimes discovered by alert patrol-division commanders or by the detectives responsible for the clearance of the crimes by the arrest of the perpetrators. Certainly of discovering the need in the early stages of its development should be further assured by an analyst who studies developments in the crime field in the same manner as does a traffic analyst in the field of traffic accidents. When the police fail to discover these needs and to take suitable action, the failure is usually called to public attention by the press.

When the police fail to discover series of crimes being committed by the same criminals, the efforts of the regular patrol force are not likely to be directed most advantageously. When a reserve squad is available to deal with such situations, the failure results in the force not being used for the purpose for which it was created. Instead, it is likely to be used in an indifferent general patrol operating without direction and purpose. Under these circumstances, the resources of the department are being squandered. The special squad might as well not have been created. Even in normal times when there is no evidence of series of crimes being committed by the same criminals, it is essential that the efforts of the special squad be wisely directed at the locations and during the hours of greatest criminal activity. To this end, a continuing analysis of the crime situation must be maintained. Only in this way is there assurance that the efforts of the special squad will be used most effectively.

The tools of the analyst are spot maps, one for each of the principal criminal specialties, with the crimes recorded by colored pins to show the hour of attack. An inspection of the maps will reveal a concentration of crimes of a type in a locality. A study of the method of operation will reveal the likelihood of the crimes having been committed by the same criminal or criminals.[1]

Some police planning units use an 8" × 5" card, for recording information relating to each crime, which is then coded by punching out designated holes that appear on all four borders so that when a rod is inserted through a selected hole, all cards may be lifted out except those on which the hole was punched out. In this way, cards on crimes having similar *modus operandi* characteristics may be selected for detailed study; a study of each crime may provide a more or less complete description of the perpetrator, his method of operation, and information as to the locality, day of week, and hour of most likely attack. This information should be disseminated, by means of a bulletin, to the police regularly assigned to the area of attack. An example of bulletins used for this purpose by the Los Angeles Police Department is reproduced in Appendix K, page 479. The crime-crusher squad, when assigned to deal with a series of criminal acts, also finds this information essential to plan their operation and to accomplish their mission effectively. Even though there is no evidence that the crimes have been committed by the same criminal, the concentration in time and place may reveal a need for the services of the reserve squad. Likewise, a concentration in time and place of criminal activity of varied types indicates a similar need; the need may be met by an intensified patrol if analysis

---

[1] See pp. 188-190.

does not indicate a more suitable procedure.

Also reproduced in Appendix K (page 482) is a weekly *Crime Summary* prepared by the Oakland Police Department that calls the attention of members of the patrol division to areas of principal criminal attack. Similar summaries of traffic accidents are used by some departments to focus enforcement attention on areas and during the hours of greatest need and against the types of violations that most frequently cause accidents.

Maps recording automobile thefts may also show the location where the cars were left; strings connecting the points of theft and abandonment sometimes reveal significant information useful in directing the efforts of the special squad.

A map used in connection with the previously mentioned questionable-character file,[1] when compared with those showing current criminal activities, may uncover suspects who should be interrogated or placed under surveillance.

Especially in large cities, more than one series of crimes are frequently being committed concurrently, each by different criminals. The series of crimes are often of different types, in different sections of the community, and at different hours of the day. For example, there may be a series of house burglaries in a select residential section during the afternoons, a series of thefts from automobiles parked in the theater section in the early evening, and a series of filling-station and liquor-store robberies on one side of the town in the late evening hours. Integrated plans must then be developed to direct the efforts of the reserve squad against each series at the most propitious time. Timing then becomes important. Transportation must be provided to move the officers from one locality to the next. Communications must be established to assure that added forces will be sent should the criminals be flushed.

The members may all be assigned to one operation; in other instances, some may be used on one operation and the remainder on another. Decisions must be reached as to the manner in which they will operate. In some instances they will be assigned to cover points of likely attack, either on the premise or an adjoining premise or outside; in others they will provide an intensified patrol by being assigned to beats designed for this special purpose. Surveillance may be provided of either suspected persons or places. One operation

[1] See p. 188.

may require plain clothes; in another, the police uniform may be demanded. Decisions must be reached on all of these points in each operation.

An example of a cover plan used by one department in dealing with a series of safe burglaries committed by one man over a period of several weeks is contained in Appendix L, at page 484. The cover was supplemented by an intensified patrol at some times. Special attention is called to the steps taken in preparing for the operations, (pages 484-489), the schedules that were drafted (pages 495-497 and 498-504), the detailed orders that were prepared for each officer (pages 490 and 504), the quality and completeness of the reports that were submitted by the officers (pages 491, 493, and 497), the coordination of the plan with other law-enforcement agencies (pages 506-508), and to the fact that letters of thanks were sent to all citizens who cooperated with the police (page 509).

Special Community Events. Special community events that attract large numbers of vehicles and pedestrians impose unusual burdens on the traffic division that necessitate the use of the special traffic squad sometimes supplemented by a crime-crusher squad and the regular force. Most special events center about a locality, such as a stadium, athletic field, or auditorium; some are in the form of parades that usually follow one of several prescribed routes. Events of this character frequently recur; plans used for one event may be adapted to meet the needs of another.

Although the events frequently vary in the number of persons attracted and some parades follow a longer route than others, these factors are predictable, and separate plans should be made accordingly. A limited number of standard basic plans may be prepared to deal with comparable situations; the basic plan is modified to meet the peculiarities of the current event. Officers who participate in the use of a plan should submit critiques of its operation; weaknesses may thus be discovered and strengthened.

Some other community events that impose unusual traffic and crowd-control burdens are not so frequent in their occurrence and do not adhere to such a precise pattern as those mentioned above. Included are street carnivals and community celebrations not hitherto undertaken. These events require careful planning; fertile imagination is needed to foretell the needs for police service; detailed instructions must be prepared to deal with each situation that is likely to arise.

Planning for Special Community Events. A number of steps must be taken to meet the needs for police service that grow out of many community affairs.

1. **The need must be discovered.** The traffic division should keep informed of pending public events that are likely to impose unusual burdens of traffic and crowd control on them and estimate the number of policemen that will be needed to deal with each. Since public affairs of this nature frequently require permits and are nearly always announced in the newspapers, an alert traffic division experiences little difficulty in keeping informed of coming events.

2. **A traffic and crowd-control plan must be developed.** Posts must be designated, and time schedules and instructions drafted. The preparation of the plan should ordinarily be the responsibility of the traffic division, although this task may be assigned to the department planning officer when the traffic division prefers to be relieved of this responsibility. In the latter case, the plan must have the approval of the head of the traffic division; the planning officer merely serves as his staff officer.

3. **Man power must be obtained to fill the need.** In some instances the special traffic squad will be adequate to deal with the situation; in other cases it will be necessary to use some or all of the traffic officers assigned to regular street duty during that time of the day; in rare instances it will be necessary to draw on the crime-crusher squad or even the regular patrol force to obtain the needed man power. Assignment from outside the traffic division must be made by the chief or an assistant.

4. **The plan must be placed in operation.** The traffic division should be held responsible for the successful accomplishment of the mission.

Public events that bring large numbers of persons together create unusual opportunities for thieves and other criminals. The situation may necessitate the use of some or all members of the crime-crusher squad. When they are used for this purpose, the patrol division should plan and control their operation. When they are used for traffic control, on the other hand, they should be assigned to the traffic division.

Plans for the special events described above should assure the rerouting of through traffic and should provide for emergency runs by fire equipment and ambulances, the posting of suitable temporary traffic directional signs, the policing of the crowd, and the prevention of criminal operations. Plans for parades should designate suitable locations, as assembly points, provide for blocking traffic into these areas and later into the parade route, and assure that traffic blocks are lifted as soon as possible. Plans for public meetings should assure the unhampered reception of vehicles and pedestrians, the blocking of vehicular traffic at points where the congestion of pedestrians and vehicles makes ready movement impossible, and the speedy and safe dispersal of the pedestrians and vehicles at the conclusion of the event. Special attention should be given to parking facilities so that they may be used to best advantage without interfering with movement.

Assignment schedules must be drafted to assure that officers are posted at the times and places needed. Since man power is nearly always inadequate, the assignments should be arranged so that officers may cover more than one post when possible, leaving the first when the need has been met and arriving at the second before the need arises.

Obtaining Concurrences. The planner must be ever-conscious of the necessity of obtaining concurrences from the heads of police units, other city departments, and outside agencies whose operations may in any way be affected by the proposed plan. In many situations, representatives of the affected groups should be invited to participate in the planning. Over-all strategy should be established in collaboration with the heads of other city departments as well as of outside agencies, and the details of the plan should be developed with their representatives. Agencies that may be concerned in a public event, for example, include: the fire department, the transportation company, the safety council, the Red Cross, the press, and sometimes merchants' organizations or the chamber of commerce. The traffic engineer, whether a member of the police department or some other city department, should also participate.

An example is given in Appendix M, page 510, of the plans drafted for the policing of a large athletic event. Attention is directed to the announcement of the event containing information as to its nature, sponsor, place, date and time, and the anticipated attendance, the facts relating to public and official parking, the reserved and no-parking areas, drives to be closed, and barricades and signs; to service vehicles, motor coaches, taxicabs, and trains, and incoming participants and special arrivals; and to the provisions for first-aid facilities, protection, and the maintenance of order (page 511. The plan also contains a map showing traffic and parking arrangements (page 512). General information and instruction to the police issued by the chief are shown on page 514. Schedules of assignment are also shown (page 519).

Disaster Plans. Disaster may strike the community at any moment. It may come as an earthquake, flood, fire, or tornado. The American Red Cross is active in preparing communities for such catastrophes. The police and other public agencies should cooperate with the local chapter of the Red Cross in developing and keeping the disaster plan up-to-date.

Excerpts that relate to police responsibilities in the disaster plan of one community are shown in Apendix N, page 528. Organization charts are shown of the disaster committee and the subcommittee on rescue (pages 529 and 531). The plans and operations of the subcommittee on rescue are also reproduced.

Civil Defense. World War II provided the police and their communities with some experience in civil-defense planning. A future war, if it comes, will bring with it the atomic bomb and perhaps other terrible forms of destruction. The civilian population of this country may then expect to be exposed to the ravages of active warfare. These reasons, coupled with the unsettled international situation, make it important that the police develop plans for civil defense and prepare themselves and their communities for any eventuality.

Police services in civil defense are described in a report to the Secretary of Defense by the Office of Civil Defense Planning titled *Civil Defense for National Security*. The Committee on Civil Defense of the International Association of Chiefs of Police and the Police Services Advisory Committee of the Federal Civil Defense Administration have also prepared an administrative guide and handbook for the police services known as AG-10-1, U. S. Civil Defense, *Police Services*. It was issued May 1, 1951. Technical Manual 27-1, *Procedure for Evacuation Traffic Movement Studies,* was issued November, 1955. These publications may be obtained from the U. S. Government Printing Office.

APPENDIX[1] A

Basic Data for Planning

The nature of data needed for planning is determined by the purpose of the plan. All-inclusive plans necessitate a survey of the entire organization and of all its operating procedures; such extensive plans require maximum information. For that reason, the information needs of the all-inclusive reorganization plan are listed below. The information has various sources and forms, and the data must be compiled in a variety of ways.

1. *Basic laws and regulations governing the department, its top control, and the control of police personnel:*
   a. City charter with amendments.
   b. City ordinances.
   c. State laws.
   d. Civil Service Rules and Regulations relating to the police.
2. *General characteristics of the community:*
   a. Area.
   b. Street mileage.
   c. Lakes, streams, parks, undeveloped areas.
   d. Population: racial, social, and other characteristics from census data.
3. *General statistics:* The following data for each of the past five years.
   a. Police strength per 1000 population compared to the average strength in cities of the same population group and to the police strength in selected cities of approximately the same population and character. These data

[1] Some material in these appendixes has its source in designated police departments, and some of it is a combination of material from many sources. This material is included in the hope that it may be used by police planners as a guide in the preparation of their own procedures.

Permission is hereby granted, without special request, to every police department to use any of this material in the preparation of their own manuals. Acknowledgment is requested of the source of any material used. Charles C Thomas, Publisher.

284

may be obtained from *The Municipal Yearbook,* The International City Managers' Association, Chicago.

b. Per capita police expenditures compared to the average for cities of the same population group and to the police expenditures in selected cities of approximately the same population and character. These data may also be obtained from *The Municipal Yearbook.*

c. Part I crime rates compared to the average rate of cities in the same population group nationally and regionally and to the rates of selected cities of approximately the same population and character. These data may be obtained from *Uniform Crime Reports.*

d. Injury accident rates and fatal accident rates compared to the average rate of cities in the same population group and to the rates of selected cities of approximately the same population and character. These data may be obtained from the National Safety Council.

e. Part I juvenile crime-rate indexes[1] compared to similar crime-rate indexes from comparable cities. These data must be obtained from the local records.

f. Per cent of juvenile offenders filed on in juvenile court.

g. Per cent of Part I crimes cleared by arrest.
   Per cent of Part I court cases convicted.
   Per cent of arrests that cleared Part I crimes that were made by beat patrolmen.

h. Per cent of stolen property recovered.
   Per cent of stolen autos recovered.
   Per cent of stolen bicycles recovered.

i. Arrests for violations of laws relating to:
   Gambling
   Prostitution
   Narcotics
   Liquor sales

j. Per cent of above arrests made by officers not members of vice division.

k. Percentage convicted on arrests for violation of laws

---

[1] A juvenile crime index is described, *Police Records,* pp. 221-222, Public Administration Service, Chicago, 1942.

relating to:
    Prostitution
    Gambling
    Narcotics
    Liquor sales

l. Per cent of convictions that resulted in probation or suspended sentences in violations of laws relating to:
    Prostitution
    Gambling
    Narcotics
    Liquor sales

m. Per cent of convictions that resulted in the actual serving of time in jail for violations of laws relating to:
    Prostitution
    Gambling
    Narcotics
    Liquor sales

n. Total amount actually collected in fines and total number of man-days actually served for violations of laws relating to:
    Prostitution
    Gambling
    Liquor sales

o. Ratio of man-days actually served to money actually paid in fines for violations of laws relating to:
    Prostitution
    Gambling
    Liquor sales

p. Traffic-arrest index by the month.
Traffic-enforcement index by the month.
Per cent of traffic citations issued for moving violations irregularly disposed of by month for the past year.
Per cent of other traffic tickets irregularly disposed of by month for the past year.
Per cent of citations for moving violations that were served by beat patrolmen.

q. Annual total mileage for (1) automobiles, (2) two-wheeled motorcycles, and (3) three-wheeled motorcycles.

Annual police deaths resulting from accidents in operation of (1) automobiles, (2) two-wheeled motorcycles, and (3) three-wheeled motorcycles.

Annual number of man-days lost from service owing to injuries resulting from the operation of (1) automobiles, (2) two-wheeled motorcycles, and (3) three-wheeled motorcycles.

Names of officers who are receiving or whose dependents are receiving pension benefits growing out of injuries or deaths in the operation of (1) automobiles, (2) two-wheeled motorcycles, and (3) three-wheeled motorcycles.

r. Monthly proportional distribution, for a recent 12-month period, of—

Part I crimes

Part II offenses

Miscellaneous reports

Accidents

Arrests

Man-days on annual relief: (1) entire department; (2) patrol division

s. Average proportional distribution, for a recent 12-month period, by days of the week, of—

Part I crimes

Part II offenses

Miscellaneous reports

Accidents

Arrests

Weekly leave: (1) entire department; (2) patrol division

t. Monthly proportional distribution of man-days lost on sick leave during the past five years.

4. *Inventories:*

a. Vehicles: (1) show the make, type, purchase date, condition, mileage, and assignment, use, or location of:

Automobiles	Wreckers	Other
Wagons		Three-wheeled motorcycles
Ambulance		Two-wheeled motorcycles

(2) if operated as a pool, describe operation.

b. Communications equipment:

Telephone (switchboards with number of trunks, stations, key boxes, call boxes, and other special equipment)

Teletypewriters and receivers

Radio transmitter; dispatcher's equipment and map (date purchased)

Mobile radios: vehicle; walkie-talkie (date purchased)

Re-call system; location of signals and call boxes

Interoffice communication devices; type and location

Sound recording equipment (not including dictating equipment)

c. Armaments: number and size

Hand guns	Riot sticks
Riot guns (shotguns)	Yawara sticks
Rifles	Batons
Submachine guns	Fighters' cups
Gas masks	Helmets
Gas grenades	Bullet-resisting shields
Gas guns	Bullet-resisting vests
Gas projectiles	Armor-plated vehicles
Other gas equipment	

d. Office equipment:

Chairs (straight; arm; executive; typist; other)

Desks (executive; typist; other)

Filing cabinets (number of drawers and size)

Typewriters (make; year purchased; carriage; condition; assignment or location)

Dictating equipment (make; year purchased; condition; assignment or location)

Tabulating equipment

Comptometers; adding machines

Other office equipment

e. Maintenance equipment:

Motor vehicle; Radio; Traffic-control devices

f. Traffic-control devices:

Description of stop signs

Description of other regulatory signs

Description of markings currently in use

Location, type, and installation date of traffic-control signals

g. Laboratory equipment

5. *Buildings:* floor plans showing dimensions and the use to which all space is devoted.

6. *Personnel information:*

   a. Roster showing: date, of appointment; birthdate; height; weight; formal education; intelligence quotient; rank; years in present rank; special training.

   b. Conditions of service: pay schedule; hours of workweek; weekly and annual leaves; sick leave; pension provisions; all compared to other cities.

   c. Turnover: number who left the service in each of the past five years classified as: deceased; retired; resigned with no pressure; resigned under pressure; dismissed while on probation; dismissed after permanent appointment.

   d. Sick leave: the average annual number of days on sick leave per member for each of the past three years.

   e. Assignments to other departments and public agencies, and to tasks that are not strictly police duties.

   f. The names of officers who are regularly assigned to street duty who are unable to drive an automobile with reasonable safety and efficiency, and the nature of their street duty.

7. *Personnel management:*

   a. What is the power of the chief of police to select, appoint, assign, promote, demote, suspend, and dismiss personnel?

   b. List the qualifications for candidates. Who set these standards?

   c. Describe the procedure of selection for appointment.

   d. Describe the procedure of selection for promotion.

   e. Who is the appointing authority? Must he have the approval of some other board or agency? Does this also apply to promotions?

   f. Describe the disciplinary machinery. Who has the final word on disciplinary action?

   g. What are the duties of the department personnel officer?

   h. Who investigates complaints against officers?

8. *Training:*

a. How many weeks are devoted to recruit training?

b. Give subject matter schedule of last school.

c. What specialized training is provided by the department?

d. List the number of officers for each of the past five years who have been sent to outside police schools (FBI Police Academy, Northwestern Traffic Institute, Juvenile Delinquency Control Institute at U.S.C. are examples) showing the number of weeks of instruction at each.

e. Describe the in-service training program.

f. Are local university or college facilities used for training members?

9. *Organization:* (Similar material from other departments is also useful for purposes of comparison.)

a. Organization chart.

b. Definition of functions of the principal divisions.

c. Rules and regulations.

d. Procedural or duty manuals of all types.

e. General Orders.

f. Beat maps for each shift showing foot, motorized, two-wheeled motorcycle and three-wheeled motorcycle beats, and points requiring traffic officers, showing the hours of assignment.

10. *Patrol Division:*

a. Personnel strength arranged by shifts and assignments.

b. Basis used in the establishment of shift hours.

c. Basis used in the organization of motorized beats.

d. Basis used in the organization of foot beats.

e. Number of shifts.

f. Number of beats on each shift covered by one-man patrol cars and by two-man patrol cars.

g. Number of foot beats on each shift.

h. Average daily number of motorized patrolmen on actual patrol on each shift during the past six months.

i. Average daily number of foot patrolmen on actual patrol on each shift during the past six months.

j. Duties of patrolmen (distinguish between foot and motorized if there is a difference) in:

The enforcement of traffic regulations

The enforcement of vice regulations

The supervision of juveniles

The investigation of crimes

The search of crime scenes for physical evidence

The investigation of traffic accidents

The checking of the security of commercial establishments

The inspection of taverns, bars, dance halls, and other licensed recreational establishments.

k. How many minutes before the beginning of their shift are they required to report for duty?

l. Do any patrolmen report on or off duty from call boxes without reporting at headquarters?

m. Are evidence technicians, equipped and trained to search crime and accident scenes for physical evidence, assigned to the patrol division? to other division?

11. *Detective Division:*

a. Personnel strength arranged by shifts and assignments with last annual case load listed for each assignment.

b. Number of vehicles assigned.

c. How many of the assigned vehicles are used by some other division and during which hours?

d. The distribution among the days of the week of the relief days.

e. The average case load for each day of the week.

f. What records are filed in the detective-division quarters?

12. *Vice Division:*

a. Personnel strength.

b. Extent of specialization of assignment.

c. Usual hours on duty.

d. Enforcement duties.

e. Inspectional duties.

f. Licensing duties.

g. Number of vehicles assigned.

h. Are any of assigned vehicles used by some other division during certain hours?

i. What records are filed in the vice-division quarters?

j. In whose custody is contraband stored?

13. *Traffic Division:*

a. Personnel strength arranged according to shifts and assignments.
b. Number and type of vehicles assigned.
c. How many of the assigned vehicles are used by some other division and during which hours?
d. Does the division have a traffic engineer?
e. If it does not have its own traffic engineer and there is a traffic engineer assigned elsewhere in the governmental organization, which engineering-type tasks are performed by the traffic engineer and which by the police?
f. What are the responsibilities of the traffic division in reference to the installation, service, and repair of signs, signals, and markings?
g. What are its responsibilities in the installation, service, and repair of parking meters? In collections from them?
h. Does it operate a schoolboy patrol? Traffic-violator school? Inspection stations?
i. Does it use chemical tests of degree of intoxication?
j. Does it use a movie camera to record actions of drunk drivers?
k. To what extent does it use warning notices?
l. What records are filed in the traffic-division quarters?

14. *Juvenile Division:*
a. Personnel strength arranged according to shifts and assignments.
b. Number of vehicles assigned.
c. How many of the assigned vehicles are used by some other division and during which hours?
d. List of classes of cases assigned for investigation.
e. Is the final disposition of juvenile offenders left to the juvenile division?
f. Are parents invariably notified of police contacts with juvenile offenders?
g. Does the juvenile division maintain some form of unofficial supervision of some juvenile offenders? Explain nature and extent.
h. What records are filed in the juvenile-division quarters?

15. Records Division:

a. Personnel strength arranged according to shifts and assignments.

b. What proportion of the records-division staff is civilian (non-police)?

c. What proportion of records-division staff is female?

d. Copy of each form or other record used anywhere in the department.

e. Reporting regulations or procedures.

f. Records division operations or procedures.

g. Copy of regularly used summaries (daily, weekly, monthly, annual, or other).

h. Copies of any special studies made in past year.

i. Are all basic records consolidated in the records division?

j. List incidents that are recorded on a numbered complaint sheet.

k. List incidents that are recorded but that are not given a serial number.

l. Who registers complaint sheets by assigning a serial number to them?

m. Who fingerprints and photographs prisoners? When is it done in reference to arrest times? Where is it done?

n. To which members of the force outside the records division are some records-division clerical tasks assigned?

16. Communications:

a. Are the communications functions under the control of the central records division?

b. How many direct-line robbery alarms terminate in the communications room?

c. How many direct-line burglary alarms terminate in the communications room?

d. Is there a direct ADT line on the switchboard?

e. Are there prepared broadcasts to be used on robbery alarms?

f. Are there floor plans available for consultation on establishments protected by burglary alarms?

g. Is there a store-report file or similar source for obtaining the name and telephone number of proprietors of business establishments for emergency purposes?

h. Describe the devices used to show the availability of officers for radio assignment?

i. Is the quadrant system used for deploying men on calls where criminals are reported to be in operation?

17. *Jail:*

   a. Which division is responsible for jail duties? Wagon runs? Ambulance runs? Booking prisoners? Custody of prisoners' property? Authorizing detention, restrictions on liberties, and release of prisoners?

   b. What duties are assigned to the wagon and ambulance crews for performance between runs?

   c. Show the average peak prisoner population by days of the week.

18. *Police Laboratory:*

   a. Is there a police laboratory?

   b. What division is it under?

   c. How many dark rooms are there in the police department?

   d. To what divisions do they belong?

   e. Who makes searches of crime scenes for physical evidence?

   f. Who photographs crime scenes?

   g. Is there a lie-detector? To which division is the operator assigned?

   h. Describe procedure used to keep the chain of possession of physical evidence as short as possible.

19. *Maintenance:*

   a. What responsibility has the police department for:
   Janitorial service?
   Building maintenance and repair?
   Servicing of transportation equipment?
   Repair of transportation equipment?
   Service and maintenance of radio equipment?
   Installation, service, and maintenance of parking meters and traffic signs, signals, and markings?

20. *Extra-departmental:*

   a. Is the community organized into a:
   Local safety council?
   Community council for the prevention of delinquency?

Local crime commission?

b. Is there a police public-relations officer?

c. What are his duties?

d. List and provide copies of all police department publications distributed to the public during the past year.

e. How many groups (totalling how many persons) have made tours of police headquarters during the past year?

f. Is there a police auxiliary? Describe its strength, organization, duties, and general operation.

g. How many commercial-type radio broadcasts have been made by police officers during the past year?

h. How many television broadcasts during the past year?

i. How many public speeches have been made by members of the department during the past year?

j. What special services has the department provided to the general public during the past year?

21. *Unsolved murders:*

a. List briefly the following information relating to each murder committed during the past ten years on which the perpetrator has not been convicted: date, name, location, hour, weapon or means used, occupation, probable motive.

b. Was the victim ever arrested for violation of gambling, prostitution, narcotics, or liquor vending laws, or suspected of such violations?

22. *In departments having district stations, the following information for the past year should be compiled for each district station:*

a. Complaints filed in person (not by telephone), not including accident reports.

b. Number of accident reports filed by citizens.

c. Lost or stolen property returned to citizens.

d. Property temporarily stored for citizens.

e. Number of fines paid in person.

f. Number of bonds posted by citizens (not by professional bondsmen).

g. Number of prisoners booked.

h. Number of foot patrolmen.

i. The sum of the difference between the distances from

the center of each motorized beat to headquarters and
to their district station, and the total number of
motorized beats on all shifts.

j. Station house complement, including weekly and
   annual leave.
k. Annual utilities cost (electricity, gas, water, telephone).
l. Annual repair and janitor cost.
m. Value of site.
n. Value of building.
o. Value of equipment (vehicles, communications, office,
   etc.).

APPENDIX B

General Information for Applicants as Patrolmen and Patrolmen-Clerks

BERKELEY POLICE DEPARTMENT
BERKELEY, CALIFORNIA

There's a future for YOU in police work in Berkeley

Career Service. Appointments as patrolmen or patrolmen-clerks in Berkeley offer able and ambitious young men a real opportunity for a career in a police department that has long been recognized as outstanding.

Officers are trained by the department to perform all phases of police work such as traffic enforcement, accident investigation, patrol methods, criminal investigation, juvenile control, and identification procedures. The training offered by the department continues throughout the officer's career.

Promotions to higher police ranks are by examination and are made from the ranks. Patrolmen-clerks who wish to do so have an opportunity to transfer to patrolman when there are openings. Patrolmen also have an opportunity to transfer to patrolman-clerk.

Requirement and Examinations. The Personnel Department establishes the qualifications that applicants must have to take the examination and to qualify for appointment with probationary status.

The Personnel Department establishes the content of the examination and administers it to the qualified applicants.

Further details relating to examinations, appointments, and working conditions may be obtained by calling at or writing to the Personnel Department, Room 19, City Hall, Berkeley.

Appointments. Employment lists resulting from examinations are in effect for one year unless sooner exhausted, and may be extended.

Individuals selected for appointment are fingerprinted and investigated concerning personal history. They must pass a medical examination by a city physician prior to appointment.

297

Candidates on the eligible list who are under twenty-one are not eligible for appointment until their twenty-first birthday. No candidate who has passed his thirtieth birthday will be appointed.

Original appointments to both patrolman and patrolman-clerk are subject to a two-year probation. This two-year work trial is part of the examining process and must be successfully completed before the officer gains tenure.

Residence. In view of the critical housing situation in Berkeley, members of the department presently are permitted, with approval of the City Manager, to reside outside of Berkeley within a reasonable distance.

Employees who live outside the city must maintain a residence telephone.

Car Allowance. Patrolmen furnish their own cars for use on city business. They are paid an allowance each month based upon the car-age classification on a standing plus running cost allowance basis.

Patrolmen-clerks do not use a car in police service and therefore receive no allowance.

Pension. A Police Employees Pension Fund is provided for members of the police department. The fund is financed jointly by employees and the City through contributions made monthly to the fund. It is possible that the provisions of the retirement ordinance may be changed in the future. This is true of most retirement systems.

Some of the more important provisions of the retirement ordinance are:

1. One-half salary is paid monthly to an officer who retires after 25 years of service, and who has reached the age of 55 years.

2. Two-thirds salary to an officer who retires after thirty years of service, regardless of age.

3. One-third salary to the dependents of a retired officer who dies while on retirement for length of service.

4. One-half salary to an officer who is retired for a disability incurred in actual performance of duty.

5. One-half salary to depedents of a retired officer who dies while on retirement for disability.

6. One-half salary to dependents if death is incurred in actual performance of duty.

If an employee resigns prior to retirement, his accumulated contributions are returned.

Sick Leave. Officers earn sick leave credits at the rate of twelve working days of sick leave with full pay for each year of service. Those with more than twenty years of service receive twenty-four days per year. Sick leave is allowed only in case of illness. Each officer is credited with 12 working days upon appointment.

Vacation and Holidays. Two weeks of vacation with pay are allowed each year. After ten years of service, vacation leave is three weeks per year. Members of the department are compensated for eleven holidays each year, either by compensatory time off duty or by pay which is in addition to their regular salary.

Duties. *Patrolmen:* Patrolmen maintain law and order by patrolling a beat during an assigned watch, or by traffic patrolling, or by working on plain clothes assignments.

A patrolman is responsible for the proper policing of the beat to which he is assigned. He investigates all assigned complaints, apprehends law violators, and maintains an active patrol to prevent crime. Part of his time is spent in the car and part on foot. No full-time foot beats are maintained at present.

Patrolman-Clerks: A patrolman-clerk works in the offices in various clerical positions. He may be assigned to perform general typing and records functions, or identification, statistical, radio dispatching, or accounting and bookkeeping work. He must also operate the patrol wagon and ambulance from time to time. When acting as jailer, he must search jail prisoners. He may be assigned to assist the patrol division in any patrol functions.

Working Conditions. Working conditions are excellent. The work week is forty hours with two days off duty each week. Officers are compensated for all overtime worked either on a basis of equal time off duty or pay on a basis of straight time.

Shifts are not rotated. The newly appointed officer begins on the morning shift. Later he is transferred to the evening shift and finally to the day shift, on a general basis of seniority.

During the last one-half hour of shift the officer types reports on all cases assigned to him. Frequently this period is not sufficient and the officer is required to work overtime in order to complete his reports. Officers must also appear in court and this frequently is during their off duty time.

Days off cannot be taken at the pleasure of the officer because of the nature of police work. The new officer will probably find it necessary to take his days off in or near the middle or the week for some time, with the possibility of the days being changed at any time.

A forty-five minute meal period is allowed during the tour of duty. Meal periods may vary because of emergencies arising during the normal lunch period.

Uniforms and Equipment. *City Furnishes:* Badge, Handcuffs, Baton, Ammunition, Radio (patrolmen). *Officer Furnishes:* Uniform, Whistle, Flashlight, Revolver, Siren (patrolmen).

Limitations. Members of the department cannot undertake any scholastic training or employment during off duty hours which affects the efficiency of their police services or which casts discredit upon or creates embarrassment for the city government.

The solicitation or acceptance of gratuities or rewards is prohibited by police regulations.

Officers are not permitted to engage in any improper political activity. Men are appointed, retained, and advanced in rank solely on merit.

Police officers must obey the same laws they are sworn to enforce. A higher standard of conduct, both on and off duty, is expected of an officer than of an average citizen.

Welfare. The Berkeley Police Association, consisting of all members of the department, is organized to protect and promote the individual and collective welfare of all officers.

The department maintains an indoor shooting range, an extensive library, and a police gymnasium. Officers are encouraged to use these facilities and may do so individually or in groups during their off-duty time.

There are opportunities to participate in shooting matches and various recreational and athletic activities sponsored by the department.

APPENDIX C

Information to Be Contained in Personnel Questionnaire

Full name, address, telephone number, age, date and place of birth, height (in bare feet), and weight (stripped).

Citizenship and whether by birth or naturalization.

The number of dependents and any additional ones expected.

Name, relationship, and department of any relatives employed by the City. Names of members of the police department who are known to the candidate.

Arrest data (including drunk, drunk driving, traffic, and all other arrest): charge, disposition, date, city, state.

The details of any civil suits brought by or against the candidate. Details of motor-vehicle accidents in which the candidate has been a driver, including the nature of the settlement.

Residence addresses for the past 10 years, with the dates, and names and addresses of the landlords.

Occupations during the past 10 years, listing for each the firm name, kind of business, street address; dates of employment and termination and reasons for termination; the starting and final salaries. If discharged, details should be given.

The position in which the candidate considered himself most proficient; the position he liked best and why; the task he enjoyed most and why; the occupation he disliked most and why.

A list of trades in which the candidate is skilled.

Financial statement, including life insurance, savings and commercial bank accounts, investments in stocks and bonds, ownership of home and other real estate. Income other than salary. The name, type of business, and addresses of firms with which the candidate has had charge accounts during the past 10 years.

Total itemized indebtedness. The names and addresses of persons from whom automobiles have been purchased on credit.

Positions held that required surety bonds; the amount of bond and the name of the bonding company.

The fairness of treatment accorded the candidate by his creditors. The fairness of treatment by his employers.

Details of anyone who is an enemy or who might attempt to injure the candidate in any way.

Ability to typewrite; the speed and whether by touch or sight. Stenographic ability: the system and speed.

Years of driving an automobile and motorcycle. Operator's or chauffeur's license number.

Hours of airplane-pilot experience.

Knowledge of radio-telephone or telegraph and license held.

Length of experience in operation of telephone switchboards and the types used.

List of gambling games the candidate is familiar with.

Hours of reading each week and type of literature.

Ability to understand, speak, read, and write foreign languages and the degree of proficiency.

Musical instruments played by the candidate and the degree of proficiency. Ability to sing, speak publicly, act, wrestle, box, swim, sail a boat, ride a horse.

Principal and other hobbies.

Experience with firearms; top score; where and when trophies and medals won in competition; the name of team or organization.

A statement of service in Army, Air Force, Navy, Marine Corps, R.O.T.C. or other military organizations: the dates of, and rank or grade at enlistment and discharge. Details of court martial or other disciplinary action. Whether a member of the active or inactive reserves.

Marital status. The following information on the present and all former wives: maiden name; previous married name; date and place of marriage; present names and addresses of former wives. If the candidate has been divorced: when and where. If widowed: the time, place, and cause of wife's death, and present arrangements for the care of any surviving children.

The name, address, occupation, present age or age at death, relationship, and cause of death of father, mother, brothers, and sisters, whether living or dead, and all other living blood relatives known to the candidate.

A list of any of the following disorders that members of the candidate's immediate family have suffered from: tuberculosis, heart ailments, stomach disorders, cancer, kidney disease, diabetes, nervous disorders, mental disturbances, drug addiction, and alcoholism.

A list of any of the above disorders plus rheumatism, scarlet fever, diphtheria, and discharging ear, that the candidate may have suffered.

Names and addresses of physicians who have treated the candidate during the past 10 years. The nature of consultation with a physician during the past year. The nature of surgical operations and injuries that required medical care, when and where they occurred, and the names and addresses of the surgeons.

A statement as to whether the candidate has ever lived with a tubercular patient.

A description of any deformities.

The quality of sleep, appetite, and bowel movement; weight gained or lost during the past year; date of last successful smallpox vaccination.

Ability to stand pain, disgusting sights and smells, and the sight of blood, with a statement of the experience on which the opinions are based.

The extent and nature of use of tobacco and intoxicating liquors.

Years of competition and letters and other awards won in football, basketball, track, baseball, rowing, boxing, wrestling, and other sports in academic institutions, athletic clubs, or as a professional.

The name and city of all schools attended: age at entrance and termination; name of principal, counsellor, or dean. Business colleges, extension or correspondence courses, night schools, and any other organized courses of study should be included.

School subjects that were most difficult; those that the candidate enjoyed most.

A statement at to whether study was easy or difficult, with an explanation.

List of other competitive examinations taken by the candidate, and eligibility lists that now contain his name.

A statement as to why the candidate makes application for police service with an explanation of any special interest he may have in police work.

Special training, experience, or ability possessed by the candidate which he considers of value in police service.

A statement as to whether the candidate knows of anything that would disqualify him for police service or prevent the full discharge of his official duties in such a position.

A statement as to whether the candidate objects to wearing a uniform or working at night.

A recent bust photograph of the candidate.

The signature of the candidate.

APPENDIX D

Tests of Strength and Agility [1]

By

LIEUTENANT L. W. NEARY
Berkeley Police Department

The following considerations should govern the selection of tests of strength and agility if they are to be practical for jurisdictions of all sizes, in many of which physical facilities are limited:

1. Score Range in Tests. Each test should show some range of accomplishment. In many of the tests collected, there were found to be events in which some participants scored a zero, while in other tests all participants scored 100.

2. Time Consumed. In running all events simultaneously, which is desirable when a large number of candidates are participating the time is controlled by the time of the slowest event. An example is the high jump, with three tries at successively greater heights.

3. Facilities Available. Events should require only those facilities usually found at the average small-town high school. The events submitted require only two pieces of equipment: a stop watch for timing, and a horizontal bar suspended between two uprights which may be varied in height to accommodate the pull-up and bar-vault events.

4. Test Should Not Require Physical Conditioning Nor Involve

---

[1] The material in this section was gathered by Lieutenant Neary at the request of the Minimum Standards Committee of the California State Peace Officers Association. A review was made of tests of strength and agility used by many law enforcement agencies, and a critical appraisal was made of the various tests used by the Berkeley Police Department over a period of years. The scoring tables for each of the events are based on the records of many thousands of achievement records of college and university freshmen, tabulated and analyzed by Professor Frederick W. Cozens, Professor of Physical Education, University of California, and revised downward after a test of 1447 applicants for law enforcement positions in three of the events (pull-ups, standing broad jump, and sit-ups) demonstrated that the higher average age of the applicants had apparently diminished somewhat their physical ability. The scoring tables represent preliminary work of the committee; further tests of applicants may reveal a need for additional revision.

Danger of Injury to the Participants. Examples of dangerous events are the "mat dive," which has resulted in broken necks, and the 440-yard run, which has resulted in heart strain in the case of participants not physically well-conditioned. The greater number available for selection, when physical conditioning in perparation for the test is not required, provides a better quality of recruit.

5. A view of candidates performing agility tests, especially the "100-Yard Dash" and the "Sit-Ups," is of advantage to oral-board members. To assist observers in the identification of candidates, each participant should be assigned an entry number attached to his trunks or shirt.

6. The events should test a maximum number of muscles and should give an index to a participant's coordination.

An aggregate score of less than 250 should disqualify.

Since fatigue has some bearing on achievement, if the events are to be run off singly, it is suggested that they be in the following order:

1. Pull-Ups
2. Standing Broad Jump
3. Bar Vault
4. 100-Yard Dash
5. Sit-Ups

Pull-Up

Description:

The contestant hangs on a horizontal bar with arms and legs fully extended, using the upper grip (knuckles to the face). He raises his body by his arms until his chin can be placed over the bar and then lowers his body to a full hang. The exercise is repeated as many times as possible.

Rules:

a. Only one trial shall be allowed unless for some reason the examiner believes that the contestant has not had a fair opportunity.

b. The contestant's performance shall be recorded as the number of pull-ups made after extension of the arms.

c. The body must not swing during the execution of the movement. The knees must not be raised.

d. No resting or change of grip is allowed.

Standing Broad Jump

Description:

The contestant stands with the feet several inches apart and with toes just back of the take-off mark or front of the take-off board. The take-off is made from both feet, and the contestant jumps forward as far as possible, landing on both feet.

Free swinging of the arms and bending of the knees is permitted but the feet must not leave the board or take-off line until the jump is made.

Rules:

a. Three fair trials (not including fouls) shall be allowed and the best of the three recorded.

b. The contestant's performance is recorded in feet and inches to the nearest inch.

c. The measurement of the jump is made from the nearest imprint (including any imprint by hands or body made by the jumper in landing) to the take-off or front edge of take-off board and at right angles to the take-off line or board.

d. Violation of any points under "Description" constitutes a foul.

Bar Vault

Description:

The contestant steps up to the bar, grasps it with the upper grip (that is, knuckles toward the face), body erect, eyes front, feet nearer than the shoulders to the vertical plane of the bar, arms and legs straight. With a spring from both feet and at the same time a strong pull of the arms, he swings his legs vigorously to one side and at the same instant straightens his arms (pushes upon them) so as to carry his body over the bar. Both arms should carry the body weight.

To save time in the administration of this test, the bar may be raised three or four inches at a time. This three or four inch rise applies only at lower heights.

Rules:

a. After a reasonable warm-up, two trials shall be allowed at each height.

b. The contestant's performance shall be recorded in feet and inches as the last height of the bar is cleared.

Scoring Scales For Peace Officers' Agility Tests

SCORE	PULL-UP	STDG. B. J.	BAR VAULT	100 YD. RUN	SIT-UP	SCORE	PULL-UP	STDG. B. J.	BAR VAULT	100 YD. RUN	SIT-UP
100	23	9'- 7"	6'- 7"	10.4	70	50		7'- 1"			20
99					69	49	6		4- 7	12.7	
98		9- 6	6- 6	10.5	68	48		7- 0			
97	22				67	47			4- 6	12.8	19
96		9- 5	6- 5	10.6	66	46		6-11			
95		9- 4			65	45		6-10	4- 5	12.9	
94	21		6- 4	10.7	64	44					18
93		9- 3			63	43		6- 9	4- 4		
92			6- 3		62	42				13.0	17
91	20	9- 2		10.8	61	41	5	6- 8	4- 3		
90		9- 1	6- 2		60	40		6- 7		13.1	
89				10.9	59	39			4- 2		16
88	19	9- 0	6- 1		58	38		6- 6		13.2	
87				11.0	57	37			4- 1		15
86		8-11	6- 0		56	36		6- 5		13.3	
85	18	8-10		11.1	55	35		6- 4	4- 0		
84					54	34				13.4	14
83		8- 9	5-11		53	33	4	6- 3			
82	17			11.2	52	32			3-11		13
81		8- 8	5-10		51	31		6- 2		13.5	
80		8- 7		11.3	50	30		6- 1	3-10		
79	16		5- 9		49	29				13.6	12
78		8- 6		11.4	48	28		6- 0	3- 9		
77			5- 8		47	27				13.7	11
76	15	8- 5		11.5	46	26		5-11	3- 8		
75		8- 4	5- 7		45	25	3	5-10		13.8	
74				11.6	44	24			3- 7		10
73	14	8- 3	5- 6		43	23		5- 9			
72					42	22			3- 6	13.9	9
71		8- 2	5- 5	11.7	41	21		5- 8			
70	13	8- 1			40	20		5- 7	3- 5	14.0	
69			5- 4	11.8	39	19					8
68		8- 0			38	18		5- 6	3- 4	14.1	
67	12			11.9	37	17	2				7
66		7-11	5- 3		36	16		5- 5		14.2	
65		7-10		12.0	35	15		5- 4	3- 3		
64	11		5- 2		34	14				14.3	6
63		7- 9			33	13		5- 3	3- 2		
62			5- 1	12.1	32	12					5
61	10	7- 8			31	11		5- 2	3- 1	14.4	
60		7- 7	5- 0	12.2	30	10		5- 1			
59					29	9	1		3- 0	14.5	4
58	9	7- 6	4-11	12.3	28	8		5- 0			
57					27	7			2-11	14.6	3
56		7- 5	4-10	12.4	26	6		4-11			
55	8	7- 4			25	5		4-10	2-10	14.7	
54			4- 9	12.5	24	4					2
53		7- 3			23	3		4- 9	2- 9		
52	7		4- 8		22	2				14.8	1
51		7- 2		12.6	21	1		4- 8			

c. A vertical measurement shall be taken from the ground or floor to the top of the bar.

d. No part of the body shall touch the bar except the hands.

e. The vault must be one continuous movement from the time the feet leave the floor or ground until landing. No double jumping is permitted, that is, a jump in place before the actual take-off. It is permissible to raise the heels off the floor or ground and to bend the knees in preparing for a vault.

f. The toes must not be on or over a line directly under the bar.

g. The diameter of the bar shall not exceed 1½ inches.

100-Yard Run

Description:

Contestant should take his mark using the customary crouching start. The starter will use the commands: "Get on your mark," "Get set," "Go." In place of the word "Go" accompanied by a downward sweep of the arm as a signal to the timer, a gun may be fired.

Sit-Up

Description:

This event should be conducted on a floor or smooth plot of ground. The contestant taking the test sits on the floor or ground with feet held by a partner or by a fixed bar six inches above the floor level. His body and head must be erect, his knees straight, and his middle fingers touching behind his head with arms parallel to a plane projected through his shoulder blades.

He then lowers his trunk backwards to a position about three inches above the floor barely touching with his shoulders the thumb side of a second partner's hand held on the floor with palm at right angles to the floor. After touching the partner's hand, the contestant immediately raises his body to the vertical position and repeats the exercise as many times as possible. The rhythm is one complete movement (backward and upward) in six seconds.

It is suggested that three men work together, one taking the test, one holding the feet, and the third holding his hand on the floor or ground. The man holding the feet counts the number of sit-ups, and the man holding his hand on the floor watches for infractions of the rules.

Rules:

a. The arms and head must remain in the original position throughout the test. Any deviation from arm or head position or from the rhythm of one complete movement in six seconds nullifies the particular sit-up in question.

b. No pause is permitted between the movements of raising and lowering the trunk.

c. Failure to touch partner's hand nullifies that particular sit-up. No momentary relaxation is permitted when touching the hand.

d. The contestant's score shall be the number of perfectly executed sit-ups he is able to do.

APPENDIX E

Lesson Plans

A course on Elements of Interrogation, included in the curriculum of a recent California Basic Peace Officers' Training School,[1] was divided into seven topics:

1. An Introduction to Police Interviews and Interrogations
2. General Interrogation Rules
3. Interrogation Techniques for the Willing and Able Subject
4. Interrogation Techniques for the Inadequate Subject
5. Interrogation Techniques for the Unwilling Subject
6. Scientific Aids to Criminal Interrogation
7. Special Techniques for Difficult Interrogations

Lesson plans on each topic for use in this school were slight revisions of those prepared for the Berkeley Police Training Bureau by Pascal C. Longaker assisted by members of the Berkeley Department. The lesson plan on the first topic is given below as an example.[2]

ELEMENTS OF INTERROGATION

TOPIC NO. 1. AN INTRODUCTION TO POLICE INTERVIEWS AND INTERROGATIONS

Materials

1. Blackboard.
2. Book, *Modern Criminal Investigation*, by Soderman and O'Connell, published by Funk & Wagnalls. Chapter II, pp. 5 to 33.

Introduction

Police work hinges on satisfactory interrogations. All other police jobs may be well done, yet an officer will not do an adequate job unless he is able to conduct effective interrogations. We shall treat

---

[1] The School was held at the Northern California Peace Officers' Training Center under the direction of the Alameda County Sheriff's Department and the Supervisor of Peace Officers' Training, Bureau of Trade and Industrial Education, California State Department of Education, February 7 to March 5, 1949.

[2] The lesson plan reproduced below was made available by John P. Peper, Supervisor of Peace Officers Training, Bureau of Trade and Industrial Education, California State Department of Education.

311

the material in such a manner that it satisfies all needs, by directing attention to each of the following:

a. The general rules and principles applying to police interrogations.
b. Illustrations drawn from experiences of seasoned interrogators.
c. The place of police interrogations in the formation of public opinion.
d. The adaptation of ideal interrogation techniques and procedures to the emergency situations under which they are frequently used.
e. It is estimated that eighty per cent of all police time is spent talking to people.

Presentation

I. Fundamentals

A. BASIC DEFINITIONS (BRIEF ON BLACKBOARD)

1. Interview:
To interview means to ask questions for the purpose of securing information. However, when the word "Interview" is used, there is an implication that the desired information will be voluntarily given.

2. Interrogate:
To interrogate also means to ask questions. But, when the word "Interrogate" is used, there is an implication that the interrogator's request for information will be met with resistance by the subject.

"Interrogate," as used in police work includes the entire contact of the officer with the subject. Reactions, time lapses, attitude, emotional responses, and many other factors may be just as important to the interrogator as the words with which the subject answers questions.

3. For the remainder of the instruction the words "Interview" and "Interrogation" may be used interchangeably. The fundamental principles apply in either case.

B. "No ONE Is LEGALLY OBLIGED TO PROVIDE INFORMATION TO THE POLICE." (Write this sentence on blackboard)

1. There are exceptions to this rule, but they are few. By law, participants in certain vehicular accidents must make reports to

the proper police authorities. There are other circumstances in which the police must be given information. We know that sexual delinquents must register, and there are other examples. But with regard to the subject of police interrogation generally, the statement is correct.

2. The important consideration is that the usual interrogation subject does not have to give the police information unless he chooses to do so. Further, it is difficult, almost to the point of impossibility, to prove that a subject has deliberately falsified, that he does in fact remember though he states that he has forgotten, or that he actually observed all that he was in a position to observe.

II. Components of the Police Interrogation

A. BASIC COMPONENTS

1. *Subjects and interrogators.*

Primary components of the police interrogation are:
   (a) Subject.
   (b) Interrogator.

The subject may be any person possessed of information needed by the police in the performance of their authorized job. It might be any of the following:
   (a) The Complainant.
   (b) The Victim.
   (c) The Suspect or Accused.
   (d) A Witness.
   (e) Any Informer or Informant.

The interrogator may be any member of the police organization who, with proper authority, seeks information possessed by another individual, so long as such information is related to and encompassed by the police jurisdiction.

2. *The Interrogator.*

   a. *The Interrogator is a constant factor.*

   The personality, capability, experience, intelligence, and other characteristics of each interrogator remain about the same from one interrogation to another. Once the interrogator has adapted general principles and techniques to his own personality, he knows the methods which operate best for him. He has an appreciation of his own limitations and special abilities. Since he always forms one half of the interrogation he is considered to be a "constant factor."

There are personality variations distinguishing one interrogator from another. These need to be considered by each individual so that general principles may best be adapted to the specific personality. Personality variations among interrogators are based in part on the following:

(1) Experience, both police and general.

(2) Attitudes springing from heredity and growing out of past experiences.

(3) The culture and education of the individual and his family.

(4) The reaction of the individual to specific situations and persons.

(5) Other untold numbers of influences, traits, and characteristics.

b. *Attitude of the Interrogator.*

The attitude of the approach to the interrogation is extremely important. There are many special reminders which might be listed. A few are specifically mentioned here. However, the most significant point to bear in mind is that the objective of the interrogation is to secure factual information. The extent and quality of knowledge to be gained is unknown before the interrogation occurs. If the outcome were a foregone conclusion, there would be little reason to conduct the interrogation.

(1) *Pre-trial tendencies.*

New men must guard against the tendency to form fixed opinions in advance of the interrogation.

(2) *Tolerance.*

No police officer can afford to be intolerant of the attitude, interest, or problems of the subject of an interrogation. Tolerance is dependent upon an understanding of the interests and problems of others. Each interrogator should seek to increase his own sphere of knowledge in this respect.

(3) *Bias.*

To be biased means to have definite leanings toward or away from a certain individual, group, or situation. The police are servants of all the public to the same degree and cannot afford to render more or less service to one group than another.

(4) *Patience.*

The interrogator must learn to be patient. Impatience may be felt and the purpose of the interrogation defeated. Time should be no element to the interrogator.

(5) *Compassion.*

To be compassionate means to feel the unhappiness or suffering of another. The interrogator who is possessed of compassion is fortunate. It springs from sincerity, which is the keynote toward establishing the support or confidence upon which the voluntary provision of information is dependent. Compassion is a rare gift, though it would be common if all men remembered always that there are few without some sin.

(6) *Self-assurance.*

This trait is apparent when the interrogator knows his job, and knows that he knows his job. Genuine self-assurance springs from an inner knowledge of truth and sincerity and from the normal development of the personality.

c. *Preparation by the Interrogator.*

(1) *Incident knowledge.*

Each interrogation has as its central interest one or more particular incidents of police business. All available information concerning that incident should be known to the interrogator before the interrogation is undertaken.

Information concerning the incident in question may furnish the basis for stimulating a lagging interrogation, evaluating the information which is secured, or the employment of a special technique to encourage the subject to volunteer complete cooperation. This knowledge should include such things as the nature and extent of the incident; the persons and objects involved; and other officers who have already been interested in the incident.

(2) *Facts surrounding the incident.*

In addition to the primary facts concerning the incident, there are other facts of great value. Some of the important secondary facts are:

(a) Knowledge of the area in which the incident occurred;

(b) Climatic condition at the time of the incident;

(c) Degree of visibility;

(d) Disturbances occurring simultaneously with the incident;

(e) The emotional, physical, and mental condition of the principals of the incident;

(f) Other coincidental and surrounding data.

(3) *Job knowledge.*

In each instance the interrogator should check his information regarding the specific matter at hand. For the new officer this is particularly important. Any single interrogation may require a knowledge not yet acquired. Time permitting, the interrogator should prepare himself by gaining the needed information.

(4) *Knowledge of the principals.*

Adequate preparation by the interrogator includes the possession of all available information concerning the persons primarily involved. A knowledge of these principals provides a basis for evaluating information given, for stimulating the interrogation, for learning of relationships existing between the subject and one of the principals, as well as many other important matters.

d. *Capability of the interrogator.*

The ability to make a rapid and accurate appraisal of the subject marks the competent interrogator. The goal of each new officer should be the attainment of this ability.

A rapid, accurate appraisal of the subject includes the following:

(1) Subject's position relative to the pertinent issue;

(2) Subject's emotional condition;

(3) Subject's general attitudes;

(4) The determination of such questions as pecuniary or mercenary liability or interest by the subject;

(5) Friendships, antagonisms, relationships, or bitterness toward the police or society as a whole.

There are other traits which identify the accomplished interrogator, but all stem from his ability to appraise and his ability to fit approaches and techniques to the specific subject and specific situation.

3. *Subjects.*

   a. *The subject is a variable factor.*

   Though the interrogator may adapt certain principles to his own personality, each subject with whom he comes in contact is a new and fresh personality. This means that the major portion of instructional periods must be directed at this ever-changing component of the interrogation. The possible range of subject personalities is as great as the range of human personalities found in the continental limits of the United States. The subject might be classified in any one of many ways for the purpose of study and analysis. As has already been indicated, treatment here will be along the classification decided by the willingness or unwillingness of the subject to provide the information which is needed. However, subjects might be considered in other ways, as illustrated by age and sex groupings.

   b. *Subjects might be considered by an age and sex classification.*

   (1) *Pre-adolescent children.*

   If a pre-adolescent child of either sex has been in a position to secure information which is needed by the police, how may he be best treated? Or, better still, can he provide any information which might be of value? He may provide very valuable information, but the interrogator must guard against damaging the information sought. Young children of either sex are very susceptible to suggestion. They should never be asked questions in such a manner as to make them believe that you want a certain answer. Young children are imaginative. Don't stir up their imaginations and expect an accurate description or story. There is no reason why children cannot provide good information if properly interrogated. They observe well, and often remember things which would never register upon an adult mind.

(2) *Adolescent boys.*

Adolescent boys are especially good subjects when information concerning such things as automobiles, airplanes, trains, or other mechanical devices are concerned. They are not given to paying close attention to the petty details of neighborhood gossip, dress, and so forth.

(3) *Adolescent girls.*

In contrast to the adolescent boy, the adolescent girl is apt to be a good subject with regard to the affairs of her neighbors, and probably could report accurately on the number of boyfriends which an older girl in the neighborhood was entertaining. The adolescent girl, while interested in hair styles, clothing, and budding romances, would be a poor subject, generally, on the make and model of an automobile involved in an accident, or the type of plane which flew over the city at a specific time.

(4) *The young adults, married or single.*

As a general rule these are poor subjects. They are preoccupied with their own problems and much involved in economic and social self-determination. Contacts tend to be limited by comparison to those of the middle-aged bracket. However, if specific attention had been called to an incident, there is no reason why accurate and reliable information might not be forthcoming.

(5) *The mature adult.*

Here is the most dependable group of subjects, for as a rule personal adjustments have been made, social perspectives have been widened, opinions are apt to be more reserved, a fuller appreciation of the police responsibility is more likely. In addition to being more fully developed and better adjusted than any other groups, their powers of observation and retention are at their peak as well.

(6) *Elderly persons of either sex.*

The very old, and some individuals not advanced in age excessively, tend to revert to childhood status mentally and emotionally. The same cautions required in handling children apply to this group. The tendency to be imaginative and susceptible to suggestion may be present. This generalization does not hold for those individuals who have retained their vigor and interests, regardless of age.

c. *Attitude, capability, and personality classifications.*

These will not be treated in detail here because specific subjects are treated according to personality, capabilities and attitudes during later hours. The significant thing to bear in mind is that, just as with the interrogators, there may be a great disparity in these factors among subjects. Some of the capabilities, personality, and attitudinal subjects treated later are, for example:

(1) The garrulous type.
(2) The drunken type.
(3) The dying subject.
(4) The born liar.
(5) The reserved type of subject.
(6) The loud blow-off subject.
(7) The remorseful type.
(8) The subject with emotional conflict.
(9) The mentally deficient.
(10) The culturally deficient.
(11) The subject suffering from loss of memory.
(12) The subject with a minority personality.
(13) The shy, diffident type.
(14) The fearful type.
(15) The know-nothing type.
(16) The disinterested type.
(17) The impudent type.
(18) The tricky type.
(19) The anti-social type.

Such personality types could be listed ad infinitum. The

interviewer must use his knowledge and experience to the best advantage with each type.

d. *The approach classification.*

Subjects might be treated according to the approach best employed by the interrogator. What is done in this instruction is to group the personality types into the approach classifications into which they usually fall. As has been indicated briefly before, the approach classifications employed during this instruction are as follows: (List italicized words on board.)

(1) Those subjects who are *willing and able* to provide the information needed by the interviewer. These subjects need to be handled in such a manner that all of the pertinent information which they possess is obtained, and that such information as they purport to provide is capable of evaluation for authenticity and accuracy.

(2) Those subjects who are *inadequate.* They are willing to provide the information needed by the interrogator, but for one reason or another are unable to do so.

These subjects need to be treated in such a way that whatever aid they require is recognized and given. It will be seen later that the treatment has been such that, for example, the subject who wants to provide the information needed but who is fearful of doing so, is considered with regard to the best manner of overcoming his fear. So it is with the timid subject, the subject who genuinely can't remember, and so on.

(3) Those subjects who are *unwilling* to provide the information they do possess.

These subjects must first be approached in such a manner that they are converted into willing subjects. Secondarily, they will be treated in accordance with the group into which they fall after they have been converted to a spirit of cooperation. In all events, it may be seen that there are numerous ways in which the subject of an interrogation might be considered, but since the chief problem is one of making unwilling subjects over into willing subjects, it has been felt that the best over-all approach is through treatment of various ways of handling the different types.

B. ADDITIONAL COMPONENTS OF THE POLICE INTERVIEW

1. *Place of interview.*

a. *Allowances for time and circumstance.*

Certain circumstances demand that the interrogation be held immediately upon contact with the subject, regardless of time or place. It is generally true that the interview should be held at police headquarters or a place of the interviewer's choosing.

b. *The value of privacy.*

Consideration of the material to be discussed or disclosed.

Effect of advertising your source of information.

Need to follow each train of thought until satisfactorily disclosed.

c. *Psychological considerations of place of interrogation.*

The police station or headquarters is generally recommended as the place of interrogation, because it places the interrogator among familiar surroundings and at the same time places the subject among strange surroundings. The interrogator is given an advantage at the outset by this condition.

(Illustrate (1), (2), and (3), below with a sketch or point out with objects in the classroom.)

There are many psychological advantages to be gained through control of the place of interrogation. Each of the following contributes to this advantage:

(1) The type and arrangement of furniture in the interrogation room;

(2) The quantity and direction of light which is present;

(3) Relative sitting positions of the subject and interrogator;

(4) Control of distractions;

(5) Protection for the interrogator;

(6) Availability of stenographic assistance;

(7) Availability of other assistance and interrogating aids.

2. *Time elements of the interrogation.*

Another secondary component of the police interrogation is the element of the availability of adequate time. If the interrogation is undertaken when the availability of time has not been properly planned, its success is jeopardized.

Questions such as follow should be raised and satisfactorily answered before the interrogation is started.

a. *Does the subject show signs of "time-pressure" distractions? Does there seem to be a need to get away and fulfill another responsibility?*

b. *Has sufficient time been allotted by the interrogator as well as the subject to permit completion of the interrogation?*

c. *Are there "time conflicts" which may decrease the attention of either the subject or interrogator?*

Generally speaking, the interrogation should be at the convenience of the subject. There are circumstances under which the interrogation time is selected purposely to inconvenience the subject. This may be true with certain classes of suspects. However, the general rule that the subject's convenience should be considered is sound.

3. *Persons present during interrogation.*

The number and types of persons present in addition to the subject and the interrogator is a real component. The matter should receive deliberate thought for the following reasons.

a. *Control.*

When more than one interrogator is present there is the constant possibility of conflict in the control of the interrogation. Even when intentions are good, the second or third interrogator occasionally speaks inopportunely. There are times when it is advisable to have more than one interrogator, but in such instances the question of control and direction of the interrogation should be clearly established in advance.

b. *Legal complications of multiple interrogations.*

The mere fact that there were several interrogators may give basis for a defense contention at a later time that there had been coercion; that the subject made statements and disclosed facts which he would not have done had he not been placed in fear by the mere fact there were numbers of persons apparently arrayed against him. (Some cases where several officers subpoenaed in one case.)

c. *Possibility of conflicting impressions and stories with multiple interviewers.*

Any person present during the interview is susceptible to examination as a witness in court to testify to what was said and done during the interview. Even though the discrepancies which might appear in statements made are slight and insignificant, any divergence in statement as to what occurred during an interview may weaken or invalidate all of the information there procured.

d. *Occasional advantage in having two interviewers present.*

Where it is necessary for an officer to question a member of the opposite sex, then his actions should always be observed (as well as heard) and made a matter of complete record. This affords protection to the officer against a later plea by the subject that the officer made an advance or otherwise behaved in an objectionable manner. Upon occasion there is a basis for believing that the personality of the interrogator is in sharp contrast and conflict with that of the subject. For that reason, it may be well to open the interrogation with two interrogators, and leave it with the one who is most successful with the particular subject.

e. *Usual situation best handled by a single interviewer.*

Subject matter often makes this policy mandatory. Exceptions as noted because of sex, and also with mental deficients and the emotionally unstable.

f. *One subject at a time.*

This is a rule to which there are few exceptions. It is based on the fact that to get true and uncontaminated information from a subject, it is well that he or she be restrained from knowing what information others have provided.

There is a great psychological advantage in handling subjects separately, too. One may be led to believe that another has provided more information than actually has been the case. There is the further consideration that one subject may dominate and restrain another if more than one is interviewed at a time.

This simple rule holds even for such routine cases as automobile accidents, where basic and preliminary information is picked up on the street at the scene and at the time of the accident. The informant or witness should be drawn aside when he is being questioned or telling his account of the facts.

In such instances as robberies where information needs to be quickly ascertained in order that a covering plan may be put into operation, when two officers are dispatched to the scene, it is a wise procedure to get the descriptions and elementary information from the victims separately, so that weaknesses in stories, descriptions, and the account of action may be recognized. If one man has gotten better information than another, the better will not be contaminated by the poorer.

There are occasional circumstances, when it might be wise to confront one subject with another.

This has been advantageously employed where women have been interrogated separately until such time as one, through suspicion or jealousy, is led to believe that the other has informed on her. Then the facing of one by the other may produce the tension required to make both tell complete and accurate stories. They should again be separated, however, for the detailed narrative.

C. HISTORICAL BACKGROUND OF INTERROGATING METHODS

 1. *There has been an unsavory past which has cast a reflection on the police.*
 Medieval methods of the rack, hot stones, etc. Contemporary methods of some police agencies.
 2. *Good Contemporary Policy.*
 Use of force is absolutely forbidden. The need to use force is an admission of incapability. At any time that a subject is under the control of a member of this department, the sanctity of the subject's person must be guaranteed.

APPLICATION: None at this point.

TEST: Oral questions to be asked of students at end of this period.

 1. Distinguish between "To Interview" and "To Interrogate" as defined in this course.

2. What is the "fundamental principle" of interrogation and what does it mean to the interrogator?
3. What is meant by a "pre-trial tendency"?
4. What group of people, as a general rule, are the most dependable subjects?
5. What is one measure of the capability of an interrogator?
6. What are some of the reasons that give value to privacy in interrogating a subject?
7. What is a good rule regarding the use of physical force in police interrogation?

APPENDIX F

Recruit Manual

WICHITA POLICE DEPARTMENT

JULY, 1937

(In addition to the following material, the Recruit Manual *contained approximately 30 pages of detailed procedure under the headings listed in this outline.)*

CLASS ROOM INSTRUCTION
RECRUIT TRAINING SCHOOL

Wichita Police Department
July 1, to August 11, 1937

SUBJECT	LECTURE PERIODS
Auto Theft	1
City Geography	1
City Ordinances	7
Criminal Procedure and Rules of Evidence	4
Discussion, Drill, and Examinations	30
Driving Instruction	4
Duty Manual	4
First Aid	18
Fraud, Bad Checks, and Counterfeiting	2
Gymnasium—Exercises and Holds	36
Investigation by Detectives	2
Investigation at the Scene of a Crime	4
Juveniles and Crime prevention	3
Laws—Kansas and Federal Criminal Laws	10
Miscellaneous	8
Modus Operandi	3
Observation	2
Organization of Wichita Police Department	1
Personal Identification and Fingerprints	5
Pistol Practice, Firearms Instruction	15
Police Problems and Patrol Investigations	3
Police Tactics	8
Public Relations	3
Reports and Records	14
Tour of Headquarters and Prison Farm	2

Traffic: Handling Violators, Warnings and
   Summons, Accident Investigation 7
Typing 15
Vice 4

                                              216

NOTE: All classroom instructors will examine the recruits by oral, written, or practical examination and will record the grades in each subject. Instructors in all subjects except First Aid, Gymnasium, Pistol Practice, and Typing shall furnish the Personnel Officer with a number of questions and problems on each subject covered, for review, drilling, and examination purposes.

INSTRUCTIONS
for
FIELD INSTRUCTORS
RECRUIT TRAINING SCHOOL

July 1 to August 11, 1937
Wichita Police Department

Plan of Operation

Each recruit will be assigned to a designated Field Instructor for the first four weeks of the recruit school. During the remaining two weeks the recruits will be rotated every night. The rotation will be progressive and regular in order of the beat numbers of the Field Instructors. The Third Platoon Sergeant will furnish the Personnel Officer a report of the assignments of recruits and a schedule of the rotating assignments.

Field Instructors will meet individually once each week with the Personnel Officer to discuss the progress of the recruits. These conferences will be in the Personnel Officer's office at 2 p.m. according to the schedule supplied by him.

Responsibility

It is hoped that each Field Instructor will accept the responsibility of the welfare of the recruit assigned to him, guiding him during his period of training, and assisting him afterward in any problems which may develop. He should give attention not only to routine training, but also to his assimilation into the department, assisting him in getting acquainted with other officers and adjusting himself to his new environment. Effort should be made to make him feel at ease and to develop the self-confidence so necessary in a police officer.

SCHEDULE
RECRUIT TRAINING SCHOOL

Wichita Police Department

July 1 to August 11, 1937

July	10 a.m.	11 a.m.	1 p.m.	2 p.m.	3 p.m.	4 p.m.
1 Thursday	Organization	Ordinances	Pistol Instruction	Driving Instruction	Duty Manual	Gym
2 Friday	Tour of Headquarters	"	Typing & Pistol Instruction	"	"	"
3 Saturday	Prison Farm	"	Crab Meeting	"	"	"
5 Monday	Observation	"	Pistol & Typing	"	"	"
6 Tuesday	"	"	" " "	Kansas Laws	Tactics	"
7 Wednesday	Discussion	"	" " "	"	"	"
8 Thursday	"	"	" " "	"	"	"
9 Friday	"	Records	" " "	"	"	"
10 Saturday	"	"	Crab Meeting	"	"	"
12 Monday	"	"	Pistol & Typing	"	"	"
13 Tuesday	"	"	" " "	"	"	"
14 Wednesday	"	"	" " "	"	"	"
15 Thursday	"	"	" " "	Federal Laws	Traffic	"
16 Friday	"	"	" " "	Federal Laws	"	"
17 Saturday	"	"	Crab Meeting	Crim. Proc.	"	"
19 Monday	"	"	Pistol & Typing	" "	"	"

Date						
21 Wednesday	Drill	"	" "	"	"	"
22 Thursday	"	First Aid	" " "	Investigation at scene	"	"
23 Friday	Exam	"	" " "	"	Ident.	"
24 Saturday	Drill	"	Crab Meeting	"	"	"
26 Monday	"	"	Pistol & Typing	"	"	"
27 Tuesday	"	"	" " "	Det. Inv.	"	"
28 Wednesday	"	"	" " "	" "	"	"
29 Thursday	"	"	" " "	Auto Theft	Juv. Crime	"
30 Friday	Exam	"	" " "	Fraud-Check	" "	"
31 Saturday	Discussion	"	Crab Meeting	Cftg.	" "	"
August 2 Monday	"	"	Pistol & Typing	Vice	Patrol Invest.	"
3 Tuesday	"	"	" " "	"	Police Prob.	"
4 Wednesday	Drill	"	" " "	"	"	"
5 Thursday	"	"	" " "	"	Public Relations	"
6 Friday	Exam	"	" " "	M. O.	"	"
7 Saturday	Drill	"	Crab Meeting	" "	"	"
9 Monday	"	"	Pistol & Typing	" "	Rpts. & Rec.	"
10 Tuesday	"	"	" " "	Miscellaneous	" " "	"
11 Wednesday	Exam	"	" " "	"	" " "	"

Assignments

The Field Instructor will cover each daily assignment as it comes up. He will follow the procedure outlined and explain the problems involved and the policies of the department. He will demonstrate the procedures listed as he encounters them. As the recruit progresses, he will be required to perform duties that have been explained to him. After three weeks, the recruits will be required to perform as many duties as possible except those of the most difficult nature.

Instructions on Reporting Regulations

Field Instructors will explain the reports that are executed at the end of each tour of duty, and as the recruit progresses, he will make these reports himself. The reports are listed in this manual with three columns headed by the letters "E," "D," and "P" respectively. When a report is explained, demonstrated, or performed, the instructor will check the appropriate column opposite the report.

Quizzes

Each Field Instructor will quiz his recruit from day to day on the instructions he has received, and drill him on any apparent weaknesses.

FIELD INSTRUCTOR'S SCHEDULE

Field Instructors will follow this schedule in recruit training. They are not limited to the schedule, however, but should, when situations arise involving items not yet covered, give instructions and demonstrations in advance of the scheduled time if such training seems timely.

As items are *Explained, Demonstrated* and *Performed,* the Field Instructor should indicate by checking the proper column of the schedule, as indicated by the letters "E," "D," and "P." These entries should be made in the Manual of the Recruit, who should also be urged to make such marginal notes as may be desirable. This manual should remain in the possession of the recruit, and will become his property following final inspection by the Personnel Officer. Field Instructors will have the manual of their recruit with them for inspection and discussion during conferences with the Personnel Officer.

JULY 1   E | D | P

  I. PARAMOUNT REMINDERS—Page 1
     A. Police and the Public
     B. Intelligent Precaution—Always Use
  II. ARREST—Page 2
     A. Information to be Gathered at Time of
        Arrest
     B. How to Search a Person (Men Only)
     C. How to Search a Woman
     D. Resisting Arrest: Book When
        Resistance is Real
     E. Using the Pistol

JULY 2

  III. GENERAL PROCEDURE—Page 3
     A. Checking on a Proprietor
     B. Checking With a Proprietor on a Suspect
     C. Obtaining Descriptions of Persons
     D. Obtaining Descriptions of Property
     E. Calling an Ambulance
     F. Handling Evidence
     G. Checking Building Permit
     H. Using First Aid
     I. Calling Headquarters
     J. Questioning a Witness
     K. Protecting a Crime Scene
     L. Taking a Dying Declaration
     M. Conducting a Raid

JULY 5

  IV. RESPONSIBILITY OF BEAT OFFICER—Page 6
     A. For Crime on Beat
     B. For Vice Conditions on Beat
     C. Patrol Technique
     D. Getting Acquainted on Beat
     E. Rules Affecting Beat Officer
     F. Follow-up on Instructions Given by
        Beat Officer
     G. Position of Officer in Civil Matters
     H. Relation with Public

E | D | P

E | D | P

E | D | P

JULY 26　　　　　　　　　　　　　　　　　　　　　　　E | D | P
XVIII.　ANIMALS—Page 33
　　　　A. Found
　　　　B. Wounded
　　　　C. Dead
　　　　D. Shooting Dogs
　　　　E. Dog Bite Cases
　　　　F. Dog Complaints

　XIX.　REQUESTS FROM CITIZENS—Page 34
　　　　A. Requests for Aid in Collecting Rent
　　　　B. To Watch Houses and Homes during
　　　　　　Vacation
　　　　C. Requests for Assistance
　　　　D. Requests for Medical Aid

JULY 27
　XX.　MISCELLANEOUS DUTIES—Page 35
　　　　A. Sweeping Wheat from Box Cars
　　　　B. Public Gatherings
　　　　C. Cars Parked in Front of Drives
　　　　D. Cars Parked in Private Places
　　　　　　Without Lot Owner's Consent
　　　　E. Noise Making Devices on Cars
　　　　F. Handbills, Pamphlets and Samples
　　　　G. Signs
　　　　H. Warnings Required
　　　　I. Trucks, Produce, etc.
　　　　J. Occupation Tax Warrants
　　　　K. Produce Ordinance
　　　　L. Taxi Ordinance
　　　　M. Milk Ordinance

JULY 28
　XXI.　INFORMATION—Page 37
　　　　A. General
　　　　B. Sources of Information Available
　　　　　　at Headquarters
　　　　C. Sources of Information in Wichita
　　　　D. Pawn Shops and Second Hand Stores

REPORTING FORMS

	E	D	P
1. Bulletin			
2. Beat Book			
3. Pickup Book			
4. Persons Wanted			
5. Investigation Report			
6. Preliminary Report			
7. Auto Injury-accident Report			
8. Daily Car Report			
9. Flat-tire Tag			
10. Lantern Report			
11. Officer's Report			
12. Visitors to Station Report			
13. Speech Reports			
14. Sick Reports			
15. Vacation Report			
16. Notice of Defect			
17. Straight Summons			
18. Notice of Violation			
19. Parking Warning			
20. Non-Injury Accident Report			
21. Accident Driver's Report			
22. Departmental Receipt			
23. Auto Red Card			
24. Injured Prisoner Report			
25. Hold for Investigation			
26. Request for Interne			
27. Store Report			
28. Property Tags			
29. Liquor Stickers			
30. Police Court Subpoena			
31. Assignment Sheet			
32. Warrant and Complaint			
33. Liquor Warrant			
34. Case Card			
35. Criminal Record			
36. Drunken Driver's Report			
37. Sergeant's Daily Report			

					E	D	P

38. Special Service Reports

39. Newcomer's Report

KEY:

  E—Explained

  D—Demonstrated

  P—Performed

APPENDIX G[1]

Duty Manual Excerpts

PART I
PORTLAND POLICE DEPARTMENT
RULES AND REGULATIONS

1000. Definitions of Terms Used in Police Department Rules and Regulations, Duty Manual, Procedures, and Orders

1001. *Organic Units*

.01 *Headquarters:* The police building that houses the head-quarters staff and the staff responsible for policing the City of Portland.

.02 *Organic Unit:* Members of a force regularly grouped together under one head for the purpose of accomplishing a specified police purpose.

.03 *Division:* An organic unit whose commanding officer reports directly to the Chief of Police.

.04 *Platoon:* The personnel of an organic unit assigned to one shift or watch.

.05 *Shift (Watch):* The period of a day during which a platoon is on duty. The first is usually referred to as the early morning, dog watch, or graveyard shift or watch; the second as the day shift, and the third as the evening watch. The precise hours of work for each are established by department order.

.06 *Detail:* Member of a force, sometimes from more than one organic unit, grouped together for the accomplishment of a specified mission. When not engaged in a continuing operation, the detail is called a special detail.

.07 *Post:* A fixed point or location to which an officer is assigned for duty. It is the desk, office, or other place to

---

[1] This appendix contains excerpts from the *Rules and Regulations and Duty Manual,* and the table of contents of General Police Procedures of the Portland, Maine, Police Department, by permission of Chief Leon T. Webber.

which an officer is assigned at headquarters; it is also the
location where a patrolman is assigned for specific duty,
such as: (a) an intersection or crosswalk for traffic duty
or (b) a spot or location for general guard duty, observation, and surveillance or for the apprehension of a person
wanted for, or about to commit, a crime.

.08   *Route:* A length of street, or streets, designated for patrol
purposes. A route is used for the assignment of traffic and
some foot patrolmen.

.09   *Beat:* An area (in contrast to length of street) assigned
for patrol purposes.

.10   *Sector:* An area containing two or more beats, routes,
or posts. The squad of officers assigned to a sector is
headed by a sergeant.

.11   *Quadrant:* The four sections created by two streets that
intersect at or near the location of a crime. Quadrants are
used to facilitate the assignment of motor patrolmen in
the search for criminals.

1002. *Command*

.01   *Order:* An instruction given by a superior officer to a subordinate. It may be either oral or written.

.02   *General Order:* Permanent written order issued by the
Chief of Police not relating to a specific circumstance or
situation but affecting or of concern to the entire force.
General Orders are published in the Daily Bulletin or
issued in writing to each member of the department. With
the exception of those relating to promotions and demo-
tions, they are ultimately incorporated into the department
manuals.

.03   *Special Orders:* Written orders issued by the Chief of
Police relating to some specific circumstance or situation,
usually of a temporary nature, that ordinarily does not
affect the entire department.

.04   *Chain of Command:* The unbroken line of authority extending from the Chief of Police through a single subordinate at each level of command down to the level of
execution.

.05   *Through Official Channels:* Through the hands of the
superior officers in the chain of command.

.06 *Staff Supervision:* The supervision by a superior of an officer not under his direct command. Staff supervision may be either (a) supervision of the man in reference to attention to duty and compliance with general regulations but without reference to the manner in which he performs his tasks, or (b) supervision of the manner in which an officer performs a specific task but without reference to his attention to duty and compliance with general regulations.

1003. *Personnel Classification*

.01 *Classified Position (or Service):* All positions and their classifications which are under civil service.

.02 *Unclassified Position (or Service):* A position that is not under civil service.

.03 *Force:* All members of the Police Department who have police powers.

.04 *Civilian Employees:* Employees in the Police Department who do not have police powers.

.05 *Officers:* Members of the Police Department who have police powers. The term is applied without regard to sex, rank, division, or duty. All officers are in the classified service.

.06 *Superior Officers:* Officers who have supervisory responsibilities, either temporarily or permanently.

.07 *Commanding Officers:* Any officer assigned to exercise command over a division or platoon. During the absence of the commanding officer, the officer designated to relieve him is in command and during that time is the commanding officer.

.08 *Rank:* Each class of members of the Force is a rank. The titles of the ranks are:
   a. Chief of Police
   b. Captains
   c. Lieutenants
   d. Sergeants
   e. Detectives
   f. Patrolmen-Policewomen
   g. Matron

.09 *Grade:* Officers are graded according to their pay step or length of service.

.10 *Patrolmen:* Regularly appointed police officers who have not been promoted to higher rank.

.11 *Detectives:* The Chief of Police is authorized to designate patrolmen to serve as detectives and to return them to patrol service at his pleasure. This designation is an assignment and not a permanent promotion.

.12 *Ranking Officer:* The officer having the highest rank or grade. Officers of the same grade shall rank according to the date of their appointment to that grade. When two or more officers are on duty together, the officer of the highest rank is in command and shall be held responsible for the operation. For a special detail and for a specific period, an officer may be designated by the commanding officer to take command without regard to rank. The beat officer is the ranking patrolman when other patrolmen are dispatched to his beat.

.13 *Acting:* Serving temporarily in a position to which the member is not ordinarily assigned, usually in a position of higher rank. All the authority, responsibilities, and duties of the officer in the higher position devolve upon the acting member.

.14 *Chief of Police:* The executive head of the Police Department.

.15 *Captains and Lieutenants:* Commanding officers of divisions and platoons.

.16 *Sergeants:* Have immediate charge of subordinates assigned to them. They instruct and assist them in their duties, and are responsible for their general appearance, good order, and discipline. Sergeants supervise activities at the operational level.

.17 *Matrons:* Women civilian employees appointed by the City Manager who have supervision of the women's jail at police headquarters.

.18 *Radio Engineer:* Licensed Radio Engineer who has charge of maintaining all police radio equipment.

.19 *Undercover Operator:* A private person of good character who is temporarily employed to associate with persons and in establishments suspected of law violations for the purpose of obtaining information that will assist the police in obtaining evidence in support of a prosecution.

.20 *Informant:* A person, usually of questionable character, who is able to give the police information to assist them in arresting a wanted person or in obtaining evidence that will support a prosecution.

.21 *Table of Organization:* A table showing the number and rank of officers and civilian employees assigned to each organic unit when each position is filled.

1004. *Personnel-Administration Terminology*

.01 *Length of Service:* The length of time an officer has been engaged in the actual performance of police duty. It includes the time served in the armed forces that is required by law to be recognized as active duty, and also sick leave and leaves of absence.

.02 *Appointment:* The designation of a person by the appointing authority to any position within the Police Department. The City Manager is the appointing authority for all positions.

.03 *Promotion:* A change in the employment status of a member to a position of greater responsibility or higher classification.

.04 *Suspension:* The act of temporarily denying a member the privilege of performing his duties in consequence of dereliction or other violation of department regulations. Suspension is either the first step in the disciplinary process or the penalty assessed. The suspended member does not receive any pay during the period of his suspension except when the Civil Service Commission rules that the suspension of an officer was unjustified.

.05 *Discharge (Dismissal):* The act of terminating the service of a member. All members shall hold office during good behavior, but may be removed by the City Manager in accordance with the provisions of City Ordinances.

.06 *Insubordination:* The willful disobedience of any order lawfully issued by a superior officer, or any disrespectful, mutinous, insolent, or abusive language toward a superior officer.

.07 *Neglect of Duty:* Failure to give suitable attention to the performance of duty. Examples include: the failure to take appropriate action on the occasion of a crime, disorder, or other act or condition deserving police attention; absence without leave; failure to report for duty at the time and place designated; unnecessary absence from his beat during his tour of duty; failure to perform duties prescribed in the Duty Manual; failure to conform to department operating procedures.

.08 *Incompetence:* Incapable of the satisfactory performance of police duties. The lack of any of the following qualities is evidence of incompetence: courage, honesty, emotional stability, sound judgment, industry, alertness, decisiveness, power to observe, initiative, energy, intelligence, ability to get along with people.

.09 *Tour of Duty:* The shift or watch during which an individual member is on duty.

.10 *On Duty:* The state of a member during the hours of the day (shift or watch) when he is actively engaged in the performance of his duties. Technically a police officer is on duty and subject to call at all times.

.11 *Off Duty:* The state of a member during the hours of the day, his day off and annual leave when he is free of the responsibility of performing his usual routine duties.

.12 *Special Duty:* Police service the nature of which requires that the member be excused from the performance of his regular duties.

.13 *Days Off:* Every member of the Police Department shall be excused from duty on designated days each week without loss of pay. The time and manner of excusing members of the Police Department from duty shall be determined by the Chief of Police.

.14 *Annual Leave:* The vacation granted to all members of the Police Department once each year.

.15 *Sick Leave:* The period of time during which an officer is excused from active duty by reason of illness or injury.

.16 *Death Leave:* The period of time during which an officer is excused from duty by reason of death in his immediate family.

.17 *Leave of Absence:* An extended period during which an officer is excused from active duty and during which time he receives no pay.

1005. *Other Terminology*

.01 *Rules and Regulations:* Directions issued by the Chief of Police with the approval of the City Manager to define the police purpose and the duties and conduct of all members.

.02 *Duty Manual:* A manual prepared under the direction of the Chief of Police with the approval of the City Manager to define the organization structure of his force and the specific duties of its organic units and members.

.03 *Procedural Manual:* A manual prepared under the direction of the Chief of Police to outline in detail the standard operating procedures of the department.

.04 *Procedure:* The official method of dealing with any given situation prescribed by General Order or by the Procedural Manual.

.05 *Daily Bulletin:* The official daily publication of the department. All directions contained in the Daily Bulletin have the force and effect of department orders.

.06 *Memorandum Book:* A book in which officers are required to record their work and official actions. The specifications of the memorandum book are prepared by the Chief of Police.

.07 *Report:* A written communication, unless otherwise specified, relating to police matters.

.08 *Patrol Wagon:* The panel truck used to transport arrested persons.

.09 *Patrol Car:* A car used to transport a patrolman from the location of one duty to that of another on his beat and to otherwise assist him in the performance of his patrol duties.

.10 *Three-wheeler:* Three-wheeled motorcycle; servi-car.

.11 *On the Air:* In service with the radio equipment in operation.

.12 *Off the Air:* In service but not available for radio communication.

.13 *Out of Service:* Not available for service because of the breakdown of the car or when withdrawan from active service for some special assignment.

.14 *Immediately:* The term "immediately" is to be construed to mean "as soon as possible and practicable."

1100. General Rules for all Members

1101. *Mission*

.01 Officers shall preserve the peace, protect life and property, prevent crime, apprehend criminals, recover lost and stolen property, and enforce in a fair and impartial manner the ordinances of the City of Portland and the laws of the State of Maine and of the United States.

.02 Officers shall serve the public by direction, counsel, and in other ways that do not interfere with the discharge of their police responsibilities. They shall respect and protect the rights of individuals and perform their services with honesty, zeal, courage, discretion, fidelity, and sound judgment.

.03 In accomplishing their mission, officers will recognize that:

a. The power of the police to fulfill their functions and duties is dependent on public approval of their existence, actions, and behavior, and on their ability to secure and maintain public respect.

b. To secure and maintain the respect and approval of the public means also obtaining the willing cooperation of the public in the task of securing observance of laws.

c. The extent to which the cooperation of the public can be secured diminishes, proportionately, the necessity of the use of physical force and compulsion for achieving police objectives.

d. The test of police efficiency is the absence of crime and disorder, and not the visible evidence of police action in dealing with them.

.04 Officers will seek and preserve public favor, not by pandering to public opinion, but by constantly demonstrating absolutely impartial service to law; by ready offering of individual service and friendship to all members of the public without regard to their wealth or social standing; by ready exercise of courtesy and good humor; and by ready offering of individual sacrifice in protecting and preserving life.

.05 Officers will use physical force only when the exercise of persuasion, advice, and warning is found to be insufficient to obtain public cooperation to an extent necessary to secure observance of law or to restore order; and to use only the minimum degree of physical force which is necessary on any particular occasion for achieving a police objective.

.06 Officers will maintain at all times a relationship with the public that gives reality to the historic tradition that the police are the public and that the public are the police; the police being only members of the public who are paid to give full-time attention to duties incumbent on every citizen, in the interest of community welfare and existence.

.07 Officers will recognize the need for strict adherence to police-executive functions, and will refrain from even seeming to usurp the powers of the judiciary of avenging individuals or the state, and of authoritatively judging guilt and punishing the guilty.

1102. *Service Requirements*

.01 Officers are held to be always on duty, although periodically relieved from the routine performance of it. They are always subject to orders from superior officers and to calls from private persons, and the fact that they may be technically off duty shall not relieve them from the responsibility of taking proper police action in any matter coming to their attention. When there is no urgent or immediate need for police action, they may request the dispatcher to turn the matter over to officers on duty in the vicinity, but they shall take such action as may be required prior to the arrival of the dispatched officers. Members off duty shall report for duty immediately on receipt of orders to do so.

.02 Members shall report for duty at the time, place and in the attire and with the equipment specified by department orders or by a superior officer, unless absence is authorized by competent authority. Inability to do so shall be reported prior to the reporting time to the desk officer or to their superior officer. Officers shall be punctual in reporting for duty and special assignments, in their court appearances, and in meeting appointments. Members shall report off duty in person at headquarters at the expiration of their tours of duty unless exceptional procedure is authorized by a superior officer. Officers in uniform while off duty shall conduct themselves as though they were on duty.

.03 All members of the department are required to reside within the limits of the City of Portland. In addition, each member shall have a telephone at his place of residence, and shall submit a report of his address and telephone number. Any changes shall be reported within 24 hours. Members shall also report immediately any change in their marital status. They shall report address and itinerary before they depart on leave. Such reports shall be submitted to their immediate superior officer who shall forward them through channels to the Personnel Officer.

.04 A member of the department seeking transfer to another division shall make a written request for such transfer through channels to his present division commander and to the commander of the division to which he wishes to transfer.

.05 When a member of the department is called on the telephone he shall respond promptly by giving his rank, surname, and the command to which he is attached. If the person calling is a member of the department, he shall promptly identify himself in the same manner.

1103. *Keeping Informed*

.01 Officers shall study and thoroughly understand the Department Rules and Regulations and the Duty and Procedural Manuals, general orders, City Ordinances, and State and Federal laws. They shall obtain the assistance of their superior officer in the interpretation of any section that is not clearly understood. They shall be especially well informed concerning the rules, regulations, procedures, and duties governing their specific assignments.

.02 Officers shall memorize the location of each police call box. They shall know the names and general locations of the streets, depots, hospitals, public buildings, government agencies, and important business establishments and associations in the city. They shall be familiar with bus lines and schedules. They shall know the state and United States highways that pass through the city and the names and distances of the principal towns on them for a distance of 250 miles.

.03 Members shall study the Daily Bulletin each day and familiarize themselves with all orders, descriptions of missing and wanted persons, and of stolen and lost automobiles and property, and with other information contained therein.

1104. *National Colors and Anthem*

.01 All members of the department shall salute the official National Colors as they pass in public parades, ceremonies, or other occasions, or when carried into any building, room, or place where they are present. Whenever the National Anthem is played at any place where any members of the department are present they shall stand at attention, facing toward the music. If in uniform, they shall salute at the first note, retaining the position of the salute until the last note of the Anthem. If not in uniform, and covered, they shall uncover at the first note, holding the head-dress over the heart, and so remain until its close, except that in inclement weather the head-dress may be slightly raised.

1105. *Salutations*

.01 The hand salute prescribed by the United States Army Regulations shall be tendered by subordinates and smartly and promptly acknowledged by commanding officers. If in civilian clothes, the subordinate shall not salute, but on entering the office of a commanding officer, he shall remove his hat. A member of the department other than the Chief of Police shall not be tendered a salute unless such member is in uniform. Members of the department lining parades or at fires, or on occasions where large numbers of patrolmen are assembled for a specific purpose, shall not salute commanding officers unless they address or are addressed by such commanding officers. In addressing or referring to a ranking officer in line of duty, his full title shall be used, and must never be omitted, altered, or abbreviated.

1106. *Obedience*

.01 Members, while on or off duty, shall respect and obey all laws and ordinances and the provisions of the Department Rules and Regulations and Duty and Procedural Manuals.

.02 As a general rule a member will be required to take direct orders from, and be directly responsible to, but one superior officer. Superior officers, however, shall exercise direct command over lesser officers outside their usual command in all situations where the police purpose or the reputation of the department is jeopardized.

.03 Members shall comply with the rules and instructions of the Personnel Officer regulating their conduct while attending school and with the rules and instructions of the Firearms Instructor regulating their conduct on the range.

.04 Members shall obey the lawful orders of their superiors and, regardless of their rank, they shall invariably obey the instructions given by the dispatcher. They shall perform all duties required of them by their superiors regardless of whether such duties are specifically assigned to them by Department Rules and Regulations or Duty or Procedural Manuals. Disagreeable duties shall be performed and unpopular orders obeyed with cheerful willingness. No member shall publicly criticize an order given by any superior officer.

.05 Should an order conflict with any previous order issued by any other superior officer or with any department order or provision of the Department Rules and Regulations or Duty or Procedural Manuals, the member to whom such order is issued shall respectfully call attention to the conflict. If the superior giving the order does not make changes to obviate the conflict, the order shall stand and the responsibility shall be his; the member obeying the order shall not be held responsible for disobedience of the conflicting order. It is sufficient for him to know that the person giving the order is in proper command. Should any lawful order appear unjust or improper to the member to whom it is directed, he shall carry out the instructions first, and afterward he may call the matter to the attention of his commanding officer or the Chief of Police.

.06   An officer temporarily filling the position of a superior, in an acting capacity, shall be vested with all the authority and responsibilities of the superior, but the acting officer shall not interfere with, countermand, or modify the orders previously issued by the superior, except in extreme emergency.

.07   The ranking officer shall take charge at fires, riots, or serious crimes. When no superior officer is present, the officer on the beat will be in charge. In his obsence and in the absence of any superior officer, the ranking patrol officer shall be in charge. At the scenes of homicides, any member of the Detective Division who may be present shall be in complete charge without regard to the rank of officers present from any other divisions.

1107. *Attention to Duty*

.01   Officers shall at all times be attentive to their duties and by their alertness and observation demonstrate their interest in their work. They shall act with dignity, maintain a soldierly bearing, and avoid a slouchy, slovenly attitude of mind or body. They shall not, while on duty in uniform or at headquarters, read newspapers, periodicals, or similar material in public view except in line of duty. They shall not show a lazy disposition, or lounge about, or sleep while on duty, or place their feet on desks or other furniture in any police office open to public view.

.02   Officers shall make diligent efforts to arrest or locate wanted persons and to recover stolen and lost property. They shall observe and investigate all persons, whether on foot or in vehicles, whose appearance, actions, or presence at a particular location seem suspicious. When so engaged they shall use tact and good judgment in speech and conduct and shall at all times remain cautious and alert to the possibility of attack or flight by the suspect. If the officer is not satisfied beyond doubt that the suspect is a law-biding citizen, he should be taken to headquarters for further investigation when the circumstances justify; otherwise the officer should summon a superior officer to deal with the situation. When the suspect is not arrested, a report of the incident shall be made.

.03   Officers shall devote their entire time and attention to the service of the department and they are prohibited from following any other calling or engaging in any other business except with the written consent of the Chief of Police.

.04   Officers shall not shop, barter, or trade while on duty nor devote any of their on-duty time to any activity other than that which relates directly to their work. Officers shall not enter places of amusement while on duty except for police purposes.

1108. *Appearances*

.01   Members shall maintain quarters, lockers, and desks used by them in a neat, clean, and orderly condition. They shall not throw cigarettes or trash on floors in the police building; they shall not store property of any kind on the floor or on cabinets or in other places open to view. Those working at desks shall clear them at the end of their tour of duty, and they shall place all material with which they have been working in its assigned cabinet or drawer.

.02   Members shall be neat and clean in appearance when in public whether in or out of uniform and whether on or off duty. They shall bathe regularly, shave once each day, and keep their hair trimmed and fingernails clean and neat. Officers in uniform shall not carry an umbrella or cumbersome bundles, nor shall they walk or stand with hand in pocket.

.03   Members shall maintain their uniforms, civilian attire, and equipment in serviceable condition. Clothing shall be clean, pressed, and shall not be noticeably patched, torn, or worn. Leather and metal equipment shall be well polished. Any officer who, when reporting for duty, is badly in need of a shave, whose uniform is badly soiled, worn, or wrinkled, or whose shoes or leather equipment is not shined, shall be given a written reprimand. A continuation or repetition of the unsatisfactory condition may justify suspension.

1109. *Relationships*

.01   Officers shall be courteous, civil, and respectful to their superiors, associates, and other persons, whether on or off duty. When addressed by an officer or citizen, they shall assume the position of attention, except when seated at a counter that places their eyes on a level with those of the other. They shall be quiet, orderly, and attentive, and shall exercise patience and discretion in the performance of their duties. They shall avoid answering questions in a short, abrupt manner; they shall maintain an even, cheerful temper, regardless of the provocation, remaining cool and collected at all times. They shall refrain from harsh, violent, coarse, profane, sarcastic, or insolent language. When requested to do so, they shall give their name and badge number in a respectful, gentlemanly manner.

.02   Officers shall develop a wide range of acquaintances among all classes of persons. In conversing to this end and for the purpose of obtaining information, they shall avoid boring their listeners and wasting the time of busy men. They shall avoid idle conversations and obscene, smutty subjects. They shall not publicly express an opinion on racial, religious, political, or other controversial subjects. They shall refrain from the public discussion of the demerits of any law. They shall use correct English, giving particular attention to their grammar and pronunciation, and they shall avoid slang and "criminalese" in conversations with citizens. They shall enunciate clearly and speak with sufficient force so that listeners can readily understand what they say.

.03   Officers shall avoid actions or conduct that annoy others. For example, they should not: touch a person or his clothing, such as fingering his coat lapel, putting the hand or arm on his shoulder, or slapping his back; stand with their faces offensively close to persons with whom they are talking; clear their throats or noses with a loud noise; chew gum, whistle, hum, sing, crack their knuckles, or beat a tattoo with their fingers or feet; or indulge in any nervous actions that tend to distract others.

.04   Members while serving the public and uniformed officers in public view shall not smoke or use tobacco in other forms.

.05   Members shall not congregate in the corridors, offices, or other places in the police building except in rooms set aside for this purpose. They shall not indulge in horseplay or in loud and boisterous conversation in public view or hearing. Officers in charge of police headquarters, or any part thereof, shall prevent loafing by persons not on police business.

1110. *Conduct*

.01   Members shall not conduct themselves in an immoral, indecent, lewd, or disorderly manner, or in a manner that might be construed by an observer as immoral, indecent, lewd, or disorderly. They shall not be guilty of misconduct, neglect of duty, conduct unbecoming an officer and a gentleman, or acts tending to discredit the department, even though such conduct is not specifically set forth in these rules.

.02   Members shall not bring intoxicating beverages into any police building or vehicle except liquor that has been seized as evidence or contraband, or that has been found unsecured, or that is the property of a prisoner. Members shall not drink any alcoholic beverages before reporting for duty or while on duty. Officers in plainclothes, with the consent of their superior officer, may drink alcoholic beverages while on duty when necessary to accomplish a police purpose. No officer off duty in uniform or in any part of uniform dress shall drink any alcoholic beverage in public view or in a place accessible to the public. No member while off duty shall drink an alcoholic beverage to an extent which renders him unfit to report for duty, or which results in the commission of an obnoxious or offensive act which might tend to discredit the department. The odor of liquor on the breath of a member while on duty will be cause for suspension.

.03   Members of this department while in uniform, shall not enter or visit any cocktail lounge, beer parlor, or other place where beer or liquor is sold, or any alleged house of ill fame, gambling house, or other disreputable house, except on official business.

.04   Members shall pay all just debts and meet all other obligations undertaken by them. No member will be permitted to take voluntary bankruptcy without the consent of the Chief of Police.

.05 No member shall willfully depart from the truth, either in giving testimony, or in connection with any legal official order received by him, or in his official duties.

.06 No member shall be guilty of oppression, favoritism, or willful wrong or injustice.

1111. *Grievances*

.01 Members shall avoid conduct or speech that is subversive to good order and discipline. They shall treat each other with the utmost courtesy and respect, and at all times refrain from making any derogatory remarks concerning each other. They shall direct and coordinate their efforts to establish and maintain the highest level of efficiency, morale, and achievement. They shall conduct themselves in such a manner as to bring about the greatest harmony among the various organic units in the department. Grouchiness, wisecracks, and flares of temper shall be avoided.

.02 Members shall not destructively criticize the department or its policies, programs, actions, or officers, or perform any acts or make any written or oral statements which tend to bring them into disrepute or ridicule, or which tend to interfere with the reasonable supervision or proper discipline of the force. Members shall not gossip about any other member to his discredit, whether the subject be true or false. Members having a grievance against any policy, procedure, or other member, shall take the matter up through official channels.

.03 Any member who feels that he has been injured or discredited by a superior officer through unreasonable, unjust, arbitrary, capricious, or tyrannical conduct, or abusive language, or any member having a grievance against another member, shall reduce his grievance to writing and direct the same, through official channels, to the Chief of Police.

.04 A member who believes himself to be entitled to official commendation by reason of an act done in the performance of police duty, may appeal within a reasonable time to the Chief of Police through official channels.

.05 Members may forward suggestions for the improvement of the service, in writing, through official channels, to the Chief of Police.

1112. *Duty to Report*

.01 Officers shall report all crimes and suicides and their attempts, and important happenings and other information of concern to the department, that come to their attention, regardless of whether the incident occurred in the city or not. They shall not repress, conceal, or distort the facts of any such incident. Officers who have reason to believe that a building or part thereof is being used in violation of the law, or as the resort or residence of persons of questionable character, or that liquor, narcotic, prostitution, or gambling laws are being violated, or who have information regarding any felony or any wanted person, shall immediately report all details to their superior officer who shall direct the action to be taken or forward the information to the proper division. However, any member of the department who has valuable information regarding an arrest or a police case other than his own, shall communicate such information to the arresting or investigating officers, either directly or through official channels and it shall be deemed neglect of duty to withhold such important information.

.02 Members shall have with them while on duty a regulation memorandum book in which they shall record on each case handled by them the names and addresses of complainants and witnesses, the identity of persons arrested, the nature of the offense and evidence, the date, time, and such other facts that may be important in the trial, as well as all alarms, calls, open doors, and information of importance relative to the discharge of their duties.

.03 Members shall make reports promptly and in the manner prescribed by reporting regulations. They shall not make a false report, either orally or in writing. Officers who receive assistance from any other officer, on a case to which they are assigned, shall note the assistance in their reports.

.04 Oral reports shall be confirmed by written communications before officers rendering them report off duty.

1113. *Property*

.01 Officers who find property that has been lost or abandoned shall cause it to be brought to the station for disposition.

.02 Before turning in any property, members shall wrap it when necessary to preserve it in good condition and label it with a shipping tag containing the following information: the name or description of the property, whether it be wrapped or not; an indication that it is found property, personal property or evidence; and the date, hour, case number, and the name of the officer. If it be one of several packages on the same case, this fact shall be noted on the tag by indicating the number of packages. The tag must be secured by a stout string and never by the use of a rubber band. Members shall not convert to their own use or have any claim in any found or recovered property or property held as evidence.

.03 Property other than weapons and evidence shall not be taken from prisoners except in the presence of the turnkey or, in exceptional cases, a second officer. Prisoners shall be given a receipt for money or other property taken from them.

1114. *Action to be Taken*

.01 Member shall be attentive to and take suitable action on reports and complaints by a private person except when circumstances make it necessary for them to report the matter or refer the complainant to a more suitable police office or other agency. Officers shall fulfill proper requests for information or assistance, or they shall aid the person in otherwise obtaining the requested information or assistance. Members shall avoid giving the impression that they are evading the performance of their duty or that they are not interested in the problems of persons who are referred elsewhere for service. Members shall not belittle a seemingly trivial request, complaint, or piece of information, but shall invariably thank the complainant or informant regardless of the value of the information received.

.02 Officers shall act promptly, with energy, firmness, and decision at the scenes of crimes, disorders, accidents, or other situations, disasters, or incidents that require police attention, and in dealing with suspects and in disposing of their assignments. When the police purpose might be jeopardized by delay, immediate action shall be taken even though the incident would ordinarily be dealt with by some other officer or division.

.03 Time is usually the essence of successful police operations. Failure to take prompt and decisive action frequently jeopardizes the success of police undertakings. Officers shall not give evidence of indecision or lack of confidence by their actions, facial expression, words, or tone of voice.

1115. *Action on Calls*

.01 Officers sent on a call shall, immediately upon the completion of the task, notify the superior officer by whom sent of the nature of the call and of the action taken.

.02 Officers sent on calls, as well as those who, in some other manner, discover incidents requiring police attention, shall obtain the names and addresses of the principals and witnesses and complete details relating to the incident. When the investigation requires an unusually long period, they shall notify headquarters by telephone or radio of the circumstances, their location, the telephone number by which they may be reached, and the facts needed for broadcast to other officers.

1116. *Disturbances*

.01 Any member observing a police emergency, or having it reported to him, shall immediately report the incident, or have it reported, to the dispatcher in as complete detail as possible.

.02 Officers shall restore order and disperse the crowd on the occurrence of a disturbance, using persuasion as far as possible. When such efforts fail, force shall be used and the principals arrested. Officers shall immediately notify or have someone else notify the dispatcher of any emergency where additional officers or special assistance is needed.

.03 Members of the department are required to perform their

duties with coolness, firmness, and determination; and in time of peril they shall act together, assist and protect each other in the restoration of peace and order, the apprehension of offenders, and the enforcement of the laws.

1117. Crime Investigations

.01 Officers called to or happening on the scene of a crime or suspicious death shall take immediate steps to apprehend the perpetrator, care for the injured, investigate the circumstances, obtain the names and addresses of the victim and witnesses, protect the area, and prevent the destruction, mutilation, concealment, or contamination of physical evidence.

.02 Officers coming upon the scene of a suspicious death or suicide shall assume that the death is homicide and proceed accordingly. They shall investigate all deaths when there are reasonable grounds to suspect that the death was not due to natural causes. In the case of suspicious death, the Commanding Officer shall be notified at once.

.03 In all cases where the victim is dead or in a serious condition as the result of gross negligence or the commission of a felony or grave misdemeanor, the witnesses shall be taken to headquarters for interrogation by the division charged with the investigation of the offense committed.

.04 The officer in charge at the scene of a serious crime shall exclude from the area all unauthorized persons and those who are not actually engaged in its investigation. Members of the department who are off duty, or on duty but not assigned to the case, shall not enter the premises or do any other thing that might interfere with the investigation, or alter physical evidence in any respect, provided, however that the officer in charge may assign such a member to immediate duty when necessary. Nothing shall be touched until the evidence technician has made a thorough search for fingerprints and for any substance, article, or material that may require scientific examination. Such evidence shall be photographed and the position of it accurately measured and recorded. When the evidence technician is not available, anything found at or near the crime scene, or on a suspect, which may be used after analysis as evidence, shall be sent to the identification officer for examination.

.05 In order to link physical evidence with a crime and to identify it for presentation in court, officers shall make detailed notes describing it, the circumstances under which they obtained it, the place where found, and its relation to other objects. The article itself should be marked by the officer to enable future identification, and a description of the mark and its location on the object shall be recorded in his notes.

.06 Officers at the scene of a homicide shall not handle any object or make a search of a body until the Medical Examiner has made his investigation, nor shall they permit any other person to do so. Particular precaution will be observed in reference to the body and effects of the victim in assault cases and to fingerprints on weapons and other articles used.

.07 Officers at the scene of an accident where it appears that someone may be prosecuted shall make a thorough investigation of the incident, ascertaining its cause and obtaining evidence of any violation for which the offender should be prosecuted.

1118. *Interrogation of Suspects*

.01 Officers shall not conduct their interrogations of suspects in a manner that tends to compel a confession. They shall not use physical violence on the suspect, or the threat of such abuse, nor shall they make any promise of immunity, probation, or lesser degree of prosecution or hold out any other inducement to a suspect, for the purpose of obtaining a confession. Officers obtaining a confession must be able to defend its trustworthiness. The conditions and circumstances under which a confession is obtained must not be considered, by a reasonable man, of such nature as to render it untrustworthy.

.02 Immediately following an oral confession, the interrogating officer shall attempt to persuade the offender to write it in his own handwriting or, if this be impractical, have it recorded by a stenographer and immediately transcribed. It shall be read to the offender who should also read it; then, the offender should be requested to sign his confession immediately. He should also inscribe his initials on each page and at each correction in the text. The signature need not be obtained in the presence of witnesses; it is sufficient for the offender to state to witnesses that the signature is his own. It is desirable to have two such witnesses sign the statement. It is also advisable at this time to ask the offender whether the confession was voluntarily made. Only a minimum time should be permitted to elapse between the oral confession and its preparation in written form and between the preparation of the written confession and the affixing of his signature by the offender.

1119. *Arrests and Prisoners*

.01 Officers shall distinguish between foolhardiness and courage in making arrests and investigating suspicious characters. While some risk is involved in police service, officers should not unnecessarily jeopardize their lives. Since their purpose is to apprehend criminals, they shall summon assistance when unaided arrest seems unlikely.

.02 Officers shall not use unnecessary force or violence in making an arrest or in dealing with a prisoner or any person. Prisoners and suspects shall be treated in a fair and humane manner. They shall not be humiliated, ridiculed, taunted, or embarrassed, although in a proper, legal, and privately conducted interrogation such verbal techniques are permitted. Officers shall not strike or use any other form of physical force on a prisoner or other person except when necessary to prevent an escape, or in self-defense, or to prevent violence to another person. Officers shall report each instance of their use of force before going off duty.

.03 In the arrest, transportation, and detention of prisoners, the officer shall take precautions to prevent an escape, injury to himself or others, or damage to property. When making an arrest, he shall search the prisoner carefully and shall immediately take possession of all weapons and evidence. If, for any reason, a prisoner has not been searched before being turned over to the patrol-wagon officer, the arresting officer shall without fail notify the officer receiving the prisoner.

.04   An officer making an arrest shall convey the prisoner or cause him to be conveyed to the police station without delay and shall at no time accompany him to his home or room or elsewhere except with the consent of a superior officer.

.05   After a prisoner who has been arrested on the street has been transported to headquarters, the arresting officer shall search the scene of the arrest for weapons or evidence that may have been concealed, dropped, or thrown away by the prisoner. The driver of the vehicle used to transport the prisoner to headquarters shall immediately afterward search the vehicle for weapons and evidence.

.06   At the time of an arrest, the person arrested has a right to know the true reason for such arrest, and the officer's authority.

.07   Every person arrested for any cause shall be brought to headquarters and the arrest properly recorded.

.08   Prisoners shall be allowed facilities for notifying their friends or the bail commissioner, or an attorney, at their own expense, if the offense is not a felony.

.09   Turnkeys shall visit all persons in their custody every half hour during the day and night, and any unusual appearance of the prisoner shall receive prompt attention and the officer in charge notified.

1120. *Women Prisoners*

.01   A woman prisoner should be kept under guard in a public room until taken in charge by a matron.

.02   Women and girls who are in the custody or under the care of the department should not be searched by male police officers unless an immediate search under one of the following conditions appears to be necessary and no policewoman, police matron or other suitable woman is at the time and place available:

    a. When there is a good reason to believe that the person has in her possession a weapon, poison, drug, or other like means of causing death or injury to herself or to another.

    b. When there is a good reason to believe that stolen property is hidden about the prisoner and there is imminent danger that it may be thrown away or destroyed.

.03 Searches in such emergency should be made with all possible regard for decency; by direction and under the supervision of an officer of rank, should one be present; and with a witness, other than the searching officer, if obtainable. After such a search has been made the facts relating to it should be reported in writing by the officer to his commanding officer.

.04 It is the duty of police officers to take possession of hat pins or other articles worn outside the clothing or carried in the hands and capable of being used as weapons, and to search bags, bundles, and other removable property.

.05 Female prisoners should not be transported in the same vehicle with male prisoners.

1121. *Juvenile Arrests*

.01 When a juvenile is arrested with or without a warrant and brought to the police station, notice shall be given by the officer in charge to the parent or guardian and to the probation officer. The officer in charge may release the child on the written promise of parent, guardian, or any other reputable person, to be responsible for the presence of such child in court at a designated time.

.02 A juvenile should not be transported in a vehicle which is occupied at the same time by an older prisoner or prisoners, except in great emergencies or when arrested in the company of an older person or for complicity in the same offense, in which case a police officer should accompany them within the vehicle.

.03 When a minor is arrested for intoxication, the commanding officer should endeavor by all proper means to ascertain the place or places at which the minor obtained the liquor.

1122. *Arrest of Postal and Common-Carrier Employees*

.01 Officers shall not take into custody, for a minor violation, a postal employee engaged in the collection or distribution of mail, or the operator of a bus or train. Instead, the offender shall be summoned to appear in court or ordered to report to a commanding officer for further investigation.

.02   The persons listed above, when suspected or accused of a felony or serious misdemeanor, shall be taken into custody, but the arresting officer shall accompany the prisoner to the post office, car barns, or depot in order that he may be relieved from duty before being brought to headquarters. When the physical or mental condition of the accused renders this procedure impractical because of the possibility of escape or of injury to the public or the arresting officer, the prisoner shall be taken to headquarters as soon as police guard can be provided for the vehicle he was operating.

1123. *Restrictions Relating to Arrests and Prisoners*

.01   Officers shall not apply for or serve a search or arrest warrant except with the knowledge and consent of their superior officer. An officer shall not apply for a criminal warrant where the offense is alleged to have been committed against himself, except with the knowledge and approval of his commanding officer.

.02   Members shall not engage in controversies nor attempt to exact police discipline or make arrests in their own quarrels or in those of their families, or in disputes arising between their neighbors, except under such circumstances as would justify them in using self-defense or to prevent injury to another, or when a serious offense has been committed. Disputes involving a member shall be called to the attention of the lieutenant. He shall investigate the complaint with the patrol sergeant and take necessary action.

.03   Officers shall not make arrests for trivial offenses when a warning would suffice, except when the violations are willful and repeated. Officers not in uniform shall not arrest traffic violators on sight except when the violation is of such a flagrant or dangerous nature that the officer is required to take the violator into custody.

.04   Whenever a person is arrested for a crime and taken to the police station, the turnkey shall immediately examine each prisoner booked and if he finds any bruises, cuts, or other injuries he shall forthwith report the matter to the Patrol Captain or lieutenant, and in their absence to the Service Division Captain or platoon sergeant and make a written report thereof to the Chief of Police. If, in the judgment of the officer in charge, the prisoner is suffering from wounds or injuries which require medical attention, a physician shall be called. If wounds or injuries appear to have been inflicted by the arresting officer, the officer in charge shall record this fact. If it appears that unjustifiable violence was used. charges shall be preferred against the offender.

.05 When a prisoner is unconscious from any cause, the officer in charge should immediately endeavor to restore consciousness; on failing to do so within a reasonable time, he should call a physician and be guided by his instructions. An unconscious person should not be placed in a cell except when it is determined by a physician that stupor was induced by alcohol.

.06 Officers shall not suggest or recommend attorneys, or any firm or place of business to anyone. They shall not obtain attorneys or bondsmen for prisoners unless the prisoner requests that a designated attorney or bondsman be notified. Attorneys desiring to see a prisoner for whom they claim to be counsel shall be permitted to do so when the prisoner is not being interrogated, providing the prisoner desires such counsel.

.07 Officers shall not dismiss the charges against an arrested person, unless there is sufficient good reason and then only with the knowledge and consent of a commanding officer in the division responsible for the arrest.

.08 Members shall not permit themselves to become involved in any promises or arrangements between a criminal and his victim intended to permit the offender to escape the full penalty provided by law. Members shall not take part, either directly or indirectly, in making any arrangements or in negotiating a compromise for the purpose of permitting any person to escape the penalty of the law or the full responsibility for his acts, except as indicated below. Neither shall they, for the direct or indirect benefit of a defendant, seek to obtain a continuance of a trial, the dismissal of a case, or leniency for the defendant in any court, except when such action enables them to obtain convicting evidences against a more serious offender, and then only with the knowledge and consent of their commanding officer, and (a) the Vice Officer in any liquor, narcotic, prostitution, or gambling case, or (b) the commander of the division charged with its final disposition in other cases. They shall not make promises that cannot be fulfilled, and when an agreement is made or a promise given, it shall be kept at all costs. They shall not, in any way, interfere with the usual procedure of any court.

1124. *Court Appearance*

.01   When a person is arrested, he must be charged with a crime, and he must be brought into court immediately if it is in session, or if not in session at its next session.

.02   In every criminal case the burden is on the prosecution to prove by relative evidence:
a.   That there is such a crime as charged.
b.   That the offense charged was really committed.
c.   That the accused committed it.
d.   That, in all crimes where criminal intent is an element, he had the necessary criminal intent at the time.

.03   The following rules should be followed while testifying before the court:
a.   Be punctual in attendance.
b.   Tell the truth.
c.   Tell your story in your own way, in plain language.
d.   Speak clearly so that you can be heard.
e.   If you make a mistake, correct it; don't try to stick to some slight mistake as to time or place.
f.   Do not hurry in giving your testimony.
g.   If assigned to the uniformed force, wear your uniform in court.
h.   Make sure your witnesses are properly summoned into court and see that they are there on time.
i.   Do not have any conversation with the defendant's attorney in the corridors of the building before the case is called.

.04   All officers should know that the prisoner has certain rights guaranteed him by the United States and Maine Constitutions. The following are some of the rights:

a. He shall not be arrested or detained except for the commission of an act or an omission forbidden by law.

b. He shall not be subject to more restraint than is necessary to hold or confine him.

c. He is entitled to be arraigned immediately if court is is in session.

d. He is entitled to communicate with friends or counsel.

e. He may request a continuance of the trial or examination, or waive it.

f. He may call witnesses in his behalf.

g. He is entitled to counsel.

h. He should have a public and speedy trial.

i. He is entitled to be confronted by his accusers and all witnesses against him.

j. The complaint must be read to him unless he waives it.

k. He shall be advised as to this right.

l. He may examine the state witnesses either himself or by counsel.

m. He shall not be twice put in jeopardy for the same offense.

n. He is assumed to be innocent until pronounced guilty.

o. He cannot be compelled to testify against himself.

p. Failure to testify himself shall not be held against him.

1125. *Sick and Injured Persons*

.01 Officers dispatched on ambulance calls or investigations shall immediately ascertain whether the ambulance is needed. They shall notify the dispatcher immediately of their conclusions.

.02 Officers may transport sick and injured persons in their police car when they can do so without neglecting their duties. Without exception, however, patients in a coma and those having head, back, or crush injuries, fractures, or hemorrhages, shall be taken to the hospital in an ambulance. Slightly sick or injured patients, such as those who have fainted or become hysterical and have recovered sufficiently as to need no further care, may be taken to their homes in a police car. Police cars may handle patients with illness or injury known to be of a minor nature, such as dog bites, as well as most sick or injured babies and children.

.03   When it is necessary to obtain additional information from a patient, the investigating officer shall notify his commanding officer who will arrange to have other officers sent to the hospital to complete the interrogation.

.04   Unusual care shall be exercised in handling insane persons or persons appearing or thought to be insane in order to guard against injuring them and also to avoid being injured by them. Force shall be used only as a last resort and then only in a measure sufficient to control the patient.

.05   All members of the department shall be required to have a thorough knowledge and skill in the application of approved first-aid methods. The revised edition of the American Red Cross First Aid Textbook shall be the approved first-aid manual of the Portland Police Department.

1126. *Sick and Injured Officers*

.01   Any member who is sick or injured shall make out or have made for him a sick or injured report which should state the nature of the illness or injury and the manner in which the injury was sustained. A follow-up report shall be submitted on his return to duty which should state the name of the attending physician and length of absence.

1127. *Fires*

.01   Officers who discover a fire shall promptly send an alarm from the nearest fire-alarm box unless the alarm can be given more quickly by telephone, radio, or in some other manner.

.02   He shall not try to extinguish the fire unless he has left some trustworthy person at the fire-alarm box to direct the fire fighters.

.03   The police at fires shall assist in the preservation of life, the protection of property, and the prevention of crime; but after the arrival of the first piece of fire apparatus they shall not enter a burning building except for the purpose of saving life, or at the request of a superior officer of the Fire Department for the performance of a proper police service.

.04 Fire lines will be established at a suitable distance from the fire by the officer in charge.

.05 From the area within the fire lines the police shall remove all vehicles that hamper or interfere with the fire fighters. No persons except those wearing exposed badges or having permits issued for the current year by the chiefs of the Police or Fire Department may be allowed inside of the fire lines.

.06 The Detective Division shall be notified immediately of fires of incendiary or suspicious nature.

1128. *Wires Down*

.01 Officers who discover a fallen overhead wire shall consider it a high-tension conductor. A wire normally carrying harmless currents may be crossed by a high-tension conductor far distant from the break and, as a result, the fallen wire may become a high-tension conductor, contact with which may cause instant death.

.02 An officer who finds a fallen overhead wire in a public place shall immediately notify the dispatcher by radio of the location and the name of the company responsible for its maintenance. He shall remain at the location to warn the public and direct traffic. In the absence of a radio, he shall request a citizen to make the notification. When this procedure is impractical, he shall notify the dispatcher from the nearest telephone and return to the scene as quickly as possible.

1129. *Drivers*

.01 A police vehicle is an authorized emergency vehicle, and the driver when responding to an emergency call or when in the pursuit of an actual or suspected violator of the law or when responding to but not upon returning from a fire alarm, may, when he sounds a siren, bell, or exhaust whistle while in motion and the vehicle displays a lighted red lamp visible from the front, as a warning to others:
a. Park or stand notwithstanding the provisions of the traffic rules.

  b. Proceed past a red or stop signal or stop sign, if he first brings the vehicle to a full stop and then proceeds with caution and due regard for the safety of person and property, unless otherwise directed by a police officer regulating traffic at such intersections.

  c. Exceed the prima facie speed limits.

  d. Disregard regulations governing direction of movement or turning in specified directions.

.02 The foregoing exemptions shall not protect the driver from the consequences of his reckless disregard of the safety of others.

.03 Members of the department shall not sound the sirens or display the red lights on police vehicles except when responding to emergencies or when it is necessary in the proper performance of police duties.

.04 When acting as escorts for parades, convoys, and distinguished persons, where no police emergency exists, members shall not use their sirens or red lights and shall observe all traffic regulations relative to speed, signal lights, and stop streets.

.05 Special care shall be taken in the operation of a police vehicle not to obstruct the free movement of traffic while patrolling or when stopped to deal with any situation.

.06 When a police car encounters an accident or other incident while en route to a previously given assignment, the driver shall notify the dispatcher and continue on the original assignment unless advised to the contrary.

.07 No member of the department shall send a patrol car on a call without notifying the dispatcher.

.08 When it becomes necessary for a member to use department motor equipment for police purposes, not on his tour of duty, or by reason of special assignment, he must first obtain permission from his commanding officer to do so.

.09 Members of the department shall not park their personal cars in the areas reserved for the parking of departmental vehicles.

1130. *Accidents Involving Police Vehicles*

.01 Members are required to report promptly to their commanding officer or the dispatcher any accident in which they become involved while operating a police vehicle. Officers shall be dispatched to make a thorough investigation and a report for further action by the Captain of the Patrol Division. Accident reports shall be filed and copies of them shall be forwarded to the Chief of Police.

1131. *City-Owned Property*

.01 Members are prohibited from using Police Department property or vehicles in the conduct of their own personal or private affairs, either on or off duty.

.02 Members shall use care in handling department equipment and property and shall report immediately any that is lost, damaged, or in bad order. Any member who willfully or negligently loses, damages, or destroys department property shall pay the cost of repair or replacement. Strict economy shall be observed in the use of fuel and lights, and city property shall be neither wasted nor destroyed.

.03 Members shall be held responsible for damages resulting from accidents where in the evidence shows carelessness, negligence, or a violation of a traffic ordinance. Members shall be held strictly accountable for damage caused by abuse or careless handling of police vehicles. Evidence of such abuse or careless handling shall be submitted daily to the Patrol Captain by the lieutenants. Each member shall examine his vehicle at the start of his tour of duty, for dents, broken glass, or other readily visible damage, and shall submit a report of such damage to his commanding officer at that time. Failure of an officer to report such damage shall be considered prima facie evidence that the damage occurred while the vehicle was in his possession, and he shall be held responsible for it.

.04 The office furniture, files, and other fixtures, furnishings, and equipment which have been officially assigned to the use of the various divisions and offices in the police building shall not be removed except with the knowledge and consent of the Division Commander.

.05 No pictures, advertising matter, or other thing shall be hung upon or affixed to the walls of the police building except such radio equipment, clocks, maps, and other essential departmental fixtures and equipment as are authorized by the Chief of Police.

1132. *Uniforms and Personal Equipment*

.01   Officers of the Patrol and Traffic Divisions and those assigned to the jail and to serve the public at a counter or desk, and officers of other divisions so ordered by their commanding officer, shall wear the regulation uniform and badge while on duty. They shall not wear any part that does not conform to department regulations. Uniformed officers on outside duty shall wear their caps in a level manner except when their removal is indicated by normal courtesy or effective police action. The overcoat, when worn, shall be fully buttoned.

.02   Officers working in plain clothes shall be prompt to identify themselves when the necessity arises, and at the scene of an emergency where it is desirable to display the badge continuously, it shall be attached to his outer-most garment over the left breast. Uniformed officers shall not recognize a member in civilian clothes unless first addressed.

.03   While off duty, officers are restricted in their use of their uniforms: (a) They may wear their full uniform in going to and from work. (b) When wearing civilian headgear, they shall not wear their uniform shirts and blouses unless the latter are under a civilian coat. (c) When bareheaded, officers shall not wear their blouses and badge unless the latter are under a civilian coat. (d) No civilian attire shall be worn with the uniform cap.

.04   Male officers on duty shall carry the following equipment on their persons: badge, handcuffs, key ring containing whistle and all issued keys, revolver, billy, fountain pen, watch, and memorandum book. Flashlights are required when officers work at night. The required equipment shall conform to department regulations. They shall carry only regulation ammunition for their service weapon. They shall carry their badge and call-box key and be armed at all times whether on duty or not. They shall not carry metal knuckles.

.05   All members of the department shall wear the official badge while on duty, and when in uniform it shall be worn conspicuously on the left breast of the outer-most garment. No other device or badge unless specifically authorized by the department shall be worn or carried.

.06 The badge shall not be altered, exchanged or transferred, except by order of the Chief of Police. When a member's badge is lost or damaged he shall report the fact to his commanding officer. The cost of replacement or repair will be charged to the member, unless he can show that such loss or damage was not incurred through personal negligence.

.07 When a member loses or misplaces his call-box or other Police Department key, he shall report the fact to his commanding officer. He shall not make or cause to be made any duplicates of call-box or other departmental keys except with the express permission of the Chief of Police.

.08 An officer shall not wear his uniform while under suspension.

1133. *Firearms*

.01 Members shall be equipped by the department with .38 special revolvers. An officer shall not carry a non-regulation firearm without approval of the Chief of Police.

.02 Officers shall not use submachine guns or gas weapons except with the approval of a commanding officer and under the supervision of a member of the department designated by him.

.03 Officers shall not draw or display their sidearms in any public place, except when they are to be used or for inspection by a superior. Officers shall not "dry fire," clean, repair, load, or unload their firearms except on the target range. Riot guns, rifles, and submachine guns shall be serviced, loaded and unloaded in the manner prescribed in the department procedures. Officers shall not place or store any firearms or other weapons in police buildings except when the place of storage is locked. Officers firing a gun accidentally or intentionally, except on a target range, shall report the circumstances to their superior officer immediately and shall file a written report of the incident within 8 hours.

.04   Officers shall not discharge firearms in the performance of their police duties except:
  a. For target practice.
  b. To defend himself from death or serious injury.
  c. To defend another person unlawfully attacked from death or serious injury.
  d. To effect the arrest or to prevent the escape, when other means are insufficient, of a convicted felon or a person who has committed a felony.
  e. To kill a dangerous animal or one that is so badly injured that humanity requires its removal from further suffering.
  f. To give an alarm or to call assistance for an important purpose when no other means can be used.

1134. *Cooperation with Other Agencies*

.01   Members shall cooperate with all agencies engaged in the administration of criminal justice and other public agencies and city departments, giving to each all aid and information that they are entitled to receive. Officers answering a call wherein another city agency or department should be notified shall, through official channels, have the appropriate agency notified of the essential details of the complaint. They shall report to their division all dog bites, and dogs alleged to be rabid. They shall give prompt attention to destitute persons, but publicity shall not be given to such cases.

.02   Officers shall investigate cases of cruelty to dogs or other animals that are observed or reported to them, and they shall take suitable action against the accused.

.03   Members shall cooperate with representatives of the press, giving them information relating to incidents that come to police attention except: (a) when the incident has been classified as "No Publicity" by a superior officer or (b) when in the opinion of the member, public knowledge of the information would jeopardize the police objective. In the latter situation, and also when questions of relationships with the press cannot be otherwise satisfactorily resolved, the member shall refer the press representative to a superior officer.

1135. *Restrictions on Action Taken*

.01 Members of the department shall not take action in any criminal cases arising outside the City of Portland and personally reported to them by any means without the approval of their commanding officer. Members of the department shall not go outside the City of Portland except in the fresh pursuit of known or suspected criminals, or when authorized by the Chief of Police, or a commanding officer on a request received by him from an outside authority because of a grave emergency and urgent need for assistance.

.02 Members who receive written communications directly from citizens, officials, or other law enforcement agencies, shall not take personal action or make personal answer, but shall forward such communications to the Records Office to be processed and answered through official channels. All official correspondence, telegrams, circulars, and other communications shall be sent over the signature or upon the authority of the Chief of Police. Members shall not use police department letterheads except for authorized department correspondence.

.03 Members shall not taunt or persecute ex-convicts. When a convicted man has paid the penalty for his offense, he is entitled to start life anew and should receive encouragement and cooperation from the police in his efforts to live a law-abiding life.

.04 Members shall not interfere with cases assigned to other officers except with the consent of the assigned officer. Officers shall not unnecessarily interfere with the operation of any other division or of the courts or with any lawful private enterprise. They shall not threaten a law-abiding citizen in the lawful pursuit of a legitimate business.

.05 Members and other persons shall not have access to department records and reports, except commanding officers and the members assigned to process, maintain, and file them. When it is necessary, in the performance of police duties, to remove departmental reports or records temporarily from the division or office where they are maintained, the member to whom they are issued shall sign a receipt for them and shall be held accountable for their return. No departmental record shall be destroyed or permanently removed from its file except on the order of the Chief of Police.

1136. *Restrictions on Revealing Information*

.01   Members shall treat as confidential the official business of the department. They shall not impart official information, such as a proposed movement of the force or regulations made for the government of the department, to anyone except to those for whom it is intended or as directed by their commanding officer or under due process of law. They shall not make known to any person, including members of the department, any order they may have received unless it is required by the nature of the order. They shall not reveal the identity of a complainant or informant to any private person.

.02   Members shall not communicate information which may delay arrest or aid a person to escape, destroy evidence, or remove stolen or embezzled goods. They shall not communicate information regarding an arrest made by them or a case to which they are assigned, except with the consent of their commanding officer. Members shall not communicate information relating to proposed or actual arrests or cases investigated or to be investigated, except to the arresting officer or the officer assigned to the case or to a superior officer. They shall not give information or refer any case to an outside department or agency except through official channels.

.03   Members shall obtain written permission from the Chief of Police to attend conventions or to fill speaking engagements or to publish articles as official representatives of the Police Department. No member shall act as a correspondent to a newspaper or periodical, nor shall he discuss, publicly or for publication, matters pertaining to police personnel, procedures, or policies without the written authority and approval of the Chief of Police.

1137. *Restrictions on Activities*

.01   Members shall not actively engage in political activities. Every member is urged to vote at all elections, but his participation must end there. Members shall not solicit or make contributions in money or other things to any person, committee, or association for political purposes. Members shall not belong to any political club or organization or take part in behalf of any candidate for political office.

.02   Upon days of election for public officers, held under the laws of the state, a member shall, whether specifically assigned to attend the polls or otherwise, do all within his power to preserve the peace, protect the integrity of the ballot box, enforce the right of lawful voters, and prevent illegal and fraudulent voting.

.03   Members shall not join a labor union nor shall they join any organization: (a) that maintains the right of its members to strike; (b) that is opposed to minority groups; (c) that attempts to interfere with the administration of the police force; (d) that might in any way exact prior consideration and thus interfere with efficient and effective police operations; or (e) that is affiliated with any of the above.

.04   Members are forbidden to solicit petitions for their promotion or change in line of duty, or for the promotion or change of duty of any other member, or for the appointment of any man to the department; or to promote any political influence to effect such an end.

.05   Members shall not solicit or accept rewards, presents, gratuities, or compensation other than that paid by the city or for approved private employment.

.06   Members shall not give testimonials or permit their names or photographs to be used for advertising purposes. They shall not seek publicity in the public press. They shall not solicit subscriptions, or sell papers, books, or tickets, or collect or receive money or other things for any purpose. They shall not participate in any public gift contest.

.07   Members shall not use their official position to solicit special privileges for themselves or others such as free admission to places of amusement, discounts on purchases, or other favors. They shall not accept free meals, refreshments, or other things from persons engaged in business. An officer may use his badge to obtain admission to any public gathering in the furtherance of his official duty. Officers in uniform may ride free on buses operated within the City of Portland but they shall not occupy seats while paid passengers are compelled to stand.

.08   Members shall not receive any article whatsoever, whether as a gift or as the result of purchase or trade, from suspects, prisoners, persons recently arrested, or known gamblers, prostitutes, or other persons of bad character or ill repute, or other persons whose vocations may profit from information obtained from the police.

.09   Officers on street duty shall not have in their possession the key to a business premise for the purpose of obtaining shelter, rest, or telephone service. Temporary exceptions may be made by commanding officers when necessary for the performance of police duties.

1138. *Civil Cases*

.01   A member of the department shall not involve himself in the civil actions or disputes of other persons nor shall he presume to adjudicate any civil dispute or give legal advice in civil matters.

.02   When called upon to act or advise in such disputes he shall respectfully inform the interested parties that the Police Department has no jurisdiction in civil disputes and shall, when requested, refer them to the proper authorities for assistance. When an eviction is made for non-payment of rent or for any other cause, or when civil disputes arise, he shall not give assistance to either party, or interfere between them, unless it is necessary to prevent a breach of the peace or to quell a disturbance.

.03   A member of the department, however, shall act to prevent or suppress any breach of the peace or disturbance which may grow or has grown out of such a dispute.

.04   Officers shall not testify in civil cases unless legally summoned.

.05   Members shall not institute civil action arising out of their official duties without first notifying the Chief of Police. They shall not use their positions with the department, as a means of forcing or intimidating persons with whom they are engaged in civil controversy, to settle the case in the favor of the member. Members shall not accept or agree to accept anything as payment for personal injury or property damage incurred in line of duty without first notifying the Chief of Police.

.06 Any member of the department who has a damage suit filed against him, by reason of an act performed by him in the line of duty, shall immediately consult with his commanding officer and the Chief of Police. The Chief of Police shall be furnished a copy of the complaint together with an accurate and complete report pertaining to the incident in question so that he may notify the City Attorney of the pending suit and relevant facts.

1139, *Annual Leave*

.01 Vacations shall be allotted to members over a period from January 1 to December 31, inclusive, and shall be distributed equally, or as nearly as possible, over the entire year, so that the number of members who are on vacation shall be the same, or nearly so, at all times.

1140. *Leave of Absence Without Pay*

.01 All applications for a leave of absence without pay shall be made to the personnel office and must be approved by the Chief of Police and the City Manager.

1141. *Violations*

.01 Failure of a member, either willfully or through negligence, incompetence, or cowardice, to perform the duties of his rank or assignment, or violation by a member of any department rule, duty, instruction, or order, or conduct prejudicial to the good order and police discipline of the department, or conduct unbecoming an officer and a gentleman, which may not be specifically set forth in department rules, may be considered sufficient cause for discharge, demotion, suspension, or other penalty.

1400. General Rules for Superior Officers

1401. *Leadership*

.01 Leadership of personnel is the primary function of a superior officer. He must realize that command imposes grave responsibilities, principal among which is the necessity for initiatve and absolute self-reliance in meeting and accepting responsibility in matters not covered by hard and fast rules of procedure.

.02 Promotion requires increased activity, alertness, diligence, and devotion to the interests of the department and the public; it shall not be permitted to bring ease. Only results count; attempts to evade responsibility will not be tolerated. The character and ability of a superior officer is reflected in the efficiency, discipline and morale of his subordinates, and the strength or incompetence of the superior is readily detected in the quality of work performed by his subordinates. General laxity, indifference, incompetence, and ineffectiveness on the part of subordinates shall be deemed evidence of incompetence and neglect of duty on the part of their superior officer.

.03 The superior officer is not only responsible for his own conduct and performance of police duties but that of his subordinates as well. He shall set an example to all subordinates in sobriety, dignity, courtesy, discretion, initiative, industry, diligence, truthfulness, courage, painstaking attention to duty, and the observance of proper discipline. He shall at all times appear neatly attired and clean in person and equipment.

1402. *Orders*

.01 A superior officer shall promptly obey all orders of his commanding officers and of the Chief of Police. He shall communicate and explain all orders and provide all necessary information to his subordinates.

.02 A superior officer shall issue clear, concise, and definite orders to his subordinates. Vague, ambiguous, and ill-defined orders, and commands that cannot be executed, are confusing to subordinates and prejudicial to the efficiency, good order, and morale of the department.

.03   A superior officer shall be held responsible for issuing improper orders. He shall not issue unlawful orders or orders in violation of Department Rules and Regulations.

.04   He is responsible for the proper execution of orders by his subordinates. The fact that an order has been given is not acceptable as an excuse when the order is not carried out by a subordinate.

.05   Communications, orders, and directives emanating from the Chief of Police or a commanding officer and all requests for assistance from one division or bureau to another shall follow the chain of command, except in emergencies where the element of time renders this procedure impractical and ineffective in the proper and expeditious performance of police duties.

.06   A superior officer shall exercise direct command over lesser officers outside his usual command in all situations where the police purpose or the reputation of the department is jeopardized. A superior officer, however, shall not unnecessarily give orders to subordinates who are not assigned to his command. When he gives such orders, he shall exercise care that they do not unnecessarily conflict with the orders of the commanding officer of the organic unit to which such subordinates are assigned. Whenever orders so given are important or require the subordinate receiving them to leave his regular post or assignment, the superior giving the orders shall, as soon as practicable, inform the subordinate's commanding officer of the action taken.

.07   During the temporary absence of a superior officer, when no other provision is made by competent authority, the command automatically devolves upon the subordinate present who is next in rank to the absent superior officer.

1403. *Performance of Duties*

.01   A superior officer shall constantly direct his best efforts toward the intelligent and efficient performance of the functions of the Police Department, namely; the protection of persons and property, the preservation of public peace and order, the prevention of criminality and suppression of crime, the detection of crime and the apprehension of criminals, the collection, identification, and preservation of evidence, the recovery of lost and stolen property, and the enforcement of the ordinances of the City of Portland and the laws of the State of Maine. He shall in turn require the same of his subordinates.

.02 He shall not perform the duties regularly assigned to a subordinate when the subordinate is available to perform them, but shall require each subordinate officer to perform his own duties.

.03 A superior officer shall familiarize himself with all police procedures, general orders, special orders, Rules and Regulations, city ordinances, and state laws, so that he may be competent to advise and instruct his subordinates in the proper performance of their duties.

.04 He shall see that all officers under his command have been supplied with copies of procedural and duty manuals and the Rules and Regulations of the Police Department and that they are thoroughly instructed on the contents. He shall frequently instruct his men in the rules of arrests and evidence and in the use of firearms. He is morally responsible for false arrests and the illegal use of firearms by his subordinates.

.05 He shall see that his subordinates make all required reports promptly, accurately, and completely, and on the proper forms.

.06 He is required to forward through channels all written communications received from his subordinates requesting a transfer or containing a grievance or suggestion.

.07 He shall carry on his person at all times the addresses and telephone numbers of each officer immediately subordinate to him.

.08 He may authorize the release of property in the possession of the police department, except property held as evidence.

.09 He shall communicate with headquarters at least once each hour during his tour of duty when on patrol, and he shall notify the dispatcher where he may be reached by telephone when he is not available by radio.

1404. *Morale*

.01 A superior officer shall give particular attention to the morale of his subordinates and shall immediately eliminate any friction or jealousy which exists in their ranks. He shall require his subordinates to maintain an even temper and cheerful disposition. He shall not permit cliques to form and he shall demand unquestioned loyalty from each subordinate.

.02 He shall constantly strive for harmony among all employees of the department and a spirit of good fellowship among his subordinates. He shall not, however, indulge in any undue familiarity with his men, or permit them to become unduly familiar.

.03 He shall sustain subordinate officers when they are acting within their rights.

.04 He shall exercise his authority with kindness, firmness, justice, and reason.

.05 He shall not censure or reprimand a subordinate in the presence of others.

.06 He shall not injure or discredit those under his authority by unreasonable, unjust, arbitrary, capricious, or tyrannical conduct, or by abusive language.

.07 Any officer who, under circumstances requiring an exceptionally high degree of courage, risks his own life in the prevention of a crime, in the apprehension of a criminal, or in saving or in attempting to save the life of another, or any officer, who, under circumstances requiring the highest degree of diligence, initiative, and ability performs a difficult and important police service, shall merit an official commendation to the Chief of Police. When an officer has performed some meritorious police service, his immediate superior shall submit to his commanding officer a written factual report of the case and make such recommendations as he deems proper.

1405. *Discipline*

.01 A superior officer is responsible for the good order, conduct, and discipline of his subordinates. Discipline is the orderly conduct of business. The ability of a police department to obtain desirable results is dependent to a great degree on the ability of superior officers to convince their subordinates that they must obey orders, observe rules and regulations, and adhere to departmental policies and procedures.

.02 A superior officer shall be responsible for the enforcement of the Rules and Regulations, for compliance with department policies and procedures, and for the maintenance of strict discipline. He shall give such close attention to this duty as to render it unnecessary for a complaint to be lodged before suitable action is taken. He will not fail to take suitable action on the discovery of any failure, error, violation, misconduct, or neglect of duty by a subordinate, and he shall act as promptly as circumstances will allow.

.03 He shall study his officers carefully, observing their strengths and weaknesses; he shall endeavor to use the strong points of his men to advantage and to shield them from their weak ones; he shall correct the faults of his subordinates and endeavor to assist them in becoming better officers in every way.

.04 A superior officer who observes or is informed of a willful neglect of duty or misconduct by an employee not assigned to his command, shall immediately bring it to the attention of the member's superior officer, who shall immediately investigate the matter to determine the facts and make a written report of his findings to his commanding officer.

.05 A superior officer shall make an impartial written report to his commanding officer in every case of misconduct, incompetency, neglect of duty, or violation of the Rules and Regulations on the part of a subordinate, or citizen-complaint lodged against a subordinate, and his failure to do so shall be deemed neglect of duty. The superior officer shall include, in this report, his recommendation as to any disciplinary action to be taken. In addition, he shall bring before his commanding officer, at once, any subordinate guilty of a serious or flagrant violation of the Rules and Regulations or of any willful neglect of duty.

.06   A superior officer shall not ridicule rules, regulations, or orders, nor shall he permit subordinates to do so.

.07   He shall exercise his authority without bias or prejudice and shall not, under any circumstances or in any manner, obligate himself to an officer of lesser rank.

1500. General Rules for Commanding Officers

1501. *Authority and Responsibilities*

.01   A   commanding officer has direct supervision and control, subject to orders of the Chief of Police, over all officers and civilian employees of the department assigned to his command. He is responsible for the efficiency and effectiveness and shall coordinate the functions and activities of the various units of his command. He shall promote harmony among the members of his command. He is responsible for the cooperation of his command with all other divisions of the Police Department. He shall act in cases not regularly assigned to his command when the delay necessary to inform the proper organic unit might result in a failure of the department to perform a police duty.

.02   The commanding officer shall so regulate his command that, at all times when he is absent, it shall be under the command of a competent officer.

.03   He shall, without specific instructions, establish the required details and assignments necessary to carry out the functions of the Police Department and of his command in particular. He shall be guided in his assignment of personnel by the number of officers available to him for assignment and the necessity for assigning his men where they will be the most useful and efficient.

.04   He is authorized to place an officer temporarily in the position of a member of higher grade.

.05   He shall not countermand an order issued by a superior officer without sufficient good reason.

.06   He is authorized to excuse a subordinate from one tour of duty. He shall notify the Chief of Police of such excuse.

.07   Commanding officer shall provide the members of their command with tentative meal schedules which shall be followed as closely as emergencies will permit. Members assigned to patrol duty over a continuous 8-hour period shall be permitted one 30-minute meal period on each tour of duty.

1502. *Operations*

.01   A commanding officer shall immediately report any emergency, serious crime, or unusual occurrence to his immediate superior.

.02   He shall personally respond to any emergency or occurrence of a serious or unusual nature which arises within his jurisdiction, unless his presence at his station would be of more value under the circumstances, in which case he shall assign a competent officer to take command at the scene of the emergency. He shall also, whenever possible, respond to calls where members of his command are involved in controversy or accident.

.03   He shall approve or disapprove all requests for communications by prisoners who have been denied this privilege. The facts in each case will be ascertained and carefully studied before a decision is made. A commanding officer shall be held responsible for the legality and justifiability of the action he takes.

.04   He is authorized to release juvenile offenders to their parents or guardians when the circumstances warrant such action. He shall notify the Juvenile Division of his action.

.05   The commanding officer shall be responsible for the prompt service of all official notices, summons, or subpoenas which may be sent him by proper authority.

.06   A commanding officer shall maintain a pleasant, courteous, and dignified attitude and shall recognize every caller's presence without unnecessary delay. He shall accord respect, courtesy, sincerity, and patient attention to every citizen calling at the police station. Under no circumstances shall he belittle a seemingly trivial request, complaint, or piece of information.

1503. *Property and Equipment*

.01   The commanding officer shall be held strictly accountable for the condition of personnel assigned to him and for the condition and appearance of their uniforms and personal equipment. He has the authority to condemn old uniforms found not fit for service and to request the purchase of new uniforms when necessary.

.02 He shall inspect, or cause to be inspected, all members under his command at the beginning of their tour of duty, and he shall at least once each month conduct a general inspection of the entire personnel assigned to his command, together with all automotive and other department equipment assigned to their use. He shall submit a written report through channels setting forth the result of the general inspection and such recommendations for the betterment of the service as he may deem proper.

.03 He is responsible for the good order and sanitary condition of the portions of the police building within his command, and for the furnishings and equipment assigned thereto. He is responsible for the proper care, economical use, and efficiency and serviceability of departmental property issued or assigned to the use of members of his command.

.04 In the event of the death, resignation, suspension, or dismissal of any member of the department, the commanding officer to whose command the member was last assigned shall take custody of all department-owned property in his possession. No resignation shall be accepted until such property is returned.

1504. *Personnel Accounting*

.01 The commanding officer shall be responsible for the punctual attendance of all personnel within his command and shall keep or cause to be kept a record of each member's attendance, overtime, court time, relief days, vacations, sick leaves, leaves of absence, and suspensions.

1505. *Personnel Management*

.01 The commanding officer is responsible for punctual attendance in court and for proper preparation and presentation of cases in court by the members of his command. He shall notify the prosecuting attorney of the inability of a member of his command to appear in court at the time scheduled.

.02 He shall assist subordinates in the preparation of their cases so that there may be no mistrial caused by neglect on the part of a member of the Police Department. When in doubt as to law, procedure, or status of a case, he shall consult suitable authority.

.03 Each commanding officer shall prepare efficiency ratings for each of the officers of his command at such intervals and upon such forms as may be required by the Chief of Police.

.04 The commanding officer shall observe the probationary patrolmen assigned to his command, and prior to the expiration of their probationary period, he shall submit through channels a detailed written report describing their appearance, intelligence, discipline, efficiency, initiative, general adaptability to police work, and their over-all ability to obtain desirable results. He shall, in his report, include a statement as to whether or not, in his opinion, each individual officer should receive permanent appointment.

1506. *Discipline*

.01 A commanding officer is responsible for the efficiency, discipline, and morale of all members of his command. He shall investigate or cause to be investigated all complaints by citizens and reports by members of the Police Department of misconduct, incompetency, neglect of duty, or any violations of the Rules and Regulations on the part of anyone under his command, and he shall submit through channels a written report of his findings. He shall also report any incompetent member who may be detailed to his command. His report shall include his recommendations as to the action to be taken.

.02 A commanding officer who initiates any disciplinary action against a subordinate has the responsibility of forwarding a complete written record of the case to the Personnel Officer for inclusion in the personnel file of the disciplined member and for entry on his service record.

PART II
PORTLAND POLICE DEPARTMENT
DUTY MANUAL

2000. Portland Police Department

2001. *Organization* (See Chart I)

.01   The Police Department shall be composed of such number of officers in the several ranks and such number of civilian employees serving in such capacities as may be provided by budgetary appropriation.

.02   The Police Department shall be divided into the Office of the Chief of Police and four divisions, the heads of which shall report directly to the Chief of Police.

.03   The Office of the Chief of Police shall contain, in addition to a secretary, the following staff officers:
Administrative Assistant
Personnel Officer
Intelligence Officer

.04   The titles of the divisions and of the commanders of each shall be as follows:

Patrol Division	Captain of Patrol Division
Traffic Division	Lieutenant of Traffic Division
Detective Division	Captain of Detectives
Juvenile Division	Commander of Juvenile Division
Service Division	Captain of Service Division

2005. *The Office of the Chief of Police*

2006. *Function*

.01   To facilitate the accomplishment of the police mission (paragraph 1101.) by:
a. Obtaining budgetary appropriations.
b. Providing essential buildings, equipment, and supplies.
c. Assuring an adequate complement of qualified policemen.
d. Preparing members for the accomplishment of their tasks.
e. Maintaining buildings and equipment in suitable order.

Chart I

ORGANIZATION OF THE PORTLAND POLICE DEPARTMENT

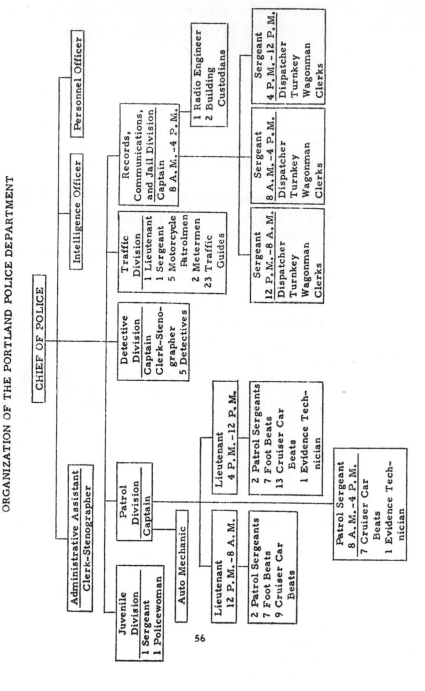

f. Analyzing the need for police service in terms of its time, its place, and its nature.

g. Planning the use of police resources to meet needs most effectively.

h. Developing sound organization of department resources and wise procedures to govern their operation and use.

i. Directing and coordinating police efforts and controlling them through adequate systems of inspection and follow up.

j. Informing the public and higher officials of police policies, procedures, and problems.

k. Controlling department expenditures and property.

l. Formulating police policies.

m. Foretelling future police needs and planning to meet them.

2010. *Duties of the Chief of Police.*

2011. *Authority and Responsibilities*

.01 The Chief of Police is the executive head of the Police Department. All orders and directives to the Police Department emanating from the City Manager, will be directed through the office of the Chief of Police.

.02 The Chief of Police shall formulate and enforce departmental policies and shall exercise such powers connected with his office as may be provided by statute, ordinance, and Charter. He is responsible for the proper and efficient enforcement of all laws and ordinances which the Police Department is authorized to enforce. He shall discharge the responsibilities imposed on his office, and he shall perform any tasks that may be assigned to him from time to time by the City Manager. He shall require the employees of his force to do likewise.

.03 He has the authority to promulgate such orders to the employees of the Police Department as he may deem proper, but the orders shall conform to law. All such orders shall remain in full force and effect until rescinded.

.04 He shall maintain records of the following:

a. Violations of federal and state laws and city ordinances.

b. Cases of lost and found persons, animals, and property.
c. Reportable automobile accidents, personal injuries, bodies found, suicide attempts, and damage to public property.
d. Cases in which a police officer is involved in any way in damage of public or private property or the injury of any person.
e. Warrants and subpoenas issued by a court and directed to the Police Department for service.
f. Arrests made by members of his department.

2012. *Planning*

.01   The Chief of Police shall predict the nature of probable emergencies and formulate procedures to be used in the event such emergencies occur.

.02   He shall formulate plans to meet both the immediate and the future needs of the Police Department.

.03   He shall recommend plans for the construction or alterations of the police building.

.04   He shall prepare annual budget estimates for the Police Department. He must translate departmental programs and needs for personnel and equipment into dollar terms. He must decide which divisions have prior need for expansion and improvement and a consequent need for additional funds.

2013. *Organizing*

.01   The Chief of police shall organize his force so that related tasks and activities may be grouped for assignment to an organic unit under the supervision of a competent superior officer. He shall establish a logical and clear-cut chain of command with definite channels of communication, responsibility, and authority. He shall prepare an organization chart of the department showing the functions and control of the various organic units and the manpower allotted to each. He shall revise the organization as needed to maintain effective operation and control, but he shall permit no change to be made in it without his consent.

.02 He shall organize personnel and equipment to meet the current needs but with sufficient flexibility so as to be readily adapted to new and changing situations. He shall approve the assignment of personnel and the distribution of equipment so as to obtain maximum results.

2014. *Staffing*

.01 The Chief of Police shall select and designate his staff officers and the commanders of the divisions of his department.

.02 He is authorized to designate patrolmen to perform detective work and at his pleasure he may return them to patrol service.

.03 He shall establish a training program for new recruits and provide an adequate in-service training program for all employees of the Police Department.

2015. *Delegating, Directing, and Coordinating*

.01 The Chief of Police shall delegate to his commanding officers an authority commensurate with their responsibilities. He shall give them full authority, within the restrictions imposed upon him by higher authority, to direct and discipline the subordinates under their command.

.02 He shall directly supervise division commanders and coordinate all departmental functions and activities through them.

.03 He shall give special attention to the coordination of the Patrol and Detective Divisions to assure that maximum use is made of the patrol force in the investigation of crimes and that the special skills and energy of detectives are not squandered on routine investigations that can be as effectively performed by the Patrol Division. The Patrol Division shall be required to perform all investigative tasks that they can perform substantially as well as the Detective Division so that the efforts of the detectives may be focused on investigations that require their special skills.

.04 He shall insist that police business be transacted through official channels, and he shall assure that each member of the Police Department is directly responsible to but one superior officer.

.05 He shall outline in a Duty Manual the duties of the organic units and members of the department. He shall formulate department procedures and publish them in one or more procedural manuals. He shall revise the procedures and duty assignments as needed to maintain a high level of effective operation.

.06 He is responsible for the publication of the Daily Bulletin and for its study by the members of his force.

2016. *Controlling and Inspecting*

.01 The Chief of Police shall establish such control devices as he may deem necessary to insure the effective administration of the department. Included are systems of inspections, efficiency ratings, activity reports, and follow-up.

.02 He shall investigate the manner of operation and the efficiency of the department and of each of its organic units. He shall investigate any charge of inadequacy against any division or unit.

.03 He shall institute a study of obstacles that prevent the department from functioning efficiently, including lack of authority or inadequate legislation, delays in prosecution, the uncooperative attitude of judges, interference by outside influences, and other morale-destroying situations.

.04 He shall conduct periodic surveys of physical equipment, arrange for the salvaging of discarded or impaired equipment, and the requisitioning of new equipment and supplies.

.05 He shall prepare, sign, and present an official commendation for meritorious service to any worthy officer. A copy shall be placed in the officer's personnel file and a suitable notation of the award shall be entered on the officer's service record and on the Daily Bulletin.

2017. *Discipline*

.01 The Chief of Police shall maintain strict discipline throughout the entire department. He is responsible for the strict enforcement of the Police Department Rules and Regulations and for the satisfactory conduct and general behavior of police officers and civilian employees. He shall require them to give close attention to their duties and to conform to department procedures.

.02 He is responsible for the investigation of all charges made against officers and civilian employees by his subordinate officers or by citizens. He shall assure that all evidence relating to alleged offenses is discovered and properly documented.

.03 He may suspend a member of the Police Department for just cause. He shall file charges against the offender with the City Manager within 48 hours of such suspension, excluding Sundays and holidays.

.04 He shall file charges with the City Manager against an officer when he has substantiating evidence of facts that justify suspending, demoting, or discharging him for just cause.

.05 He shall submit to the City Manager a carefully prepared and completely documented case-study of each disciplinary matter on which he files charges.

.06 When the facts do not justify suspending, demoting, or discharging the offending officer, the Chief of Police is authorized to take the following disciplinary actions without filing charges with the City Manager:
   a. Oral reprimand.
   b. Written reprimand.
   c. Transfer to another assignment.

.07 When a commanding officer reports that a member detailed to his command is incompetent, the Chief of Police may, at his discretion, transfer the member to another command. If the commanding officer to whose command the member was transferred declares that the member is incompetent and can cite instances of incompetency, the Chief of Police may, if he deems such action desirable, prefer charges against the incompetent member.

.08 The Chief of Police has the responsibility of assuring that a complete written record of each disciplinary case is made a part of the personnel file of the disciplined member and that an entry of the action is made on his service record.

2018. *Official and Public Relations*

.01 The Chief of Police shall represent the Police Department in all external relations, including contacts with other public officials and law enforcement agencies. He shall maintain personal contacts with the public and represent the department when citizens feel that they have been unjustly treated.

.02 He shall create and maintain favorable relations between the public and the police and he shall, for the guidance of the members of the Police Department, establish basic policies governing the various phases of public relations.

2019. *Reporting*

.01 The Chief of Police shall confer with the City Manager before taking the following action:

a. Making important changes in the duties of key positions.

b. Changing the assignments of captains.

c. Making important changes in the organization of his force.

d. Making important changes in operating procedures.

e. Leaving the city for a longer period than his weekly relief.

f. Preferring charges before the Manager against a member of the department.

.02 He shall report immediately to the City Manager any of the following incidents:

a. The appointment and removal of detectives.

b. The suspension of a member or civilian employee of the Police Department.

c. The death of any member.

d. The injury in line of duty of any member.

e. The injury of any person in consequence of any police action.

f. The injury by a police officer of a prisoner while in custody or when being arrested.

g. Damage to police vehicles or other police property in excess of $100.00.

h. The damage of public or private property (other than

police property) in consequence of any police action.

i. Unusual occurrences and crimes.

j. Offenses committed by the City employees and State and Federal officials.

k. Serious complaints by private persons or subordinate officers against members of the department or its operation, and the results of the investigation thereof.

.03 He is responsible for the preparation of record forms and for daily, monthly, and annual reports. The report forms shall contain all information required in the Uniform Crime Reports and in the National Safety Council Reports. Copies of the monthly and annual reports shall be forwarded to the City Manager.

.04 The annual report shall contain the following information:

a. Personnel information (distribution among organic units of the department, changes in strength, number of sick and injured and days lost, number of separations and reasons).

b. Information regarding police buildings and equipment.

c. The number and rates of Part I and Part II crimes, and clearances by arrest of Part I crimes.

d. The amount of stolen and recovered property and the number of lost and found persons, animals, and property.

e. The number and nature of investigations made for other jurisdictions.

f. The number, age, sex, and charge against persons arrested.

g. The number of traffic accidents, persons killed, persons injured, and other pertinent traffic accident data.

h. The number of traffic accidents investigated and other pertinent data on the safety activities of the police.

i. The number of arrests for traffic offenses by type of violation.

j. The plans and recommendations of the Police Department for future activities in traffic safety, crime and vice control, and delinquency prevention.

2020. *Duties of the Administrative Assistant*

.01   The Administrative Assistant shall serve as the personal representative of the Chief of Police.

.02   He shall conduct open inspections of personnel, equipment, property, police buildings, procedures, and results of police operations.

.03   He shall make his inspections at irregular and unusual hours.

.04   He shall accomplish his purpose by observation and by interviewing members of the department, persons involved in police incidents, and the general public, and also by analyzing police reports and statistical summaries.

.05   He shall correct without reference to the Chief such unsatisfactory conditions as he is able to remedy.

.06   He shall inform the Chief on (a) action taken by the Administrative Assistant and (b) action desired of the Chief.

.07   He shall promote and stimulate supervision on the part of operating personnel by:

    a. Devising well-conceived inspection reports for their use that will require a positive statement that a condition is satisfactory or unsatisfactory.

    b. Instructing supervisory officers in the use of the inspection reports and the nature of authoritative and staff inspections.

    c. Spot checking on inspection reports.

.08   He shall inspect and effect correction of conditions reported unsatisfactory.

.09   He shall maintain satisfactory relationships with subordinate and commanding officers.

.10   He shall focus his attention on the tasks of appraising such intangibles as public relations, conditions in the community affecting police operations, and the morale of the men.

.11   He shall seek the underlying cause of any unsatisfactory condition with a view to its correction.

.12   It shall be the responsibility of the Administrative Assistant to ascertain whether:

    a. Department morale is satisfactory.

    b. Morale-destroying influences are at work.

c. The attitudes, actions, reactions, and accomplishments of the members of the force are satisfactory.

d. Training, direction, and supervision are satisfactory.

e. Rules governing the care of the body are complied with.

f. The integrity of all members is above reproach.

g. The moral standards of the members are satisfactory.

h. Regulations governing the maintenance and use of equipment and property are complied with.

i. Equipment and property require repair or replacement.

j. Impaired condition of equipment and property has resulted from improper use or inadequate maintenance.

k. Equipment and space are adequate.

l. Department procedures are suitable and are being followed.

m. Operations are carried out as planned.

n. Department resources are used to best advantage.

o. Department organic units are operating satisfactorily.

p. Any part of the police job is being neglected.

q. Community conditions affecting operations against crime and vice are satisfactory.

r. Public reaction to department policies, programs, methods, and officials is satisfactory.

s. Persons and incidents are satisfactorily dealt with.

.13 He shall provide the Chief of Police and the heads of organic units with statistical reports at periodic intervals and with special statistical studies that may be requested by them.

.14 He shall undertake the study of any matter that may be referred to him by the Chief of Police, the head of any organic unit, or that may be initiated by him.

.15 He shall be held responsible by the Chief of Police for the soundness of all departmental operating procedures, for the suitability of its organization, and for the direction of its resources in the most productive manner.

.16 He shall analyze incidents that call for police service to ascertain where, when, why, and how the incidents occurred and who was involved, in order that the need for police service in all sections of the city, at all hours of the day, and in all fields of police activity may be measured.

.17   On the basis of the average or year round need, he shall plan and recommend the distribution of the force among the functional units, the shifts, and territorially in proportion to the need for service.

.18   He shall discover unusual needs for police service that exceed the average need in any field of police activity and in any specific area of the city and during any specific time. He shall develop and recommend a plan to cope with the unusual situation which will usually not be of long duration.

.19   He shall analyze all department operating procedures with a view to discovering weaknesses so that the procedure may be improved.

.20   He shall develop a long-range program for the improvement of police service and an annual work program for the succeeding year. He shall convert the annual work program into terms of man power, equipment, and supplies needed for its accomplishment. These represented in terms of money shall be the proposed department budget.

.21   He shall supervise the Chief's Secretary in the preparation of payrolls, the processing of requisitions, and the maintenance of accounts.

.22   He shall maintain liaison with City and County Attorneys; he shall review all proposed legislation of concern to the police; he shall review all incidents in which the police may have a moral or financial responsibility for damages.

.23   He shall review all proposed changes in forms and records procedures and make recommendations on them to the Chief of Police.

2030. *Duties of Personnel Officer.*

.01   The Personnel Officer shall be responsible for the administration of all police personnel matters:

   a. Recommendations relating to selections for appointment, promotion, and assignment.

   b. Recruit, in-service, and roll-call training.

  c. Supervision of the appraisal of the value of the individual officer to the service by his superior officers.

  d. Improvement of conditions of service and welfare of the officers.

  e. Supervision of departmental disciplinary machinery.

  f. Supervision of departmental grievance machinery.

  g. Assistance to the heads of all organic units in dealing with personnel problems.

  h. Liaison with the City Personnel Director.

.02 The Personnel Officer shall (a) evaluate public opinion and attitudes in reference to the policies, methods or procedures, and personnel of the department, (b) advise the Chief of Police with regard to the public relations aspect of new or revised department programs, policies, procedures, and activities, (c) plan and carry on informational activities to keep the public informed on police activities, and (d) furnish staff supervision of all police activities that may influence public support.

.03 The Personnel Officer shall assist the Chief of Police and the heads of organic units in dealing with personnel problems and morale-damaging situations.

.04 He shall do all in his power to improve the selection procedures in order to avoid the appointment of persons who are below average intelligence.

.05 The Personnel Officer shall promote a recruitment campaign designed to attract larger numbers of better qualified candidates to police service.

.06 He shall require an intensive investigation of the character and personal qualifications of each candidate on the eligible list before recommending him to the Chief for appointment.

.07 He shall instruct, assist, and supervise superior officers in the rating of their subordinates.

.08 He shall devise measures of accomplishment of the individual members of the department and supervise their use.

.09 He shall advise the Chief of Police in the promotion and assignment of personnel and in the development of harmonious working relationships between all members and employees.

.10   He shall deal with all grievances and recommend correc-
      tive action to the Chief of Police. He shall act as counselor
      to any member whose attitude or conduct is likely to bring
      discredit to the department.

.11   He shall strive to improve the conditions of service and
      to promote the welfare of all members and employees.

.12   He shall supervise the department disciplinary machinery.
      He shall assure the recording and registration of all com-
      plaints against members of the department and a thorough
      investigation and suitable disposition of each.

.13   He shall maintain and keep up-to-date all department per-
      sonnel records. He shall compile data on each member
      relating to his description, education, special skills, in-
      terest, training, assignments, efficiency, accomplishments,
      and breaches of discipline.

.14   He shall establish, and maintain up-to-date, a library of
      all books, periodicals, reports, and proceedings of associa-
      tions in the fields of law enforcement. He shall promote
      the use of the library by all members.

.15   He shall evaluate public opinions and attitudes with re-
      spect to the policies, programs, methods or procedures,
      and personnel of the department and advise the Chief of
      Police regarding the public relations aspects of proposed
      police action.

.16   He shall provide a staff supervision of all police activities
      that may influence public support.

.17   He shall provide staff supervision of superior officers in
      reference to their supervision of the public relations as-
      pects of the work of their subordinates.

.18   He shall devise programs of police activity designed to im-
      prove police relationships with the public.

.19   He shall analyze all police procedures with a view to dis-
      covering features that may have an undesirable effect on
      public attitudes toward the police and modifying the pro-
      cedures to assure the most desirable public reaction to
      them. He shall give special attention to procedures for
      dealing with complainants and with traffic and other minor
      offenders.

.20   He shall plan and carry on informational activities to keep
      the public informed on police activities.

.21 He shall promote police information and assistance-rendering activities.

.22 He shall advise the Chief of Police in reference to police-press policy. He shall supervise the implementation of the policy. He shall do all that he can within the framework of the policy to facilitate news gathering by reporters. He shall establish and maintain desirable relations with the members of the press.

.23 He shall search for material, not relating to current individual news items, suitable for feature stories and give it to the head of the appropriate organic unit for delivery to the press.

.24 He shall advise the Chief of Police in reference to the publication of a monthly news letter or house organ for distribution to all members as well as to selected citizens. Should such a publication be undertaken, the Personnel Officer shall be responsible for its publication.

.25 He shall establish a police speakers bureau and promote speaking engagements before civic and other groups.

.26 He shall promote the use of radio and television for the dissemination of information relating to police activities.

.27 He shall promote a close and friendly relationship between the police and the children of the community.

.28 He shall assist all organic units of the department in carrying on their public-information activities, and he shall provide a staff supervision of them.

.29 He shall prepare, for the approval of the Chief of Police, programs of training designed to meet current needs in the department.

.30 When a training program has been approved, the Personnel Officer shall be responsible for placing it in operation. He shall prepare school schedules and seek and obtain the services of qualified instructors, utilizing the members of his department, representatives of Federal and State Police agencies, the faculty of local schools and colleges, and other persons in the community and state who may be qualified to assist. He shall arrange for space, teaching aids, and other facilities that may be needed by the instructors.

.31 He shall have direct supervision of all men who are attending the Training School or instructing in it.

.32   Recruits shall be given instruction in a pre-service training school for a period of time to be determined by the
Chief of Police.

.33   The Personnel Officer shall state in writing his opinion
of the fitness for permanent appointment of each recruit
who has been assigned to the school.

.34   He shall prepare roll-call training bulletins to guide supervising officers in the continued training of their subordinates on the job.

.35   He shall supervise the Instructor of Firearms and require
him to prepare suitable rules to govern the operation of
the range, with special attention to safety, and shooting
schedules to be approved by the Chief of Police.

.36   He shall supervise the instruction in close order drill and
riot control of members selected for that purpose by the
Chief of Police.

2040. *Duties of the Intelligence Officer*

.01   The mission of the Intelligence Officer is to ferret out
facts for the Chief of Police relating to conditions in the
city in the following areas:

a.   Subversive activities.

b.   Minority-group tensions.

c.   Industrial and labor tensions.

d.   Organized crime and racketeering.

e.   Commercialized vice.

f.   Corruption in public office.

g.   Police integrity.

.02   The Intelligence Officer is a fact finder, not an enforcer.
He shall take no direct action beyond reporting his findings to the Chief of Police except in the enforcement of
vice laws.

.03   He shall be under the direct command of the Chief of
Police and shall report directly to the Chief.

.04   He shall be held to account for any failure to keep the
Chief informed regarding conditions in the city in the
areas of activity listed in paragraph 2040. 1. He shall keep
the Chief constantly informed of his activities and findings.

.05 He shall make contacts with persons who are likely to have, or are able to get, the desired information.

.06 He shall use undercover operators to assist in the accomplishment of his mission.

.07 He shall not reveal the identity of informants nor require them to appear in court as witnesses except with the approval of the Chief of Police.

.08 He shall be cautious in his relations with informants (a) to lessen the likelihood of the informant taking or being given unjustified privileges, and (b) to increase the effectiveness of their service. He shall not grant anyone the right to violate any law.

.09 He shall keep himself informed as to the identity of all commercialized vice operators in the city, the nature of their activities, and their operating relationship, both in the community and outside of it, to each other, to public officials, and to private persons. He shall use every legal means to convict vice operators and shall focus his attention on higher echelons.

.10 He shall make frequent inspection of all places where commercialized vice may be suspected, and places where prostitutes, gamblers, and narcotic addicts and dealers may congregate. He shall use every lawful means to arrest and convict the offenders, to suppress their illegal operations, and to drive them from the community. He shall rid the city of narcotic addicts by focusing his attention on individual offenders.

.11 He shall guard himself against being forced into ill-advised action against minor non-commercial violators that may result in arousing public indignation; raids on church buildings, homes, and privately occupied hotel rooms not used for commercial purposes are occasionally examples.

.12 He shall cooperate with the Captain of the Detective Division and shall report to him all information obtained that does not involve vice operations but that relates to:

a. Newly arrived criminals and criminals in hiding as well as activities of local offenders.

b. Felonies regardless of where they may have been committed.

     c. Persons arrested on vice offenses who are suspected of having committed felonies or being wanted by the police anywhere in the country.

.13   He shall maintain a close surveillance on taxi drivers, hotel clerks, and bell boys for possible violations of the laws against procuring, directing, or transporting any person for the purpose of prostitution.

.14   He shall inspect all clubs, houses, or other places reported to be, or suspected of being, kept or resorted to for the purpose of prostitution. He shall check all hotels and roominghouses for violations of the city and state ordinances aimed at the suppression of prostitution.

.15   He shall investigate all complaints brought to their attention relating to sexual perversions, including any complaints against exhibitionists, fetishists, masochists, lesbians, homosexuals, and reports of crimes against nature, the taking of indecent liberties, or the assault or abuse of minors.

.16   He shall investigate any person or place suspected of displaying or placing on sale any pornographic material, pictures, or films; and he shall seize such contraband.

.17   He shall cooperate with Federal Narcotic agents in the suppression of illegal traffic in narcotics and in the arrest and prosecution of offenders and shall enforce all laws relating to hypnotic or somnifacient drugs.

.18   He shall check all public events, where a considerable number of persons gather, for ticket scalpers, pickpockets, pimps, procurers, etc.

.19   He shall check all circuses and carnivals for confidence men, pickpockets, strip shows, and other lewd performances, and for pornographic pictures or materials.

.20   He must be especially circumspect in his conduct. He must avoid the appearance of evil; he must avoid situations that may permit a frame-up; he must be constantly on the alert not to step inadvertently into a plot to incriminate him on false evidence.

.21   He shall maintain suitable records of his activities and findings and shall keep them constantly under lock.

2050. *Duties of the Chief's Secretary*

.01 The Chief's Secretary shall maintain a system of book-keeping that will assure suitable budgetary control.

.02 She shall process all department requisitions and shall encumber the appropriate account whenever a requisition is issued.

.03 She shall process and file attendance records (call sheets) and prepare department payrolls.

.04 She shall maintain accounts of all monies handled by the police department.

.05 She shall perform secretarial and clerical work for the Chief and his staff assistants.

.06 She shall maintain attendance records on all persons assigned to the Chief's Office.

.07 She shall perform such duties as may be assigned to her by the Administrative Assistant.

The following sections are omitted:

2100. Patrol Division

2101. *Functions*
2102. *Organization*
2110. *Duties of the Captain of the Patrol Division*
2120. *Duties of Patrol Lieutenant*
2150. *Duties of the Patrol Sergeants*

2200. Duties of Patrolmen

2201. *General Duties*
2202. *Learning His Beat or Route*
2203. *Manner of Patrol*
2204. *Leaving His Beat or Route*
2205. *Security Measures*
2206. *Business Establishments*
2207. *Suspicious Persons*
2208. *Vice Control*
2209. *Protection of Children*
2210. *Public Welfare*
2211. *Traffic Control*
2212. *Nuisances and Obstructions*
2213. *Signal and Street Light Outages; Fires*

.01   The dispatcher shall be under the direct control of the Service Division platoon commander.

.02   He shall be in command of the Service Division during the absence of the Captain and platoon sergeants.

.03   He shall operate the police telephone, the Gamewell board, and the police radio transmitter. He is responsible for prompt, efficient, and courteous performance of all communication tasks.

.04   He shall exercise extreme courtesy and extend maximum consideration, understanding, and cooperation to both the public and members and employees of the department. He shall recognize that in many instances he will be the first, and in some cases the only police contact by many citizens, and that good or bad impressions thus gained will influence the attitude of the citizen toward the police.

.05   He shall not permit unauthorized persons to enter, or authorized persons to idle or loaf in, the Communications Office. Authorized persons are members of the department who find it necessary to enter the office in the conduct of official police business and others who have been granted permission by the Captain of the Service Division or a platoon sergeant.

.06   In matters relating to the dispatching of officers, he shall take orders directly from the Patrol Division Captain and lieutenants. He shall relay instructions, relating to radio broadcasts to their subordinates, that are received from any superior officer.

.07   He shall not dispatch officers or police vehicles outside the city limits except on the order of the City Manager or Chief of Police.

.08   He shall dispatch immediately, without waiting for specific instructions, such officers, ambulances, patrol wagons, and other equipment as may be needed to deal with all complaints and requests for police assistance that ordinarily require this action. He shall conform to outlined procedures in making such dispatches.

.09   When in doubt as to the procedure to follow in dealing with a call, he shall consult the Captain or lieutenant of the Patrol Division.

.10   He shall maintain either a sound-recorded or written radio log, a record of the time each officer is off the air and the reason, and enter the radio call numbers of officers dispatched on the Assignment Report and also time stamp it.

4312. *Telephone Duties of Dispatcher*

.01   The dispatcher shall answer promptly all calls on the telephone by announcing "Police Department" in a pleasant and courteous manner. When he is unable to answer promptly, he shall signal the Records Office.

.02   The dispatcher shall record on an Assignment Report all requests for assistance on which officers are to be sent, and immediately time stamp it.

.03   In the event the complainant reports that criminals are in operation, he should keep the complainant on the line while dispatching officers, obtaining all details that may be helpful in deploying officers at the scene. He should inform the complainant that officers are on the way.

.04   He shall receive all descriptions of stolen cars and missing persons. When the complainant has reason to suspect foul play or injury to the missing person and when a child under 8 years of age or a person who is senile or mentally deficient is reported missing, the dispatcher should send an officer to interview the complainant and make the investigation.

.05 He shall transfer the calls to the office charged with providing the service or information requested.

.06 He shall accurately record the name of each member of the department reporting by telephone or from call boxes, listing the time and number of the box.

.07 When any officer fails to report over the call-box system or by telephone within the regular appointed time, the operator shall notify the member's commanding officer at once and make a memorandum on the back of the call sheet.

.08 When an officer reports, the dispatcher shall transmit to him any orders, descriptions, or information received from his commanding officer.

.09 He shall record complaints regarding inoperative or damaged street lights and traffic signals and signs and shall inform the agency responsible for their repair.

.10 He shall notify the telephone company repair department when any repair or maintenance service is needed.

.11 While on duty, the dispatcher shall not leave the desk without first being relieved by a competent person.

4313. *Duty of Dispatcher to Inform*

.01 He shall invariably notify dispatched officers of such information relating to the nature of the call as to enable them to take suitable precautions. He shall so advise the officers when such information is not available.

.02 When informed by investigating officers of a fatal or serious injury accident, he shall notify the traffic sergeant when he is on duty. He shall notify the officer in charge of the Traffic Division of all fatal accidents. When requests are made for tow service, he shall notify the garage requested by the owner of the car or one of the approved garages in the area.

.03 When informed by investigating officers of the description of persons wanted and their cars and of property they may have stolen, he shall immediately broadcast the information to all members.

.04   In homicide cases, and in other cases of violent death, the dispatcher shall notify the Medical Examiner, when requested to do so by investigating officers. He shall give the officer in command in the Detective Division, and the Patrol Lieutenant, information relating to the incident and the action taken.

.05   He shall dispatch the lieutenant to the scene of an accident involving a police vehicle or of an altercation involving a member of the department.

4314. *Calls Not Requiring Pursuit or Capture of Criminals*

On calls in which immediate capture or pursuit of a criminal is not required, the dispatcher need send only the motor-beat patrolman except:

.01   When a crime or accident scene should be searched for physical evidence, in which case an evidence technician shall also be dispatched.

.02   When there may be an attendant need for guarding the premises, or controlling a crowd or diverting traffic, as at the scene of an accident or other incident that may cause traffic to be blocked, in which event additional officers should be dispatched for these specific purposes.

.03   In cases involving drunken or deranged persons, family quarrels and other fights, at least two officers should be sent, with a greater force when the reported conditions indicate greater need.

.04   In cases where the principal objective is to save a life endangered by accident or some non-criminal act, when the force sent should be sufficient to accomplish its purpose.

4315. *When Criminals Are In Operation*

.01   In the event of a direct-line robbery alarm, he shall dispatch officers in the manner outlined in a prepared broadcast.

.02   In cases where criminals are reported to be operating but there are no prepared broadcasts, he shall divide the area surrounding the point of attack by the nearest intersecting streets into quadrants designated as northwest, northeast, southeast, and southwest. He shall send, as a minimum, the motor-beat patrolman and four officers, each assigned to the quadrant that lies closest to his beat. Additional officers shall be dispatched when the size of the premises or other conditions indicate a greater need. All officers shall be instructed to go directly to the scene to surround the premises, four or more of them having their quadrants designated at that time so that they will know that they are to make a search of the designated area in the event the criminals escape.

.03 In cases where the criminals have left the crime scene so recently as to justify pursuit, assignments shall be made substantially as above except that officers assigned to quadrants shall not be sent to the scene but shall be required to institute an immediate search of their areas.

.04 The dispatcher shall notify the detective captain of all major felonies.

.05 When the offense has just occurred in all major felonies, such as murder, robbery, rape, and other serious offenses, the dispatcher shall alert all officers by broadcasting the nature of the call and the address twice.

The following sections are omitted:

4316. *Dispatching the Police Ambulance*
4317. *General Operations of the Dispatcher*
4350. *Turnkey's Office*
4351. *Duties of the Turnkey*

.01 The turnkey shall be under the direct command of the Service Division Captain or platoon commander; he shall perform such additional tasks as his commanding officer shall require.

.02 He shall keep the quarters, equipment, and supplies of the jail and turnkey's office clean and in good order at all times.

.03 He shall book all prisoners, recording accurately and completely all information required by reporting regulations.

.04 He shall require a thorough search in his presence of each prisoner before he is admitted to the cell room. He shall take from the prisoner all valuables, and property with which he might injure himself or others; give the prisoner a detailed receipt for the property; and deliver the property to the prisoner on his release or transfer to jail, obtaining his receipt for same at that time.

.05 He shall maintain a cell register to show the cell number in which a prisoner is placed, a record of their transfer from cell to cell, and the time of their release.

.06 He shall not permit an unconscious prisoner, or a prisoner who gives any evidence of illness or injury, or a prisoner arrested by forcible means, to be locked in a cell until he has been examined by a physician. He shall notify the platoon commander of any prisoner who becomes ill or injured while in custody.

.07 The turnkey shall be watchful for arrests made with doubtful legality.

.08 He shall immediately report the cases described in the two paragraphs above to the Patrol Division Captain or lieutenant.

.09 The turnkey shall fingerprint all prisoners and photograph designated categories of them.

The following sections are omitted:

4355. *Duties of the Matron*
4360. *Duties of the Radio Engineer*
4370. *Duties of the Building Custodians*

PART III
GENERAL POLICE PROCEDURES

The following sections are omitted:

7000. Procedures

7001. *Procedure When Criminal Is In Operation*
7002. *Dispatcher*
7003. *Officers*
7004. *Rank at the Scene of a Crime*
7005. *Duties of the Ranking Officer at the Scene of a Crime*
7006. *Duties of Beat Officer*
7007. *Duties of the Evidence Technician*
7008. *Duties of All Officers on the Case*
7009. *Duties of Officers Assigned to Quadrants*

APPENDIX H

Selected Procedures

(These are included only as examples)

I. General Instructions on Bank Robberies

1. Officers approaching the scene of a bank robbery reported to be in progress will stop their cars at a safe distance in such a manner that they will block traffic as much as possible.[1] Cars are not to be left with motor running or with keys in the switch. They will advance on foot, taking advantage of all possible cover such as parked cars and buildings.

2. On approaching the bank, a sharp lookout will be kept for the get-away car, making every possible attempt to capture it and the driver. Officers shall keep in mind that the driver will probably be armed and that a mob big enough to tackle a downtown bank probably will have a guard on the sidewalk armed with a machine gun. Officers will not attempt to get such a guard or driver to surrender if he has arms in sight, but will shoot first, taking deliberate aim.

3. Officers equipped with shotguns or machine guns will have them drawn and ready for use when they arrive at the scene.

4. Any unassigned officer arriving on the scene, including the patrol sergeant and the evidence technician,[2] will determine whether the posts specified are occupied and if not he will take one of them and cover the exit specified. As other officers arrive they will join any officer on one of the posts assigned. If possible to cover one of the exits from a bank from another post, it is permissible to do so when that post is not in the line of fire from some other officer.

5. Only officers equipped with bullet-resisting shields are to enter the bank until it is determined that there are no bandits present. These officers shall have their shields adjusted, a tear gas grenade in their pocket and pistols drawn before they leave cover. They will turn their shotguns over to some other officer before entering the bank.

---

[1] On receipt of bank robbery alarm, all traffic signal lights in the downtown area were turned on amber from a central control point.

[2] Originally called "special investigator."

6. The ranking uniformed officer will be in charge until it is determined whether the call was a false alarm, the bandits have escaped the scene, or are captured.

7. Should officers who go into the bank find the call was a false alarm, the evidence technician will call the station immediately and the patrol sergeant will go outside the bank and notify all persons there that it is a false alarm. Officers will not leave posts even though so directed by radio until this is verified by the sergeant.

8. Officers assigned to positions one block away from the bank will park in such a manner that they will be facing the street which passes the bank and capable of seeing down that street to the bank. Officers will get out of their cars and stop traffic and direct the drivers in such a way as to block all exits from that intersection.

9. The detective assigned to the alley one block from the bank and the uniformed officer on the intersection nearest him will watch doors and roofs of the buildings adjoining the bank to see that bandits do not escape that way.

10. The detective-division secretary will assign one detective to take gas rifle and shells and report to officer in charge at the scene and another to take a rifle and post himself at end of the alley one block from the bank. On arriving at the scene, if it is certain that the robbery is still in progress the detective assigned will immediately fire a tear gas projectile through a window of the bank.

NOTE: The radio dispatcher is supplied with a sample radio broadcast for each bank; in event of alarm he will select the proper broadcast sheet and proceed with the dispatch. The detective division secretary is supplied with written instruction sheets assigning two detectives, one to proceed with the gas gun, the other with a rifle; in event of alarm these assignments will be handed to any two detectives at headquarters and the detective division secretary will then take a position by the gun cabinet, closing same properly after detectives have left.[1]

II. Jail Emergency

When the jail buzzer sounds while the jailer is in the jail area, the information clerk will proceed as follows:

1. He will immediately notify the station lieutenant or patrol sergeant if they are available; if not he will get the three officers

---

[1] The radio broadcasts and detective assignment sheets are shown in *Police Records,* pp. 246-250.

who are most easily available, calling them in from beats if necessary, giving them the keys to court holdover rooms.

2. If one of the three is not a superior officer, the ranking officer will be in charge. One of these men will obtain a hand gas grenade and another a machine gun and ammunition. They will go to the courtroom where one man will take the keys and the gas grenade and go to the foot of the spiral stairs in the men's jail. He will not open the door at the foot of the stairs until he has looked over the situation in the jail. If everything appears to be satisfactory and the jailer is in sight, he will call the jailer and talk to him before opening the door, making certain that everything is safe before he does open the door.

3. If the jailer is not in sight, he will call to him before opening the door. In case he is unable to locate the jailer he will go into the jail to determine the trouble. When the spiral stair door is opened he must keep in mind that just to his right as he goes through is the door to the physician's room and prisoners might be there. He should, when entering under these conditions, have the gas grenade in one hand and a side arm in the other, ready for action.

4. The other two men will remain in the court room with firearms ready for action in case the prisoners make any attempt to get out that way.

III. An Extreme Emergency Requiring the Calling Out of Every Officer Where Criminals Are at Large in the City on Foot

1. Traffic squad on duty will continue working their regular beats unless otherwise assigned.

2. Traffic squad off duty will cover their regular beats working in private cars, unless otherwise assigned.

3. Third platoon officers will take their usual cars and work their regular beats unless otherwise assigned.

4. First and second platoons will cover regular beats in private cars unless otherwise assigned.

5. Detectives will relinquish cars and drive private cars as third platoon officers report for duty.

6. In the event chase centers in some definite section, unless time be important, the first and second platoon officers will be dispatched by recall lights and the third platoon in radio cars shall be left to cover for any new emergency.

7. All dispatchers will remain on duty at the desk. The dispatcher

regularly on duty during the tour of duty will be in charge and the others will assist in the PBX operation, assignments, etc.

8. The extra jailers and evidence technicians will obtain private cars and cover areas assigned by the lieutenant in charge. The off-duty lieutenant will cover the entire city in a private car.

9. Commanding officers will require all patrol sergeants and officers to remain on the street away from headquarters, working diligently until they are recalled.

IV. Dealing With a Traffic Violator

1. Have an accurate check on the speed.

2. Never drive recklessly. Be certain that your vehicle is properly lighted at night. Never drive directly behind and never stop directly in front of the violator. Do not park too close to the violator's car. At night stop the car under a street light or near an open business establishment.

3. Immediately on stopping him, tell him why you stopped him and the action you have determined to take.

4. It is not usually necessary to get the occupants out of the car. It is not always necessary to arrest the violator. He might be confused. All violators can't be handled alike. Use best judgment. If cautioning, make a friend; do not lecture, scold, or reprimand. Emphasize the danger rather than the wrong, especially the danger to the other man.

5. Do not ask any question or try to be "smart." Be pleasant but businesslike. Make no unnecessary delay. Do not waste time; the violator may really be in a hurry.

6. Ask the driver for his operator's license and check with name, address, description, or other identification.

7. Explain the violation notice to the violator. Be sure he understands that further action may be taken after his driving record is checked at headquarters. Inform him that in the event further action is taken in the matter he will be notified by mail. Never tell a violator that "this is only a warning and will cost you nothing."

8. Be courteous but firm at all times. Never lose your head. Do not argue. Do not take the violation as a personal insult. Do not permit a quarrelsome violator to ruffle your feelings. Be impersonal.

9. Give any reasonable information asked. Give the violator your badge number and name on demand, courteously and without rancor or sullenness.

10. Be alert for any emergency that may arise. Do not stick your head inside the car. Do not make threats of violence.

11. Do not refer the violator to anyone for leniency after arrest.

12. When dealing with a woman be especially careful that nothing you say may be misconstrued. Ask if she be "Miss or Mrs." rather than ask bluntly, "Are you married?"

13. Always obtain the full first name, middle initial and last name, asking proper spelling.

14. Operators of U. S. mail trucks or drivers of Transportation Company buses shall not be stopped at the time traffic violation is observed by officer. The number of truck or bus, license number of vehicle, and other information shall be noted on a traffic ticket and handed to the captain of the division who will notify the company to have driver come to headquarters and sign the ticket.

V. Operation of the Public-address Car

A. GENERAL RULES

1. Obey absolutely all traffic regulations. Do not exceed limit except while pursuing a violator. Come to a dead stop at all stop signs. Signal properly all turns and stops. Give the other fellow the right-of-way, whether he be motorist or pedestrian. Be courteous at all times.

2. Use the loudspeaker for police purposes only. Do not speak to acquaintances through it. Say absolutely nothing which might in any way be construed as a "wisecrack." Never use the loudspeaker when angry. Use the best grammar you can command at all times. Never "bawl out" a violator. Tell him as pleasantly as possible of his violation and what he should do to correct it.

3. If you wish to talk to a violator coming toward you begin talking when he is about 100 feet distant. First turn on the red light to attract his attention.

4. When talking to a violator going in the same direction as you, get within a car's length of the rear of his car (or closer) and on his left if possible. Keep the front of the loudspeaker to the rear of the violator.

5. Never warn a violator when he is turning except where left and U turns are prohibited; wait until the turn is completed then tell him about it.

6. Keep a record showing the number of violators warned and the nature of the violations.

B. For Use in a Crowd or Mob

1. Maneuver the car into such a position that the driver will be face to face with the crowd as nearly as possible.

2. Statements made should be firm and concise so as to leave no doubt about instructions or orders.

3. In the case of a mob these statements should be made and public-address car immediately withdrawn.

VI. Servicing Department-owned Firearms

1. Each Sunday morning all second platoon officers who drive cars in which department-owned firearms are installed, will take such arms from their respective cars and take them to the runway between police station and city hall and there unload them. While unloading, arms will be pointed toward the ground in such a manner that should one be accidentally discharged the ricochet will strike the blank west wall of the police station. Officers will not get too close to another officer while unloading these pieces. Arms and ammunition will be turned over to the mechanic after they are unloaded.

2. The mechanic will clean these pieces as soon as possible, cleaning the machine guns first.

3. As each piece is cleaned the officer driving the car in which it belongs will be called to the station and gun and ammunition delivered to him. He will reload it in the same place and manner as above prescribed for unloading and return it to his car.

4. As the mechanic completes cleaning the other pieces he will take them singly to the runway, reload them as above prescribed and place them in the proper cars.

5. All guns in gun cabinet will be unloaded by mechanic as above prescribed, cleaned, reloaded as above and replaced in gun cabinet.

6. Shotguns will be carried loaded at all times.

7. Each officer equipped with a shotgun should inspect same, as soon as safely possible, after leaving station each day, to be sure that it is properly loaded.

8. Mechanic will clean guns on wrapping table in garage. Should he be called away while cleaning a gun, he will lock the weapon in the storage room until his return.

APPENDIX I

Civil Disturbances

Congregations of persons contain all the potentialities for group panic and tumultuous riot. Consequently, any crowd deserves police attention. The action and behavior of the police toward a crowd influence the development of its potentialities. The police, therefore, should analyze the crowd and the circumstances of its formation; they should learn its purpose, appraise its temper, and estimate the likelihood, nature, and extent of immediate disorder. Police action toward the crowd should be based on this analysis.

Crowds vary in their purposes and attitudes. They may form, either conventionally, in a peaceful and orderly manner for some lawful purpose, or casually to satisfy normal curiosity concerning an unexpected incident or situation. Genuine leadership is conspicuously absent in these crowds although they may contain agitators intent on arousing the group to unlawful action. Lawful assemblies left to themselves are usually harmless. They do not present serious police problems so long as they are supervised with tact and good humor. They are readily susceptible to direction and control unless they become emotionally disturbed. Well organized and skillfully led crowds with a well-developed plan for accomplishing an unlawful purpose are more difficult to control.

The general test to identify an unlawful assembly is the existence of violence, threats of violence, or other unlawful acts. The police must recognize the right of the public to assemble for lawful purposes. When no crime is planned or attempted by the crowd, it should not suffer because of police action. When the assembly is unlawful, on the other hand, it must be dispersed. The police may disperse the crowd quietly by the use of diplomacy and good temper, and so preserve the peace. On the other hand, they may provoke a disturbance by poor judgment, by giving evidence of enmity, prejudice, fear, or indecision, or unnecessary interference, or by the use of more force than is needed.

A crowd, in contrast to a mob, is cowardly. It hesitates to commit itself to a course of unrestricted violence, even though some of its members may commit illegal acts when they think they will not

423

be apprehended. The cowardice of a crowd is due to its lack of unity and definite purpose. The members have only half-hearted enthusiasm for an enterprise that involves danger; they are hesitant and uncertain of the action they should take. It is this fact that gives a disciplined police unit its power to control and direct them.

A mob is distinguished from a crowd by the fact that, under the stimulus of intense excitement, its members have lost their collective sense of fear. They no longer respect the law or fear the consequences of its violation. Rational, respected, timid, and even cowardly persons frequently lose their sense of responsibility, reason, and fear when mob spirit permeates the crowd. Homicidal tendencies of the mob develop in a form of blood madness that demands more blood. A mass craze sways the group; its members go temporarily insane together. The members of the mob are unable to resist the madness; they deeply regret their actions when they recover their sense of responsibility and once more become normal. It is the duty of the police to see that a crowd is not transformed into a mob. When a mob forms, bloodshed and destruction usually result before the influence of fear of the law can be restored to its proper power.

Any crowd may become emotionally aroused by fear- or hate-provoking incidents or situations, or by the words or acts of its own members or of the members of an opposing group. When blind, unreasoning fear prevents a sufficient number from controlling their desire to flee, group panic results; frantic efforts are then made to reach safety. The panic of one is often quickly transmitted to others; their frenzied behavior becomes inappropriate to the needs of the situation. Clever agitation may exaggerate a fancied grievance of the crowd and so intensify its hatred and desire for revenge that the members will vent their fury on anyone who interferes with their purpose as well as on the object of their hatred.

The police, being human, are also subject to emotional stresses. Profane and indecent remarks directed at them by members of the crowd may arouse hatred. The approach of several persons armed with clubs, stones, and other weapons may create fear. Officers who permit such actions of the crowd to upset them emotionally may become panicky. They then fall to the level of the crowd and are no longer effective in its control.

Inquisitive and expectant spectators usually constitute a large part of a disorderly crowd; while perfectly harmless in the beginning, they are good material for the mob spirit to work on. The courage of the members of a mob increases with its size; the leaders consequently attempt to convert passive members and spectators to their mood and to attract others to their group. Hate and revenge, which are mob characteristics, thrive on speedy action; delay causes the mob to disintegrate. The leaders, therefore, exhort the mob into immediate action.

As long as a crowd is kept in hand, no matter how noisy and threatening it may be, its collective cowardice remains its most distinguishing characteristic. If not controlled, however, a crowd may commit assaults and depredations which will excite it to a mob pitch. A crowd also may be transformed into a mob by such apparent trivialities as a momentary weakening of the forces holding it in check, a harangue by a fiery leader, or the appearance of a hated figure. The subtle change from confusion to unity, from hesitation to determination, may occur in a few seconds.

Riots and lesser disturbances may have their origin in economic, industrial, labor, racial, cultural, religious, or political differences. Disorders associated with strikes and industrial unrest cause the police the most frequent difficulty.

Preventive Measures

Major riots do not occur spontaneously. They result from emotional tensions that have been built up in members of minority groups over an extended period. They usually start with a small crowd that grows into a large and disorderly mob. The time involved in the development of differences of opinions and interests and in their discussion usually affords the police an opportunity to become aware of impending disorder. Suitable police action may lessen emotional tensions and prevent the growth of a small group into a large crowd and its transformation into a mob.

1. **Intelligence.** Procedures should be established to assure that police executives will be informed of (a) signs of tensions and (b) circumstances that will cause the formation of a crowd.

Beat officers have an opportunity to hear comments and rumors and to observe other signs of tensions. They should report their observations so that the information may be evaluated on a city-wide basis.

Other sources of information should also be developed. Plant security officers, labor officials, minority group leaders, and officials of welfare and other agencies are in positions to gain significant information that should be given to the police for evaluation and action.

Police executives must organize their information sources to assure advance notice of crowd formations. Crowds seldom form without warning; the times and locations where crowds are most likely to form can be foretold with considerable accuracy.

2. Conferences. When a disturbance seems imminent, the city manager or mayor with the chief of police should hold conferences with responsible leaders to analyze the situation, plan action designed to resolve the differences peacefully, discuss likely action of the participants, outline policy in reference to the police enforcement program, and explain the legal aspects of the situation so that all may understand the legality or illegality of probable acts. The problems of law enforcement should be discussed freely and frankly. Legal restrictions on picketing, carrying weapons, making threats, and other likely acts should be discussed, and the legal rights and responsibilities of the contending groups should be clarified.

The initial conference should be held before passions have been so aroused that the contending leaders become unreasonable when conferring. Representatives of both sides of the controversy should be present at conferences to assure them of the impartiality of the public officials. The police should not themselves arbitrate the differences; they must remain impartial if they are to perform their tasks of law enforcement most effectively.

The circumstances may justify the creation of a committee of community leaders charged with continuing efforts to resolve differences, correct unsatisfactory conditions, and counter inflammatory propaganda.

3. Prompt and Decisive Police Action. Prompt and decisive action taken by the police under justifiable circumstances may prevent disorder. Since mobs start as crowds, the likelihood of disorder may be reduced by preventing the formation of a crowd. The police may not molest lawful assemblies, but they should disperse crowds before they get out of hand when there is evidence that they have gathered for an unlawful purpose or are attempting to commit unlawful acts. Inflammatory publications should be investigated and effort made to curb their influences. False rumors should be exposed. Surveillance should be maintained of persons who are believed to be instigating disturbances so that they may be apprehended at the outset of any disorders in which they are involved.

Should rioting occur, the area should be closed off to vehicular and pedestrian traffic. Should there be arsenals in the vicinity of the disturbance, the commanding officer should be notified to post a guard to prevent their seizure. Stores carrying guns in stock should be properly protected. Crowds should not be permitted to congregate; persons should be kept moving. Circumstances may justify a curfew to keep people off the street and a prohibition of the sale of liquor in the neighborhood of the disturbances.

4. Positive Police Action. The police cannot be weak or vacillating in dealing with disorders. They must outline their program of law enforcement in detail, assure themselves of its legality, and instruct all members in the planned course of action. Participants in the disturbance should be informed of the police program of enforcement, as far as it is possible to do so, and they should be convinced of the sincere determination of the police to carry it out impartially and without prejudice. Individual officers on assignments of this nature must perform their duties with confidence and poise; they must avoid giving evidence of uncertainty or fear.

5. The Presence of the Police. The presence of the police to preserve the peace at the scene of a potential disturbance may prevent disorder. Two cardinal principles of crowd control are to get there first and in sufficient force. If a crowd can be legally prevented from forming, the problem is solved before it has developed. The mere presence of officers at the scene may prevent violence or other unlawful acts by either side of the controversy.

Under some circumstances, however, it may be undesirable for the police to make a strong show of force; the display may incite the antagonism of the crowd and thus cause a disturbance the presence of the police was intended to prevent. It may be desirable, therefore, to maintain a strong force in reserve on a nearby side street with a relatively small number of men to police the crowd.

6. Preparation. The police should prepare themselves to deal promptly and decisively with disorders. Units of selected officers should be organized, equipped, and trained in crowd- and riot-control tactics to assure suitable police action at the scene of any actual or potential disorder. Leaders who plan riotous demonstrations familiarize themselves with the preparedness of the police to deal with mob action, and they will avoid violence when police opposition is likely to be strong.

The Riot Squad

The size and organization of the police unit created to deal with civil disturbances are influenced by the size of the department and the probable number of persons it may be directed against. Officers assigned to the squad should be temperamentally suited to this type of work. The stress and excitement of a civil disturbance subjects them to unusual emotional strain. The importance of the judgment used by the police and the serious consequences of their unwise action and behavior make it important that the officers who are assigned to such tasks should be selected from the most competent and stable. An officer should be rejected for this service when there exists any doubt as to his emotional stability, courage, and ability to disregard insulting language and to remain calm under the most trying circumstances. Officers whose prejudices are likely to affect their judgment and actions in dealing with a group should also be rejected.

The question of suitable arms for the riot squad may be summed up in two words: "Never bluff." Give the men weapons they can use and which the crowd knows they are ready to use. A crowd is encouraged to violence by a feeling that the force attempting to hold it in check is bluffing, and rifles and shotguns in service against a crowd, except when held by reserves, are patent bluffs. With firearms virtually barred from such tactics, the riot stick becomes the chief offensive weapon.

Properly used by disciplined bodies of men, riot sticks will suffice to overcome any crowd not extensively equipped with firearms and will disperse an unlawful gathering without bloodshed, whereas a single shot might entail the most disastrous consequences. There is no element of bluff about the riot stick, for any trouble maker knows that it will be used freely and without hesitation, whereas, unless the situation is acutely serious, a commanding officer hesitates to give his men the order to fire; and the crowd is perfectly well aware of this attitude. A man is in an awkward position when he is equipped only with a weapon which he quite properly hesitates to put to its correct use.

These men should be equipped with helmets, riot sticks, and fighter's cups and thoroughly trained in close-order drill. Frequent drills in the use of riot sticks are necessary, for much of their effectiveness in service depends on proper handling. The men should be trained in resisting attempts to wrest their riot sticks from them. The thrust and cut are two simple movements which should be practiced. The thrust is a quick, short jab, aimed at the opponent's stomach or ribs, followed by a quick recovery. The thrust should never be aimed at the face. A cut should be aimed at the junction of the neck and shoulder. In cases of unwillingness or stubbornness rather than actual violence, the thrust should be used rather than the cut. The thrust can be delivered with any degree of force that the circumstances warrant, but the cut should always be hard.

A detail of officers in plainclothes to infiltrate the crowd must complement the work of uniformed officers. They are more effective than uniformed officers for intelligence and reconnaissance assignments. They should locate, obtain evidence against, and arrest the leaders. When this has been done, the uniformed officers should move in to help them control their prisoners.

The commanding officer should maintain as large a reserve as possible. The reserve is his most effective means of making his will felt; without it he is greatly handicapped in the event affairs take a sudden adverse turn. The reserve should, in addition to carrying gas supplies, be armed with riot guns (sawed-off shotguns) in case conditions become such as to necessitate the use of firearms. It should normally be held in close order in the rear of the riot squad, and in a position where its flanks and rear can be readily protected. In the event the police are compelled to split their forces in order to cover several points, a sufficient reserve force armed with riot guns should be detailed to cover all movements of the squad.

The riot gun is the most effective weapon for short-range work. Its effective range is considerably greater than that of a revolver, and its spreading discharge covers a large target. The most effective load for this work is No. 0 buckshot, of which there are twelve pellets in each shell. The shocking power of No. 0 buckshot is sufficiently great, although not as great as No. 00 buckshot. The greater number of pellets, however, has the advantage of spreading into a larger pattern and lessens the chance of a miss. When firing into a mob it should be remembered that a wounded member is just as discouraging to his fellows as a dead one. Firing should be concentrated at the knees, in an effort to stop a member but not to kill him.

Proper and timely use of gas is the most humane method of dispersing an unlawful assembly. The most riotous mob is unable to stand against suitably dispensed tear and sickening gas. The use of gas will be governed entirely by existing conditions, with regard to location and wind. In attempting to disperse a group with tear gas, it should be kept in mind that tear gas is colorless, and that smoke should be used in conjunction with the gas. The smoke should be released first. The gas bomb or grenade should be thrown to the edge of the mob on the up-wind side. The smoke and gas should be released on a sufficiently wide front so that the entire mob is covered. Three-wheeled motorcycles especially equipped to throw a mixture of tear gas and pyrene smoke have been used with success to gas crowds that were in locations where the machines could be successfully maneuvered into position. With the aid of such machines it is possible to thoroughly gas a large area in a short space of time. The riders are equipped with gas masks to avoid being caught in their own barrage.

Both still- and motion-picture cameras should be used from the earliest possible moment at disturbances to gain and preserve evidence for court, to assist in the investigation of offenses, and to refresh officers' minds in preparing a case for court. The sight of the photographer taking pictures also has a tendency to retard the action of the rioters; it instills fear in the leaders that they may be identified by this means and made to pay the penalty for their lawlessness.

The laws of most states not only permit but require police officers to prohibit and disperse unlawful assemblies, by commanding persons who have unlawfully or riotously assembled to disperse and arresting those who fail to comply with the order. The command should be made in an audible tone of voice so that all persons present may have due notice. Public-address equipment is useful for this purpose. Following the issuance of the order, all necessary force may be used to accomplish the dispersal. Those who remain after the dispersal order has been given, especially the leaders, should be arrested.

In labor disturbances the police should make a special effort to be absolutely neutral. They should take no action against the members of either side until the law has been violated or violence threatened.

Personal contact between police officers and members of the crowd should be avoided until tactical operations require it. When officers are in bodily contact with a crowd, a slight blow or shove either by the members of the crowd or by the police, whether accidental or deliberate, may provoke violence.

Force should not be used against the members or the leader of a crowd unless necessary to prevent violence or to make an arrest that cannot be delayed until the crowd has dispersed. When it is necessary to strike a rioter, the blow should fall on a muscle, not on a bone or the head, in order not to permanently injure them. The officer should not strike a woman, an old or infirm man, or a child. He should not strike a man who is running away unless he has committed a serious offense and cannot otherwise be apprehended.

The use of excessive force to effect a dispersal or an arrest is not only unlawful, but it is poor police strategy. Police brutality will cause a crowd to resist all police action and the effectiveness of the police will be correspondingly hampered. Officers must remember that it is not their duty to punish those who oppose their action.

In dealing with a crowd, the making of arrests requires sound judgment. The amount of force used should be proportioned to the seriousness of the offense. It is better to allow one who has committed a minor misdemeanor to escape for the time being than to use violence on him. Arrests should be made in cases of actual violence. On the other hand, it is undesirable to make arrests for stubbornness or slowness in obeying orders. Once an order is given, it must be enforced absolutely, but in dealing with the initial stages of a disorderly crowd, a combination of tact, coolness, and determination may make arrests unnecessary. At times, however, an arrest is exceedingly desirable, either to remove a persistent trouble maker from the scene, or for its effect on the crowd. An arrest, if ordered, should be made at once. The more rapidly it is executed, the greater will be the effect on those who witness it.

Whenever it is necessary to make an arrest in neighborhoods where rioting is anticipated, the prisoner should be removed immediately. The quicker he is removed, the less danger there is of a crowd gathering and getting out of hand.

The members of the unit should be trained to fight back-to-back in groups of four. Singlehanded combat should not be undertaken. One officer must not be allowed to struggle with one person. Should any person lay hands on an officer, other members of the unit must instantly and unhesitatingly spring to his assistance. Their actions must be vigorous. Each member of the crowd must be made to feel that if he resists he will have to fight the entire unit.

Special formations are needed to control crowds. In infantry combat tactics, it is essential that no man in the firing line should ever partially mask a comrade so as to interfere with his field of fire; the single deployed firing line, with supports and reserves to re-enforce it, is basic. Crowd tactics, on the other hand, are based on shock action and personal contact. Not only is it harmless to have the men partially mask one another, but it is often an added source of power.

The tactics used should include the wedge, the diagonal, and the deployed line—three standard formations. The first two may be formed by a squad, section, or platoon; the third may be formed by a unit of any size. The wedge is the normal offensive formation, with the diagonal primarily adjunct thereto; the deployed line will be used chiefly for defensive purposes. These three formations form an adequate basis for all crowd tactics. Their effectiveness depends very largely on the precision and speed with which they can be executed, and on the steadiness with which the men can retain them in the face of opposition.

The Squad Wedge is to be used when the crowd is small enough not to require more than a squad. This is used in splitting a crowd in order to apprehend a ringleader.

The Squad Diagonal, like the squad wedge, is to be used in dealing with small groups. The purpose of this movement is to move men away from a wall or building or to clear a street. In the event the crowd is large, the wedge and diagonal will be executed by the entire group of men as a section movement.

The Deployed Line is strictly a defensive formation and will be used in case the police have drawn fire, or have gained an objective and wish to hold it. The reserves who are not engaged in any squad or section movement should be drawn up in a skirmish line in the immediate rear of the action.

The object of the commanding officer in dealing with a mob should be to settle the affair with a minimum of delay. A mob should be attacked, if possible, from two sides at once. If a mob has formed because of the failure of applied tactics, the commanding officer should endeavor to send a flanking force from his unit to work around to a position whence it can deliver a flanking attack.

The attack should be hard and delivered with sufficient force so that it will instill fear in the members of the mob. In most instances the attack should effect a splitting up of the assembly. This will cause disunity and loss of courage among the members.

There is no absolute rule whereby the commanding officer can tell when the efficacy of applied tactics is at an end and the need for stronger tactics begins; but in general, the use of firearms against the police will be the determining factor. Disorderly assemblies in their initial stages are crowds and should be dealt with by the tactics outlined. Once the bullets begin to fly, however, the further maintenance of such tactics is nothing short of a criminal risk of life. It is when the commanding officer sees that many of the men facing him have firearms, and are ready to use them, that the time for the use of firearms has arrived. With such tactics, the wedge and diagonal pass into uselessness and the deployed line is the tactical basis. These tactics differ from other tactics in that a battle with a mob is almost sure to be short, sharp, and decisive, whereas it may take considerable time to disperse a crowd.

Duties of Observers[1]

The following orders are to be observed by all members of the Department when assigned to obtain information at the scene of any threatened civil disturbance. The men selected for this work are the eyes and ears of their Troop Commander, and the report of their observation may greatly influence the action that will be taken.

1. Two men in civilan clothes will always be assigned to work together. These men should *dress to fit the occasion,* so that they can mingle with the crowd without attracting undue attention. No part of the State Police uniform will be worn while on a detail of this type.

2. Men assigned will obtain a map of the municipality affected in order that they will be in a position to outline the disturbance area when a conference is called by the Troop Commander. A study of the terrain shall be made so that important physical conditions surrounding the threatened area can be accurately drawn on the map. A large-scale map showing the following shall also be prepared:

    a. Best entrances and exits to the area; names and widths of streets.

---

[1] This section has been extracted from *Riot Control Manual,* New Jersey State Police, 1947, by permission of Colonel Charles H. Schoeffel, Superintendent, pp. 12-25.

    b. Type of buildings (factories, warehouses, stores, private dwellings, etc.).

    c. Any vacant spaces between the buildings.

    d. Location of alleys, driveways, railroad sidings, employees' entrances, etc.

    e. Location of any fences, type and height.

    f. Height of buildings and type of their construction.

    g. Location of any vacant lots or fields.

    h. How well the area is illuminated at night.

    i. Locations where groups are congregated.

3. Upon approaching the disturbance area, the vehicle will be parked at the safest location obtainable. The location selected should be several blocks from the scene so that the men will not be observed entering or leaving the vehicle.

4. Upon arrival at the scene of the disturbance, note the proximity of the nearest telephone that is available for use. Use care in making this selection so that you will have maximum security in concealing your identity when the phone is used.

5. Make report of conditions hourly, unless instructed otherwise. Immediately report any important change in conditions, particularly whether the disturbance is increasing or has lessened in intensity.

6. Make mental notes, until such time as the information can be written down. Ascertain the size of any group, or opposing groups, if more than one. Identify ringleaders or persons who appear to be inciting or agitating the crowd and record their names, nationalities, descriptions, and dress or other identifying marks. State whether they are local persons or strangers; if not local, ascertain point of origin. State the degree of success each leader seems to have in handling the crowd; give, in your opinion, the importance of the individual leaders in relation to each other.

7. Observe the type of persons who comprise the group or groups, their reaction to suggestions of violence, whether carrying concealed weapons, sticks, bats, wrenches, bricks, nuts, bolts, etc. Report the type of placards or standards being used, the phaseology appearing on the same, and how they are being carried, *i.e.* nailed to a thin stick, bat, pick handle, two-by-four, etc. Report approximate number of each sex.

8. Report the number of spectators, type, probability of disorders being committed by them, number of each sex, whether or not they

are local people or from out of town, whether they are friendly or opposed to disorderly elements.

9. Report equipment used by leaders, such as sound trucks, other vehicles, loud speakers without sound trucks, or soap boxes for their orators.

10. In industrial disturbances report the following:

a. Name of plant.

b. Location.

c. Name of owner or head of firm.

d. Name of superintendent or manager.

e. Union affiliations.

f. Names of representatives.

g. Cause of strike and matters at issue.

h. Product manufactured (description).

i. Number on strike.

j. Number and average age of employees.

k. Enforcement officers in charge at scene, etc.

l. Proximity of the headquarters of the strikers to the disturbance area.

m. Other data.

11. In reporting on a vehicle, note the model, color, year, registration number and other identifying marks, occupants, and the use made of it.

12. Obtain copies, if possible, of all literature being passed out by the factions concerned.

13. Observers will ascertain the number of shifts working at an industrial plant having a disturbance, the number of persons employed during each shift, hours of shift changes, probability of disturbances being created at the time of such changes, and which shift change would bring the greatest disorder. They will ascertain the number of employees striking, number of pickets who are employees, number of pickets not employees, number of spectators who are employees, number of spectators who are not employees, whether the leaders are local persons or imported to the area.

14. Observers will report on all remarks or conversations overheard relative to the disorder, which may assist in determining (a) degree of violence which may be expected; (b) attitude of the more important leaders toward the situation; (c) methods groups may use in attempts at intimidation; and (d) probable trend of future developments.

15. In order to prevent looting in the event the disturbance starts, observers should ascertain what type stores are in the vicinity and the character of the merchandise they handle.

16. Members assigned to duty of this type must be mentally and physically alert at all times. They will not consort with the factions involved, except as it may be necessary to obtain information. They will not engage in any unwarranted conversation or social activity while on duty, except in extreme necessity to obtain information.

17. All facts should be reported without prejudice, bias, or partiality.

18. If in doubt about any condition or situation, immediately call your superior officer. Keep in mind that many seemingly unusual occurrences may be normal. Therefore, learn to evaluate all matters, actions, and information observed while on this duty.

DISPENSING TEAR GAS AND SMOKE AT RIOTS[1]

By

MAYNARD H. FINLEY

Criminalist, Wichita Police Department, Wichita, Kansas

In dealing with mobs and riots, the police department must always keep uppermost in mind the fact that physical violence to participants does not meet with acceptance on the part of the general public. To avoid the creation of resentment, therefore, a means which has the least possible physical after effect must be used in quelling the riot or dispersing the mob.

The use of tear gas has been recognized for some time as a superior method of mob control, having no deleterious after effects. The present procedures used in dispensing tear gas are restricted to guns and grenades. These procedures have definite limitations:

1. Area effectively covered by a single officer is relatively small.

2. Area is not covered uniformly.

3. The time required to cover a large area is great.

4. The number of officers required to cover an extensive area is large.

The needs, then, of any adequate dispensing system are these:

1. The system must be capable of covering a large area.

---

[1] Reprinted from *The Journal of Criminal Law and Criminology*, Vol. 29, No. 2, 1938, pp. 254-260.

2. It must cover this area in a minimum amount of time.

3. It must cover the area completely, leaving no spaces where there is no gas present.

4. The gas must be of sufficient density over the area covered to produce the desired results.

5. It should require a minimum number of men to effectively cover the area.

In addition to the above points, it is also advisable to provide a means for breaking up certain mobs, as in the case of minor disturbances, without the use of tear gas. For this purpose a smoke screen may be used, provided the smoke screen is (1) dense enough to obscure vision, and (2) light enough to rise to a height of 8 or 10 feet, and at the same time heavy enough so that it will not float away rapidly.

Covering a large area with gas in a minimum of time requires greater speed than is possible on foot. While an automobile would speed up the dispensing process, its operation would be limited to street use. If the gas is distributed through the exhaust or by air pressure, or if the automobile passes through an area which has already been gassed, the car has a serious disadvantage due to the creation of air currents which bring the gas into the vehicle itself. The air stream under the motor and dust pans of the car tends to stay at the same level, and due to the difference in height between the bottom of the motor and pans and the floor boards, a partial vacuum is created next to the floor boards which causes a swirling motion of the air and tear gas up toward the floor, resulting in some gas leaking into the car. A partial vacuum is created at the back of the car, due to the air stream over the top and sides setting up a swirling motion at the back which has the same effect as the one under the car, and, in addition, tends to make the gas rise more rapidly, which spoils the effectiveness of the barrage by lifting the gas off the ground.

These difficulties are overcome by the use of a motorcycle. The "three-wheeler" is particularly well suited because (1) it can be used at slow as well as high speeds; (2) it is more stable than a "solo" machine, especially where members of the mob may attempt to grab the handlebars or capsize the machine; (3) it is small and easily handled and can be used over terrain not passable for an automobile; and (4) it does not create the swirling motion of gas since there is less vacuum created.

The distribution of gas and smoke from the motorcycle is accomplished by mounting two cylinders above the gas tank, one for liquid tear gas, the other for the smoke liquid. Each of these cylinders is connected to the exhaust pipe by copper tubing; the connection for the tear gas cyclinder is at a point in the tail pipe below the saddle, the smoke cylinder being connected to the two manifolds just below the exhaust ports. The full heat of the exhaust is thus used on the smoke liquid to insure complete vaporization, less heat being used on the tear gas as it is volatile at the average temperatures encountered in its use. The impelling force of the exhaust is used for the distribution of the vapors through a specially constructed "V" tail pipe, which is attached in place of the muffler.

The cylinders are made of three-inch pipe twenty inches long. They must be constructed of extra heavy, seamless pipe in order to withstand the pressure of 150 pounds which it is necessary to apply to force the liquids from the cylinders. The lower ends of the cylinders, next to the rider, are made by welding an end plate into the pipes, while the front or top ends are threaded so that steel caps can be screwed on the full length of the cap threads. The caps are placed on the front ends as a protection for the rider in case the threads should give way after continued use and wear, and the caps be blown off. Each cylinder is provided with a screw-type regulating stop valve screwed into the end plate at the lower end and then welded into the plate so it will withstand the pressure in the cylinders. These valves, and also the fittings and tubing, are of the type commonly found on gasoline stoves and appliances, and were purchased from a concern specializing in the manufacture of this equipment. The tubing size used is 3/16″ and all fittings and valves correspond in size. This equipment may be purchased from any store selling repairs for gasoline appliances. A valve stem of the type used in old inner tubes is threaded into each cap at the top end and then welded in. These valves are used in the application of the air pressure to the cylinders and are provided with regular valve stem caps, besides the valves.

The cylinders are mounted above the motorcycle gas tank by double U clamps, the rear clamp being bolted directly on the frame of the motorcycle just in front of the saddle, while the first clamp is mounted about six inches above the tank by an angle bracket bolted to the frame. This is done in order to clear the speedometer and controls. The 3/16″ soft copper tubing is connected to the valves by

3/16" compression fittings on one end of the valves. The other end of the valves are screw type which are welded into the cylinder ends. The tubing from the tear-gas cylinder extends downward from the valve, past the rear cylinder of the engine, to the exhaust pipe at a point approximately under the rear edge of the saddle. It is connected to the compression end of a fitting which has been welded into the pipe at this point. One or two loops were provided in this line to avoid strain and breaks due to vibration. Introducing tear gas at this point in the tail pipe avoids excessive heat and chances of breaking the gas down chemically, but provides sufficient heat to aid in complete volatilization and consequent even distribution. The connection from the smoke cylinder is brought down from the valve and forward across the top of the rear cylinder of the engine to a point midway between the two exhaust manifolds, where it branches in a 3/16" compression T fitting, one branch running to each manifold, where it is connected by a male screw 3/16" compression fitting, the screw end being welded into the manifold as close as feasible to the exhaust port. Loops are included in these lines to avoid breaking due to vibration. This arrangement provides equal distribution of the smoke mixture to each manifold and thereby equal vaporization of the total mixture. The liquid mixture is introduced as near the exhaust ports as possible in order to provide maximum vaporization.

The tear-gas cylinder cannot be filled at ordinary temperatures because a large portion of it will be lost as vapor due to its volatility. The method used to prevent loss of the gas was to immerse the liquid tear-gas container and the cylinder to be filled in a solution containing ice and rock salt, as used in freeing ice cream. If enough time is allowed, the temperature of the containers and liquid may be reduced by this method so that very little is lost by vaporization, if the transfer is quickly made. The lower the temperature the smaller the vaporization loss. An electric refrigerator may also be used to reduce the temperature of the liquid and containers by placing them in or on the freezer coils to obtain quick reduction in temperature. If the refrigerator is a walk-in type, the person charging the cylinder may do so in the box, provided there are no foodstuffs or other articles in the box which would be ruined by the tear gas. Whichever method is used, the person charging the cylinders should invariably be equipped with a tear gas mask.

The liquid smoke mixture is composed of three parts motor flushing oil, as used in service stations, to one part of pyrene, by volume.

This may be increased to a mixture of two parts of oil to one part pyrene, with satisfactory results, the exact proportions depending on the weight of oil used. The pyrene holds the flash point of the mixture high enough so that the oil is vaporized without burning. Penetrating oil may also be used, but is more expensive. The mixture may be made and kept in a closed container for some time without deterioration. This liquid produces a dense white fog due to the pyrene in the mixture, and is heavy enough, because of the percentage of oil used, so that it will not rise rapidly and float away, but the mixture is purposely made so it is light enough to rise gradually above the average person's height, thereby obscuring vision and confusing the mob. Two or more machines may be used in tandem where a heavier screen is desired.

The riders should always be equipped with tear-gas masks so that they may return to any section where a gas barrage has been laid, and because the quick action so often necessary in handling a mob requires clear eyesight. A steel helmet should also be regular equipment, as a protection against stones and clubs. Any attempt to dislodge him from the cycle can be successfully repelled by cutting the front wheel at right angles and spinning the machine in a circle, which will gas all persons in the vicinity of the machine.

When not in use, the equipment is readily removed for storage by disconnecting the copper tubing at the exhaust connections, unbolting the brackets from the frame and lifting the whole assembly off the machine. The exhaust port connections are then closed by dead heads, the special "V" tail pipe unclamped and replaced by the regular muffler and the machine is ready for regular use. Because of its corrosive effect on metals, the tear gas is removed from the cylinders and kept in rubber-stoppered glass bottles, sealed with adhesive tape. The gas cylinders are then flushed out with alcohol, swabbed with light oil and capped. All the equipment except the tail pipes is stored in a metal box two feet square by four feet long.

Here, then, is a means, effective with a small number of officers, of quickly providing a smoke screen in case of minor disturbances, and of dispensing tear gas rapidly and effectively in case of mobs and riots. This method fulfills the requirements set forth in the first part of this article, and yet is flexible in its use, since both the speed of the cycle and flow of tear gas and smoke may be varied at will. It is felt that, due to its flexibility, this apparatus, once tried, will be a welcome addition to the equipment of all departments.

Police Duties at Crime Scenes

By Don J. Finney
Laboratory Technician, Police Department,
Wichita, Kansas

[Reprinted from *The American Journal of Police Science, incorporated in* THE JOURNAL OF CRIMINAL LAW AND CRIMINOLOGY, Vol. 27, Nos. 2-3, 1936]

In order to understand the assignment of specific duties to certain officers in the Wichita Police Department it is necessary to understand the organization of the department and the relationships between the various officers. The city is divided into beats, each covered by one officer in an automobile equipped with two-way radio and a riot gun. The size of the beats vary from a few square blocks to several square miles, according to the need for police service. The number of beats varies according to the time of the day, the force being distributed among the shifts according to need.

Each patrolman is restricted to his own beat unless he is dispatched from headquarters or is in actual pursuit of an offender. Covering the city at large are two cars, one driven by the patrol sergeant, the other by an evidence technician.[1] The patrol sergeant has supervision of each beat officer as well as of the technician. As far as he is able, the patrol sergeant answers the more important calls to determine that the officers are handling their assignments properly.

The evidence technician is a patrolman selected and trained in the examination of crime and accident scenes for the purpose of discovering, identifying, recording, preserving, and transporting physical evidence to the crime laboratory. This point differentiates the duties of the evidence technician from the duties of the beat officer. It is the duty of the latter to investigate persons: to interview, question and cross-examine principals, witnesses, and all other people who might have some knowledge of the crime. He reconstructs the

---

[1] The evidence technician was originally called a "special investigator" but because of the greater suitability of the title "evidence technician" to the tasks he performs, he is called an evidence technician in this appendix. The number assigned was later increased to two patrol sergeants and two evidence technicians on the third (evening) shift.

crime and attempts to identify the criminal by getting information from people.

The evidence technician is not concerned wih people; his attention is limited to things. He searches the crime scene, not only the interior of the building in which the crime was committed, but the space surrounding it as well, for some trace of the criminal, some physical clue which may establish his identity, some mark which may be identified as having been made by him or by some tool, instrument, or device in his possession. It is the duty of the technician to reconstruct the crime solely from the physical evidence he finds at the scene; he must take photographs and measurements which will enable him to re-enact the crime in the imagination of the court.

When a call is received that a criminal is in operation, the dispatcher immediately dispatches the beat officer, the evidence technician, and such number of other officers as he deems necessary.[1] These officers proceed to the scene following the procedure outlined in the department's "Tactics" with a view of capturing the criminal rather than frightening him away. If the criminal has left the crime scene, officers are assigned to quadrants radiating from the scene of the crime. Because of the small size of the beats and the relatively large number of motorized officers, it is always possible to surround a building or an area within a minute's time.

The beat officer, usually being nearest to the scene, is almost always the first officer there; if not, he arrives at so nearly the same time that the first officer usually has no time to accomplish the duties outlined for him. Since the beat officer may be detained, however, it is necessary that the first officer to arrive know what he is to do. As soon as the uselessness of immediate pursuit of the criminal becomes apparent, the beat officer and the evidence technician proceed with the duties outlined herein.

The evidence technician is required to investigate every crime scene where there is any likelihood of physical evidence being found. He is dispatched on all accident cases, all cases involving dead bodies, all felonies except cases of fraud, and any larceny where it is believed that physical clues may exist.

The evidence technician drives a car which, like the patrol sergeant's, is equipped with a bullet-resisting shield, a sub-machine gun, gas supplies, and a mask. In addition, this car carries paraphernalia useful in searching for, recording, collecting and preserving physical evidence, as well and a rope and a broom. It is also equipped with a

[1] See p. 85.

metal case containing fingerprint powders, atomizers and brushes for applying powder, lifting tape, material for making comparison prints, film holders for a fingerprint camera, and stickers for labeling all evidence. In another compartment of the same case are tools such as pliers, scissors, tweezers, files, screw drivers, chisel, tape measure, and other articles necessary for collecting practically any kind of evidence. Another metal case contains a Speed Graphic Camera with flash synchronizer, reflector, film holders, and flash bulbs. These are for photographing evidence and crime scenes and for making any other photographs necessary in investigation. A third case contains extension cord, reflectors, flash gun, flood bulbs, flash bulbs, and other equipment necessary in taking night photographs. Still another contains material for making casts of plaster, moulage, and modeling clay, with containers for mixing and heating the casting material. The fifth case contains a set-focus fingerprint camera, and a Graflex camera for emergency work or in the event it is more practical for use under certain conditions.

INVESTIGATION AT THE SCENE OF A CRIME

General Duties

There are some rules of investigation at the scene of a crime which every officer should know. If he observes the following general rules, as well as those specifically assigned to him, his investigation will be thorough and efficient:

(1) **Cooperate.** Close cooperation of all officers is essential to successful investigations. Regardless of whether you are the first at the scene, the beat officer, the evidence technician, or the detective or an officer who just happened along, it is your duty to cooperate with the others to the best of your ability.

(2) **Consult Superior Officer.** If in doubt in any phase of the investigation, consult your superior officer, and in his absence confer with your co-workers. Talk things over between yourselves and decide what is best to be done.

(3) **Preserve Evidence.** If you discover anything that might be physical evidence, do not touch, or disturb it, but note its character, position and relative location to the crime, and see that it is preserved in its original state for the evidence technician.

(4) **Note Conditions.** Upon your arrival at the scene of a serious crime, note the weather condition, position of sun or moon, direction of wind, as well as the exact time.

(5) **Notify Coroner.** In the case of murder or suicide remember that it is not permissible to remove a body without the permission of the coroner.

(6) **Notify Policewoman.** If the crime involves rape, or the murder or attack of a female person, the policewoman should be notified.

(7) **Bar Relatives.** Never allow members of the family involved to assist in the investigation, or to search for clues, especially in case of homicide. Should the search uncover a clue or lead that might implicate or point toward a member of the family, there is always a tendency to conceal the clue or otherwise protect the suspected member.

(8) **Listen.** Be alert for unguarded remarks made by witnesses or others having knowledge of the case. Some unintentional hint may furnish a clue that will result in the solution of the case.

(9) **Assist.** If you are an officer off duty, or an officer who happens to be at the scene and not one of those sent on the call, it is your duty to assist in every way possible. Never leave the scene, whether you were sent on call or not, until you are certain there are sufficient officers there to handle any situation that might arise. In no case should you intrude upon the scene, especially in civilian clothes, any more than any other person.

(10) **Do Not Talk.** Do not disclose valuable clues to any one. If you come into possession of a clue preserve it and give it to your superior officer at the earliest possible moment.

(11) **Crime Must Be Proved.** Bear carefully in mind the elements of the crime you are investigating and undertake to find proof for each.

(12) **Write Report.** It is important that each officer take careful notes during the investigation. His investigation report must contain a full and complete account of all that he did and of all that he observed and learned during the course of the investigation.

Duties of the Superior Officer

(1) **Determine the Facts.** Ascertain from the first officer at the scene the nature and status of the case.

(2) **Apprehend the Criminal.** Determine if immediate pursuit of the perpetrator is advisable; if so detail officers to this task. If necessary to dispatch officers from the scene on this mission, see that the crime scene is properly protected, posting a civilian guard if neces-

sary. In searching for the criminal, remember that he may hide on the premises or in the immediate vicinity. A thorough search is necessary.

(3) **Protect the Crime Scene.** See that the officers are properly performing their duties in protecting the crime scene. Rope off the area if advisable.

(4) **Obtain Reenforcements.** Determine if there are sufficient officers present to handle the situation, and if not, ask for further assistance from headquarters.

(5) **Assign Officers.** If there are officers present who have no specific duties outlined, assign them to given tasks, either at the scene or elsewhere. If there is nothing for them to do on the case, detail them to cover the districts of the officers who are detained on the case. Do not permit officers not actually engaged in the investigation to loiter at the scene. There is always something which they can do, such as checking information at other locations and questioning possible witnesses with a view to determining if they saw or heard anything. This applies to officers off duty as well as to those on duty. As soon as an officer completes his work at the crime scene, assign him to other tasks or have him report to the dispatcher and return to his beat. Do not permit officers to leave the scene until you are sure they have done everything possible on the case.

(6) **Advise** the beat officer and the evidence technician as to the proper action to be taken in case of doubt.

(7) **Assist** the evidence technician in his search for physical evidence in the more serious cases. Assist the beat officer in questioning witnesses when necessary. See that all possible information is obtained.

(8) **Notify** the detective to be assigned and the captain of your division, when the seriousness of the case warrants such action.

(9) **Report to Headquarters.** Report to the dispatcher when you leave the crime scene, advising him as to the status of the case and informing him as nearly as possible of the length of time that will be required to complete the investigation so that he may arrange to have the beats that are open covered by other officers.

Duties of the First Officer to Arrive at the Scene of the Crime

(1) **Arrest the Perpetrator.** Ascertain the identity of the criminal and arrest immediately if possible.

(2) **Pursue if Apprehension Likely.** When flight of criminal has been sufficiently recent, notify dispatcher so that officers may be as-

signed to quadrants or, when information is available as to the course of his flight, in actual pursuit. When advisable, join the pursuit and search.

(3) **Give Description to Headquarters.** When the perpetrator has escaped, obtain his identity and a detailed personal description. Establish means of escape, whether by car, taxi, bus, on foot, etc., with a description of the vehicle used. As soon as sufficient information has been obtained, give the dispatcher either by telephone or radio the necessary details for a broadcast.

(4) **Preserve Evidence.** Protect the crime scene against any intrusion or molestation. Give definite instructions that nothing is to be touched until the evidence technician arrives and takes charge.

(5) **Inform Other Officers.** Perform the duties of the beat officer until his arrival. Upon his arrival and the arrival of the evidence technician give them a brief outline of the nature of the case, the central point of attack, and the progress of the investigation.

(6) **Report to Headquarters.** Do not leave the scene until you are sure there are sufficient officers present to cope with any situation that might arise. Report to your superior officer for further instructions. In his absence inform the dispatcher that you have finished.

(7) **Specific Duties of the First Officer** to arrive at the scene are listed under specific crimes.

INVESTIGATION AT THE SCENE OF A CRIME OF VIOLENCE AGAINST THE PERSON

Duties of the First Officer to Arrive at the Scene

(1) **Care of Victim.** Ascertain the condition of the victim and arrange for immediate medical attention if it be needed.

(2) **Observe Carefully.** If the victim is to be moved immediately note carefully the location and position of the body and the condition of the clothing. Outline the position of the body with chalk or other contrasting material before moving.

(3) **Protect the Scene.** Protect the crime scene from any intrusion or change. Prevent the touching of the body. Give instructions that nothing is to be disturbed until the evidence technician arrives and takes charge. Prevent unauthorized persons from entering the crime scene. Post a civilian guard if necessary. Clear the room or the immediate area of all persons except those on official business or detained on the case.

(4) **Guard Witnesses.** Hold everyone who was at the scene at the time of your arrival. Allow no one to enter or leave until questioned. Be tactful and courteous. If it becomes necessary to permit any one to leave the scene obtain his name, address, and telephone number.

Duties of the Beat Officer

(1) **Determine the Facts at Once.** If the first officer to arrive at the scene, perform all of the duties outlined above. If not, contact the officer who first arrived at the scene and obtain from him a brief outline of the nature and status of the case. Eliminate repetition and backtracking as much as possible.

(2) **Separate the Witnesses** to prevent their conversing with one another. This should be done at the earliest possible moment. In the event it is not possible to separate all witnesses, then the more important ones should be separated and the others left in one room in charge of an officer.

(3) **Identify Those Present.** Obtain the name, address, and telephone number of everyone present at the time the crime was committed, of those who discovered the crime, and of those who came in immediately after its discovery.

(4) **Notify Headquarters.** Relay to dispatcher or station lieutenant any information that will assist in pursuit, search, or investigation of leads.

(5) **Question Principal Witnesses First:** (a) Eye witnesses, (b) Persons present at the time of the commission of the crime. (c) Those who discovered the crime, or came in shortly thereafter. (d) Witnesses who saw the perpetrator leaving the scene. (e) Witnesses having knowledge of events leading up to the crime. (f) Hearsay witnesses. (Hearsay witnesses cannot testify in court, but their statements may be of value in the investigation.)

(6) **Question Witnesses Separately.** Interrogate witnesses one at a time and separately. Be tactful and courteous. Be careful in talking to witnesses not to reveal unnecessarily facts relating to the case; keep in mind that the person you are questioning may prove to be a principal. Make notes on the statements of each individual questioned. Any statement made by a witness relative to the guilt of another party should be made in the presence of that party so that the officer hearing the statement will be permitted to repeat it as evidence in court in the absence of the witness.

(7) **Be Suspicious.** It should be remembered that a great many

crimes are simulated for one reason or another; i.e., to create sympathy, to defraud insurance companies, to cover losses sustained in other ways, to deceive spouse, etc. In questioning witnesses, simulation can often be detected by contradictory and inconsistent statements as to the sequence of events, amount of loss, etc. Remember, however, that memory is fickle and, although the story of the victim does not ring true, the fact of the commission of a crime should be accepted as true until sufficient evidence has been obtained to substantiate a theory of falsification. Be suspicious of the victim who has a ready answer to every question; no person sees all there is to see, hears all there is to hear, and remembers all he sees or hears. This applies to the witness as well.

(8) **Get the Story Immediately.** Obtain definite statements as soon after the commission of the crime as possible. Get the story from the victim and from the principal witnesses before they have had time to think over what they are going to say. Then, at some later time, get their story again. They may have remembered some important detail or may tell the same story in a very different way, so as to throw an entirely new light on the facts.

(9) **Question Witnesses Thoroughly,** obtaining detailed information as to: (a) The number of criminals involved. (b) The identity and description of each; whether he was wounded or his clothing torn; who are his associates, relatives, friends, enemies, sweetheart; what places he frequents; his hangouts; what are his habits, etc. (c) The route taken in escape; vehicle used and dscription. (d) Any inquiries made by the perpetrator prior to the crime; words spoken and statements made at the time of the crime. These should be recorded verbatim. (e) The general conduct, attitude, tone of voice, and language characteristics of the criminal; attempt to commit suicide; false statements, etc. (f) Any suspicious person or thing noted in the vicinity of the crime immediately prior to its commission. (g) The movements of both the victim and the perpetrator of the crime.

(10) **Identify the Victim** (if deceased or unconscious). Obtain: (a) Complete and correct name. (b) Complete and correct names of witnesses who make the identification. (Witnesses who make the identification must be produced at the inquest.) (c) Record the means of identification for future reference. (d) Description of body, clothing, letters, photographs, moles, birthmarks, scars, teeth, etc.

(11) **Obtain a Dying Declaration** if the victim is seriously

wounded. Proceed as follows: (a) What is your name? (b) Where do you live? (c) Do you believe that you are about to die? (d) Have you no hope of recovery from the injuries you have received? (e) Are you willing to make a true statement as to how you received the injuries from which you are now suffering? (f) Record statement. (Dying declarations are admissible as evidence.)

(12) **If Property Stolen,** obtain a complete list and detailed description.

(13) **Make Inquiries** of neighbors and bystanders.

(14) **Assist the Evidence Technician** in his work when needed.

(15) **Notify Headquarters.** Remain at the scene until you are certain that there is nothing more to be done. Notify the dispatcher when you leave.

Duties of the Evidence Technician

The **primary function** of the evidence technician is to **search** for physical evidence. Having found such evidence it is his duty to take steps necessary to identify it; establish its exact location by measurements, sketch and/or photograph; reproduce it by photographic and casting methods; preserve it in an unchanged and uncontaminated form, and label it in its proper sequence; and also to interpret its relation to the crime. It is his duty to note the general facts of the case. In order to do this properly it is necessary that he have the cooperation of the other officers as outlined in the preceding sections. The questioning of persons and obtaining facts from people is the duty of the beat officer. The evidence technician is only concerned with what he finds at the crime scene in the form of physical evidence. The beat officer investigates **persons;** the evidence technician investigates **things.**

Internal Examination

(1) **Determine Facts.** Upon arrival at the scene obtain a brief outline of the nature and status of the case from the officers who were first there.

(2) **Conduct a Preliminary Survey** of the entire crime scene in order to: (a) Choose a point from which to start the search for evidence. (b) Determine equipment that will be needed in the search and in the photographic work to be done, but do not leave the scene unless there is some other officer there to protect it.

(3) **Examine Area Around the Body.** Make an examination of the area immediately surrounding the body before the coroner makes his examination. There may be evidence that otherwise would be destroyed by being trampled upon.

(4) **Examine the Victim.** This examination should consist of the following: (a) Photograph the body. Note carefully the location and position. Outline the body with chalk, or some other contrasting material, so that if it should have to be moved before the photographs are taken the position will not be lost. The exact location and position of the body should be shown in the photographs. Should the coroner arrive before you have finished this task, ask him to wait until you are through. (b) Examine body. Assist the coroner in making his examination, searching the body for marks that may assist in identifying the instrument used, noting carefully the type and location of wounds, their dimensions in all directions, blood and seminal stains, and the general condition of the body. Examine carefully fingernails, hands, hair, and arms. Obtain debris from under the fingernails. Samples of hair from the head should be obtained in all cases. Ask the coroner for an opinion as to the time and probable cause of death. Close-up photographs should be taken at this time. (c) Examine clothing. Before the body is removed make a thorough examination of the clothing. When there is any possibility that evidence may be lost or destroyed during the process, the clothing of the victim should be thoroughly examined before the body is moved. In some instances it may be necessary to remove an article of clothing before the body is moved. Search carefully for hair, fibers, tissue, stains, and foreign matter. (d) Procedure in sex cases. Have victim examined thoroughly by a physician, to determine whether penetration was effected, to search for evidences of semen, and for signs of blows, choking, scratching, or other evidences of force. Have the physician examine the body for hairs that might be from the perpetrator. Samples of the victim's hair should also be obtained from head and body, including the genital region.

(5) **Examine Area Under the Body.** Examine the area which was directly under the body for blood stains, vomited matter, semen, bullets, and marks of any weapons. The presence or absence of certain things may establish or disprove a murder theory. Certain conditions found under the body may even influence the degree of the offense committed.

(6) **Start from the Body.** In most cases the body of the victim will be the starting point for the search. From this point work outward in ever widening circles, making careful examination of the floor, walls, ceiling, furniture, and all exposed surfaces. This examination should be very thorough and critical. The smallest piece of foreign matter may prove to be a clue.

(7) **Search for What:** (a) Lethal weapon. If found, examine it for traces of hair, tissue, and fibers, as well as for fingerprints, dirt, rust, blood, and any foreign substance that might serve to identify it as having come from a certain location or belonging to a certain person. It is important that the lethal weapon be handled by no one except the technician. This is especially true in the case of a gun. (b) Bullets and cartridge cases. Search carefully for fired bullets and shells at the scene, and when found observe all the precautions outlined subsequently in section on "Care and Preservation of Evidence." (c) Poison. In poison cases search for the poison container, preserve contents, and search for latent prints; if evidence of poisoning, obtain samples of vomit, samples of food, and examine carefully contents of all containers. (d) Marks. Search carefully for a mark of any description left at any place by the criminal. Such possible marks include fingerprints or any other prints made by contact of the criminal's body; knee, foot, or heel prints, or other marks left by his clothing, etc.; tool marks, whether made by a bullet, a weapon, a jimmy or other tool in forcing a door or container, etc. (e) Articles left by criminal. Search for matches, toothpicks, etc., which criminal may have dropped, or a tool, weapon, or other device used by him in committing the crime, or a hat or other article which he may have lost in his flight. The scene of struggle should be examined carefully for articles which might have been dropped. (f) Hair, fibers, dirt from shoes, dirt from clothes or hands, etc. Especially should points of entry and exit be examined for fibers from snagged clothes. (g) Blood, excreta, sputum, and other stains. (h) Disorder. Signs of struggle. (i) Procedure in sex cases. Search carefully for cloth, towel, handkerchief, or paper, and examine them and all garments, bedding, and other material for signs of seminal stains, blood stains, hair and other material.

(8) **Search Where:** (a) Openings to room. Search all openings to the room for evidence of tool marks, footprints, fingermarks, and evidences of forcible entry. If there was forcible entry, examine the

point of entrance for signs of fibers from clothing, blood stains, fingerprints, tool marks, dust, and heel prints. (b) Unexposed places. After all exposed surfaces have been thoroughly gone over, search the unexposed places diligently, inside books, behind pictures on the wall, behind furniture, in waste baskets, under rugs, in vases; in fact, everything at the scene should be searched with care. The most valuable evidence may have been purposely hidden. (c) Ascertain condition of scene. Determine from the person who discovered the crime if there has been any change in the crime scene prior to your arrival. Some one may have pulled down a window shade, closed the door to a book case, shut a drawer, or have done most any little thing, unthinkingly hiding valuable evidence. If you are unable to determine definitely whether any of these things have been done, then it is best to proceed as though they had, raising and lowering windows and window shades, opening doors, etc., carefully examining the portions that would be hidden by any change. (d) The hiding place. In the search for evidence, do not overlook clothes closets, attics, vacant rooms, etc., where the perpetrator might have lain in wait for his victim.

(9) **Reconstruct Crime:** (a) Location of victim. Determine as nearly as possible the location and position of the victim at the time of the commission of the crime. If the course of the bullet can be traced it will assist in locating the point from which the death missile came. If possible, to show the course of the bullet fairly accurately, a white string may be used in a photograph. (b) The struggle. Carefully examine all blood stains to ascertain the amount of struggle, distance covered, whether the victim crawled or walked after being assaulted, etc. Reconstruct the sene as nearly as possible.

(10) **Record Evidence** in the order found, and where it was found. Be able to state definitely its relation to a fixed point, giving at least two measurements. When the evidence is not originally found by the technician, it is important to record by whom it was found, and to trace possession up to the time it came into the hands of the technician.

(11) **Search for Latent Prints.** Ascertain whether any article on the premises was handled by the perpetrator, and search it especially. When latent prints are found, take elimination prints of everyone who might have made them.

(12) **Photographs to Be Taken:** (a) General photographs of the scene, including the location and position of the body, location of

weapons and other important points. It may be necessary to take these from several angles. Pictures should be taken from the point where the scene first came into your view. It is important that these be taken as early as possible, as some of the articles will of necessity be moved during the investigation. When this is done, the moving or disturbance of some of the evidence will not destroy its value. (b) Close-up photographs of the body, showing the location and character of wounds, condition of clothing, etc. (c) Photograph showing relative position of weapons and body. (d) Entrance and exit to crime scene. (e) Evidence in its original position and condition. (f) Close-up photographs of weapons, showing serial or other numbers if present. (g) Photographs of blood stains after body is removed. (h) When firearms have been used, photograph all bullet holes and marks. (i) In taking photographs where distances are of importance, some measuring instrument should be placed where it will show in the photograph. This measure should be on the same plane, or at the same distance from the camera, as the object you are photographing. Every photograph should contain some identifying mark. If there is nothing on which a mark may be placed one should obtain some object upon which his initials and the date may be placed and place the object where it will show clearly in the photograph. Do not leave yourself open to the possibility of having your pictures thrown out as evidence.

(13) **Measurements to Be Taken:** (a) Exact measurements of the room or building in which the crime was committed. (b) Location of the more important articles of furniture. (c) Distance of perpetrator from the victim, when possible to ascertain. (d) Height of openings (windows, etc.) from ground or floor. (e) When doors or windows are open, measure the extent of the opening. (f) Measure the location of the wounds from some fixed point of the body. (g) Height of blood spots on the walls. (h) When instruments are found, their exact size should be measured. (i) Take all necessary measurements for making diagrams and accurately locating the more important objects in them. In taking measurements it is advisable that a graduated instrument be used. However, if this is impractical and one distance is measured by steps, or by hand spans, then all measurements should be taken in the same manner. When a measurement is taken by stepping, it should be recorded as so many steps, and not in feet and inches. Usually it will be necessary to show at least two measurements in relation to any one object or location of evidence. It is

better to show too many measurements than too few.

(14) **Leave Nothing to the Imagination.** Do not depend upon word pictures where photographs can be obtained. Photographs in conjunction with scale drawings will explain more in a few minutes than a person can relate in hours. When photographs and scale drawings are used, the jurors are more nearly of the same opinion than when they must depend upon the interpretation of spoken words.

(15) **Search the Suspect.** Any suspects should be searched in the light of what has been found at the crime scene. **Thoroughness** should be the watchword. Fingernail debris should be obtained and the body should be examined carefully for scratches, bruises, and wounds. A suspect's clothing, including the cuffs of his trousers, should be examined for dirt, fibers, stains, etc., which may have come from the victim or the crime scene. In sex cases his body and his clothing should be examined for seminal stains and for fibers from the clothing and hair from the body of the victim. When an animal is involved in unnatural sex crimes, the suspect should be searched for hair from the animal, and any blood stains should be examined to determine whether they are human or animal. In such cases, hair from the animal should also be preserved.

(16) **Trademarks.** Be particularly watchful for peculiar characteristics and evidence of acts of an unusual nature performed by the criminal. Many criminals, because of superstition, will do things which will identify their jobs as definitely as though they left their card. These unusual acts are known as trademarks, and, when considered in conjunction with other characteristics of the job, establish the **Modus Operandi** (method of operation) of the criminal, which is often useful in identifying him, or in connecting up his several jobs.

External Examination

(1) **Select a Starting Point,** preferably the point of entry or exit. From this point work outward in the same manner as in the interior examination.

(2) **Determine the Manner of Approach** and the means of reaching the point of entry, whether by ladder, fire escape, adjoining roof, trellis, crawling, concealing behind hedge or tree, etc.

(3) **Crime in the Open.** If the crime occurred in the open, a careful search should be made of the area for several hundred feet

around for signs of footprints, tire tracks, objects being dragged, or other signs of struggle.

(4) **Search the Immediate Grounds.** Examine the grounds thoroughly as you go, searching for any matter foreign to the premises, such as tools, weapons, articles, dropped in flight or purposely thrown away. Search all places where a weapon might have been thrown or concealed either before or after the crime.

(5) **Search the Surrounding Grounds.** Cover the surrounding grounds for some distance. One should not stop the investigation at the border of the premises on which the crime was committed, but should continue to farther points, in some cases covering blocks. Note the vegetation, texture of soil, and substances common to the vicinity.

(6) **Search for Fibers.** If fences, hedges, or underbrush are crossed, search them carefully at the point crossed for fibers, tissue, or hair that might have been caught on them in flight. Search for unusual substances with which the criminal may have come in contact, which might have adhered to his clothes. Take samples.

(7) **Concealment.** Search all outbuildings, shrubbery, hedges or other places where the perpetrator might have concealed himself while waiting for the victim. Search for footprints, fingerprints, cigarette stubs, matches and other substances or marks that might lead to identification of the criminal. If there is a large quantity of dust in a place where the criminal concealed himself, a sample of this should be taken for comparison.

(8) **Means of Escape.** Ascertain the means of escape from the crime scene and search for tire tracks and footprints. If a vehicle was used the intervening space between where this vehicle was parked and the point where the actual crime was committed should be searched carefully for articles dropped in flight, such as part of the loot, weapons, hat, or some article from the pocket. Examine driveways and roadways for signs of tires or other vehicle marks. Protect these with boxes or other objects until they can be photographed or be preserved by means of casts.

(9) **Evidence.** Do not confine your collection of evidence to that which may be admissible in court. Evidence which would not be admitted to court may furnish a good clue, and may also serve to break down the perpetrator and cause him to confess.

(10) **Photographs to Be Taken:** (a) General photograph of premises, showing entrance and exit used in the perpetration, together

with surrounding grounds. (b) Close-up photograph of exit or entrance. (c) Roadways and driveways used in gaining access to premises. (d) Photographs showing any building, shrubbery, or other objects used for concealment. (e) Photograph evidence as found.

(11) **Measurements to Be Taken** (The taking of measurements will vary somewhat according to the nature of the case and the evidence found): (a) Height and size of opening used as entrance or exit. (b) Distance from outbuilding or other place of concealment to the point of entry. (c) Distance traveled on foot after leaving vehicle used. (d) Accurate location of all evidence, with reference to fixed points.

(12) **Casts to Be made** (All casts should be marked in such a manner that they can be identified and connected with the case at any future date. They should be marked so that others will be able to identify them if you are not present): (a) Make casts of all tire tracks which cannot be accurately recorded by photograph. (b) Moulage casts of unidentified dead. (c) Moulage or plaster casts of all tool marks. (d) Casts of footprints. (e) Any other evidence where a definite imprint is shown should be recorded by the casting method, especially if it cannot be shown to best advantage by photograph.

(13) **Report to Headquarters.** Stay on the job until you are sure that all has been done that can be done. Notify the dispatcher when you leave.

INVESTIGATION AT THE SCENE OF A BURGLARY

Duties of First Officer to Arrive

(1) **Burglar Seen Entering.** Nonresidence burglaries reported at night are usually discovered by some party who saw the burglar enter or leave the building or saw him in operation. The first officer to arrive at the scene should immediately contact such person and ascertain: (a) If the burglar was seen entering the building, is there a probability of his still being there? What was the point of entry? Has the witness been out of sight of the building since seeing the burglar enter? When there is evidence that the burglar is still in the building, radio the station and request assistance. When radio is not available, request the witness to telephone the station while you keep watch. (b) When the burglar has escaped, ascertain the direction of flight, means of escape, detailed personal description and description of the

vehicle used. Give this information to the dispatcher for additional broadcast.

(2) **Burglary Discovered Later.** When a burglary is reported at opening time by some employee, warn all employees entering the place not to touch or move anything until the investigation is completed. When the crime is of a serious nature, keep the store closed to the public until the investigation has progressed to the point that they will not destroy evidence or hamper the investigating officers. When the report is received after the store has been opened for business, ascerain the central point of attack and exclude all persons, employees, and customers from that area.

(3) **Safe Burglary.** In safe-burglary cases, the owner or manager usually desires to learn whether the cash is missing. To permit them to examine the contents endangers valuable evidence. See that no one approaches the safe prior to the arrival of the technician.

(4) **House Prowls.** In residence-burglary cases request all occupants, servants included, to remain in one room until the investigation is completed. The occupants interfere with the work of the investigator when permitted to follow him around.

Duties of the Beat Officer

(1) **Contact Officer Who Arrived First.** Obtain from the officer who first arrived at the scene an outline of the nature and status of the case. Make certain that the scene is properly protected.

(2) **Identify Criminal.** Obtain a detailed description of the perpetrator and information relating to his place of residence, friends, enemies, hangouts, places frequented, means of transportation, and where he is likely to be found. As information is obtained telephone it immediately to the dispatcher.

(3) **Determine Facts.** Ascertain as accurately as possible the hours between which the crime was committed, amount of loss, and other information necessary for the preparation of the offense report.

(4) **Suspicious Persons.** In residence-burglary cases, inquire regarding peddlers, agents, garbage haulers, trash haulers, meter readers, or other persons who may have called at the home for any purpose other than friendly visits. Check on persons who have visited the servants on the premises. Ascertain if they had an opportunity to examine the premises without the knowledge of the occupants.

(5) **Inquire of Neighbors** to learn whether peddlers, agents, or others were in the neighborhood during the absence of the occupants

of the premises burglarized. Frequently burglars will gain entrance after knocking to see whether anyone is at home. If such persons were seen, obtain a description and an account of the story they told in explanation for being there.

(6) **Investigate Servants** of the premises as to length of time employed, general character, and previous record. Ascertain whether servants of neighbors or their friends might be suspects in the case. Such servants might have an opportunity to know of the absence of occupants and may have given the necessary information to the perpetrator.

(7) **In Burglaries of Hotels** and apartment houses question the bell boys, porters, engineers, elevator operators, and clerks concerning persons seen about the halls and corridors at unusual hours or under suspicious circumstances.

(8) **In Nonresident-Burglary Cases** question employees to determine whether suspicious persons were in the place prior to closing time on the previous day or at any other time. Inquire regarding salesmen, building inspectors, prospective buyers, or others whose business appeared in any way out of the ordinary.

(9) **Make Inquiries** among persons living in the vicinity to learn whether suspicious cars or persons were seen or unusual noises heard. Obtain descriptions. If noises were heard, determine as nearly as possible the exact time of their occurrence.

(10) **Check Watchman.** Make inquiries as to insurance protection, burglary-alarm systems, watchman service and private police. If a watchman or private police is maintained, ascertain the name of the firm or individual through whom the service was obtained.

(11) **In Safe-Burglaries** and other crimes of a serious nature, determine whether it is advisable to notify the detective assigned to that class of crime.

(12) **Anything Unusual.** In cases of large losses, ascertain whether the presence of the large sum was unusual. Ascertain which persons had an opportunity to know of its existence. When the presence of a large sum is unusual, facts concerning persons having knowledge of it are important.

(13) **Stolen Property.** Obtain an accurate and descriptive list of the loss, including serial numbers, names, initials, monograms, and other marks of identification.

(14) **Assist the Evidence Technician** in his work when needed. When a clue or any physical evidence is found note its character, lo-

cation and position, but do not touch or move it. Notify the technician of its existence and location.

(15) **Do Not Leave** the scene, except in case of urgent necessity, until you are certain that the investigation has been completed.

(16) **Report to Your Commanding Officer** for instructions as soon as your work is completed. In his absence inform the dispatcher that your work is finished.

(17) **Do Not Remain** at the scene any longer than is necessary. Idleness and inactivity present a bad appearance to the public, and there may be other crimes occurring in your district.

Duties of the Evidence Technician
Nonresident Burglary

(1) **Protect the Scene.** When no other officer is present at the time of your arrival, take necessary steps to protect the crime scene. Give instructions that nothing is to be disturbed. Do not undertake to conduct the investigation until other officers arrive to assist you. When it is necessary for you to leave the crime scene to obtain your equipment from your car, arrange for some other officer to protect the scene during your absence. Never leave the scene unattended.

(2) **Determine the Facts.** When other officers are present at the time of your arrival, obtain from them a brief outline of the nature of the case. Ascertain the central point of attack and points of entrance and exit.

(3) **General Survey.** Make a general survey of the crime scene for the purpose of selecting a starting point and determining what equipment will be needed in the investigation.

(4) **From the Central Point Work Outward.** The search should not be hurried but should be thorough, searching for any trace of footprints, fingerprints, articles left at the scene, and any other evidence. Minute evidence is easily overlooked and destroyed. Care should be taken that nothing is overlooked.

(5) **Hair and Fibers.** Not infrequently a criminal will sustain slight injuries in the commission of a burglary, such as skinned hands or slight cuts. Search carefully for traces of blood, hair, fiber, and stains. The location and position of such evidence will sometimes indicate which hand or arm they came from; this should be noted. Tissue can sometimes be identified as having come from certain portions of the body. Hair and fibers furnish excellent clues to identity.

(6) **In Clothing-store Burglaries** the perpetrator will frequently

change clothes on the job, leaving articles of old clothing on the premises. These should be carefully preserved, using the method outlined in the handling of evidence.

(7) **Examine Underneath Counters** and other fixtures, searching for tools, gloves, or other articles unintentionally left at the scene by the perpetrators.

(8) **Locate the Point of Entry** and examine for traces of toolmarks, heel-prints, fingerprints, blood, fibers, and tissue. If there is dust of an unusual character, such as powdered putty, powdery paint, and the like, take samples for comparison with similar material that may be found on the clothes or person of the suspect.

(9) **Determine Exit.** Frequently entrance to a store will be gained through a high window or a skylight, and it will be found more convenient for the perpetrator to make his exit by unlocking a door. Determine whether such is the case and search the point of exit as well as the point of entry.

(10) **Exterior Examination:** (a) Ascertain method of entry. Determine the method employed in reaching the point of entry, whether by fire escape, ladder, adjoining roof, use of boxes to stand upon, accessibility from ground, rope ladder, or other means. When access was gained over an adjoining roof, ascertain the means of reaching the roof, whether through adjoining building, fire escape, ladder, rope, over top of car, and others. (b) Trace movements. Try to trace the criminals from the point of entry or exit to the point where a car was parked. Search for traces of footprints, tire tracks, and articles lost or dropped in flight. Search alleys, roadways, driveways, and vacant lots adjoining the premises for traces of vehicles. When the point where the vehicle was parked can be located, attempt to trace it to a point where a turn was made, in order to obtain an impression of all four tires.

(11) **Safe Burglary:** (a) Make a critical survey of the condition of the safe and of the surrounding area, observing any tools present, the method used in opening the safe, the position and condition of the outer door and, when open, the condition of the inner door or compartment. This should be done before the safe is touched. Form a definite plan of procedure before beginning the actual examination and search. (b) Carefully examine the outer door and inner compartment for traces of toolmarks and fingerprints. When the doors bear marks that may be identified they should be removed and taken to the laboratory for final examination. (c) Collect, examine, and care-

fully preserve all parts of dials and locks that are broken from the safe. If tool marks appear on them preserve them in such a manner that the marks will not be changed in any way. Wrapping paper will usually protect them. (d) Plaster dust will usually be found scattered about the floor around the safe. Samples of this should be taken for comparison with dust found in the clothing of suspects. (e) Papers scattered about, and those in the safe, should be examined to determine if they have been handled by the perpetrators. Usually the papers will show dirty finger marks if they have been handled and will easily be detected. Handle them as little as possible and preserve them for examination in the laboratory. (f) Tools left at the scene of the crime should be carefully preserved. Traces of fingerprints, paint, stains, hair, fibers, tissue, blood, and toolmarks on any object should be protected until they have been thoroughly examined. The imprint of a hammer blow on the end of a chisel or punch may serve to identify that tool. (g) Considerable time will generally be consumed in the commission of a safe burglary, and the perpetrators will frequently smoke on the job. All matches and cigarette and cigar stubs should be collected. (h) The method used in opening a safe, and the amount of damage done in the process, will give a clue to the perpetrators' knowledge of such jobs and their experience. Study them carefully and, if advisable, call in a safe expert to assist in determining the extent of the criminals' knowledge of that particular type of safe.

(12) **Photographs to Be Taken** (All photographs should contain some means of identification and should show a scale where the measurements are of value): (a) General photographs, showing damage to premises, or any portion of them, damage to safe, and the general scene as you first saw it. (b) Close-up photographs showing the central point of attack, including tool marks and other marks of violence. (c) Photographs of all evidence in its original location and position. (d) Points of entrance and exit, from both inside and out, showing the method of reaching them. (e) Photographs showing the instrument used in gaining access to the point of entry.

(13) **Measurements to Be Taken:** (a) Accurate location of all points of physical evidence. These should be located by actual measurements from fixed points. (b) Size of the opening through which entrance was gained. (c) Height of the opening from the ground or adjoining roof. (d) Height of the opening from inside the floor or other footing. (e) Height and size of articles used in gaining access to the

point of entry. (f) Size of safe and of safe door. (g) Length and breadth of tool marks. (h) Sufficient measurements to permit an accurate reproduction of the essential points in a sketch or a scale drawing. This should enable the location of the central point of attack and the more important articles in the building.

(14) **Casts to Be Made of:** (a) tool marks, (b) footprints, (c) tire or vehicle marks.

(15) **Collect All Evidence** as you come to it, properly labeling and marking it in its proper sequence.

(16) **Make Notes as You Go.** Do not depend upon memory for anything. At the time each piece of evidence is found, enter its character, size, general description, when and where found, the relative location to the center of the crime scene, how marked for identification, and how disposed of.

(17) **Hold Evidence.** Do not surrender evidence to anyone other than authorized persons. Evidence should be taken directly to the laboratory by the technician himself. When this is done there will be no difficulty in establishing an unbroken line of possession from the time it was found until it is presented in court.

(18) **Stay on the Job** until you are sure there is nothing more to be done. Check your activities to see if there is anything you have missed in the investigation.

Duties of the Evidence Technician
Residence Burglary

(1) **Ascertain the Facts.** General instructions relating to the search for physical evidence at the scene of a nonresidence burglary will be applicable at the scene of a residence burglary. At the start see that the scene is properly protected, and ascertain the facts necessary to your investigation from the first officer at the scene.

(2) **Object of Attack.** Ascertain whether the search was for some definite object, such as the hiding place of money.

(3) **Type of Work.** Note carefully the amount of disorder and the extent to which the place was ransacked. Watch carefully for unusual characteristics or "trademarks."

(4) **Starting Point.** Select a definite starting point and work slowly and carefully, making notes as your examination progresses. The extent of the investigation will have to be determined from the facts, the extent of the search made by the perpetrator, the amount of disorder, etc.

(5) **Entry.** Locate the point of entry and make an examination as before outlined. Examine the screens, doors, or windows to ascertain the type of tool used to gain entrance.

(6) **The Exterior Examination** can be more thoroughly done, and probably with better results, than in the case of a nonresidence burglary. Starting at the points of entry and exit, trace the path of the criminal as far as possible, watching carefully for traces of footprints and articles that may have been lost or dropped in flight. Keep watch for tools that may have been used in effecting entrance.

(7) **Fibers.** When fences, hedges, or other barriers have been crossed by the burglar, examine them for traces of tissue, blood, and fibers.

(8) **Search** all shrubbery, outbuildings, and other places where any object might be hidden. Search for traces of the perpetrator having been concealed. Be on the lookout for loot that might have been hidden with a view of returning for it later. Look for purses discarded after being looted.

(9) **Tracks.** Search roadways, driveways, and alleys for traces of vehicles, tire tracks and footprints.

(10) **Photographs to Be Taken:** (a) When there is an unusual amount of disorder, or other unusual occurrence, photograph the crime scene, showing the important detail. (b) Photograph tool marks at the point of entry and any other evidence showing its position in relation to the crime scene. (c) Take close-up photographs of the point of entry, showing, if possible, the method used in gaining entrance and the size and shape of the opening. (d) Take photographs of any evidence of an unusual nature or the character of which is likely to be subjected to change in the course of time.

(11) **Measurements to Be Taken:** (a) The size of the opening through which entrance was gained, especially when only a portion of an aperture was opened, such as partly raising a window, breaking a panel from a door, etc. (b) When the case is of a serious nature, take sufficient measurements to permit an accurate reproduction in a scale drawing, locating the more important articles of furniture and evidence. (c) The size of all tool-marks. (d) The height from the ground of the opening through which entrance was gained. (e) The accurate location of the main points of evidence. (f) When footprints, tire tracks, or other traces are found that are suspected of having a connection with the case, their distance from the point of entry should be ascertained.

CARE AND PRESERVATION OF EVIDENCE

General

(1) **Court Presentation.** The success or failure of an investigation and of the prosecution of a criminal will often hinge on the manner in which physical evidence is handled. From the time the evidence is found until it reaches the court it is subjected to much handling, and often mishandling, with the result that it is somewhat changed by the time the route has been covered. Frequently the slightest change will render the evidence incompetent.

(2) **Preservation for the Laboratory.** Proper handling of evidence is of the greatest importance from the point of view of the criminalist. Mishandling may so change the substance that a complete and satisfactory examination is impossible. Portions which would be most valuable to the investigation may be lost or so damaged as to be valueless.

(3) **Training Necessary.** The only solution of this problem is the training of technicians in the proper handling of evidence. Most officers realize the necessity of properly protecting the evidence, but often they are not versed in the methods that should be employed. Various kinds of materials require different handling. For example, glass on which there are fingerprints should not be transported in the same manner as a document, and dust should not be handled in the same manner as a piece of metal.

(4) **Preservation.** When an article to be held as evidence is found, it should immediately be placed in the container that is to be used in its transportation. The container should be labeled with the initials of the officer, the date, hour, and the identification mark which he has employed. Immediate entry should be made in his notebook, giving the nature of the evidence, when and where found, the names of those present when found, the identifying mark used, the relative position to the scene of the crime, and its suspected relation to the crime.

Specific

The following outline will explain how certain evidence should be handled, and from it may be devised means of preserving other kinds of evidence:

(1) **Hair.** Hair which is to be taken for examination or for comparison should be handled with the fingers exclusively. Instruments

of any sort will damage the hair, bruise, mash, or split it; their use should be avoided. Should it ever become necessary to use any kind of forceps, two pieces of wood, such as toothpicks or matches, may be used. Occasions of this kind, however, will be rare. Injuries of any kind will be misleading to the examiner. Hair, which is found at the scene of a crime, should be picked up with the fingers and placed in clean white pieces of paper. The paper is then folded in the manner in which druggists wrap powders. Should the hair be too long to make a convenient package it should not be folded, but should be coiled loosely about the finger, removed carefully and placed in the paper in a coil. If this is done no pressure should be exerted against the folded paper that may cause the hair to be mashed together and bruised. Care should be taken not to dislodge any dirt or other matter that might cling to it.

The paper used should be clean and preferably white. If there is dust on the paper used, it may be mistaken for dust that has come from the hair, or particles may adhere to the hair, causing erroneous conclusions in the examination. In the absence of paper, a glass vial may be used, but this is not desirable for the reason that it is usually necessary to use instruments to extract the hair from such containers. Also, any particles which are dislodged from the hair will probably be lost in the bottom of the vial, while if paper is used it can be spread out and its surface examined after the hair is removed.

Hair removed from the head of an individual for comparison should be pulled out by its roots with the fingers. The bulbous end of the root is often valuable in comparison. Never cut specimens of hair that are to be used for comparison.

(2) **Metals.** Metals are handled according to the size and number of pieces. In referring to metals, tools, which will be discussed later, are not included.

Small pieces of metal which are not considered filings or dust, and which are not too large for placing in small containers, should be packed in small boxes of cotton. Line the boxes with cotton, place the pieces of metal in the center, and cover it with more cotton. It should be packed tightly enough so that it will not shake around in the box. If the pieces are small and the size of the box permits, two or more pieces may be packed in the same box, provided they are packed so as to prevent their coming in contact with one another. If cotton is not available, a piece of cloth or handkerchief may be used. If cloth is used, it should be wadded around the metal, not folded. Extreme care should be taken with pieces of metal to be used for comparison which have ragged edges or broken surfaces. The ragged edges will chip very easily, and should be properly protected.

Larger pieces of metals, such as iron bars which have been sawed out of windows, wire grills which have been cut or removed, rods used as a weapon, or pieces of metal used in any other way should be inspected carefully for traces of hair, tissue, fibers, blood, or dirt, and should be protected in such a manner that any substances adhering will not be dislodged. In such cases the surface bearing the evidence must not be allowed to come in contact with the wrapping or container in which it is carried. Suspend the rod or other metal in a box in such a manner that this portion will not touch. An iron may have hair or blood on one side. In this case it can be protected by wrapping several layers of cloth around the rod on each side of the stain, laying a piece of board over it and tying the board in place.

Pieces of metal bearing tool marks should have that portion of the surface, on which the tool marks appear, protected. Wrap several thicknesses of newspaper around that portion of the surface. If on the end wad a paper or cloth and fasten it in place over the end.

(3) **Tools.** Tools and other instruments which are suspected of having been used in the commission of a crime should be so protected that the surface which is thought to have made the mark will not come in contact with any object which might so change it that identification would be rendered more difficult. The minute lines and grooves, caused by the grinding of the tool, are easily damaged, and extensive changes may result from improper handling. The face of a hammer, the point of a punch, and the cutting edge of a chisel or screw driver, or any other portion of the tool which might have left a mark on a surface must be protected. Tools used as a jimmy may leave the impression of the shank in the wood sill of a window. This must also be taken into consideration.

In many cases, the entire tool must be examined for traces of foreign substances, such as particles of paint, putty, bits of wood fiber, grease, and other matter which may be identified as having come from the crime scene. These bits may be easily dislodged, and lost. Precaution should be taken against unnecessary handling.

Place the tool in a cardboard box, preferably one slightly larger than the instrument, and, if advisable, place wads of paper in the top of the box to hold it in place. The box should be covered, and the evidence delivered to the laboratory at the earliest possible moment. Tools should never be placed loosely on the floor of an automobile or in any way handled so that additional foreign substances are collected or evidence specimens lost. If advisable they may be wrapped in a clean paper before being placed in the container.

(4) **Dust, Dirt, and Filings.** Minute particles, metal filings, dust, and dirt should be collected in small glass vials. These must of necessity be clean and free from dust and dirt. Clear glass is preferred as it permits more thorough inspection prior to inserting the specimen. Wipe the vial with a piece of clean soft tissue paper before using it. The freer the specimen is from other substances the easier and more accurate will be any examination or comparison. Care should be taken that there is no dust already in the vial, as a few particles may be misleading to the examiner. Also, if the evidence specimen contains something not found in the comparison specimen it may be attacked in court as improper evidence. In the absence of glass vials a piece of clean white paper may be used, folding the specimen into it in the manner previously outlined.

(5) **Tissue.** Tissue, or specimens suspected of being tissue, should be handled with extreme care. If not entirely dry they will adhere to almost any surface, and difficulty will be experienced in extracting them without loss of some of the evidence. The full surface and thickness of the tissue is valuable in the examination; therefore it should be delivered to the examiner exactly as it is found.

In most cases when tissue is found, it is adhering to some other object. If this object is too large to remove, use a sharp knife and shave away, where possible, the portion of the surface to which the tissue adheres, disturbing it as little as possible. Be careful not to cut the tissue in the operation. As in the case of hair and other articles, tissue should be handled with the fingers when possible. In no instance should it be handled with any instruments that will bruise or mash it. A needle, at times, may be used in picking it up.

Tissue can best be transported on glass slides. Protect the tissue from dust and dirt as much as possible. Glass bottles or containers should not be used, as tissue will adhere to their walls and difficulty will be experienced in removing it from the vial.

Blood, hair and fibers which are found clinging to tissue must not be removed or disturbed, but the entire specimen should be preserved just as it is found.

(6) **Fingernail Scrapings.** Debris from under the fingernails have been known to contain a wide variety of substances from blood to

dust. Fibers, tissue, grease and many other substances have been scraped from the fingernails, and have proved valuable evidence.

In scraping the fingernails the instrument used should be very clean and one that will not bruise or break the small particles. The investigator must be able to testify positively that none of the specimen examined could have come from the instrument which was used in scraping away the particles.

Place a piece of clean white paper under the hand from which the scrapings are to be taken. Hold the hand close to the paper and scrape all loose matter from under the nail. Do not try to work hurriedly, and do not exert any more pressure than is necessary. As each finger is cleaned deposit the debris on the paper. When all the evidence has been collected fold the paper in the manner used by druggists in wrapping powders. Mark the package for identification purposes, indicating also whether from the right or left hand. Make note of the date and hour and the names of the witnesses who were present. When the debris is dry, a vial may be used for transporting the evidence. However, there is some danger of losing part of the evidence in transferring it to and from the vial.

(7) **Firearms.** As previously suggested, any gun found at the scene of the crime, including the clips or magazines of automatic weapons, should be examined for finger prints. Make a record of caliber, make, and serial number of such firearm, and keep notes as to the relative location in which the arm was recovered. Mark the firearm by scratching an initial or other distinctive label.

When it is necessary to remove loaded cartridges or fired cartridge cases from the weapon mark each one so that the relative positions of all will be known. Cartridge cases which may be found either in the gun or elsewhere should be marked in the following manner: An initial or other distinctive mark should be scratched on the surface of the shell near the mouth or, in the case of paper shot shells, an inked mark should be made in the same relative position. Where fired cartridge cases are recovered on the floor or ground, notes should be taken of the exact location of each shell so found. All shells should be separately wrapped in paper for proper preservation.

In recovering fired bullets, which may have lodged in surrounding woodwork or other material, do not use any instruments which will damage the surface. When recovered, mark each bullet by scratching an initial or other distinctive mark on the "nose" of the bullet; no mark should be placed on the base or side. No attempt should be made to wash or clean the bullet; it should be wrapped in cotton or other soft material in its original state. Complete notes should be kept regarding the place, relative location, date, and time of the recovery of each bullet.

Any shot pellet or pellets recovered should be placed in small cardboard pill boxes, envelopes, or vials for preservation.

Where shot or powder patterns are evident, either on the body or elsewhere, scaled photographs should be taken as near 1 to 1 as size of film will permit.

(8) **Liquids.** Ordinarily very little difficulty is experienced in handling liquids. It is only necessary that the container be clean and free from dust. Liquids are usually found in containers, and there is no necessity for changing them. In some instances, however, liquids that have been spilled or poured out will have to be collected. If the quantity is small some difficulty may be experienced. This will depend somewhat upon the nature of the liquid. If the quantity is so small that a sponge cannot be used and squeezed out a clean cloth may be used to absorb the fluid. The cloth is then placed in the container. First wash and dry the container to be used for such a purpose.

If evaporation will not diminish the value of the evidence, blotters or filter paper may be used. If blotters are used they should be clean and white, because the dye of colored blotters may materially change the character of the evidence. When it is desirable to preserve as much of the moisture as possible, use a small container and seal it tightly. In collecting evidence with a cloth or blotter, it should be blotted, not wiped.

It is advisable to collect as little dirt as possible with the liquid. In some cases it may be advisable to wash the hands, especially if perspiring, before handling it. If the hands are washed they should be rinsed thoroughly to remove the soap, which may affect the results of the tests subsequently made.

Unless you know what is in the liquid you are handling, you should not get it on your hands, especially when it is suspected of being a poison. In such cases it is advisable to use filter papers handled with tweezers.

(9) **Fibers.** While some fibers are not damaged by handling with tweezers or other instruments, others are, and for this reason, unless you are familiar with fibers, it is desirable to handle all of them with the fingers as much as possible. Handle them as lightly and as

little as possible. They may be transported in glass vials, or in white paper.

The dyes in some fibers are affected by different things, such as moisture, air, etc. They should be placed in vials that are perfectly dry, and in wet weather should be sealed in. Blood and other stains in fiber should be protected fully. Do not permit others to handle them through curiosity.

(10) **Clothing.** Carelessness in the handling of clothing which is suspected of belonging to the criminal may cause much evidence to be lost. Therefore, it is necessary to handle it with care and to preserve it intact until it reaches the examiner.

Never inspect clothing at the scene. To do so causes it to be shaken, dislodging minute evidence, such as hair, fibers, dust, and other small particles. Place a large piece of clean paper, such as heavy wrapping paper, or preferably a large clean paper sack, as close to the clothing as possible, then gently lift it onto the paper. Fold the paper over it from all sides and secure it in place. In moving the bundle handle it right side up at all times, and do not throw it around. Carefully inspect the area which was directly under the clothing for traces of hair.

If it is necessary to search the pockets of the clothing, this should be done after it is placed on the paper in order that any particles which are dislodged will fall on the paper and will not be lost. If the necessity of searching the pockets is not urgent, it should be done after reaching the laboratory.

It is wise to wrap each garment separately. This is imperative when the clothing belongs to both the victim and the suspect.

(11) **Documentary Evidence.** There is probably more mishandling of documentary evidence than of any other kind. It seems to be generally considered that no harm is done by handling a document. This is entirely erroneous. Each time a document is handled its value as evidence is diminished.

Documentary evidence should never be folded. Even though it has been previously folded, once it is straightened out it should be preserved in a flat position. Each time it is folded and unfolded that portion which is in the fold is damaged. Also, it is necessary to handle a piece of paper considerably in folding and unfolding, and this also does its share of damage.

To properly preserve documentary evidence, it should be placed between two sheets of cellophane. The sheets should be larger than the document and the edges should be sealed as soon as possible. This will prevent the papers from being rubbed in handling, keep out the air, and permit their being inspected without great damage.

Cellophane or other such material is sometimes not available at the time a document is found. In this event it may be safely transported to the laboratory by placing it between two sheets of clean white paper and then in a book or magazine. This will hold it flat and it will be easy to handle.

It is common practice to permit anyone who so desires to examine a document. This should never be done until it is properly protected. Moreover, it may contain valuable latent prints. Other officers should not request the officer who is in charge of the document to "let me see it." They can usually do no good by seeing it, and they may do much harm.

(12) **Latent Fingerprints.** Great care must be exercised in searching for fingerprints lest they be destroyed by superimposing your own prints over them or by rubbing them in a manner that results in the prints being obliterated or partially destroyed. It is important to search all smooth surfaces for finger marks and latent prints; special care should be used in the treatment of objects known to have been touched by the criminal as well as of those objects which he might have handled.

A water glass, a bottle, a small box, and some utensils may be picked up for more careful examination by touching only the edges, tilting the object by pressure with the finger extended on an upper edge such as the rim of a glass, the mouth of the bottle, etc., thus permitting the extended fingers of the other hand to be inserted under and against the lower edge, thus enabling the object to be raised by pressure applied at opposite edges of the diagonal. Caution must be taken to keep the fingers on the edges and not permit them to come in contact with the sides.

Many latent fingerprints have been rendered useless by the manner in which they were handled while being transported from the scene of the crime to the place where they are to be developed and examined. It is a common and a very poor practice to wrap articles suspected of containing fingerprints in paper. It is estimated that only four ounces of pressure is necessary to make a print, and probably less to eradicate it. The paper rubbing against the print will destroy one-half to three-fourths of the pattern. Again, the oils from the finger, which are in reality the fingerprint, will be absorbed by the paper, rendering development with powders more difficult. After they have been in contact with paper they will react very much the same as prints that are several days old. The powder brushes away, leaving very little on the ridges.

Glass and other flat objects which are suspected of containing latent prints can be successfully transported from one point to another without damage to the prints. From an ordinary piece of tire patch or lifting tape cut several small pieces about one-half inch square. Examine the surface of the object to be transported and select spots where you are sure there are no prints, sticking four or five of the squares of rubber to the surface. Place the object in a heavy cardboard box, allowing it to rest on the pieces of rubber. This will prevent the flat surface from touching the box, and will protect the prints. The box should be covered to keep out dust and air currents, which will tend to evaporate the moisture in the prints.

If no rubber tire patch is available, select a cardboard box which is a little smaller than the glass to be carried. Cut slits in the sides of the box about one inch above the bottom, insert the corners of the glass in these slits, and tie a string around the box to prevent them from slipping out.

A gun should be picked up at the scene of a crime by inserting a pencil or a wooden stick in the barrel holding the gun in place by placing the index finger of the other hand against the outer "edge" of the butt, after first assuring yourself that no accidental discharge can be occasioned thereby. A gun which is to be examined for latent prints may be easily transported a short distance in this manner. For longer distances it may be suspended in a box by three strings: one through the trigger guard, one through the barrel, and the third through the upper part of the frame. Use a wooden box and drive small nails on the inside at the desired points to which to secure the strings. The box should then be carried in such a manner that the gun will be suspended by one or two strings and steadied by the other. In other words carry the box on edge.

By giving a little thought to the matter a means can be devised to transport successfully any object suspected of containing latents.

In the development of latent fingerprints there are a number of things to be taken into consideration, particularly as regards fingerprints on glass and metal surfaces. Atmospheric conditions and the condition of the surface will play an important part in the success or failure of the developments.

On any surface, if the fingerprint to be developed is inside a building where there is much cooking, or where open gas fires are used extensively, deposits of grease are very likely to be found. Fingerprint powder applied to surfaces on which there is grease will adhere to the entire surface, as well as to the ridges of the print, and completely eradicate the latent print. If there is any possibility of such being the case, test prints should be made and thoroughly tried out before attempting to powder the print. Similarly, surfaces on which there is moisture, as a result of dew, or damp weather, will have a like effect, and tests should be made before the powder is applied.

Glass and metals which are exposed to the elements will, in cold weather, present some difficulty, even though no moisture is present. Powder applied to a cold glass or metal surface will adhere in lumps, and in many instances cannot be brushed away sufficiently to develop the print. The brushing requires so much pressure that, when all the powder between the ridges is removed, the ridges themselves are destroyed.

In all the above mentioned cases the object on which the print appears should be moved, if possible, to a warm, dry place and allowed to remain for several hours before an attempt is made to develop the print. In some instances, where the coating of grease is heavy, the print will never dry sufficiently to permit powdering. However, the portion between the ridges will be reduced to such an extent that a very good photograph may be obtained.

When fingerprints appear on painted surfaces, those surfaces must be tested to determine if the paint is entirely dry before applying the powder. Particularly with enamels, some portions never dry completely and may cause the powder to adhere between the ridges as well as on them.

When prints appear on both sides of a piece of glass it is advisable that only one side be powdered at a time. If both sides are powdered the powder will show through the glass, giving a blurred appearance in the photograph. Develop and photograph the prints on one side, then wipe that side clean before working on the other side.

Broken glass and other like objects, which can be conveniently removed, should be preserved until the prints are developed and the pictures finished in order to assure good photographs, In some cases it is advisable to preserve the object with the print intact, for presentation in court. If this is done, the print should be covered with cellophane to keep out the air and moisture.

If there is the least doubt as to the contrast which will be obtained in the use of one color of powder, test prints should be made and developed with the different powders until the proper contrast is obtained. Test prints are easily made and require only a little time.

Do not depend upon snap judgment or guess work to determine if a certain substance will "take" a fingerprint. The only sure way is to test it. If you have the remotest idea that the object might have been handled, and the prints cannot be developed with the equipment you have at hand, take the object to the laboratory to be tested further.

APPENDIX K

Focus on Crime

I. **Mobile Reserve.**
II. **Special M. O. Bulletins,** Los Angeles Police Department.
No. 38, December 18, 1953; No. 44, April 2, 1954.
(Reproduced by permission of Chief William H. Parker)
III. **Weekly Crime Summary,** Oakland Police Department.
Bulletin No. 57-12, week of 8-14 April, 1957.
(Reproduced by permission of Chief Wyman W. Vernon)

MOBILE RESERVE

SUBJECT:

The formation of a Mobile Reserve.

PURPOSE:

To attack unusual or special concentrations of crime by a special striking force designed to be shifted in time and area with the movement of such concentrations.

COMMAND:

The Mobile Reserve will be under the command of a captain who will report to the Assistant Chief of Police. Strategic plans are subject to approval by the Chief of Police. The Mobile Reserve will operate in the Patrol Division under District Command in accordance with its agreed mission. In operations, the squads will be under the supervision of the Mobile Reserve Assistant Commander who is authorized to withdraw any or all squads from any district for immediate reassignment, in order to deal with situations that may develop which require a modification of the original plan.

PERSONNEL:

Complement

    1—Captain (Commander)
    1—Lieutenant (Assistant Commander)
    6—Sergeants (Squad Leaders)

475

1—Sergeant or patrolman

30—Patrolmen

10—Reserve: these officers will be selected, trained, and used when needed to replace other Mobile Reserve members. They will perform normal District activity until recruited for Mobile Reserve duty.

Qualifications

Officers selected for Mobile Reserve duty must appreciate that a crime problem exists; they must recognize the need for a reduction in crime; and they must be in sympathy with the objective and method of operation of the Mobile Deserve. The Captain, Lieutenant, and Sergeants must have administrative ability commensurate with their rank. Patrolmen must have proven their ability to work as individuals as well as in teams, and they should have above average ability with firearms and should be outstanding officers in excellent physical condition.

Selection

Personnel for the Mobile Reserve will be selected by the Chief and Assistant Chief of Police and the Commander of the Mobile Reserve from the roster of commissioned officers.

WORKING CONDITIONS:

Members of the Mobile Reserve will work the usual 8-hour day unless conditions occur which cause the work day to be extended. They will receive the usual four days for recreation each month and, as nearly as practicable, an entire squad will have the same recreation days and the recreation days will be at times of minimum need.

EQUIPMENT:

Eight nonmarked automobiles with three/two-way radio equipment. Accessory radio, firearms, and other equipment as may be required from time to time.

ORGANIZATION:

Strategy Board

Chief and Assistant Chief of Police, Commanders of Records and Communications Division, Detective Division, Mobile Reserve, and Districts concerned. The Strategy Board will assign daily missions to the Mobile Reserve.

Operational Planning Unit

The Mobile Reserve Commander and a sergeant or patrolman. This unit will be responsible for strategy implementation.

Field Unit

The Mobile Reserve.

PROCEDURES:

Strategy Board

1. To receive from Commander of Records and Communications Division a daily report on concentrations of crime in time and area which may be considered susceptible to attack by the Mobile Reserve. The report will include data relating to location, hour of occurrence, day of week, date of month, and M.O. pattern of the crimes under consideration.

2. To designate the crime series against which the Mobile Reserve will be directed. The designation may cover operations over consecutive days, or any designated days of the week for a number of weeks. More than one series of crimes may be attacked on any one day. Missions will be so assigned to the Mobile Reserve that it will be fully occupied for its full tour of duty on every day of the week.

3. The Commander of Records and Communications Division will maintain a journal of crime situations considered by the Strategy Board at each meeting and a statement of missions agreed upon.

Operational Planning Unit

1. To plan the details of each mission, including the preparation of assignments, schedules, and instructions.

2. To distribute copies of the details of each plan to the members of the Strategy Board, District Commanders concerned, and the Mobile Reserve.

3. To brief the Mobile Reserve, giving a detailed explanation of the nature of the crime situation being dealt with and the manner of attack.

4. To maintain a journal of missions assigned to the Mobile Reserve, giving a brief description of the plan of operation of each, the dates in operation, and the results.

Field Unit

1. Will assemble at the Police Academy or at other designated lo-

cations at an hour established for each day by the Mobile Reserve Commander.

2. Will be given detailed instructions by the Mobile Reserve Commander or Assistant Commander, and in some instances a squad will be briefed by its leader.

3. After briefing, each squad leader will transport his squad to their posts and assure himself that each man understands his mission.

4. The Assistant Commander will maintain an up-to-date list of telephone numbers of his squad leaders, and in the event of sudden change in hours of duty or other plans, he will notify each squad leader by telephone or other means. Each squad leader, in turn, will maintain the telephone numbers of his squad members and will transmit the same information to each.

5. Mobile Reserve squad leaders will supervisethe members of their squads to assure strict attention to duty and conformity with instructions relating to the mission. They will use their cars in supervision only when conditions warrant.

6. The Mobile Reserve Assistant Commander will supervise his squad leaders and assure himself that each clearly understands the mission to which he is assigned and that each effectively supervises the members of his squad.

7. The Mobile Reserve Assistant Commander will be alert to the occurrence of serious crimes and other incidents which may justify the withdrawal of one or more squads and their assignment for a part or the remainder of the tour of duty and their return to their previous assignment in the event time permits.

8. The Mobile Reserve Commander will obtain armaments, communications, and other equipment needed for each mission. The Assistant Commander will distribute the equipment among the squads and maintain a record thereof.

9. No member of the Mobile Reserve will deviate from an agreed plan except when conditions clearly warrant. Deviations will be reported to the immediate superior so that notations may be made for future planning.

10. When an arrest is made, the Mobile Reserve may continue to gather evidence and prepare the case for court presentation up to the end of their tour of duty, when it will be turned over to the special division having ultimate responsibility for its court presentation. The principal arresting officer will be assigned to continue the investigation and assist in the preparation of the case for court.

Los Angeles Police Department Special M.O. Bulletin

W. H. PARKER, *Chief of Police*

Published by Crime Analysis Unit, Planning and Research Division,
Michigan 5211, Station 2925

Bulletin # 44   *April 2, 1954*

The Newton Collection Bandit. Approximately twenty robberies have been committed in Newton District and adjacent areas in the past two months by one male negro suspect, who lures salesmen and deliverymen to an off-street location by the pretext of getting a new customer for the victim.

Description: One male negro, 35 to 45 years, 5'9" to 6', 175 to 190 lbs., medium to dark complexion, smooth talker, clean shaven, wide nostrils, possible scar on right cheek. Suspect always wears a brown or grey felt hat. He is neatly dressed and has worn brown sport coat, brown suit, brown or grey slacks, faded blue denim pants and sport shirts. (See Artist's composite sketch on reverse side.)

Method of Operation: Approaches as victim is completing a collection or delivery. Tells victim that his (suspect's) *relative* (sister, mother, brother, etc.) is opening a place of business and wishes to buy from victim.

Lures victim to an off-street location (alley, yard, Hotel, Apt. House).

Produces gun and takes victim's collection money.

Usually takes victim's pants and shoes.

Has robbed various victims who were delivering eggs, beer, TV sets, oil, bread, tobacco, meat, dairy products, vegetables, auto accessories, canned goods, etc.

Most robberies have occurred in the area bounded by 33rd Street, Avalon, Slauson and Central. Six robberies have also occurred in the adjacent county area. One has occurred in 77th Division and one in University Division.

Weapon: Suspect is armed with a nickel-plated .32 or .38 cal. revolver, possibly an H & R with a 4" barrel.

Vehicle: One victim saw suspect again several days after the robbery, entering a 1951 Cadillac 4-door sedan with Illinois license plates, number unknown, at 36th and Western Avenue.

Any Information Pertaining to this Suspect for: HARRIS AND DAVIS, Newton Division Detectives, MI 5211, Ext. 2533 or Police Complaint Board, MA 7911.

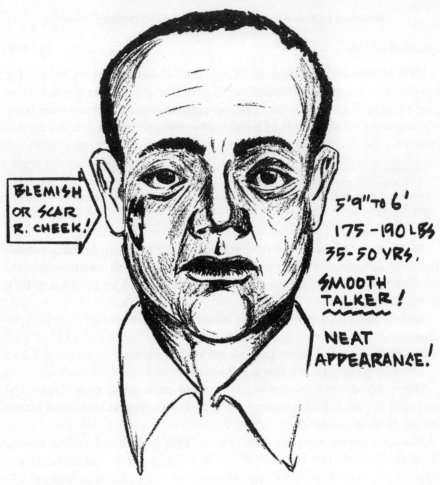

BLEMISH OR SCAR R. CHEEK!

5'9" TO 6'
175 - 190 LBS
35 - 50 YRS.
SMOOTH TALKER!
NEAT APPEARANCE!

Suspect has been identified as:
    Robert Taylor, AKA, Bobe Taylor, Bob Estes, Bob Easter, male negro, 40 to 50 years, 5'11", 180 lbs., medium dark complexion. Formerly resided at 2021½ 2nd Avenue.
Closely resembles above drawing. Blemish or scar on cheek not too noticeable (possibly non-existent).
1951 Cadillac in custody.

Los Angeles Police Department Special M.O. Bulletin

W. H. PARKER, *Chief of Police*

Published by Crime Analysis Unit, Planning and Research Division,
Michigan 5211, Station 2925

Bulletin #38   *December 18, 1953*

On December 14, 1953, at about 7:40 P.M., on Santa Ynez Street between Bonnie Brae Street and Glendale Blvd., three male Mexicans alighted from a 1940 Ford 4-dr. sedan and attempted to rob one male victim. Suspects #1 and #2 approached victim and asked him for a dollar. When victim refused to give them the money, both suspects attacked him. At this time, suspect #3 got out of the car with a knife in his right hand and attempted to stab victim in the back. Victim, who is a professional wrestler, broke the right arm of suspect #3 at the elbow, then tripped over suspect #3 and fell to the ground. Suspect #2, in attempting to kick victim while he was down, was tripped and it is believed that his right leg was possibly broken at the knee. Suspects then got in their car and left the scene.

Description of Suspects. #1, male Mexican, 18 to 19 years, 5'7" to 5'8", 150 lbs., brown hair and eyes. #2, male Mexican, 18 years, 5'8", 150 lbs., brown hair and eyes, medium complexion, *right leg possibly broken at the knee.* #3, male Mexican, 25 to 30 years, 5'11" to 6'0", appeared to be a homosexual as his eyebrows seemed to be plucked, *right arm possibly broken at the elbow.* #4, male Anglo-Saxon or light complexioned Mexican in his twenties, was the driver of the car.

Vehicle Used. Described as a 1940 Ford 4-dr. sedan, brown or maroon in color, with two rows of louvres on each side of the hood. Vehicle is equipped with *twin pipes.* The rear license plate bracket has the words *SAN BERNARDINO* written across the top and a 4" by 5" tab attached to the upper right corner with the word *VACS* running diagonally from lower left to upper right. The letters are silver against a dark background. Because of a cracked and discolored celluloid covering over the face of the license plate, no number was obtained. *There is no handle or emblem on the trunk.*

Oakland Police Department Crime Summary

Bulletin # 57-17   *Week of 22-28 Apr 57*

There were some pleasant changes last week in more than just the weather. Reports of Part I Offenses dropped to 241 from 268 the previous week, and 296 the week before that. This represents the first major drop from the peak winter crime rates and we are glad to see that spring is finally here. Burglaries and Auto Thefts are looking better, and Auto Thefts, particularly, were down during the last few days; but these continue to be major problems. Auto Burglary has shown a tendency to rise lately, and special attention to known "hypes" is indicated.

Residence Burglary seems to be increasing very slightly and Beats 3, 5, and 25 were the target areas last week, with some action in Beats 13, 22, 29, and 33. A substantial number of these cases were late afternoon and early evening; however, we'll have to watch this pattern for a few weeks to see how burglars react to Daylight Saving Time. Electrical appliances and clothing are the types of loot taken most frequently (except, of course, money). Non-Residence Burglaries have been decreasing pretty steadily, but we still have more than enough of them. These are especially difficult cases to clear because most of them are "small-time" and there isn't much to go on. Patrol personnel have apparently been doing a good job on security checks recently, and continued emphasis on this kind of activity should help. Last week's biggest problems were in Beats 21, 27, and 28, with a sprinkling of activity in Beats 4, 5, 14, and 15.

Auto Thefts were down to a real respectable level last week, but they won't stay there without some positive police action. The thefts which were reported last week were well spread around town, except that Beats 4 and 31 were pretty hard hit. Half of the reported thefts occurred on Friday night and most of these between the hours of 1800 and 2400. Nearly all of the stolen vehicles were 1946 to 1952 models, and Fords and Chevys are by far the most popular. If every patrol and traffic officer on the 3rd Watch would check the registration of one or two juveniles who are driving 1946 to 1952 cars on Friday night, we'd cut our 503 VC rate in half.

Auto Burglary has been fluctuating considerably of late, and last week these offenses were up a little. Most of the action was in West Oakland, especially in Beats 1 and 7. Auto Clouts were way down and no concentrations in either time or area were noted.

Auto Accessory Thefts were down from previous weeks, but hub-caps and tires continue to be stolen with discouraging frequency. Beats 23 and 24 were hardest hit last week, and reasonable activity was reported from Beats 14, 21, 28, 30, and 31. About 50% of the reported thefts occurred on Monday night.

PART I BAROMETER

Offense	Last Year to Date	This Year to Date	2 Weeks Ago	Last Week
Rape	45	69	3	4
Robbery, Armed	102	105	6	6
Robbery, Strongarm	122	130	9	4
ADW	285	267	12	13
Burglary	1163	1111	56	59
Burglary, Auto	297	247	13	16
Auto Clout	248	253	10	8
Auto Accessories	578	506	38	29
Bicycle Theft	293	284	10	16
Auto Theft	577	593	32	24
Other Thefts	1348	1389	79	62
	5058	4954	268	241

W. W. VERNON, *Chief of Police*

APPENDIX L

Cover Plans[1]

The action taken by the Midland Police Department against some safe burglars is used here as an example of plans made to cover hazardous locations for the purpose of apprehending the burglars should they repeat, and also as an example of action taken when the safe men were surprised in operation and were being pursued. Quoted excepts from reports on the case cited are examples of complete, detailed, and well written reports which reflect the quality of the investigation they related.

On Monday night, 5 July, the Elm Restaurant was entered, the safe successfully punched, and about $1850 cash taken. On Sunday night, 18 July, a safe containing about $400 was taken from Gold's (one of a chain of candy stores). Both stores were in Midland.

The police made a re-survey of all safes in the city and urged the merchants to illuminate them at night and to place them in easy view of patrolmen. They selected the nine most hazardous ones and covered them for the following seven consecutive Sunday nights and also on Monday September 6th (Labor Day). The following reports are illustrative of the action taken.

Det. Fry   *Case No. 69615*

For commercial burglary apprehension we have 16 officers available for special duty. Using two each at the Palm, Midland, and Ross theatres and at Wood Bakery and the Triangle restaurant, and using one man for Washington-Apple Market Group, one for Lords Market-Rock Furniture, and one for the Elm-Wards & Lee-Pierce-Sun Store group, we have one man left.

Will you, forenoon of July 23, do following, which I have not been able to do:

1. Look over Rules store (Stafford Square), where the safe will have $3500 according to manager, and Dunn's Restaurant, to see if safe in

---

The city involved is in the 100,000 class, in a metropolitan area, adjacent to several other municipalities, some larger and some smaller. All proper names and addresses have been made fictitious in the interest of commercial security.

either place can be taken without explosives and whether we should cover either one.

2. See Mr. Wood or his son at Wood Bakery and make arrangements for us to leave guns there Sunday afternoon and to get in before closing time, and find out how we lock up. Wood has been on vacation for two days.

3. See manager Triangle and make arrangements for us to cover, find out what time they close and ask where guns can be delivered.

4. Obtain key from Mrs. Ford, 4020 Bank, Real Estate Office. She has been cooperative in past and probably will let us use her office again.

5. See Mrs. Beebe in office on Alford above Suns and borrow her key so officer posted in hall there can use her phone.

HOLMES LT. No. *10*
7-23
11:00 P.M.

Case 69615

FOLLOW-UP ON LT. HOLMES REQUEST FOR ADDITIONAL INFORMATION RE CERTAIN SAFES

Contacted Frank C. Steele, Manager of Rules Store, Stafford Square (also in charge of operations at the Morse Ave. branch) and with him looked over his safe. The safe is one about 20″ wide, about 16″ high, and about 18-20″ deep, single door, combination type lock. This is a cast safe and quite a formidable one but still is of the type that two or three men might carry away. Safe is situated in the mezzanine office about the center of the store on the WS and not visible from the street.

Three thousand would not be an unusual amount to find in this safe over a weekend, and any night it would be good for about 1500 to 2000 dollars.

The fact that this is a sub-station Post Office might be a deterrent to the gang we are looking for when their previous activities are considered but we still have this hazard in the city.

I talked at some length with Steele and obtained his promise to make every effort to have the Rules install at least in their two Midland stores, the two-door type of concrete-imbedded safes visible from the street. Steele seemed sincere in his statement that he would take every means available to him to have the situation improved promptly. I will check further in a reasonable time on the progress he is making.

With the lineup of men already organized for the cover, other places might appear to be more worthy of attention at this time, but we should surely take steps to prevent the Stafford Sq. safe from being worked on.

Next I checked with Adolph Benton, the manager of the Morse Ave.

branch, and learned from him that the safe in the basement, of a type I would judge easily entered, usually contains from 750 to 1000 dollars over a weekend. I told him of my discussion with Steele, and then advised that for the time being, and until something could be done to improve the present hazardous situation, that he bring his money to the Police Station, under Police Escort on Saturday nights, and leave his safe open.

At Dunns I looked the situation over and learned that Mrs. Black lives in the same apartment building, but on the 3rd floor, and it is believed that they could hear any hammering done on the safe. The safe is in the office on the United St. side of the building, through which entrance the early and late employees travel, and through which Mrs. Black and some employees go to and from their living quarters. This much traffic, and being in a residence building might be a deterrent to a safe mob; we cannot overlook the fact that 1500 to 2000 plus would not be an unusual amount to have in this safe over a two or three day weekend.

For the purpose of this cover we can skip this one, I believe, but Mrs. Black has authorized me to contact Bill Dean, an electrician, to rig up some sort of a buzzer arrangement, to the sleeping quarters above, which would be set off by anyone tampering with the safe. I will contact this electrician as soon as I can.

At the Wood Bakery I talked with the son of the owner, the latter being out of town, and the former leaving town today at 3 P.M. to go to Pineville for the weekend. I made known to him our problem and he assured me of cooperation. I then talked with Mrs. Ida Depew the manager and from her OBTAINED A KEY TO THE MEZZANINE OFFICE WHICH IS TO BE RETURNED TO HER ON MONDAYS. This key, labeled properly, will be turned over to Lt. Holmes along with this report.

A girl named Ethel at the Bakery will be contacted by me so that arrangements can be made for the delivery of guns and storing of them in the mezzanine office by officers who will cover that night, and who will be equipped with the office key so that they may put the guns in the office, and later, just before they close at midnight, go there, and as inconspicuously as possible, drift up to the mezzanine and get out of sight.

A cook or baker comes to work at about 5:30 A.M. and I will try to get word to that person regarding the officers so that there will be no misunderstanding when she comes to work in the morning and finds them there.

Judging from this setup, if the burglars continue with their MO already established, this would be one of the most likely places (I have looked over so far) to kick in and take the safe away. The safe looks large but much of the largeness is due to asbestos packing and not to steel walls.

In covering this place weekly, the key could be obtained each Sunday afternoon from Mrs. Depew and returned the following day.

I contacted Mrs. Ford at 4020 Bank Way, made my purpose known to her, and received a key for her office which we may keep in our custody until such time as we have no further need for it. It will be found accompanying this report, properly labeled.

I contacted Mrs. Beale at her office and obtained a key from her which is properly labeled, and we may keep this key until such time as we have no further need for it.

I called at the Triangle cafeteria shortly after noon this date and without making my purpose known to anyone, learned that the manager will not be available there until after 5 P.M. this date. Under those circumstances I am presuming that there will be time enough for the Sgt. on the Evening Watch to obtain needed information and to make necessary arrangements.

CCDD
CC Sgt. Coles (Please notify your desk about Morse Ave. Rules Bros.)
CC Sgt. Wales
CC Case 69810

A. R. Fry Det. No. *33*
1:20 P.M. *7-24*

Preparation for Special Detail, of Sunday   *Case No. 69615*
Captain Lee:

Please assign plain-clothes officer to deliver two wrapped shotguns with 18 rounds of ammunition for each to the following locations during the early afternoon of Sunday July 25:

No. 1. Palm Theater. Deliver to manager who has agreed to lock them up in the office. He will be contacted by two plain-clothes officers shortly before midnight.

No. 3. Wood Bakery. Make similar deliveries to Mrs. Ida Depew or a girl named "Ethel" who will admit the officer to the mezzanine office. The key to this office is attached and should be returned to Lieut. Holmes' desk as soon as deliveries have been made so S.D. officers will have it to use in getting into the office.

No. 8. Midland Theater. Same instructions as for No. 1.

No. 9. Ross Theater. Same instructions as for No. 1.

/s/ D. J. Holmes
Lieutenant
7-24
10:40 P.M.

Reply:

Deliveries made to posts 1, 8 and 9 between 1:30 and 1:50 P.M. this date, being delivered to Managers at Midland and Ross and assistant manager at Palm (mgr. is on vacation).

On post 9 (Ross) Manager gave me two of his cards and requested that when Officers enter the front door they display the cards and walk in without any discussion. Cards herewith.

On Post 3 (Wood) will be necessary to deliver after 3:30 P.M. as Mrs. Depew is gone for the day and Ethel does not arrive until 3:30 P.M. Delivered at 3:40 P.M.

LEE 7-25

LIEUT. HOLMES   *Case 69615*

12 GAUGE AMMUNITION

I have this date personally checked all ammunition which is issued with the Riot guns stored in Arms lockers. Some of the ammunition which was in the small canvas sacks was bulged at the neck as result of many loadings and, in such cases, that ammunition has been taken out of service and will be used for practice or instruction at some future date. All ammunition which is now in the canvas bags is in serviceable condition. Eighteen rounds are in each bag.

ADDITIONAL

This ammunition should be watched in order that ammunition which might be faulty can be eliminated. Ammunition which is now being issued has a black wad which extends beyond the crimped end of the shell and which is OK as long as the protruding wad is well set and does not become soft or splinter off. I have removed a number of these today and on others have split them. Unless they are checked, part of the wad might fall off when shell is being carried from magazine to chamber and foul the operating mechanism. All of these possibilities are remote but can be prevented by care.

TAKE-DOWN GUNS

The five take-down guns have been packed in the suit boxes and are on cabinet in Captain's office. Officers who take these guns out *must* be familiar with their assembly even to point of being able to assemble in the dark. Unless you are certain that each man knows how to assemble, have him take one of the other guns.

DISTRIBUTION OF GUNS

Eight (8) guns have been delivered to four locations, each gun being supplied with 18 rounds of ammunition. Both guns wrapped in one package.

Five (5) take-down guns packed as above indicated. Eighteen shells.
Six (6) guns still in arms locker. Eighteen shells with each.

LEE *4:30* P.M. *7-25*

SPECIAL ORDER
SPECIAL DETAIL, SUNDAY, JULY 25.   *Case 69615*

Morning Watch Report for Duty at 9:00 P.M. and take over radio car beats at 9:30 P.M., at which all Evening Watch beat patrolmen will be relieved. Special to be recalled at 4:00 A.M.

9:30 P.M.-*4:00* A.M. *Patrol Duty*		When Scheduled to 4:00 A.M. *Special Detail*
Desk Sgt. Pedder	No. 1 Palm Theater	A. Pastor; B. O'Malley
Ptl. Sgt. Wales	No. 2 Roof Mayland Storage	Logan (RIver 2158)
Office Jones-Parks	No. 3 Woods	A. Mears; B. Ladue
No. 1 Gainese	No. 4 Triangle	A. Corey; B. McVeigh
No. 2 Ford	No. 5 Red & White Market	A. Huddle
No. 3 Grand	No. 6 4020 Bank Way	Brooks
No. 4 Clune	No. 7. Elm's Alley	Nolds
No. 5 Connor	No. 8 Midland Theater	A. Fraser; B. Bowdon
No. 6 Williams	No. 9 Rivoli Theater	A. Morton; B. Berle

At Large

Car 33 Capt. Lee, Sgt. Wales
Car 22 Lt. Holmes, Sgt. Coles

At Large: Patrol store fronts in an inconspicuous manner. On radio constantly. To answer all suspicious-character calls in vicinity known safes assisted by patrolman. To be detailed geographically by desk.

Special: Observation Points

Be definite when you phone in. Keep line open and report events to desk who will keep open radio line to "At Large" cars. Regardless of events keep communication open.

Inside Posts

A. Position depends on cover afforded and view obtained. Officers not more than few feet apart.
B. *Officer designated as "A" in charge, make all moves, give all orders and commands in event of entry.*
C. Remember possibility of third or fourth burglar.
D. Unless impossible, let suspect or suspects commit definite overt act, before challenging.

Sgt. Morning Watch: Notify all officers listed above to report for duty at 9:00 P.M. Will work to 8:00 A.M.

Sgt. Evening Watch: Notify all officers listed above to come into station 9:30 P.M. at which time Morning Watch Officers will take over beats.

Special Detail—Sunday Night—July 25   *Case 69615*

No. 1 Palm Theater—(A) Pastor (B) O'Malley. Arrive not later than 11:00 P.M. See manager who has guns locked up in office. Last two people out of theater are manager and janitor. Avoid janitor and pick position commanding office door after manager leaves. Use exit door in leaving; return guns to station.

No. 2 Roof Mayland Storage—Logan. Arrive by 10:00 P.M. Take position on South West corner of roof, using large packing box either for shield or backstop so you will not be visible against the sky. Regular telephone has been installed, unlisted, RIver 2158. Washington to Apple Market group under observation. Bells on phone are muffled so you may be called from police station if desirable. Apple Bakers due to arrive at 2:00 A.M. No bakers at Washington.

No. 3. Woods Bakery—(A) Mears (B) Ladue. Arrive by 11:00 P.M. Take key to mezzanine office. Mears, contact waitress "Ethel" and then make your way to office. Ladue, join about 10 minutes later, without contacting anyone if possible. After store closes pick desirable location. Guns will be found in office, having been delivered earlier in day. Return guns and key to station.

No. 4. Triangle Cafeteria—(A) Corey (B) McVeigh. Arrive by 10:00 P.M. Take guns in suit boxes. Pick position. Take key and return it to station.

No. 5. Red and White Market—Huddle. Arrive by 11:00 P.M. Take gun in suit box. Pick own position. Take key and return it to station. Object is to watch Burton's Candy Store which closes at midnight. Floor safe under cash register near front door, hangs down into basement.

No. 6. Ford's Real Estate Office, 4020 Bank; commanding rear Rocks Furniture and side Lords Market, Bank and Stafford. Brooks— Arrive 10:00 P.M. Phone is MI 2349. Take gun and key and return both.

No. 7. 4085 Alford—On Roof—Nolds. View of Alley behind elm, wards, grands. Use phones in Beales Real Estate Office.

No. 8. Midland Theater—(A) Fraser (B) Bowdon. Arrive not later than 11:00 P.M. Contact manager, who has guns in his office which were delivered earlier in day. Pick own location after employees leave. Leave by exit door. Return guns.

No. 9. Ross Theater—(A) Morton (B) Berle. Arrive by 11:00 P.M. Contact manager who has previously delivered guns in his office. Arrange for him to be last out. Pick own position. Leave by exit door. Use manager's cards to gain admittance.

D. J. Holmes
Lieutenant
7-25

Footnote: Carried out as planned; but see Case 72725 re suspicious circumstances at the Palm Theater. DJH-7-26.

———————

At 5:56 A.M., 7-26, Officer H. W. Gaines found a rear exit door of the Palm Theater open. The circumstances were as follows:

To: *Lt. D. J. Holmes*   Case 72725
Subject: *Suspicious Circumstance—Palm Theater. July 26, 1:00-5:00
a.m.*

At 1:00 A.M., I checked all of the doors and exits to the theatre and they were all locked tight.

At 4:20 A.M., following a report of special duty officers Pastor and O'Malley of someone being heard on the roof, a detail including Lt. Holmes, Sgt. Coles, Captain Lee, Sgt. Wales covered the place which was given a thorough inspection. The officers of this detail had been at the exit on stairs on the south side of the building in the alley behind the stores facing on High Ave., and had checked the entire place through from all sides, even climbing up onto the roof and checking all possible sources of entry, with negative results.

We left this detail at 4:40 A.M., and at that time I went to breakfast.

At 5:30 A.M., I passed by the front of the theatre and thence north on Columbia to take care of some routine work. At 5:45 A.M., I drove into the service station at the NW corner of High and Allen where I left my car and walked down the street to the alley which connects State Place with High. I went to the North end of the theatre and checked all of the exits. Coming around the West end of the building I went up the alley to check the South end. As I started up the iron stairs I noticed that the exit at the top was standing about ¾ inch ajar. I immediately went to the police box (56) and called for a detail which arrived shortly. Officer Williams was sent to the rear to cover at Station Place. When Grand arrived I sent him to cover the front from High, and Ford was also detailed to cover the front. Sgt. Wales having arrived, I went with him again into the alley and up the stairs. The door had not been forced from the outside, but had been opened from the inside. A search of the building was made, and nothing found to indicate forced entry. The door to the office had not been "made" so I went up onto the roof above the marquee and dropped down onto the marquee. The windows leading into the office had not been forced, and the safe appeared to be intact. Climbing out again I went up onto the roof proper. There at the extreme West end, I noticed a 2x6 plank laid up against the roof which is directly over the stage. Up there are two large trap doors, both of which were locked. In the extreme N.W. corner is a smaller trap door which was not locked. Opening that I found that footprints had been made on an iron gallery and on the rungs of the ladder which went straight down to the floor of the show. This place was extremely dusty and except for the FRESH marks in the dust, had not been used for a long period of time. Sgt. Wales and myself climbed down this, locking same after us. Once again in the theatre proper we awaited the arrival of keys to let us into the office. About this time the janitor, Fred GASPAR (45), 2230—8 St. NP, arrived and told us that he had left at 12:15 A.M. and that the place was locked tight upon his leaving. He admitted us to the office, where we found that nothing had been bothered. I then went to the home of Frank Weeks (18), 1841 Drake, NP, who is the Asst. Mgr. He stated that he had locked the doors himself and left the theatre at 12:05 A.M. He said that he had left the money in the safe, and to make sure that it was still there I asked to have him come out there with me and verify this. Arriving at the theatre we found that the money was there (about $500). He stated that he did not go back to the theatre between 4:40 A.M. and 5:50 A.M. The janitor says the same.

OPINIONS: (Herewith is the only possible solution that I can offer. As Sgt. Wales and myself tried to put facts together we arrived at the following as being the only possible solution at the present time.) Evidence is indicative that the exit was made from the upper exit door. Entry must have been made from the trap door of the roof as that is the only way unless someone went in the front door with a key.

Someone entered the theatre during the performance and sneaked behind the stage via one of the many doors to same, climbed the ladder to the roof and unlocked the three hooks which held the door secure. As Officers O'Malley and Pastor claim that they heard someone on the roof, I believe that the culprit walked up the stairs on the outside of the South side of the building, climbed the fire ladder to the roof, across the gravel roof, (heard by the officers at 3:40 A.M.) became frightened by my driving up across the street (several blocks down) and laid low for awhile. After awhile Officers Pastor and O'Malley left and the subject started again to make his entry. Within a few moments of this time the alarm had been given out and the building had been covered. Knowing that if he ran out he might be spotted, and if he went down into the theatre he would be found, he hid on the small gallery just inside the trap door. After the search had been made, he dropped down into the theatre and out the exit.

Another angle might have been the place was being "worked" when I returned to check it about 5:30, and while I was away for the few moments, escape was made.

The doors had been locked at 4:40 and I found the door open at 5:50; therefore only an hour and 10 minutes had elapsed.

CC:DD

Capt. Lee   W. H. GAINES NO. 26

Sgt. Wales   7-26 8:55 A.M.

During the weeks a similar Sunday night cover was being maintained on the safes in Midland, a $20 traveler's check taken from the Elm's safe early in July was cashed at a Metropolis bank by a known safe man, Peter Joseph Battoni, who was arrested and brought to Midland on August 13th for investigation as to his complicity in the two safe burglaries. The police were unable to obtain further evidence and he was returned to the Metropolis police who held him for forgery in connection with the cashing of the traveler's check. He was indicted and released on bail, his attorney succeeding in having the case set for trial in January.

The next development was reported as follows:

ELM RESTAURANT   *Case 69615*

Lieut. Holmes: Please note following report and bring to attention Night Watches. CONFIDENTIAL: (LEE):

While in Ridge City today, I talked with Detectives Bridge and Brown who told me the following story:

About 4:20 last Monday morning, Ridge City patrolman was standing in a doorway on 17th Street near Morse Avenue and he noticed one suspicious person idling about the corner and an automobile parked in front of the Royal Theatre. At the same time, this officer seemed to hear what appeared to be the hammering of a heavy sledge or hammer. The officer remained in the doorway watching proceedings and, since he could determine nothing of any great consequence taking place, he walked out onto the sidewalk into view. The suspicious person on the corner disappeared over towards Broadway and the automobile was driven away, giving the policeman an opportunity only to take the license number.

Nothing more was thought of this incident until the following day when a report from the Cape Restaurant revealed that yeggs had worked on the safe without completing entry. Apparently efforts had been made using a Stilson wrench to twist the cylinder lock on the front door. This effort was given up in favor of breaking into the restaurant through the back entrance.

No tools were found on the job but the knob of the safe was knocked off and the combination partially punched back. Apparently the job was given up because of the activity and interest of the officer referred to previously.

The Detective assigned to the case checked up on the license number and found that it was registered under the Acme Auto Rental Service, 25-11th Street, Metropolis.

In checking at the Acme Rental Service they found information of a rather interesting nature. The automobile seen in front of the Cape restaurant at the time the hammering was heard by the officer had been rented by Pete Battoni at about 7 P.M. Sunday night and was turned in by the same person at 6:28 A.M. Monday morning after having been driven 58 miles.

Of more interest in this investigation was the fact that Pete Battoni has been renting automobiles quite regularly for the past two years and I looked over a detailed record of such rentals dating from October 3rd of this year and from the nature and character of this record I would not be surprised if we could not almost associate certain facts shown there with safe burglaries or other crimes in this State. I intend going to Metropolis tomorrow and, with the assistance of the burglary detail there, obtain a detailed record of all such rentals by Pete Battoni or any of his known associates during the past two years.

I have cited the details in connection with this burglary attempt of a safe at a restaurant in Ridge City for several reasons, not the least of which is to refresh the memory of our own officers with the need for more attention to safes during this Christmas holiday. Pete Battoni is, at present, out on bond in Metropolis and, no doubt, a defense attorney sufficiently successful in keeping Battoni from coming to trial thus far is going to demand something in return for his services, and I daresay that if we are not on the alert, some of our local merchants may unwillingly and unwittingly aid Battoni in paying his attorney's fees. If possible I will furnish more details in connection with this problem tomorrow.

CC:DD   A. R. FRY, DETECTIVE No. 33
                                               12-15, 4:30 P.M.
                                               /s/ A. R. Fry

––––––––

A check of the dates on which Pete had cars from the rental agency revealed that he had one at the time of the previously reported incident at the Palm Theatre.

A list of the license plate numbers of all automobiles owned by this rental agency was obtained from the motor vehicle department and given to all patrolmen with suitable explanation and instruction. In addition a special detail, as outlined in the following report, was arranged for Sunday night, December 26th.

———

SPECIAL DETAIL *of 12-26*   *Case 69615*

A file in the office of undersigned contains reasons for this detail and background for anyone uninformed on subject.

Surveillance will be provided by three squads consisting of three unmarked radio cars with two officers in each car, on both watches operating this detail.

Three squads of the Morning Watch officers will report for duty at 9:35 P.M., 12-26, get notebooks in shape, read bulletin and have riot guns issued them by Sergeant in charge. They will go out on street at 10 P.M. A list of locations requiring attention has been provided for each car. Locations and vicinity of those locations will be inspected in the order listed, by surveillance from auto unless an unusual condition warrants getting out of the car. In looking for license numbers furnished on attached lists, special attention shold be given to cars parked on street, in driveways, lots and yards. Officers should remember that so far persons we are looking for have used Plymouth automobiles and perhaps may not use one with license corresponding to the list. Consideration should be given possible lookouts on foot. Each squad will return to station at midnight.

Each car will tour entire city, following the list of locations in the tour, and should make one complete circuit each hour. It is necessary to follow the schedule to insure the inspection of any given location at least once each 20 minutes.

Car No. 1 will begin at box No. 54 and ring in from that box on each even hour. Ring on half hour from any box listed.

Car No. 2 will begin at Box No. 27 and ring in from that location on each even hour. Ring on half hour from any other box listed.

Car No. 3 will begin at Box No. 18 and ring in from that location on each even hour. Ring on half hour from any box listed.

Special Detail officers from the Evening Watch will report to station 10 minutes before midnight, remove uniform caps and blouses, have riot guns issued them by Sgt. in charge, be given information of procedure to follow and be out on street at midnight. They will follow above plan from that point returning to station at 4:00 A.M. IN NO EVENT EXCEPT EMERGENCY IS ANY SPECIAL DUTY OFFICER TO RING IN FROM ANY BOX OTHER THAN THE SIX LISTED ON THE OUTLINE OF LOCATIONS, NEITHER IS ANY CAR TO COME INTO STATION DURING SPECIAL DUTY TOUR EXCEPT IN EVENT OF EMERGENCY.

Officers on regular duty should wear uniforms and officers on Special Duty may wear uniform trousers only. Effort toward looking as little like police officers on the prowl as possible will lend success to this assignment.

Officers should make every effort to be as inconspicuous as possible. Tour sheets for each car are attached.

HOLMES
LIEUTENANT
12-26

BOXES AND PERTINENT SAFE LOCATIONS—Route of inspection tour:

BOX NO. 54—*Columbia & King*
  Palm
  North Midland Coal Yard

BOX NO. 46—*Oak and Cedar*
  Apple's
  Woods
  Washington
  Thriftway
  MacDaniels
  Maxwell
  Kreig
  Rules
  Lees
  Wards
  Elm

BOX NO. 83—*Magnolia & Taft*
  Seaside Oil
  Standard
  Heath's
  Ross
  River Lines

Electric Company
Burtons
Golds
Samptons
Doughnut Shop
Masons
Triangle
Dunns—South Gate Apparel

BOX NO. 27—*Bank & Ellton*
  Lords
  Rocks

BOX NO. 18—*Ellton & Linden*
  Alpine Coal
  Daniels—Magnolia

BOX NO. 39—*Cedar & Taft*
  Water Company
  Southern Auto
  Midland Theatre
  Fidelity Loan
  Oultons

USE ONLY BOXES INDICATED. IN EMERGENCY USE SOME RESIDENTIAL AREA BOX. AVOID BOXES IN BUSINESS AREA OR AN ARTERIAL UNLESS ABSOLUTELY NECESSARY TO USE THEM. TURN OFF YOUR LIGHTS WHEN PHONING.

TURN IN THIS SHEET AT END OF DAILY DUTY TO THE CAPTAIN'S OFFICE.

HOLMES
LIEUTENANT
12-26

An incident that occurred during the operation of this special detail was reported as follows: (Later investigation revealed that Pete had rented the car that was observed.)

SAFE SPECIAL   *12/27*   *Case 69615*

At about 1:20 A.M., 12/27, Officer Williams and I were cruising West School at Stafford. Just as we were about to make a left turn on Stafford we both spotted one of the cars bearing one of the license as we recognized the license number and immediately followed it. It was a Plym. Sedan A/G 2433, and it had just turned South on Stafford off School. It stopped on the west side of Stafford alongside the curb in front of Freids' Paint Store and the following man got out: Male, large, about 6' 2, heavy, looked like an Italian, wore a dark hat, brown suit, and white shirt.

He got out of the right side of the car from the rear seat and walked North on Stafford from School. Our attention was directed to the car as we recognized the license number and immediately followed it. It was about two blocks ahead of us by the time we started. We stopped at Alford & Stafford long enough to inform the desk by phone of what we had seen. The car by that time was about opposite John Oulton's at Carle & Stafford. It was very foggy there and we lost sight of the car. We went straight down Stafford and picked it up again at Ward & Ada where it turned left into Stafford. We were then about 50 feet behind it. It was going at a very slow speed, I would say not more than 10MPH. It was hugging the west curb and there were two men in the front seat both with dark overcoats. The one on the right side thrust his hand out giving a signal like they were going to pull over to the curb. We then passed them and proceeded South on Stafford to Ashton where we made a left turn to Newton. Then a U turn back to Stafford. Then North on Stafford, past the car where it was parked about 50 feet north of the coal yard. We went North to Orange and turned around (U) and went back to Ashton & Stafford to ring in and let the desk know where we and the other car were. Then we went back to the Coal yard but the car was gone. It was very foggy and we were not able to see more than about 50 feet ahead of us. We believe that the car turned West on Ruswin. We searched the vicinity but found no trace of it.

/s/ *John A. Logan*
JOHN A. LOGAN NO. 17
5:05 A.M. *12/27*

SAFE SPECIAL   *1227*   *Case 69615*

Summary

Six members of Evening Watch, Offs. Dayton, Wilde, Nolds, Logan and Williams, Sgt. Wales, plus Capt. Lee, and Sgt. Akers, in four cars, two men to a car, covered the safes in a circuit.

At 1:25 A.M. Offs. Williams and Logan saw a large Italian get out of a Plymouth sedan at School and Stafford. Followed car and ascertained license to be A/G 2433, one of the Acme Auto Rental sedans. Notified desk immediately from box 81 and tried to trail car. Saw same containing two additional men stopped at Ruswin and Stafford. Car went west on Ruswin from that point. Logan then notified desk from Ashton and Stafford.

Offs. Wilde, Nolds, Capt. Lee and Sgt. Akers, myself and Dayton covered main part of town looking for anything suspicious or the car in question. At 2:10 A.M. conferred with Capt. Lee and decided to start shaking main beat down at 3 A.M. if nothing was uncovered in the meantime. At 3 A.M. we divided the main part of town consisting of both sides of Stafford Ave. from Midland Way to Doran into small beats, put two men on each with instructions to shake down the hot safes. This was done without results.

At 3:15 A.M. I called Det Fry at his home, and he agreed with this procedure. At 4:40 A.M. called Evening Watch men off street and went home. Nothing further was seen of either the large Italian or the car.

Later in the morning Capt. Lee picked up an Italian driving around the main beat, but he was cleared by Insp. Fry. Off. Logan will write a detailed report on his observations of the car in question. Perhaps men "pegged" Logan and Williams at Ruswin and Stafford and drifted. No one knows what happened to the large Italian who got out of the car at Stafford and School.

4:50 A.M. 12-27

H. F. WALES SGT. *No. 4*

/s/ H. F. Wales

cc 2

CONFIDENTIAL   HOLIDAY SPECIAL DETAIL   *Case 69615*

On December 31 and January 1st, 2nd, and 3rd, some Special Details, Extra Hours, and Transfers will be necessary:

The public reason for unusual movement of the force is that "Our high fatality rate coupled with the two-day holiday makes it necessary to provide some extra men." Officers are authorized to make such a statement on any occasion where providing a reason seems in order. Any other reason than this is not to be given nor intimated to *any* person.

Conversation about other problems which will be encountered over the holiday is strictly forbidden. Conversation in public places, at home, and particularly in restaurants, is to be strictly avoided. Members of the department who will be working regular duty need not be concerned about this Holiday Special Detail.

All persons whose names are listed below are affected, and check marks ON THE ORIGINAL indicate that they have been notified about hours of duty, and given specific information on the various means of handling the problem at hand:

Captain Lee—notify all day men.

Captain Jones—notify D.D. & V.D.

Lieutenant Holmes—notify all others.

DD Jones, W. J.	Nolds	Connor
Fry	Brooks	Houser
Howe	Ford	Near
Thomson	Williams	Clune
	Ladue	Gaines
VD Parke	Wilde	O'Malley
Lowan	Huddle	Rowse
	Stuart	Bly
Evening Watch	Bavidon	
Holmes	Dutton	*Day Watch*
Coles		Lee
Wales	*Morning Watch*	Manton
McVeigh	Kerr	Sampson
Layton	Morton	Baines
McGay	Jones, E. C.	Grand
Beale	Parks	Pedder
Fraser	Severe	Corton
Logan	Bischam	

Arrangements appearing in this file have been organized by Captains Jones and Lee, Lieutenant Holmes, and Inspector Fry, with the approval of the Chief.

It is requested, that any suggestions about organization or any revision of plans be cleared through the undersigned for the sole purpose of having a central clearing point for arrangements.

D. J. HOLMES
LIEUTENANT
12-29
11 P.M.

L1/35
Orig.: Lee-Holmes
Dup Chief
Trip D.D.

SCHEDULE FOR HOLIDAY SPECIAL DETAIL

Friday	December 31
Saturday	January 1
Sunday	January 2
Monday	January 3
Tuesday	January 4

DAYS OFF CANCELLATION:

Morning Watch:	All days off cancelled Jan. 2 and Jan. 3.
Day Watch:	No days off will be concelled except for officers listed under "Transfers" below.
Evening Watch:	All days off cancelled January 1, January 2.

REGULAR AND SPECIAL DUTY:

West Side Traffic Officers:		Follow schedule posted at desk.
Morning Watch:	Jan. 1	(Regular shift—Strength to be increased by Sgt. Coles, Officers Pedder, Mears, Grand, as ordered in New Year's Eve Special.)
Uniform at all times:		
(Days off cancelled,)	Jan. 2	Report for duty 9:00 P.M., Jan. 1, out on street at 9:30 P.M. on regular beat assignment. Off duty 8:00 A.M. Strength to be increased by Grand, Pedder, Mears.
(Days off cancelled.)	Jan. 3	Report for duty 9:00 P.M., Jan. 2, on street at 9:30 P.M. on regular beat assignment. Off Duty 8:00 A.M.
	Jan. 4	Regular Duty.

Day Watch 1, 2, 3, 4:		Regular duty except that Sgt. Manton, Officers Baines, Grand, Sampson, Pedder, Mears, Capt. Lee, will be transferred as shown below, also Corton.

Evening Watch:	Dec. 31	Regular Shift.
(Days off cancelled.)	Jan. 1	Regular duty 4-9:30 P.M. (All officers will report for duty today and tomorrow at 4:00 P.M., IN UNIFORM. At dinner time will change to plain clothes. At 9:30 P.M. will come in from street. At 10 P.M. will go out on Special Detail to be concluded at 5:00 A.M. WEAR WARM CLOTHING.)
	Jan. 2	Same as Jan. 1st—days off cancelled.
	Jan. 3	Regular shift again.

Detective Division: Dec. 31—Special Duty 10 P.M.-5 A.M.
                               (Jan. 1st.)
                               Jan. 1—Special Duty 10 P.M.-5 A.M.
                               (Jan. 2nd.)
                               Jan. 2—Special Duty 10 P.M.-5 A. M.
                               (Jan. 3rd.)
                               (For all three days this includes *Capt.*
                               Jones, Detectives Fry, Howe, Thomson,
                               Parks, and Lowan.

TRANSFERS

Morning Watch—None, but see additional duty hours above.
Evening Watch—Sgt. Coles only, others see additional duty hours above.
Detective Division—None, but see additional duty hours above.

CONFIDENTIAL

TRANSFERS

"U"—Uniform, "C"—Civilian clothing
December 31, Friday
January   1, Saturday
January   2, Sunday
January   3, Monday
January   4, Tuesday

EVENING WATCH

Sgt. Coles   December 31   Excused
              January   1   U   11:30 P.M. 12-31 to 8:00 A.M. 1-1
              January   2   C   9:00 P.M. 1-1 to 5:00 A.M. 1-2
              January   3   C   4:00 P.M. — Midnight

DAY WATCH

Capt. Lee   December 31 C Regular Duty
                January   1 C Off Duty
U-Uniform   January   2 C 9:00 P.M. 1-1 to 8:00 A.M. 1-2
C-Pl. Clothes   January   3 C 9:00 P.M. 1-2 to 5:00 A.M. 1-3
                January   4 C Regular Duty

Sgt. Manton   December 31 U Regular Duty
                January   1 U 8:00 A.M. 1-1 to 2:00 P.M. (Exc. 2-4)
U-Uniform   January   2 C 9:00 P.M. 1-1 to 5:00 A.M. 1-2
C-Pl. Clothes   January   3 C 9:00 P.M. 1-2 to 5:00 A.M. 1-3
                January   4 U Regular Duty

Off. Sampson December 31 U Regular Duty
                January   1 U 8:00 A.M. 1-1 to 2:00 P.M. (Exc. 2-4)
U-Uniform   January   2 C 9:00 P.M. 1-1 to 5:00 A.M. 1-2
C-Pl. Clothes   January   3 C 9:00 P.M. 1-2 to 5:00 A.M. 1-3
                January   4 U Regular Duty

Off. Baines December 31 U Regular Duty
              January 1 U 8:00 A.M. 1-1 to 2:00 P.M. (Exc. 2-5)
U-Uniform   January 2 C 9:00 P.M. 1-1 to 5:00 A.M. 1-2
C-Pl. Clothes January 3 C 9:00 P.M. 1-2 to 5:00 A.M. 1-3
              January 4 U

Off. Grand December 31 U Regular Duty
              January 1 U
U-Uniform   January 2 C 9:00 P.M. 1-1 to 5:00 A.M. 1-2
C-Pl. Clothes January 3 C 9:00 P.M. 1-2 to 5:00 A.M. 1-3
              January 4 U Regular Duty

Off. Pedder December 31 C 8:00 A.M. 12-31 to 2:00 P.M. (Exc. 2-4)
              January 1 U 11:35 P.M. 12-31 to 8:00 A.M. 1-1
U-Uniform   January 2 C 9:00 P.M. 1-1 to 8:00 A.M. 1-2
C-Pl. Clothes January 3 C 9:00 P.M. 1-2 to 5:00 A.M. 1-3
              January 4 C 8:00 A.M. 1-4 to 4:00 P.M. 1-4

Off. Corton December 31 U Regular Duty
              January 1 U 8:00 A.M. 1-1 to 2:00 P.M. (Exc. 2-4)
U-Uniform   January 2 C 9:00 P.M. 1-1 to 5:00 A.M. 1-2
C-Pl. Clothes January 3 C 9:00 P.M. 1-2 to 5:00 A.M. 1-3
              January 4 U Regular Duty

On Friday night, December 31st, a special detail limited to three cars was used to cover the city at large, as indicated in the following report.

SPECIAL DETAIL *of 12-31 10 P.M. to 1-1 5 A.M.*

Case 69615

Surveillance will be provided by three squads consisting of three radio cars with two officers in each car.

Will report for duty 9:30 P.M., go out at 10 P.M., return to station at 5:00 A.M.

A list of locations has been provided. These locations will be inspected in the order listed, by surveillance from the auto unless an unusual condition warrants getting out of the car. Special attention should be provided vicinity of each location. License numbers have been furnished and the responsible car may be found on streets, alleyways, driveways or parking lots. It should be remembered that Plymouths have been used so far and it is possible that one might be used which does not correspond in license number to the list.

On this night there will be no plants inside any store.

Car No. 1. Jones-Howe will begin at box No. 54 and ring in from that box on every even hour.

Car No. 2. Fry-Thompson will begin at box No. 27 and ring in from that box at 20 minutes past each even hour.

Car No. 3. Parks-Logan will begin at box No. 18 and ring in from that box at 40 minutes past each even hour.

Beginning at boxes indicated locations will be inspected as listed on the location sheet. By this method it is anticipated that a circuit of the city will be made each hour and each location will be passed every twenty minutes by one of the three cars.

IN NO EVENT EXCEPT EMERGENCY IS ANYONE TO RING FROM ANY BOX EXCEPT THOSE LISTED ON THE LOCATION SHEET.

Needless to say every effort should be made by officers concerned to appear as little as possible like officers on the prowl.

All three special detail cars will immediately respond to "Car No. 22, Call your station." This particular radio car number will not be in service and one number is used to avoid attracting attention to unusual number of radio cars in service.

No attention should be paid by any special detail car to any police business, or radio broadcast, unless they are specifically called. In event detailed covering is necessary these three radio cars will respond to their own radio number assignment.

HOLMES
LIEUTENANT
12-31

———————

On Saturday and Sunday nights a detail was posted in 12 locations somewhat as indicated in the report on a similar cover used in August. The orders issued follow:

Case 69615   SPECIAL ORDER
SPECIAL DETAIL

Saturday Night, Sunday morning, Jan. 1-2
Sunday Night, Monday morning, Jan. 2-3

In Station	On Location	Location	Officer	
7:30 P.M.	10:00 P.M.	Desk	Holmes	Morton
9:30 P.M.	10:00 P.M.	Squad No. 1	Lee	Baines
9:30 P.M.	10:00 P.M.	Squad No. 2	Fry	Ladue
9:30 P.M.	10:00 P.M.	Squad No. 3	Wales	Thomson
9:30 P.M.	11:00 P.M.	1. Palm Theater (inside)	A-Coles	B-McHugh

9:30 P.M.	10:00 P.M.	2. MacDaniels from Elec. Store—1985 Stafford	Berle (listening post not visible)
9:30 P.M.	11:00 P.M.	3. Woods (inside)	A-Manton B-Bowdon
9:30 P.M.	10:00 P.M.	4. Triangle (inside)	A-Nolds B-Grand
9:30 P.M.	11:00 P.M.	5. Doughnut Shop	A-Sampson B-Corton
9:30 P.M.	11:00 P.M.	6. Gold & White Hotel	A-Jones B-Parks
9:30 P.M.	11:00 P.M.	7. Burtons R & W Mkt.	Huddle
9:00 P.M.	9:30 P.M.	8. Lords & Rocks	Dayton
9:30 P.M.	11:00 P.M.	9. Midland	A-Pedder B-Wilde
9:30 P.M.	10:00 P.M.	10. Alpine 2905 Stafford	Howe
9:00 P.M.	9:30 P.M.	11. MacDaniels	A-Logan B-Brooks
9:30 P.M.	11:00 P.M.	12. Ross	A-Ford B-Lowan

Same set-up both nights.

Care in parking autos, leaving and entering.

DETAILED ORDERS

1. PALM. Arrive before 11:00 P.M. One man see manager, arrange to avoid janitor. Guns will be found behind desk in office. Cover from outside office itself behind curtain. Before leaving tie up guns again and replace. Advise manager they will be there on Sunday. On Sunday night return guns to station.

2. MACDANIELS. No gun. Take key to Midland Electric Company, 1985 Stafford. Key will open door at 1985 but not 1987 Stafford. Remain in back room near phone, where you can hear activity in MacDaniels primarily and Thriftway incidentally. Bring key back with you both nights and turn it in. Telephone MI 8747. An emergency might bring one of the owners into shop, but unlikely. (Try phone upon arrival.)

3. WOODS. Guns will be found in office on mezzanine. Arrive before 11:00 P.M. Drift in singly. Return key. Cover from mezzanine.

4. TRIANGLE. Arrive 10 P.M. Cover from partition on S/s store or balcony in rear. Night watchman has been told to turn off sign at 9:30 P.M. and stay away thereafter. Take key and return it each night. Take shotguns and return them. Manager may possibly come in one of the nights. Locate the telephone. *If manager comes in he will be instructed to turn*

on lights upon his entry and by this means you will know who is coming.

5. DOUGHNUT SHOP. Arrive 11:00 P.M. Take guns broken down. "Margaret" will be in charge Saturday night and owner Kilman on Sunday night. A Filipino stays cleaning up till 1:30 A.M. Have Margaret or Kilman tell him some plausible story. In leaving, closing the door locks the place. Return the guns.

6. GOLDS. Arrive 11:00 P.M. Take key and gun. Try phone. *A*. Gun to be taken wrapped. Post in rear near special extension telephone. Another officer will watch front from across the street. You will cover alley. Phone first, keep communication open. If opportune and can be done with safety to yourself may be able to take them when they load safe into car. Safety to self and other officers closing in of most importance. *B* Watch front and alley of Golds from Room No. 237, White Hotel, MI. 2319. Keep communication open all times. Your only job is to observe regardless of what may happen on street.

7. BURTONS. Cover from R & W Market. Take key. Cover from mezzanine at back of grocery department at North wall. Special extension telephone will be at elbow (try phone). Keys for both grocery division and front door will be provided. No gun needed. Stay by phone at all times.

8. LORDS & ROCKS. Arrive 9:30 P.M. Take key. Post inside small window in Rock's N wall opposite entrance to Lords. Phone will be installed there. Try phone upon arrival. Your job to watch entrance to Lords basement. If basement light out, phone and we'll try to turn it on. If any noise of anyone working on Rocks safe, phone in. Be specific. You are not to move from telephone for any reason, regardless of what may happen inside Rocks or outside, until 5 A.M. or until instructed to do so.

9. MIDLAND. The same as for Palm Theater above, guns will be in manager's office. Leave them there wrapped Sat. night. Return them here Sunday night.

10. ALPINE. Arrive 10 P.M. at Ornamental Iron Works, 2905 Stafford. Key is for padlock on front door, north half of which slides open. Try telephone, which is MI 0463. Door on N/s never locked as owner lives next door—he knows about covering plan. Your assignment is to watch safe at Alpine. In event someone gets in there you are to telephone station and keep communication open. Under no circumstance are you to go outside if something breaks but are to stay at telephone, giving information where it will do the most good.

11. MACDANIELS, Magnolia Avenue. Guns will be delivered to manager's office. Take key with you. Store open until 10 P.M. Girl does not get out until about 11 P.M. Norma Dayton and Carol Rose will be girls on duty and know officers are coming. Officers to drift in separately and after proper identification walk upstairs. Telephone is MI 2212, but should not be answered by officers as burglar may telephone to see if place covered.

Key will permit access to all doors of building. Replace guns on Sat., bring them in on Sunday.

OFFICERS TO BE PARTICULARLY CAREFUL TO LEAVE NO SIGNS OF HAVING BEEN THERE. PLANT WAS VERY DIFFICULT TO ARRANGE. LEAVE *EXACTLY* AS YOU FIND IT, DO NOT LEAVE CIGARETTE BUTTS, SANDWICH WRAPPING, AND NO UNNECESSARY TRESPASS ABOUT THE PLACE.

12. Ross. Same as Palm. Wrap guns and leave them on Sat. Return on Sunday. Janitor there late; avoid him if possible.

Sergeant Clyde D. Beers of the State Police later reported the following information:

"About Tuesday, Dec. 28th, Inspector Fry of the Midland Police Department came to the State Police local Headquarters and told us, Captain F. M. Stevens, Sgt. G. W. Clark, and myself, of expected operation of a safe gang the following week-end, most likely the Sunday night of Jan. 2nd.

"Fry said he would provide us with a list of license numbers on a card already printed. I immediately went to the Bridge Toll Plaza to check all cars bearing license plates in that series.

"At approximately 8:40 P.M., I was posted at that location when a blue Plymouth Sedan bearing license plates AG2567 went through going east with two occupants in the car. The driver was wearing a dark overcoat like a camel's hair overcoat and the passenger also had on a light hat. I can say only that I judged them both to be adults, 30 years old or thereabouts.

"The passenger paid toll and then turned halfway toward me and glanced at me as they drove on out. After they got out of sight and before I came to the toll plaza to phone, I made a pen mark opposite the license number AG2567 to be sure it was the one I had seen. The tail light was burning and illuminating the license plate when this car went through."

C. D. BEERS, SGT.
JAN. 2, 8:40 P.M.

CC:DD

Subsequent events are recorded in the following report:

SUMMARY—DESK ACTION   *Case 69615*

This is a summary of the action taken by the Sergeant's Desk and the Patrol Division on the morning of 1/3 in line with attempted apprehension of two men who were responsible for an attempted safe job at JONES Restaurant at 19th and Morse in Ridge City and the subsequent gun battle with Ridge City Police officer in which he was not injured.

On the date as the result of preparation by Detective Bureaus of several police departments in cooperation with our own we had 12 locations covered by members of the evening watch who were not involved in the Ridge City case and who were not successful locally. During this time at the desk was Lt. Holmes assisted by acting Sergeant Morton with three men in records office and a full crew of patrolmen on the street.

A list of license numbers owned by the rental agency whose car was used by the suspected burglars in the past was furnished by Insp. Fry.

8:40 P.M. 1/2, Serg. Beers, State Police, informed that Plymouth Sedan AG2567 had crossed the Bridge with two men in the car, one wearing a gray overcoat. This information was immediately given to all first and third platoon Midland officers by telephone with instructions to merely observe and not follow the car until after a job had been pulled.

12:18 A.M. 1/3, Officer Clune reported that license AG2432, one of the listed cars, was parked beside the Tunnel grocery. This place was covered and the car was checked out as being operated by a boy who had rented the car and brought his girl home to Midland. The Bridge was telephoned and informed that they should not stop this car on the way back to Metropolis.

1:30 A.M. Sergeant Clark, State Police at the Bridge removed coverage from the Toll Station which had been maintained continuously as it was felt it was too late for any other car to come from Metropolis.

4:27 A.M. Ridge City Central requested all points, particular attention North Ridge City and Midland cars, be on the lookout for a blue-colored sedan headed north on Broadway which had been involved in a candy store burglary at 19th and Morse.

4:28 A.M. this message was verified as to the location of the candy store.

4:30 A.M. all cars, call your station.

4:32 A.M. Ridge City Central stated that this was a safe job and there had been a shooting. By this time the Ridge City-Midland line had been covered and at this time from our own list all points were informed that the probable license was AG2567.

4:35 A.M.—this information was repeated.

At this point acting Sergeant Morton, Officer Williams and Officer Parks took over the emergency call list and immediately started verifying to all outside points by telephone the radio broadcast. At this time the Bridge was closed to traffic momentarily and each car checked going through. *Metropolis Detective Jackson* was notified to cover the coal yard and the auto rental agency in Metropolis. Following this, with the aid of other men who came in, all police agencies and radio stations in the surrounding counties were notified by telephone.

4:37 A.M. Eastern Station reported car going east on 14th Street at 8th Avenue at a high rate of speed.

4:38 A.M. we covered Bear Peak bivd.

4:45 A.M. Highland Sheriff's office reported the car was lost by one of their cars which had been following it in Neal's Canyon.

4:50 A.M. Eastern reported the car had gone through Piketown.

4:58 A.M. Car 205, Sheriff's Office was detailed to Southern Alton County. THE LICENSE NUMBER WAS VERIFIED BY THE SHERIFF'S OFFICE IN HAYMAND. This was the first time we had a verification.

5:15 A.M. Midland cars were recalled to their beats and incoming evening watch men were sent to covering points in Coulton County because they had only had one car in service there.

5:30 A.M. we cancelled the coverage at Bear Peak Blvd. and substituted two officers for the Sergeant who had been there formerly.

Insp. Fry's report will show that he learned from the Ridge City Police Dept. that a patrolman observed the blue sedan parked in front of Jones' with the door open, that he went along side the car to investigate the man behind the wheel and suddenly someone told him to hold up his hands. He turned and faced the man with the gun. Then he jumped behind the corner of a building, pulled his own gun and started firing. There was an exchange of shots. A taxi driver across the street thought the burglar doubled up holding his stomach. The car left going north. It passed an officer at 18th street, did not fire at him, indicating possibly that one of the men was wounded. Possibly some Ridge City car followed it part way out 14th Street but lost it and subsequent to this time its movements were shown above and from the time it was lost Insp. Fry has been in touch with a number of outside detective bureaus. We plan to pull our own coverage from Coulton County at daylight.

D. J. HOLMES, LT.
1/3, 7:10 A.M.

At 8:10 A.M., a detail of detectives headed by Inspector Jackson of the Metropolis Police Department, arrested Peter Joseph Battoni as he parked Plymouth Sedan AG2567 in the Acme Auto Rental in Metropolis. Speedometer mileage indicated he had driven about 100 miles and had not returned via the Bridge.

All agencies previously contacted were during the forenoon notified by telephone, to verify radio cancellation that the wanted car had been returned to its owner, and the suspect apprehended.

The file also contains a report of the conviction of Peter Joseph Battoni and copies of innumerable letters of thanks sent to the business men who had cooperated in the venture by permitting the police to use their premises for observation (and included in the lot was one to the owner of the auto rental agency) and to cooperating law enforcement agencies.

APPENDIX M

Plans for a Large Athletic Event[1]

When a permit is granted for such an event as the 15th Annual All Star Football Game, a statement is prepared by the Chicago Park District traffic engineer and chief of police, approved by the general superintendent (the equivalent of a city manager) as to where and when the event will be held, the anticipated size of the crowd, and the identity of the sponsor. This bulletin also contains information as to parking restrictions to be imposed, transportation facilities to be operated, streets and drives to be closed, and first-aid facilities to be provided, as well as information relating to incoming participants and special arrivals and the identifying stickers that will be displayed on their vehicles; the responsibility of the traffic engineer to furnish and place barricades and signs; the maintenance of law and order, and some general remarks.

General information and instructions to the police are issued over the signature of the chief of police, and a Station Order assigning designated officers to specific duties at selected locations is issued over the signature of the traffic captain. A similar assignment sheet is prepared for the signature of the chief of police directed to the captain commanding the City of Chicago police detail assigned to the Chicago Park District police for assistance. Information regarding special movements for the event are also distributed. At the conclusion, a special event report is prepared; comments on it prove helpful in correcting weaknesses when planning for future events.

The documents described above are reproduced in the following pages; the names and assignments of some 150 patrolmen have been omitted from the Station Order in the interest of brevity. In addition to these bulletins and orders, a special instruction sheet is read at roll call.

A truck equipped with a portable public-address system and another with a power generator are in attendance at all such events, to be placed in service in the event of a break in the power line. Also

[1] The material in this section was obtained through the courtesy of Captains George A. Johnstone and John D. Leonard of the Chicago Park District Police.

at each event, the fire department, at police request, sends one pumper (two when fireworks are to be displayed), one special squad, and one ambulance. Another ambulance is available at all times to transport patients to the two hospital rooms, one located on each side of the field. The sponsors of the event are requested to staff the hospital rooms with doctors and nurses.

CHICAGO PARK DISTRICT
Traffic Section   •   Engineering Division

15TH ANNUAL ALL STAR FOOTBALL GAME

SPONSORED BY | The Chicago Tribune Charities, Incorporated. For further information contact Mr. William Sturm at Superior 0100.

PLACE | Soldier Field, Burnham Park.

DATE AND TIME | Friday, August 20, 1948. The kick-off will be promptly at 8:30 P.M. and the game will end at approximately 11:00 P.M. The game will be played rain or shine.

General Admission tickets will be placed on sale at 8:00 P.M. at ticket booths.

Admission to Soldier Field will be permitted after 7:00 P.M. with as many gates open as is necessary at that time.

ATTENDANCE | A capacity crowd is expected to attend this event, weather permitting.

SEE MAP ATTACHED

PUBLIC PARKING | A charge for parking in the Soldier Field area will be made and collections will be under the direction of the Department of Finance and Property of the Chicago Park District.

OFFICIAL PARKING | Official cars will be parked in the Chicago Park District Administration Building Garage and will enter Soldier Field via ramp 41. These cars will exit from the garage via ramp 42. GRAY colored Official Car Stickers will be issued by the

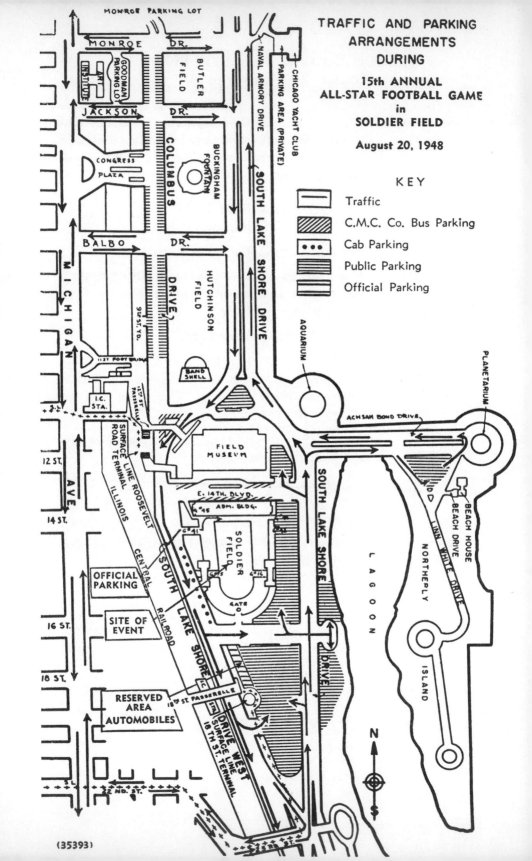

TRAFFIC AND PARKING ARRANGEMENTS DURING

15th ANNUAL ALL-STAR FOOTBALL GAME in SOLDIER FIELD

August 20, 1948

KEY

Traffic	
C.M.C. Co. Bus Parking	
Cab Parking	
Public Parking	
Official Parking	

(35393)

Chicago Park District to the sponsor for distribution.

RESERVED AREA

An area will be set aside in the northwest corner of the parking lot south of Soldier Field for automobiles displaying the LAVENDER "Reserved Area" Sticker.

POSITIVELY
NO PARKING

No parking will be allowed at any time on Columbus Drive, south of 11th Street, South Lake Shore Drive West, South Lake Shore Drive, Waldron Drive, or 14th Boulevard.

AT ALL TIMES TUNNELS INTO AND UNDER SOLDIER FIELD ARE TO BE KEPT CLEAR OF PARKED VEHICLES

SERVICE VEHICLES

Those trucks and other vehicles servicing the event will display a GREEN "Service Vehicle" Sticker.

TRANSPORTATION

MOTOR COACH

The Chicago Motor Coach Company will operate several buses on each line, as well as all No. 26 Jackson Boulevard buses, direct to Soldier Field.

Passengers coming from the north may transfer at the southwest corner of Jackson Boulevard and Michigan Avenue to any No. 26 bus marked "Grant Park." Those passengers coming from the south may transfer at the southeast corner of Balbo Drive and Michigan Avenue.

A 1-minute shuttle service starting at 6:25 P.M. will operate from Randolph Street and Michigan Avenue to Soldier Field and return.

ALL CHICAGO MOTOR COACH COMPANY BUSES WHEN LEAVING MICHIGAN AVENUE WILL PROCEED EAST ON BALBOA DRIVE TO SOUTH LAKE SHORE DRIVE AND SOUTH ALONG THE EAST CURB OF SOUTH LAKE SHORE DRIVE TO 14TH BOULEVARD, DISCHARGING THEIR PASSENGERS

IN FRONT OF THE ENTRANCE TO THE ADMIN-
ISTRATION BUILDING ON EAST 14TH BOULEVARD
OR AS DIRECTED.

Arrangements have been made to store as many
Chicago Motor Coach Company buses as possible
on East 14th Boulevard for the break of the
event. Buses will be parked on East 14th Boulevard as directed.

TAXICABS

Northbound taxicabs on South Lake Shore Drive
will turn west at Waldron Drive, discharging
their passengers along the north curb of Gate O,
Soldier Field and exit via South Lake Shore
Drive West and 23rd Street.

Southbound taxicabs from the west and north
will discharge their passengers along the east
curb of South Lake Shore Drive West between
Gate 29 of Soldier Field and Waldron Drive and
exit via South Lake Shore Drive West and 23rd
Street.

TAXICABS SERVING THIS AREA AT THE BREAK
OF THE EVENT WILL BE PARKED ALONG THE
EAST CURB OF SOUTH LAKE SHORE DRIVE WEST
FROM GATE 29 TO WALDRON DRIVE OR AS DI-
RECTED.

TRAINS

Spectators using the ILLINOIS CENTRAL SUB-
URBAN LINES will arrive and depart at the 18th
Street Station.

CHICAGO TRANSIT
   AUTHORITY

SURFACE
DIVISION

The CHICAGO TRANSIT AUTHORITY, SURFACE DI-
VISION will serve Soldier Field in the following
manner: Cermak Road street cars terminating in
Burnham Park at the 18th Street terminal on
South Lake Shore Drive West; Roosevelt Road
street cars terminating in Grant Park at the
Roosevelt Road terminal on Columbus Drive.

RAPID TRANSIT DIVISION	Those arriving via the ELEVATED or SUBWAY LINES will transfer at the Roosevelt Road Stations to any eastbound Chicago Transit Authority, Surface Division street car terminating in Grant Park at the Roosevelt Road terminal on Columbus Drive.
DRIVES TO BE CLOSED	The Chicago Park District Police Division in co-operation with the Traffic Engineer will determine the time, if and when, traffic will be detoured around the site of the event.

In the event the decision is made to close off traffic in the area, northbound traffic on South Lake Shore Drive will be detoured west at 23rd Street and thence north. Southbound traffic on North Lake Shore Drive will be detoured west at Ohio Street to Michigan Avenue, thence south.

No traffic will be permitted to enter Grant Park from Michigan Avenue between Balbo Drive and Randolph Drive during this time, EXCEPT CHICAGO MOTOR COACH BUSES OR TAXICABS.

The above traffic arrangements, if necessary, will be put into effect in ample time to have the drives cleared of traffic at the end of the event or at approximately 10:50 P.M. and will remain in effect until it has been decided by the Chicago Park District Police Division and the Traffic Engineer that the drives should be opened.

FIRST AID	The sponsor of this event will arrange for first-aid equipment and attendants to be stationed in the hospital rooms at Gate 15 and 16 in Soldier Field.
INCOMING PARTICIPANTS	The College All Star team will use the dressing rooms at Gate 16 of Soldier Field and the Chicago Cardinals will use that at Gate 15.
SPECIAL ARRIVALS	A contingent of War Veterans will enter the ramp at Gate 41 at approximately 6:30 P.M. The vet-

erans and their assistants will be seated on the field. These cars will display the GRAY "Official Car" Sticker.

A special bus displaying a BLUE "Official Press" sticker transporting Press Representatives will make two trips to Waldron Drive where the passengers will unload at Gate O. After the second trip in, this bus will park on Waldron Drive east of the entrance at Gate O until the end of the game.

Chartered buses and automobiles displaying a YELLOW "Official Car" sticker transporting special groups will enter Gate 45 and park in the Chicago Park District Administration Building vehicular tunnel until after the game.

BARRICADES AND SIGNS

The TRAFFIC SECTION, ENGINEERING DIVISION, will also furnish and place barricades across the south sidewalk on Waldron Drive on a line with the inside of the sidewalk on the east side of South Lake Shore Drive West. Those barricades will be placed for the start of the event and will be maintained during the early stages of the event, but will be removed prior to the break of the event.

The TRAFFIC SECTION, ENGINEERING DIVISION, will erect the necessary directional signs reading, "Odd-Number Gates," "Even-Number Gates" on the south sidewalk of East 14th Boulevard at the entrance to Gate 45, and at the point where the Chicago Motor Coach Company buses will discharge their passengers in front of the entrance to the Administration Building. Signs reading "No Outlet—Please Use Sidewalks" will be placed on the sidewalk directly in front of the Administration Building entrance.

The TRAFFIC SECTION, ENGINEERING DIVISION, will furnish, erect, and place the necessary signs, barricades and lanterns to direct pedestrians and vehicular traffic around this area in the interest of public safety.

MAINTENANCE
OF ORDER AND
PROTECTION

The CHICAGO PARK DISTRICT POLICE DIVISION will have sufficient police in the vicinity of the event to direct and control traffic and pedestrian movements.

GENERAL REMARKS

THE SPONSOR OF THIS EVENT SHOULD CALL HARRISON 1190 IMMEDIATELY IF ANY EMERGENCY ARISES NECESSITATING A REVISION OF THE SCHEDULE HEREIN LISTED.

Traffic
Section: /s/ VICTOR G. HOFER,
TRAFFIC ENGINEER
Police
Division: /s/ ROGER F. SHANAHAN,
CHIEF OF POLICE
Approved: /s/ GEORGE T. DONOGHUE,
GENERAL SUPERINTENDENT

CHICAGO PARK DISTRICT
DIVISION OF POLICE
15TH ANNUAL ALL STAR FOOTBALL GAME
AUGUST 20, 1948
GENERAL INFORMATION

Sponsored by the Chicago Tribune Charities Incorporated. Sponsors' Representatives: Arch Ward and Bill Sturm, Phone Superior 0200.

Preliminaries start at 8:15 P.M. (Introduction of players as they enter the field.)

Game starts at 8:30 P.M.

Special program between the halves. (Massed band formations and presentation of most valuable player awards.)

It is expected that the game will be concluded by 11:15 P.M.

Participants, College All Stars and Chicago Cardinals, Champions of the National Professional League.

The College All Stars will use the dressing room at Gate 16 and occupy the players bench located on the east side of the field.

The Chicago Cardinals will use the dressing room at Gate 15 and occupy the players bench located on the west side of the field.

400 Andy Frain ushers will be in attendance and will form a cordon around the field at the end of the game.

General Instructions to Police

1. Police Headquarters is located in Soldier Field just east of Gate "O." Phones dial 480—485—493—PAX. 442 Bell: Harrison 5188—5189.

2. The Chicago Health Dept. will man the hospitals located at Gate 15, dial phone 478 and Gate 16, dial phone 479.

3. Personnel and apparatus from the Chicago Fire Department will be located at Field Gate 42, dial phone 470 and in the west exhibition hall dial phone 480—485 or 493.

4. All lost persons or property shall be delivered to Police Headquarters, Gate 4 Soldier Field.

5. Chicago Police will furnish a pickpocket and scalper detail.

6. Positively no spectators are allowed on top of colonnades, press boxes, photographers' stand, scoreboard or public-address system towers.

7. Police in citizens dress shall make frequent visits to toilets and to be on the alert for hijacking of refreshments vendors, and especially alert for pickpockets.

8. Police are to remain on their posts until relieved by a supervisory officer.

9. Police assigned to the stands shall stop anyone from standing on walls and parapets and shall keep wells and aisles free of spectators at all times.

10. Police assigned to the field shall extend every effort to prevent occupants of field seats from leaving their seats and rushing onto the field. They shall also be responsible for the protection of the goal posts and bunting at the end of the game.

11. Holders of field badges shall remain on the paved track unless they are performing duties on the field or players' bench.

12. Police shall prevent the throwing of bottles, drinking of intoxicating liquors, urinating in unauthorized places and be especially alert for pickpockets.

REMEMBER THAT THOUSANDS ARE WATCHING YOU AS WELL AS THE GAME, THEREFORE, PERFORM YOUR DUTIES ACCORDINGLY.

/s/ ROGER F. SHANAHAN,
CHIEF OF POLICE

CHICAGO PARK DISTRICT
DIVISION OF POLICE
—CENTRAL—

FROM   : Captain George A. Johnstone
To   : Supervisory Officers
SUBJECT : STATION ORDER #200

DETAIL : CHICAGO TRIBUNE 15TH ANNUAL ALL STAR
FOOTBALL GAME, FRIDAY EVENING,
AUGUST 20, 1948—SOLDIER FIELD

CHIEF ROGER F. SHANAHAN IN COMMAND

Captain George A. Johnstone #4—Outside Soldier Field, Car 807
Captain George A. Otlewis   #8—Inside Soldier Field, West Side
Captain Kenneth Fossier   #7—Inside Soldier Field, East Side

The following men will report to Captain George A. Johnstone at Gate 4, Soldier Field at 4:00 P.M. Friday, August 20, 1948 for roll call and assignment. Roll call will be held before and after the event. After instructions are read, men will report to the Sergeant to whom they are assigned as their names are called.

Men whose names are preceded by an asterisk will report directly to their posts at the time indicated. Men who are assigned to Michigan Avenue, or to posts north of 14th Boulevard, will be excused by the Sergeant in charge of their area. Names preceded by double asterisks will report to Captain George Otlewis at Field Gate "O" at 10:00 P.M. for assignments inside Soldier Field.

Uniform of the day and batons will be worn. Men will be required to present the best possible appearance.

SUPERVISION OFFICERS TO REPORT NOT LATER THAN 3:45 P.M.

Lieutenant Ralph Riley	#10	Outside—Grant and Burnham Parks. Car 802
Lieutenant Walter J. Balcom	#1	Inside Soldier Field—West Side
Lieutenant Robert V. Keleher	#9	Inside Soldier Field—East Side
Sergeant William O'Neill	#84	Inside Soldier Field—Playing Field, East Side
Sergeant Arthur Judson	#54	Inside Soldier Field—Playing Field, West Side
Sergeant William Wheatley	#70	Burnham Park, Waldron Drive to 23rd Street also South Parking Lot

Sergeant Fred McDonald	#53	Outside—East Side of Soldier Field, 14th Street to Waldron Drive—also 14th Street Boulevard (Court of Honor)
Sergeant Lou Steinberg	#76	Parking Lots—East of Soldier Field and Museum, east lot. Also East Lawn Parking, 14th Street to 20th Street
Sergeant Patrick Diggins	#87	Exhibition Halls and beneath stands. After start of game, Exhibition Halls and beneath stands, East Side, Gate "O" to Gate 50
Sergeant Onnie Walker	#35	Outside Soldier Field—West Side and Outside Gate "O." After game is started, Exhibition Halls and beneath stands, West Side, Gate "O" to Gate 50
Sergeant Leo Wm. Powers	#65	1st and 2nd Districts. Grant and Burnham Parks. Car 804
Sergeant James O'Neil	#27	Jackson Boulevard-Michigan Avenue to the River (Walking)
Sergeant John Sodini	#44	Central Section Police Headquarters
Patrolman Elmer Burt	#132	Central Section Police Headquarters, Messenger.

CIVILIAN DRESS PATROLMEN

#305	Raymond Earsman	#315	Herbert Strobel
#605	James Riordan	#652	James Keegan

POLICEWOMEN

#4	Alice McCarthy	#6	Marcia Wistort

MOTORCYCLE PATROLMEN

STAR #	NAME		ASSIGNMENT
168	John Thieke	(8 to 4)	All Parking Areas—12th St. to 23rd Street
117	Arthur Heidmann		Messenger—Central Section Headquarters
676	Everett Walsh		Messenger—Central Section Headquarters
592	William Jorgenson		East Parking Lot
136	Arthur Swanson		South Parking Lot
560	John Olson		Waldron Dr. to 23rd Street—Outer Dr. NO PARKING

484	Everett Begy	12th Street to Waldron Drive—Outer Dr. NO PARKING
506	John Long	12th Street to Waldron Drive—Outer Dr. NO PARKING
554	Harry Hogan	Northerly Island and East Lawn Parking Lots

AMBULANCE CARS

STAR #	NAME	CAR	ASSIGNMENT
476	Harvey Hart	804	2nd District
439	John Goldrick	804	2nd District
299	Edwin Westhouse	806	1st District
545	Albert Heitman	806	1st District

1st and 2nd DISTRICTS: GRANT AND BURNHAM PARKS
SERGEANT LEO WM. POWERS

STAR #	PATROLMAN	TIME	ASSIGNMENT
376	* Lee Sawyer	4 to 12	Michigan Avenue at Monroe St.

(Note: The names have been omitted here of 27 other patrolmen similarly assigned to intersections of Michigan Avenue, Columbus Drive. North Lake Shore Drive, and South Lake Shore Drive.)

JACKSON BOULEVARD-MICHIGAN AVENUE TO THE RIVER
SERGEANT JAMES O'NEIL

STAR #	PATROLMAN	TIME	ASSIGNMENT
382	* James Coyle	4 to 12	Jackson Boulevard at Wabash Ave.

(Note: The names have been omitted here of 7 additional patrolmen assigned to other intersections on Jackson Boulevard.)

OUTSIDE: EAST SIDE OF SOLDIER FIELD—14TH STREET TO WALDRON DRIVE
ALSO 14TH STREET (COURT OF HONOR)
SERGEANT FRED McDONALS

STAR #	PATROLMAN	ASSIGNMENT
465	James Mackie	Court of Honor—West Half

(Note: The names and assignments of 15 additional patrolmen have been omitted here.)

PARKING LOTS—EAST OF SOLDIER FIELD AND MUSEUM EAST LOT
ALSO EAST LAWN PARKING—14TH STREET TO 20TH STREET
SERGEANT LOU STEINBERG

STAR #	PATROLMAN	ASSIGNMENT
192	Clarence Binder	So. Lake Shore Drive—Waldron Drive entrance to temporary parking lot

(Note: The names and assignments of 14 additional patrolmen have been omitted here.)

Burnham Park—Waldron Drive to 23rd St. and South Parking Lot
Sergeant William Wheatley

Star #	Patrolman	Assignment
240	Walter Schulz	Waldron Dr. entrance to South Parking Lot

(Note: The names and assignments of 18 additional patrolmen have been omitted here.)

Outside Soldier Field—West Side and Outside Gate "O"
Sergeant Onnie Walker

Star #	Patrolman	Assignment
198	James Spencer	Gate "O" Outside

(Note: The names and assignments of 23 additional patrolmen have been omitted here.)

NOTE: Men assigned to Exhibition Halls are to see that everyone is out of the STANDS and the EXHIBITION HALLS cleared before leaving their post for roll call.

Exhibition Halls and Beneath Stands
Sergeant Patrick Diggins

Star #	Patrolman	Assignment
651	Phil Yablong	Gate "O"—Inside

(Note: The names and assignments of 13 additional patrolmen have been omitted here.)

Soldier Field—Inside West Side
Sergeant Arthur Judson

Star #	Patrolman	Assignment
664	Thomas Gordon	Inside Soldier Field—West Side at the Television Booth

(Note: The names and assignments of 17 additional patrolmen have been omitted here.)

Soldier Field—Inside East Side
Sergeant William O'Neill

Star #	Patrolman	Assignment
492	Edward Moore	Inside Soldier Field—East Side at the Photographers' Stand.

(Note: The names and assignments of 17 additional patrolmen have been omitted here.)

THE FOLLOWING MEN WILL REPORT TO THEIR REGULAR ASSIGNMENTS AT 8:00 A.M. AND LEAVE THEM IN TIME TO REPORT TO SERGEANT JOHN LEEN AT GATE 4, SOLDIER FIELD, FOR ASSIGNMENT AT 9:30 A.M.

Star #	Patrolman	Time	Assignment
191	Thomas Burns	8 to 4	Gate "O" Inside and Outside

(Note: The names and assignments of 4 additional patrolmen have been omitted here.)

RESERVE:
4:00 P.M.

    #538   James Fick
    #629   Arthur Proskin

DETAIL CONSISTS OF:

    1   Chief of Police
    3   Captains of Police
    3   Lieutenants of Police
  10   Sergeants of Police
    4   Civilian Dress Patrolmen
    4   Squad Car Patrolmen
    9   Motorcycle Patrolmen
 167   Foot Patrolmen
    2   Policewomen

TOTAL DETAIL: 203

By order of

/s/ GEO. A. JOHNSTONE
CAPTAIN OF POLICE
COMMANDING CENTRAL SECTION

CHICAGO PARK DISTRICT
DIVISION OF POLICE

To   :   Captain Michael J. Ahern, Chicago Police Detail
FROM   :   Chief of Police, Roger F. Shanahan
SUBJECT :   Assignments for All Star Football Game

ASSIGNMENTS FOR CHICAGO POLICE DETAIL

Assign the men under your command as follows:

Forty-six (46) patrolmen to the stands and wells as indicated on the attached diagram of Soldier Field.

Forty-two (42) patrolmen to outside gates as indicated on the attached diagram of Soldier Field.

Twelve (12) patrolmen to be assigned to the playing field to augment Park Police Detail.

ASSIGNMENT INSTRUCTIONS

Patrolmen on these assignments are to be instructed to keep wells and aisles free of spectators at all times.

Patrolmen on these assignments are to be instructed to stop spectators from standing or sitting on the walls forming the outer part of the stadium. Prevent spectators from standing or sitting on any parapet around the colonnades or stairways and keep all aisles clear.

Instruct the patrolmen on this assignment to stop anyone from climbing on top of the scoreboard, standing or sitting on walls or parapets, or blocking aisles.

Instruct all patrolmen assigned to Gate Detail to post themselves at the crash door behind the turnstile on the outside of the stadium in order to prevent gate crashing. It is important that the members of this detail remain on their posts as ticket takers have a tendency to leave after the game starts. The closing of the crash doors does not prevent gate crashing as the doors may be opened by anyone from the inside thereby permitting those on the outside to enter.

The forty-two (42) patrolmen on Gate Detail shall be arranged into five (5) groups with each group designated in advance and instructed to leave their gate assignments at the beginning of the third quarter of the football game and proceed to one of the five local transportation terminals listed as follows:

1. Illinois Central Railroad, Roosevelt Road Platform.
2. Illinois Central Railroad, 18th Street Platform.
3. Chicago Surface Lines Terminal, Roosevelt Road.
4. Chicago Surface Lines Terminal, 18th Street.
5. Chicago Motor Coach Terminal, 14th Boulevard between South Lake Shore Drive (East) and South Lake Shore Drive (West).

ROGER F. SHANAHAN,
CHIEF OF POLICE.

SPECIAL MOVEMENTS FOR THE
15TH ANNUAL ALL STAR FOOTBALL GAME
SOLDIER FIELD

Friday, August 20, 1948

1. Two hundred and ten patients from the Veterans Hospitals under the direction of Morris Handel will move into Soldier Field via six (6) buses, one (1) station wagon and three (3) private cars which are to be parked north of the temporary bleachers at the north end of Soldier Field. Before parking, these veterans will unload at the south end of the field where they will be seated for the game. This group should arrive at 7:00 P.M.

2. Forty-five cars owned by amputees and paraplegics in charge of Terry Rose will leave the Sherry Hotel for Soldier Field and will enter Gate 41 at approximately 7:00 P.M. These cars will be parked at the north end of Soldier Field and the occupants of these cars will be seated with the other veterans at the south end of Soldier Field.

3. There is a possibility that patients will arrive from Battle Creek, Michigan, via bus and they should be parked in the South Parking Lot in the area at the northwest corner, known as the Reserved Area. These buses will not have "Reserved Area" stickers.

4. Four (4) bus loads of enlisted men from Great Lakes will be parked in the Reserved Area of the South Parking Lot. They will display "Reserved Area" stickers.

5. Arrangements have been made to store four (4) coaches in the Administration Building Tunnel. Two of these coaches will carry guests of the Chicago Motor Club, one coach will carry guests of the General American Transportation Company and the fourth coach will carry guests of the Coca-Cola Company. Eight (8) other official car stickers have been issued for this tunnel to the officials of the Chicago Park District.

6. Arrangements have been made to store four (4) coaches transporting the players of the opposing teams. These buses will be stored opposite Gate 16 in the East Parking Lot of Soldier Field.

7. Forty (40) Reserved Area Stickers have been issued to the Willett Motor Coach Company for special charter groups and thirty (30) Reserved Area stickers have been issued to the Chicago Motor Coach Company for charter groups.

8. Twenty-four (24) Service Vehicle Stickers have been issued to the sponsor. These vehicles will be parked in the northwest corner of the East Parking Lot of Soldier Field.

9. Two (2) Official Press stickers have been issued to the sponsor and theses vehicles will be parked opposite Gate O in the South Parking Lot.

10. It is expected that twelve (12) official cars transporting the Governor's Party will enter Soldier Field via Ramp 41 and will park in the tunnel leading to Gate O along the west side of the Stadium.

11. Three (3) Gate 41 stickers have been issued to the Mayor's Office and these cars will park in the same tunnel as the Governor's Party.

12. Six (6) Ramp 41 Stickers have been issued to Mr. Mertz of the American Red Cross and they will also park in the lower tunnel at Gates 15 and 16.

Issuance of Car Stickers
15th Annual All Star Football Game
Soldier Field

Friday, August 20, 1948

Name	Gate 41	Gate 45	Re-served Area	Service Vehicle	Official Press
File	3	3	3	3	3
Sponsor	47		75	24	2
Evan I. Kelly	1		31		
John Chamberlain, 6518 Vernon Ave.	1		1		
Miss O'Neill, Mayor's Office	2		2		
Sgt. John Connor, Mayor's Detail	3				
Wm. McKenna, Assistant to the Mayor	3		3		
Fred C. Worden, Supt. Waukegan-North Shore Transit, 1400 Tenth Street, Waukegan, Illinois			5		
Patty Leydon, C.M.C. Co.	4				
Terry Rose	45				
Morris Handel, 2610 W. 25th Place	12				
G. T. Donoghue	5	3	8	1	1
D. L. Flaherty	5	1	3	1	1
Chief Shanahan	7	3	17	1	1
Capt. Johnstone	1	1	6	1	1
V. G. Hofer	1	1	1	1	1
R. G. Fencl	1	1	1	1	1
M. F. Connelly	1	1	1	1	1
Ray Thompson (Publicity)	1				
Joe Demask	3				
Thomas L. Beem, 917 W. 77th Street	5				
J. A. Mertz, 8111 Stewart Avenue	6				
Ed. Welch			10		
Jacob Arvey	2	1			
I. S. Bernstein (Coca-Cola)		1			
LeRoy Woodland	1	1	1	1	1
Phil Lozowick	8	1	2		
Comm. Cremin		1			
Comm. Levin	4	1			
Comm. McFetridge		1			
James H. Gately		1			
Mr. Eckleman—C.M.C. Co.			30		
Elmer Layden—General Amer. Transportation Co., 135 S. LaSalle St., Room 2805		2			
R. S. Knapp	1		1		
Jos. E. Love			9		
Dan Collins			3		
S. Wyer—Willett Coach Co.	3	2	40		
Wm. E. Doan, Jr.—Referee	1				
Al Kemp			1		
Tony Destefano			1		
Adolph Rasmussen	1				
Glenn Stromberg	1				
Terry Rose			1		
Mary Walsh			1		
Shore Line Buses, 4923 Columbia Ave., Hammond, Indiana			6		
Sam Pecoraro	2		15		

CHICAGO PARK DISTRICT
DIVISION OF POLICE

SPECIAL EVENT REPORT

Date: *August 20, 1948*

Event: *15th Annual All Star Football Game.*

Location: *Soldier Field.*

Date: *August 20, 1948.* Beginning Time: *8:15* P.M. Ending Time: *11:15* P.M.

Sponsor: *Chicago Tribune Charities Incorporated.*

Sponsor's representatives: *Arch Ward and Bill Sturm.*

Address: *435 N. Michigan Avenue.* Phone: *Sup. 0100.*

Attendance: Anticipated *90,000;* Police estimate *90,000.*

Nationality of groups attending: *Mixed.*

Weather conditions: *Warm Clear*—Temp.: *75 Degrees.*

Number of Park police present: Captains *3;* Lieutenants *3;* Sergeants *10;* Patrolmen *184;* Policewomen 2. Total *203.* Under direction of *Roger F. Shanahan.* Rank: *Chief of Police.*

Number of City police present: Captains *1;* Lieutenants *4;* Sergeants *8;* Patrolmen *100;* Policewomen *0.* Total *113.*

Were arrangements satisfactory? If not, give reasons and recommendations for future assignments: *Men should be detailed on the lawn area directly east of 14th Street for parking cars. Also men should be stationed to patrol both the Lake Shore Drive north and Lake Shore Drive south between 12th Street and 20th Street, to prevent cars from parking in this area.*

Chief Roger F. Shanahan
Captain George A. Johnstone   ROGER F. SHANAHAN
Captain George A. Otlewis   CHIEF OF POLICE.
Captain Kenneth Fossier
CITY: Captain Michael Ahern
CARS PARKED: 6029

INSTRUCTIONS: Fill out this report after any special event in the Chicago Park District to which one or more members of the Division of Police are assigned; attach a copy of the bulletins and the program. If the event is held on more than one date, submit a separate report for each date.

APPENDIX N

Disaster Plan

KANSAS CITY AND JACKSON COUNTY CHAPTER

AMERICAN RED CROSS

The Disaster Preparedness and Relief Manual prepared by the Kansas City and Jackson County American Red Cross contains an organization chart of the Disaster Committee, Chart I, a detailed index (7 pages), general instructions, and detailed plans and operating instructions for each of the subcommittees shown in the organization chart. There is also an alphabetical list of key assignments, giving the residence and business telephone numbers of personnel, and a similar list of the telephone listings of key personnel of other organizations that may participate in disaster relief, including:

Adjutant General's Office (Mo.)	Police Department
American Legion	Power and Light Company
American Red Cross Area Office	Public Works Department
Boy Scouts of America	Real Estate Board
Broadcasting Stations	Salvation Army
City Health Department	Sheriff's Office
Civil Air Patrol	Street and Sewer Department
Council of Social Agencies	Traveler's Aid
Federal Bureau of Investigation	U. S. Coast Guard
Fire Department	U. S. Engineers
Highway Commission (Kansas)	U. S. National Guard
Highway Commission (Missouri)	U. S. Naval Reserve
Nurses Registry	U. S. Weather Bureau
Park Department	Veteran's Administration

The manual also contains an itemized list of disaster equipment owned or stored by the Red Cross Chapter, with additional pages devoted to resources available on short notice, listing the agency and telephone numbers through which key officials may be reached. These are arranged under the following headings:

Acetylene Torches (welding and cutting)
Ambulances

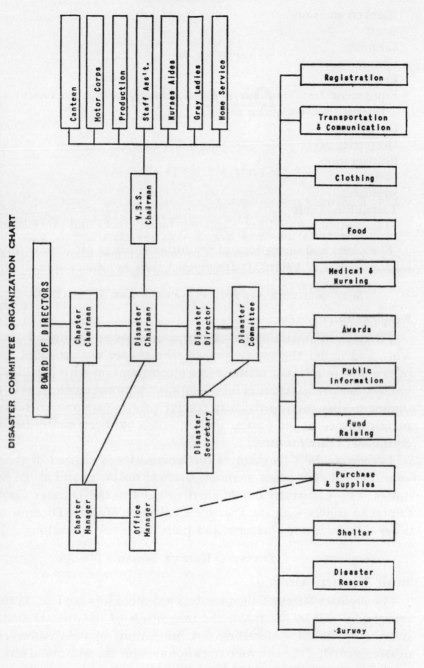

KANSAS CITY - JACKSON COUNTY CHAPTER AMERICAN RED CROSS

DISASTER COMMITTEE ORGANIZATION CHART

Canteen
Motor Corps
Production
Staff Ass't.
Nurses Aides
Gray Ladies
Home Service

V.S.S. Chairman

BOARD OF DIRECTORS

Chapter Chairman
Disaster Chairman
Disaster Director
Disaster Committee

Disaster Secretary

Chapter Manager
Office Manager

Registration
Transportation & Communication
Clothing
Food
Medical & Nursing
Awards
Public Information
Fund Raising
Purchase & Supplies
Shelter
Disaster Rescue
Survey

Blankets and Cots
Boats
Cleaning
Communications
Engineers
Equipment List (bulldozers, cables, chains, crowbars, crosscut saws,
    lanterns, shovels, picks, ropes)
Generators
Hospitals
Refrigeration
Shelter
Sterilizers
Tarpaulins, Tents
Transportation (air lines, airplanes, buses, trucks and miscellaneous)

The plans and operations of the Subcommittee on Rescue (organization shown in Chart II) are given below as an example.

Subcommittee on Rescue—Plans and Operations

Responsibility

To assist in rescue and evacuation of disaster victims. To work
with, and under the supervision of, the properly constituted forces
of law and order. To maintain close coordination with the subcommittees on transportation and communication, medical aid, and
shelter so that the injured may receive proper care and all refugees
be transported to the nearest shelter which has been established and
equipped to care for them.

As soon as the Chairman of this committee is advised of the disaster, he will alert other members deemed necessary and assign their
duties. The Chairman should then proceed to the Disaster Control
Center to confer with the Disaster Chairman, Disaster Director, and
other subcommittee chairmen and plan the entire operation.

Disaster Rescue Squad

Small Disaster Alerts

The Disaster Rescue Squad renders a twofold service; first, as an investigation unit to determine the magnitude of the disaster at hand
and the advisability of calling out other units of the disaster committee; second, if the situation does not warrant the additional services
as outlined in the Disaster Manual, the squad alerted proceeds to give
such services as may be deemed advisable under the circumstances and
in accordance with the Disaster Rescue Squad Plan.

CHART II

KANSAS CITY-JACKSON COUNTY CHAPTER AMERICAN RED CROSS

DISASTER COMMITTEE—SUBCOMMITTEE ON RESCUE

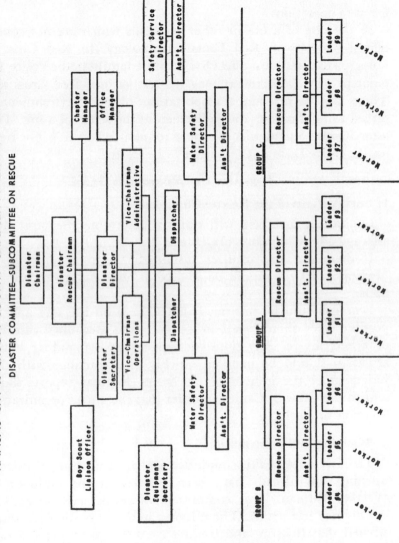

As soon as the chairman or vice chairman and/or Disaster Director have been advised of the disaster (or accident bordering on disaster) the chairman and director should immediately proceed to Chapter Headquarters to receive calls at the telephone number HARRISON 2353, which has been set up for this purpose until the PBX Board is put in operation.

In the case of a fire or other accidents which are not considered official disasters in Red Cross terminology (in Red Cross terminology, a disaster must affect five or more families), the Police Department or Fire Department may request various Red Cross services. These may be first aid, transportation, or even refreshments to be served to the firemen and policemen at the scene of a fire. The Disaster Rescue Squad will fill these requests when it is not necessary for the entire Disaster Committee to be alerted.

Tornado or Windstorm Plan

1. Survey Plans of the Rescue Committee

Committee members will quickly determine the most devasted area and advise the Control Center.

If there are any injuries sustained, the subcommittee of the Medical Aid Unit should be advised at once and given full instructions.

People should be informed that help is on the way and that, if possible, they should wait in, or near, the area until case workers or others arrive. Any unusual happenings demanding immediate attention should be handled quickly in accordance with the best judgment of the individual in charge. Regular reports should be sent to the Control Center in order that the entire organization will function properly.

2. Warning and Information

The first duty of this committee is that of warning although such warning may already have been given over the radio or by the Weather Bureau. This committee, however, will be active after the disaster has struck. Those living in the Disaster Area should be advised that housing and feeding centers will be erected near the devastated section and that they should not leave without permission unless they are injured.

While waiting, those affected by the disaster should be requested and instructed how to get their personal possessions together preparatory to evacuation, should that be necessary.

Should evacuation of household belongings be necessary, or desired, that fact should be reported at once to the Transportation Committee through the Control Center. It is the duty of this committee to determine the areas for evacuation.

All people in the area should be directed to the nearest Disaster Field Office registration desk.

3. Evacuation

The Rescue Committee must report immediately to the Disaster Area when it is known that evacuation is necessary. Any estimate as to the number of trucks needed should not be made on a "conservative" basis. (For Truck sources, see "Trucks.")

The committee should proceed systematically with the task of evacuation, using every worker available.

All persons sent to R. C. Shelter Houses *must* be listed by workers. All data and instruction listed under "Flood Plans—Evacuation" will apply in case of Tornadoes or Windstorms—particularly as they relate to listing of property, handling of livestock, etc.

FIRE AND EXPLOSION PLAN

1. Warning and Information

Unless disaster is extremely widespread, this committee will not be active.

2. Evacuation

The biggest job in case of a fire or explosion disaster is to get injured persons to medical aid—and in the proper manner.

Ambulances, buses, and trucks will be used if normal channels and resources are not adequate. A list of all people given service must be kept as in Flood and Tornado Plans.

All injured persons involved in the disaster should be taken to the nearest suitable hospital or safe place and kept there until ARC refugee shelter is established or until permission to leave is given.

3. Rescue Crews

The Fire Department will function in accordance with their usual procedure. If they should need help, the Rescue crews should report to the Chief of the Fire Department, or whoever is in charge, upon arrival at the scene of the disaster for instructions. First-aid workers, as well as the medical committee, should be called out to help injured victims and workers.

Index